Contents at a Glance

Cascading Style Sheets:
Separating Content from Presentation
Second Edition

Owen Briggs
Steven Champeon
Eric Costello
Matt Patterson

with contributions from

Dave Shea
John Simons
Michael Switzer
Dan Rubin
Michael Pick
Cornelia Lange

friendsof

DESIGNER TO DESIGNER™

an Apress® company

Cascading Style Sheets: Separating Content from Presentation, Second Edition
Copyright ©2004 by Owen Briggs, Steven Champeon, Eric Costello, and
Matt Patterson

ISBN (pbk): 1-59059-231-X

Printed and bound in the United States of America 9 8 7 6 5 4 3 2

Trademarked names may appear in this book. Rather than use a trademark symbol with every occurrence of a trademarked name, we use the names only in an editorial fashion and to the benefit of the trademark owner, with no intention of infringement of the trademark.

Technical Reviewer: David Powers

Editorial Board: Steve Anglin, Dan Appleman, Ewan Buckingham, Gary Cornell, Tony Davis, Jason Gilmore, Chris Mills, Dominic Shakeshaft, Jim Sumser, Karen Watterson, John Zukowski

Lead Editor: Chris Mills

Consultant Editor: Bruce Lawson

Assistant Publisher: Grace Wong

Project Manager: Beth Christmas

Copy Editor: Nicole LeClerc

Production Manager: Kari Brooks

Production Editor: Laura Cheu

Proofreader: Thistle Hill Publishing Services, LLC

Compositor: Kinetic Publishing Services, LLC

Indexer: Brenda Miller

Artist: Kinetic Publishing Services, LLC

Cover Designer: Kurt Krames

Manufacturing Manager: Tom Debolski

Distributed to the book trade in the United States by Springer-Verlag New York, LLC, 233 Spring Street, Sixth Floor, New York, NY 10013 and outside the United States by Springer-Verlag GmbH & Co. KG, Tiergartenstr. 17, 69112 Heidelberg, Germany.

In the United States: phone 1-800-SPRINGER, email orders@springer-ny.com, or visit http://www.springer-ny.com. Outside the United States: fax +49 6221 345229, email orders@springer.de, or visit http://www.springer.de.

For information on translations, please contact Apress directly at 2560 Ninth Street, Suite 219, Berkeley, CA 94710. Phone 510-549-5930, fax 510-549-5939, email info@apress.com, or visit http://www.apress.com.

The source code for this book is freely available to readers at http://www.friendsofed.com in the Downloads section.

Contents

About the Authors

Owen Briggs is an independent web designer based in Victoria, Canada. Like so many people, he was introduced to personal computers in 1978 with the Commodore PET and hasn't stopped playing with them since. Online he's currently a member of the Web Standards Project and perpetrator of http://www.thenoodleincident.com. Offline he tries to maintain his privacy.

Steven Champeon is CTO at hesketh.com/inc. (http://hesketh.com) in Raleigh, North Carolina; founder and list mom of the popular webdesign-L mailing list community; author of *Building Dynamic HTML GUIs*, as well as dozens of articles on web technology and culture; development and technical editor; speaker on the web conference circuit; and member of the Web Standards Project, a grassroots effort to raise the bar on standards support and education. In spite of it all, Steven has time to make his own salsa. He would like to thank Eric, Owen, and Matt for asking him to be a part of this book.

Eric Costello is a web developer for hire, working out of his company Schwa. He's currently helping to build The Game Neverending (http://www.gne.net). He maintains a personal site at http://glish.com, where he links to articles on web standards, Flash, DHTML, CSS, XML, and other topics of interest to web developers. He helped usher in the era of CSS page layouts by offering information and CSS templates for free download. He's an emeritus of the Web Standards Project steering committee and the developer for Stewart Butterfield's 5K Contest, along with being a guitar player (a pretty lousy one), photographer, husband, and father.

Matt Patterson is an independent typographer/coder based in Reading, England. Introduced to the Web in 1996, he started building sites immediately and became interested in CSS when he realized it meant you could do actual typography on the Web. These days, he mostly spends his time designing and building websites and web applications based on open standards at the front- and back-end. He runs Reprocessed (http://reprocessed.org), where he writes about design, web stuff, and whatever else strikes his fancy. He is married to Clare.

Dave Shea is the cultivator of the CSS Zen Garden (http://www.csszengarden.com) and a member of the Web Standards Project. Working as a graphic designer in beautiful Vancouver, British Columbia, Canada, Dave writes about all things web-related on his daily weblog, mezzoblue (http://mezzoblue.com).

John Simons has been floating around Seattle, Washington, since 1998, doing various jobs and projects in writing, programming, and design. He has a computer engineering degree from the University of Washington, and his current interests (aside from twiddling <div>s) include typography, newspaper design, and web server administration.

Michael Switzer has been programming since the fourth grade in 1983. Since 1996, he's been involved in various roles of web development, most recently directing Propaganda by Design, a web development firm in Buffalo, New York. He gets an adrenaline rush from the challenges and demands of creating sites that use standards, are accessible and user-friendly, and function across multiple browsers and platforms.

Dan Rubin is a graphic designer and web developer from Fort Lauderdale, Florida. Working with the Web since Mosaic was released, Dan publishes his thoughts on design and the Internet via his weblog SuperfluousBanter (http://superfluousbanter.org). He is the president of Webgraph (http://webgraph.com) and cofounder of SineLogic (http://sinelogic.com), agencies specializing in brand development and building usable, accessible websites.

Michael Pick lives in New York City and is now finally gainfully employed at a really cool multimedia company, after a few years spent working as a freelance web and print designer. Mike came into the field when he returned to college to earn a bachelor's degree in design (with honors) from Nova Scotia College of Art and Design (NSCAD) in Halifax, Canada, after a somewhat successful (depending on the yardstick) career as a musician. He writes periodically on web design issues for his own website, http://mikepick.com, exploring CSS and the structural web design strategies that have proven to be so lucrative.

Cornelia Lange has more than 25 years of experience in different trades (tourism and advertising among them). After studying economic science, she started her own telemarketing and new media agency, clkm (http://www.clkm.de). Since 2000, she has specialized in web and CSS design. In 2004, she's joining up with Olaf Gleba to form the agency http://www.x-appearance.com, with the aim of achieving technical web content accessibility/usability in accordance with sophisticated graphic design through the creation of new websites or the modification of existing websites.

Cornelia would like to thank the members of the German CSS-Design mailing list (operated by Michael Charlier) for their suggestions and assistance. Without them, the CSS resource http://www.css-technik.de would have never been developed. Also, she would like to thank Beth Christmas for her friendly care, Chris Mills for asking her to join the project, and David Powers and Olaf Gleba for their adept notes.

About the Technical Reviewer

 **David Powers** is a writer and broadcaster on international affairs, specializing in Japan, who also just happens to have a passion for web design. As editor of BBC Japanese TV, he created his first serious website in 1995 after recovering from the shock of hearing how much it would cost for the IT department to do it for him. Instead, he persuaded them to let him have a bit of server space for nothing, and he built it himself. He kept the 80-page site in both Japanese and English updated on a daily basis until leaving the BBC in 1999 to set up his own business, Japan Interface (http://japan-interface.co.uk).

David now concentrates on writing, translation (he has translated several plays from Japanese), and bilingual web design. He is coauthor of *Foundation Dreamweaver MX 2004* (friends of ED, 2004).

Acknowledgments

Many thanks to all the people at Apress who have been involved in the second edition of this book. Particular thanks to David Powers and Nicole LeClerc, without whom you'd have a much harder job understanding what we were trying to say, and to Beth and Laura, without whom the book wouldn't exist. Thanks also to Ben, Jack, and others who have made useful comments, critiques, and requests that have pushed and shaped my chapters. Finally, thanks to Owen, without whom there wouldn't be a book; to Eric and Steve, without whom the book would be poorer; and to Bruce and Chris, glasshaus survivors who have been with the book through two editions and two publishers.

—Matt Patterson

Introduction

CASCADING STYLE SHEETS (**CSS**) enable developers to add color, typographic style, positioning, and much more to plain HTML and XHTML pages.

Prior to CSS, developers were resigned to squeezing the last drop of presentation from HTML elements that were designed simply for structure or from markup that was added to the language with complete disregard of its original intention. Many also used true hacks, such as invisible GIF files.

CSS has many advantages over those techniques, most of which stem from the fact that CSS is a complete separation of the document's presentation from its content and structure. With CSS, the developers' style choices no longer limit web pages to specific browsers, and instead allow full access across all platforms and devices, as was always the intention for the Web. Developers can also change the entire design of a site by modifying one stylesheet, rather than updating the markup in every HTML document the site uses.

This book covers what you need to know to understand and use CSS. This is no small task because understanding CSS requires that you fully understand how the World Wide Web Consortium (W3C) means markup to be used, something that has been largely glossed over by developers for years. Nor is it always easy to apply CSS because browser vendors have had similar poor respect for the W3C recommendations, resulting in many inconsistencies and incomplete support of CSS properties. On top of these two hurdles, CSS itself is suitably large and flexible enough to allow a full range of design and style; there's a great deal for developers to learn, and to continue learning.

To make this task manageable, this book doesn't attempt to cover every possible CSS property or all nuances of the language. Instead, it takes a direct approach to the core techniques of CSS, staying within what works across current browsers as much as possible and providing solutions to browser failings where they're unavoidable. The intent of this book is to give you the real-world grounding and guidance needed to accompany the complete CSS specifications online at http://www.w3.org/TR/REC-CSS1 and http://www.w3.org/TR/REC-CSS2.

The book flows as follows:

First, we cover the necessary background to CSS: why it was introduced and what advantages it has. We follow this with separate chapters on the concept of presentation and the structure of XHTML to provide the key background to applying CSS successfully.

Next, we delve into the meat of CSS: the syntax. Included are chapters on how CSS rules work, how to write them, and how to attach them to your XHTML. These are followed by a chapter dedicated to CSS layout.

The third major topic is real-world issues of using CSS. We cover the main browser defects you must look out for, and we discuss techniques that will enable you to quickly detect and resolve bugs on your own.

With this practical foundation in place, we finally bring you into the realm of more advanced CSS with an in-depth chapter on typography and several complete CSS design projects to amaze and inspire you— these are modern web pages by professional developers.

Who Is This Book For?

This book is for everyone who creates web pages from the code up, whether they come from a design background or a coding background.

The book assumes readers are experienced in using HTML. Knowledge of XHTML is also useful (all examples will use this markup language), but it isn't essential, as HTML and XHTML are closely related. No other skills, such as scripting or programming languages, are needed.

What Do I Need to Begin?

As with HTML, you can write CSS using nothing more than your favorite text editor, and you can display CSS using your favorite web browser. There are other products you can use to edit CSS, just as there are more complex HTML editors, but these aren't essential to use and learn CSS.

To test and debug your CSS-based pages, it's useful to have access to a number of different web browsers on a variety of operating systems. In Chapter 11 the various options are discussed in full.

Lorem Ipsum . . .

Throughout this book you'll see sample text beginning "Lorem ipsum dolor sit amet, consectetuer adipiscing elitinclude . . . ." This nonsense text, and slight variations on this theme, is commonly used in the early stages of designing a web page, before the real content is specified, to focus the eye on the design rather than the content. Using text such as this is commonly called **greeking**.

The text itself is reported to be a garbled portion of Cicero's Latin text *De Finibus et Malorum* (*The Extremes of Good and Evil* in English). Having an origin in a real language means that the text "looks" real, at least compared to English and most European languages, because it has words of appropriate lengths, and an average numbers of ascenders and descenders on the letters.

Style Conventions

We've used a number of styles in the book to help you understand what's going on:

We've used **this style** to flag new or important subjects.

To talk about code within text we use this style.

New blocks of markup and stylesheets are in the following style:

```
<html>
<style type="text/css">
  p {
    font-family: Verdana, Arial, sans-serif;
    }
</style>
<body>
  <p>Text to be styled</p>
</body>
</html>
```

If we're amending XHTML markup or CSS stylesheets, perhaps adding in a new line or making changes to an existing one, we use a white background for the code that you've already seen together with bold typeface to highlight the new code:

```
<html>
<style type="text/css">
p {
  font-family: Verdana, Arial, sans-serif;
  color:red;
  }
</style>
<body>
  <p>Text to be styled</p>
</body>
</html>
```

NOTE *Essential, not-to-be-missed information is indicated by this element.*

friends of ED

For news, books, sample chapters, code downloads, author interviews, and more, point your browser to `http://www.friendsofed.com`. Be sure to sign up for our monthly newsletter to get the latest gossip about upcoming books!

You can also visit our support forums at `http://www.friendsofed.com/forums` for help with any of the tutorials in this book or just to chat with like-minded designers and developers. Here, you'll find a variety of designers talking about all manner of tricks, tips, and techniques, and they might even provide you with ideas, insights, and inspiration.

Even if you don't have problems, e-mail `feedback@friendsofed.com` to let us know what you think of this book—we'd love to hear from you! Whether it's to request future books, ask about friends of ED, or tell us about sites you've created after reading this book, drop us a line!

CHAPTER 1

Foundation Concepts

THE WORLD WIDE WEB ("the Web" for short) is a massive media revolution empowering individuals and organizations with self-publishing capabilities and a ready-made, worldwide audience. Whereas the printing press gave us the ability to record and distribute information, the Web has increased those abilities exponentially, removing the barrier of the commercial publishing system from the production of self-published materials.

But the ease of publishing on the Web, an integral part of the Web's success, has also contributed to the creation of significant hurdles that threaten to keep the Web from developing to its full potential.

Recall that the Web is an interconnected group of computers, from the army of small iMacs and PCs on the desktops of homes and offices around the world to massive web server farms that feed pages to an ever-increasing audience. On these web servers are documents (web pages), each of which can be connected to other documents via hyperlinks. Web surfers use web browsers, such as Netscape Navigator, Microsoft Internet Explorer, or the Opera browser, to retrieve and view these web pages from the web servers that serve them.

As you know, web pages themselves are constructed with a simple markup language called Hypertext Markup Language (HTML). Using a markup language, an author "marks up" a document with structural and other metainformation right alongside the document's content. This system is designed to make Web publishing simple. But as innocuous as that may sound, HTML is at the center of a significant struggle in the Web publishing world: Is HTML to be used as a *presentation* language, used to define the visual appearance of a web page, or is it to be used as a traditional markup language, defining the *structure* of documents and leaving layout and visual design to a style language? It's a complicated question, and at its heart lies the subject of this book: Cascading Style Sheets (CSS).

> **NOTE** *To understand the difference between "structure" and "presentation," consider the following sentence: "William Faulkner's <u>Sanctuary</u> is one heck of a scary book." Structurally speaking, the word "Sanctuary" is a book title; in terms of presentation, on the other hand, the word is underlined. This distinction is lost on many because of the ubiquity of word processing applications such as Microsoft Word, which blur the line between structure and presentation. In a word processing application, you don't select the text "Sanctuary" and click a Book Title button. You click the Underline button on the toolbar, which underlines the title as you wish. In the following sections you'll see why marking up text structurally produces powerful documents.*

CSS is a style language that you can use in conjunction with HTML to define the visual presentation of a web page. "If that's the case," you might ask, "then why is there any question of using HTML as a presentation language?" The short answer is that CSS didn't exist until 1996, 5 years after the birth of the Web, and even now it's not fully supported by the dominant web browsers. Thus, web professionals have taken to twisting HTML to suit their own design and presentation purposes, misusing the markup language and adding elements to pages that contribute nothing to the content.

Style languages may also be used to control more than just the visual presentation of documents. For instance, aural browsers can use stylesheets to guide inflection and intonation when reading documents aloud to people with visual impairments. This book deals nearly exclusively with stylesheets used for visual browsers, but it's important to note that the markup practices recommended herein will also allow you to attach other types of stylesheets to your documents. The Web is bigger than what we can see.

A Short History of the Web

To understand why using CSS is vital to the health of the Web, you must know a little history. You may be tempted to skip this section, having probably read similar accounts of the Web's short life countless times. However, we encourage you not to skip ahead, but to instead read on and think about the implications of the Web's short but rapidly evolving past.

In 1990, Tim Berners-Lee released the world's first web browser and launched the world's first web server, on which he published for discussion the specifications of many of the technologies that run the Web today (over 10 years later!). His goal in releasing this software was to facilitate the sharing of research documents among scientists. He created a Standard Generalized Markup Language (SGML) application that he called Hypertext Markup Language (HTML), which was a document format suitable for transmission over his new protocols.

The truly distinctive element of his whole system was the *hyperlink*, which put the "hyper" in Hypertext Markup Language. The hyperlink may not seem all that revolutionary to you now, and in fact even before the Web it had been around as a concept for decades. Experiments in hypertext systems were not new, but before Berners-Lee, no hypertext application had been a part of a network the size of the 1990 Internet, and it was the combination of the network and hypertext that made his experiment a success.

As you know, the hyperlink's power is that it allows random connections between disparate bits of data. It escapes the traditional hierarchical data storage systems of computers and allows documents to be "linked" to one another in arbitrary ways. It mimics the associative nature of the human brain, which connects memories, thoughts, and information through a complex web of neurons.

The hyperlink's usefulness is limited to the pool of data that it links together. Berners-Lee developed a system for linking data from any computer on the Internet to any other computer on the Internet, and in so doing maximized the power of hypertext. For this reason, an essential requirement for the Web as Berners-Lee envisioned it is *openness*. In his own words,

> *"I have fought since the beginning of the Web for its openness: that anyone can read web pages with any software running on any hardware. This is what makes the Web itself."*[1]

As openness increases, so does the power of hypertext, and therefore the power of the Web as a whole.

Berners-Lee invented HTML in order to maximize openness. A simple text document format could be transmitted easily using his new Internet protocols to any computer platform that implemented those protocols. Using standard American Standard Code for Information Interchange (ASCII) text as a file format ensured that existing computer platforms would have no problem handling HTML documents, and choosing to build HTML as an SGML application, which was a platform-neutral system for describing the contents of a document, created an open environment for platform-specific browser makers.

HTML documents in 1990 were radically different from how they are today. In the early '90s, the familiar look of today's Web, with flashing images, animations, and multimedia files, was an unimagined thing of the future. To understand how HTML got where it is now, we have to take a closer look at where it came from.

Where Did HTML Come From?

As stated in the previous section, Berners-Lee based his new markup language on SGML, which has a wonderful history of its own.

In the late 1960s, Charles Goldfarb left the legal profession to work with IBM, where he established the principles of modern markup languages. His goal was to create a system that would enable the specification of documents that could be stored in a database, edited, and output for printing with a minimum of difficulty. The documents themselves were to be stored without any presentational information; they were to contain only content and structural information. Goldfarb's work, together with that of Ed Mosher and Ray Lorie, resulted in Generalized Markup Language (GML), an ambitious effort that overcame incredible obstacles.

---

1. See http://news.com.com/2100-1023-275248.html?legacy=cnet&tag=tp_pr.

A markup language is used to mark up, or tag, a document's elements with information regarding the elements' structural position in the document. A page header in a markup document, for example, might look like this:

```
<header>On the Nature of Markup</header>
```

However, before GML, markup (then called *procedural markup*) was application specific—the text editor and the page composition program of Goldfarb's project required their own unique markup to process the documents. What GML did was to establish a uniform set of markup tags. Documents so marked up could then be "understood" by *all* the different applications needed to process the documents. The goal was platform and application neutrality, a system whereby different applications on different platforms could share documents freely.

SGML, the next step in the evolution of markup languages, pushed GML even further with the introduction of document type definitions (DTDs), which allowed the creation of new sets of markup tags for any given set of documents. A validating parser could then read the DTD, which defined a specific markup system, and ensure the accuracy of the marked-up document. Applications could use the DTD to make sense of the document.

So what does that have to do with HTML, you ask? Well, HTML is an SGML application: a markup language defined according to the rules of SGML. As such, it's intended to communicate the structural meaning of HTML document elements with a set of tags defined in the HTML DTD. The following is a simple example of a web page, starting with the document type declaration (<!DOCTYPE...) and followed by the HTML markup:

```
<!DOCTYPE html PUBLIC "-//W3C//DTD XHTML 1.0 Transitional//EN"
     "http://www.w3.org/TR/xhtml1/DTD/xhtml1-transitional.dtd">
<html>
  <head>
    <title>An HTML document</title>
  </head>
  <body>
    <p>Herein is the lone content of our web page.</p>
  </body>
</html>
```

As you can see, the content of the page is contained within a series of nested tags, which provide a structural framework for the content. The markup of the page is intended to communicate the semantic relationships of the page's elements to one another.

In this book, we use Extensible Hypertext Markup Language (XHTML) as our markup language in all examples. XHTML is a reformulation of the HTML vocabulary as an Extensible Markup Language (XML) application, which is itself an

SGML application. XML was developed to sit in between HTML and SGML, retaining the simplicity of the former while providing some of the power and flexibility of the latter. The Web of the future will rely heavily on XML, and so the World Wide Web Consortium (W3C) has discontinued the development of HTML, recommending instead the migration to XHTML, which will allow documents authored today to be forward compatible with the XML-heavy Web of the future.

What Happened to HTML?

As we've already mentioned, when the Web was but a toddler, there was no style language available to web authors to instruct browsers on how to display the elements of a page. Instead, browsers had internal rules that governed all presentational aspects of a web page. For instance, a piece of content marked as a section header would be typically rendered in a relatively large font with bold text, and something tagged as a `<blockquote>` would usually appear with indented left and right margins.

The user was given access to some of these rules through the browser's preferences. For example, a web surfer could select what color a link should be and what typeface the browser should use. These preference settings are applied globally, to all web pages, not to specific pages or sites.

However, web authors had no way to control layout or typography. They were totally at the mercy of the browser's internal page rendering engine, and these engines differed from browser to browser. For instance, take the `<em>` tag, which is used to mark up a bit of text intended to be emphasized. Some browsers choose to represent the `<em>` element with *italicized* text, and others use **bolded** text.

Now, this situation wasn't particularly problematic for the first web audience—the scientists who shared the first web pages were much more interested in the content of the documents than the typeface and color with which they were displayed. But, as the Web began to build an audience that wasn't exclusively research scientists sharing scientific results, the desire to control visual design of web pages grew accordingly. Early extensions to the HTML language therefore included `<b>` and `<i>` tags, which allowed the author to specify whether text should be bold or italic, respectively. Such minor additions were relatively benign, and didn't seriously affect the structural value of a document, but many more additions were to come that would have more problematic results.

When Netscape introduced version 1.1 of its popular Navigator browser, a new element was added to the HTML author's arsenal: the `<table>` element. An HTML `<table>` is intended to hold tabular data, with column and row headers organizing a grid of information.

The `<table>` tag was a great addition to the HTML language, and it was especially useful for displaying scientific results data, but it quickly became an innocent victim in a nefarious plot to twist the usage of the HTML language, which resulted in the dot-com collapse of the year 2000 and the loss of thousands of Web-related jobs. Well, not really. . . . However, web authors did see something in the `<table>` tag that it wasn't intended for: The `<table>` tag could be used to create multicolumn web page layouts.

Tables were quickly put to use controlling page layouts. Instead of containing tabular data, web authors used tables to contain whole pages. With no other way to define page layouts, and with an army of web authors arriving on the burgeoning web design scene without an inkling of what a markup language was supposed to be, the `<table>` tag quickly became the poster child for abused HTML elements.

In addition, Netscape and Microsoft, then the dominant web browser makers, engaged in an all-out battle to win users to their respective browsers. As the Web rose to prominence in the computing world, the browser quickly became one of the most important pieces of software on a computer. Some said the browser would replace the operating system; others said the Web itself was a new platform. Also, the dot-com explosion of the 1990s brought commercial interests to the Web with a force that no well-meaning technologist could combat. The need for companies to maintain a consistent brand image on their new web sites was greater than any concern for the integrity of HTML as a markup language. A good-looking web site was more important than correct markup.

Sensing this need of the commercial web page author to control page presentation, and using that as a way to attract both developers and users to their software, both Microsoft and Netscape encouraged the use of the `<table>` tag for layout and introduced a series of HTML extensions, such as the abominable `<blink>` and the obnoxious `<marquee>`. These elements were, of course, not universally supported, and they represented a willful disregard for HTML as a structural markup language. The `<blink>` element, for example, communicates nothing of structural value about the text it tags—it merely instructs the Netscape browser on how to display it.

Perhaps the worst of all such extensions, however, was the egregious `<font>` element. Although today all browsers support the tag, which allows a web author to define the color, size, and typeface of text, its use encourages the common thinking that HTML is intended to communicate document presentation. Combine the `<font>` element with the `<table>` element and the fact that the once-dominant Netscape browser didn't carry `<font>` specifications into `<table>` elements, and you find the explanation for the morass of markup nearly devoid of structural information that passes for an HTML document even today.

In addition to using semantically meaningless tags such as the `<font>` element and abusing tables for page layout purposes, web authors have attempted to overcome the shortcomings of HTML by placing text in images that are then loaded into the page via the `<img>` element or by building whole sites in proprietary technologies such as Macromedia Flash, a plug-in application that loads in a browser window. Both of these techniques afford the designer much greater control over presentation than HTML does, especially typographically speaking, as they basically give free rein on typeface, color, and layout. When compared to the meager presentation control HTML affords, even when using `<font>` and `<table>`, a web site built with images instead of text is indeed very attractive.

However, such practices have negative consequences. They destroy the structural meaning of a web page's markup. This results in the following problems:

- **Inaccessibility:** The Web's audience isn't limited to users of Internet Explorer and Netscape Navigator. In addition to these premier visual browsers, there are a plethora of other visual browsers that have smaller but not insignificant groups of users. Opera, Konqueror, Mozilla, Firebird, Safari, and countless other browsers are used by a growing number of web surfers, who chose them because they typically render pages faster than the "big two," have a smaller disk footprint, or are less prone to security hole exploits. In addition, the Web has already spread to the television with the WebTV browser, web browsers are now a standard feature on digital phones, and web browsers are currently even being built into household appliances. Perhaps most important, special software, such as a screen reader, helps the blind to access web content. Web pages with presentation-oriented markup designed exclusively for Internet Explorer or Netscape Navigator are often rendered unusable by such devices.

- **Degraded performance:** Bad HTML practices used to achieve page layout and design goals can actually make web pages load more slowly in the browser. Using `<table>` and `<font>` elements or inserting site copy into images adds bulk to each web page. Not only does that bulk require more time to download, but also it slows the browser's rendering engine down when it tries to display the page. It's a double whammy. Nested tables, which were almost a necessity when trying to achieve complicated table layouts, increase rendering time logarithmically in many common browsers.

- **Increased production work:** Reliance on HTML presentation hacks can seriously affect the maintainability of a site. Not only does the site risk future obsolescence as new browsers are introduced, but also simple changes to a large site can become a nightmare of "search and replace," with fingers crossed. Inserting presentation rules directly into HTML documents with `<font>` and `<table>` tags creates a maintenance headache, as any changes to the site presentation must be made to each document.

Later in this chapter we explore how the use of CSS and structurally sound markup solves all of these problems.

Introducing Cascading Style Sheets

The full adoption of CSS for web page layout and typographical design is the next step in the evolution of the Web. Tired of abusing HTML by using it to control the presentation of web pages, web professionals are turning en masse to a technology that first made its official appearance as far back as 1996 in the hopes of rescuing the Web from fracture and the Web's content from unnecessary obsolescence.

CSS has finally garnered enough support from browser makers and generated enough excitement from web professionals to start making a difference on the Web. With the helpful nudging of advocacy groups such as the Web Standards Project (WaSP), browser makers Microsoft and Netscape have recently released versions of their browsers with CSS support orders of magnitude better than previous releases. And Opera has of its own initiative put forth arguably the most complete CSS implementation in its flagship browser, owing in no small part to the fact that Håkon Lie, the company's founder and chief engineer, was a member of the group that issued the first CSS recommendation.

Even with great strides in CSS browser support, the adoption of CSS by developers is no simple task, especially for those who have earned their bread and butter relying on the ubiquitous `<table>` hack and "single-pixel GIF" tricks (which use invisible images inserted in a page's markup to stretch page elements to the desired dimensions) to force browsers to present their page designs consistently in a varied and inconsistent field of browsers. For such a group of wizened developers, deciding to use CSS is more than a choice to change methods of defining page presentation. To be successful and rewarding, the use of CSS must be motivated by a thorough understanding of the deficiencies of the Web as we know it, as well as the promise that CSS and new design methodologies hold as we try to push the world's largest and most important media revolution forward into the twenty-first century.

For young developers, the generation of people who are the first to have grown up with the Web as a household name, we must find ways to teach proper development practices, lest they continue the unfortunate trend of the early Web toward the use of proprietary HTML extensions and invalid markup. The view-source school of web design, once a great boon as web professionals learned from, shared, and expanded upon the work of their peers, has become a dangerous teacher. Its classes are filled with bad examples—creaky old markup and questionable development techniques that hinder progress.

That's why we wrote this book: to train and educate the builders of the Web to use the appropriate technologies for the task at hand, so that the Web in 10 years will be the Web that Tim Berners-Lee intended when he invented it and not an ever-increasing morass of unstructured information.

The Birth of CSS

It may seem to you at this point that stylesheets are an afterthought, a change in plans for the Web. But the world's first web browser (called "WorldWideWeb" and built by Tim Berners-Lee) included an internal style language the browser used when rendering HTML pages. In fact, many first-generation web browsers had their own style languages, some of which were even considered when the CSS recommendation was first under development. A style language is a natural— even necessary—partner for a markup language, for as you know, a markup language isn't intended to define presentation.

However, these early HTML style languages were internal; they were used by the browser and weren't available to the document author. It quickly became apparent to the Web's early architects that control of presentation must in some way be wrested from a browser's internal presentation rules and handed to the web author. In 1994, Håkon Lie published the first draft of the Cascading HTML Style Sheets proposal (`http://www.w3.org/People/howcome/p/cascade.html`).

As Lie envisioned it, the style language for the Web must somehow combine author and user preferences. His proposal accomplished this with a *cascade,* which allowed for multiple sets of style rules and a well-defined system for determining the weight of competing rules. This cascade set Lie's style language apart from other style languages of the day and made it the natural choice for a presentation language to accompany HTML.

The W3C was formed in 1994 to establish technical standards for the growth and development of the Web, and it published the first CSS recommendation, known as CSS1, in December 1996. In May 1998, the W3C released CSS2, which improved and expanded upon the first recommendation. CSS2.1 should be released in 2004, and CSS3 is currently under development.

These recommendations, although not actually "standards," provide browser makers with the necessary information to implement CSS in a uniform manner. Internet Explorer 3.0 was the first browser to implement CSS in August 1996, before CSS was even an official recommendation. Netscape followed suit, and since then nearly all web browsers have implemented it.

As you'll learn, browser implementations of CSS vary widely, a problem that causes many web professionals to run screaming from stylesheets with their hair afire. We hope in this book to keep you from that fate by presenting CSS as it currently works in modern browsers, advising you where older browsers may fail, and suggesting where future browsers may improve on CSS support. In the next section we take a look at CSS as it exists in its natural environment: the web page.

What Is CSS?

CSS at its core is extremely simple and powerful. It allows you to attach style rules to HTML markup elements, such as the <p> or <a> element. These rules

9

define the presentational aspects of the HTML elements to which they apply, such as color or typeface.

Take a look at the following sample page, YeOldeCheeseShop.htm, which includes style rules embedded in the page markup:

```
<!DOCTYPE html PUBLIC "-//W3C//DTD XHTML 1.0 Transitional//EN"
      "http://www.w3.org/TR/xhtml1/DTD/xhtml1-transitional.dtd">
<html xmlns="http://www.w3.org/1999/xhtml" xml:lang="en" lang="en">
<head>
<title>Ye Olde Cheese Shop</title>

<style type="text/css">
body {
  font-family: Verdana, Arial, sans-serif;
  }

a {
  color: red;
  text-decoration: none;
  font-weight: bold;
  }

#Header {
  position: absolute;
  left: 25px;
  top: 10px;
  }

#MainText {
  position: absolute;
  left: 225px;
  top: 100px;
  margin-right: 25px;
  }

#SiteNav {
  position: absolute;
  left: 25px;
  top: 100px;
  width: 175px;
  }
</style>

</head>
<body>
```

```
<div id="Header">
  <h1>Ye Olde Cheese Shop</h1>
</div>

<div id="SiteNav">
  <h3>Choose a Cheese</h3>
  <ul>
    <li><a href="">Beaufort</a></li>
    <li><a href="">Bleu d'Auvergne</a></li>
    <li><a href="">Brie de Meaux</a></li>
    <li><a href="">Brillat Saverin</a></li>
    <li><a href="">St Maure de Touraine</a></li>
    <li><a href="">Chabichou de Poitou</a></li>
    <li><a href="">Camembert</a></li>
    <li><a href="">Cantal Entre Deux</a></li>
    <li><a href="">Chaource</a></li>
    <li><a href="">Comte</a></li>
    <li><a href="">Crottin de Chavignol</a></li>
    <li><a href="">Emmenthal</a></li>
    <li><a href="">Epoisses</a></li>
    <li><a href="">Langres</a></li>
    <li><a href="">Mimolette</a></li>
    <li><a href="">Morbier</a></li>
    <li><a href="">Munster</a></li>
    <li><a href="">Picodon</a></li>
    <li><a href="">Pont l'Eveque</a></li>
    <li><a href="">Reblochon</a></li>
    <li><a href="">Rocamadour</a></li>
    <li><a href="">Roquefort</a></li>
    <li><a href="">St. Marcellin</a></li>
    <li><a href="">St Nectaire</a></li>
    <li><a href="">Tomme de Chevre</a></li>
  </ul>
</div>

<div id="MainText">
  <h2>Cheese: it's not just for the French anymore</h2>
  <p>Lorem ipsum dolor sit amet, consectetuer adipiscing elit, sed diam nonummy nibh
euismod tincidunt ut laoreet dolore magna aliquam erat volutpat. Ut wisi enim ad
minim veniam, quis nostrud exercitation ulliam corper suscipit lobortis nisl ut
aliquip ex ea commodo consequat. Duis autem veleum iriure dolor in hendrerit in
vulputate velit esse molestie consequat, vel willum lunombro dolore eu feugiat
nulla facilisis at vero eros et accumsan et iusto odio dignissim qui blandit
praesent luptatum zzril delenit augue duis dolore te feugait nulla facilisi.</p>
```

11

```
<p>Li Europan lingues es membres del sam familie. Lor separat existentie es un
myth. Por scientie, musica, sport etc., li tot Europa usa li sam vocabularium. Li
lingues differe solmen in li grammatica, li pronunciation e li plu commun
vocabules. Omnicos directe al desirabilita de un nov lingua franca: on refusa
continuar payar custosi traductores. It solmen va esser necessi far uniform
grammatica, pronunciation e plu sommun paroles.</p>
</div>

</body>
</html>
```

This page displays as shown in Figure 1-1.

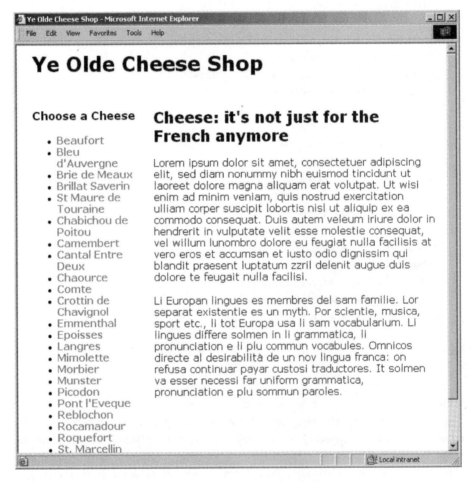

Figure 1-1. YeOldeCheeseShop.htm rendered in a browser

Now let's take a closer look at the markup and style rules. We go into this in much greater detail in future chapters, so don't worry if not everything makes sense. It's enough now to get a general sense of how stylesheets interact with XHTML markup. The first thing to notice is the `<style>` element itself:

```
<style type="text/css">
...
</style>
```

The `<style>` element appears in the `<head>` element of an XHTML document. Its `type` attribute declares that the style language is CSS, and it overrides the default stylesheet language used by the browser when rendering stylesheets. Actually, there are no other style languages in use by browsers today, except for Netscape Navigator 4.*x*'s proprietary JavaScript Stylesheets (JSSS), which use the `type` attribute value `"text/javascript"`, now virtually obsolete as the browser fades from existence. However, as with many things in CSS, the `type` attribute looks forward to a time when browsers provide support for multiple style languages.

Contained within the `<style>` element are the style rules that define certain presentational aspects of the page. Each rule contains two main parts: a *selector* followed by a list of *declarations*. The selector defines which XHTML page element(s) the rule applies to, and the declarations define the presentational aspects that are to be applied to those elements.

The first rule in our sample page (as shown in the following code) selects the `<body>` element and declares that text within it should be presented in the Verdana typeface. If that font isn't installed on the system, then Arial should be used. If the Arial typeface isn't available either, a sans-serif typeface should be used:

```
body {
  font-family: Verdana, Arial, sans-serif;
  }
```

The next rule in our stylesheet declares that all `<a>` elements are to be displayed with bold, red text with no text decoration (underlines, overlines, and so on):

```
a {
  color: red;
  font-weight: bold;
  text-decoration: none;
  }
```

The final three rules in our stylesheet are quite different from the first two:

```
#Header {
  position: absolute;
  left: 25px;
  top: 10px;
  }

#MainText {
  position: absolute;
  left: 225px;
  top: 100px;
  margin-right: 25px;
  }

#SiteNav {
  position: absolute;
  left: 25px;
  top: 100px;
  width: 175px;
  }
```

Each of these three rules doesn't apply to all elements of any one type, such as all links in the preceding example, but instead applies to elements with a specific id attribute value. The # character is used to indicate this type of rule, followed by the id attribute value itself. So, the following rule:

```
#Header {
  position: absolute;
  left: 25px;
  top: 10px;
  }
```

applies to the following element:

```
<div id="Header">
  <h1>Ye Olde Cheese Shop</h1>
</div>
```

and instructs the browser on the exact location that the <div> element should appear onscreen.

The preceding example is, of course, quite simple and doesn't even really scratch the surface of what CSS is capable of. In subsequent chapters we explore how CSS gives you powerful typographic control over your pages, allowing you to specify not only the font, but also the relative size, the line height, and numerous other presentational aspects of your text. You'll also learn how to select broad areas or certain specific elements of your document with a given rule, along with how to use CSS to define complex page layouts.

The Separation of Structure and Presentation

In this chapter we've presented a short history of the Web, told you how using HTML as a presentation language is injurious to your sites and the Web as a whole, and introduced you to the basics of using CSS for web page presentation. We want to leave you with perhaps the most important information so far: the reasons you as a web professional should want CSS. What will you get out of it?

An important principle that underlies all the arguments in favor of CSS is referred to as "the separation of structure and presentation" or sometimes "the separation of content and presentation." This separation of markup (structure and content) and style rules (presentation) is valuable to web professionals in many ways, as you'll soon see. (Chapters 2 and 3 expound more completely on these topics.)

Earlier you learned how HTML used as a presentation language results in several negative consequences, including decreased accessibility, degraded performance, and increased production work. Now we detail how the separation of structure and presentation, using sound structural HTML markup with CSS for presentation, results in the following benefits:

- Increased accessibility

- Improved performance

- Decreased production work

Accessibility

Accessibility is all about making your web pages available to the maximum number of users and Internet devices. With sound structural markup, your HTML pages are accessible to and understandable by the widest possible audience, including site visitors with older browsers, next year's visitors using new browsers that are yet to be released, blind visitors who rely on screen readers to access your site, and last but not least, indexing agents.

"What is sound structural markup?" you may ask. Well, let's take a look at an example of *bad* markup:

```
<font size="5" face="Arial" color="green">My Page Title</font><br /><br />
```

In this example, the `<font>` element has been used to give a page header a certain typeface, color, and size. Two `<br />` elements follow to give the text the proper bottom margin. This will look as desired in most major browsers today, which gives the false impression that all is well. In fact, by using the `<font>` element, which communicates no information about the text "My Page Title" other than presentational directions, we've rendered the text less intelligible to both old browsers, screen readers, and indexing agents.

On the other hand, the following markup communicates a great deal of information:

```
<h2>My Page Title</h2>
```

By using the `<h2>` element, we've instructed all devices that parse the HTML that "My Page Title" is a header. Screen readers can give special emphasis to the text; old, current, and future browsers can render it appropriately onscreen (with or without further style rules); and indexing agents, such as the spider for the search engine Google that crawls the Web to add pages to the Google database, can give extra weight to the header text in their search result algorithms, which leads to our pages appearing higher in the search results for the most relevant search terms.

"But you've removed the presentational cues, and now the text is no longer green or displayed with the Arial typeface," you say. Adding the following style rule to the document solves this problem:

```
h2 {
    font-family: Arial;
    color: green;
    font-size: 1.4em;
    }
```

In addition, now that the rule has been declared, all `<h2>` elements will share the same presentation without the need to surround each one with extraneous markup. This leads us to another benefit of the separation of structure and presentation.

Improved Performance

By providing one level of indirection, or abstraction, CSS embedded in the head of a document streamlines document markup, improving download times and speeding up page rendering. Instead of relying on markup to instruct browsers on how to display each separate instance of an element, CSS allows you to declare a style rule once and have that presentational cue apply to all such elements. Such file-size savings really start to add up as the number of times a styled element appears in a document increases. Generally speaking, the larger the document, the more it benefits from CSS.

Even more file-size savings can be achieved with slightly more advanced CSS techniques. For instance, CSS allows you to group selectors, so that one style rule can apply to multiple elements, like so:

```
h1, h2, h3, h4, h5, h6 {
  font-family: Arial;
  color: green;
  }
```

Furthermore, another level of abstraction can be added by using external stylesheets, creating even greater download time reductions. The examples you've seen in this chapter use embedded stylesheets, which are contained within the <head> element of the page to which they apply. Using external stylesheets allows you to link a stylesheet to multiple XHTML pages. This can significantly improve performance on a site, because the stylesheet needs to be downloaded only once per visitor. It's then stored in the visitor's browser cache, and subsequent page loads from the site by that visitor require only the download of the XHTML markup.

Smaller file sizes and cached external stylesheets not only mean a speedier site, which makes your visitors happy, but also can result in lowered hosting costs for you, as your site takes less bandwidth to serve.

In addition to bandwidth savings and the speed increases your site visitors will enjoy when you use well-structured markup and CSS, you as a web professional will have at your disposal a powerful style language that allows much greater control over the appearance of your pages than the <font> and <table> elements could ever provide.

As if that wasn't enough, CSS and solid markup are the foundation for dynamic HTML (DHTML), with which you can add dynamic behaviors to your web documents. With DHTML, JavaScript is used to manipulate page elements and their style properties to create dynamic pages that can react to user input, animate page elements, and provide new and innovative interfaces to your site visitors. We won't be talking much about DHTML in this book, but the skills you'll learn here will set you well on the path to understanding how to build dynamic sites with DHTML.

Decreased Production Work

It may be hard to believe, but not only does the use of CSS and sound structural markup improve the experience of your site visitors and provide you with cost savings and a powerful style language, it actually makes your job easier as a web professional. By separating presentational directions from your HTML, especially when using external stylesheets, you make it easier to build and maintain sites. Your clean markup will be easier to develop initially, because the job of marking up the information in your HTML pages can be a discrete task, unfettered by concerns about color and typeface. Maintaining pages with clean HTML becomes a simple task also, saving you from the headaches of searching through lines of bloated HTML for that one simple link you want to change.

Redesigning a site also becomes a much simpler task. When you use an external stylesheet for a whole site, redesigning involves changing only that one document instead of editing each individual HTML page.

All of these improvements that you gain through the use of CSS result in cost savings that make your clients happier and your wallet fatter.

Summary

CSS is an important part of the future of the Web. It's unfortunate that a style language wasn't available to the Web's early document authors, as it might have helped change the problematic route that HTML took, which was driven by author desire to control page presentation and fueled by shortsighted browser vendors eager to attract developers to their platform. But CSS is ready for the masses now, and it provides great improvements to web professionals in many areas.

In the chapters that follow, you'll take a detailed look at the ins and outs of developing pages with CSS. You'll learn good markup practices, how to control typography, and how to use CSS to lay out pages. You'll also look at troubleshooting and developing CSS for multiple web browsers. We'll round off our tour by presenting some advanced CSS projects to give you inspiration for your own projects and show what can really be achieved with the awesome power of CSS. When you've finished this book, you'll be prepared to develop the Web as it was intended to be developed—not only making your job easier and your clients happier, but also making the Web a better and more useful place.

CHAPTER 2

Overview of Presentation

IN CHAPTER 1, you were introduced to the idea of distinction between a document's *structure* and *semantics* on the one hand and *presentation* on the other. Structure refers to how the various parts of the document are put together, and semantics refers to what meaning they convey. Presentation refers to the way that those parts are manipulated, delivered, and displayed to the user. CSS provides a means of manipulating a document's presentation—whether by visual means, or through the use of sound and voice—and that's what we tackle in this chapter. In Chapter 3 we go on to discuss the structural side of the XHTML documents to which we apply CSS in this book.

As we noted in Chapter 1, we assume that you're working with XHTML documents. However, CSS was designed to be relatively language independent, meaning there is nothing in the CSS specifications that forbids its use with other markup languages, so long as they're founded on SGML and XML, the markup metalanguages that gave rise to HTML and XHTML, respectively. A *metalanguage* is, as its name suggests, a step above specific languages (variously known as *document types, tagsets,* and *vocabularies,* depending on who you ask) such as HTML and XHTML. Rather than defining what elements and attributes can exist in a given document, metalanguages define the rules by which those more specific markup languages are created, described, and managed.

Presentation

The presentation of a document may be affected through manipulation of color, typography, layout, and other factors, such as whether it's in print or on an electronic display, or even using sound and voice through the use of sophisticated text-to-speech readers. More sophisticated transformation languages such as Extensible Stylesheet Language Transformations (XSLT) may actually modify the document's structure and contents; CSS merely affects the display of the document's contents based on its structure and semantics.

As mentioned in Chapter 1, in the early days of HTML, the document author had very little control over such presentation-related characteristics. Here's a simple example of the sort of page you might have found on the Web circa 1994:

```
<html>
<head>
  <title>Steve Champeon's Home Page</title>
</head>
<body>
<h1>Steve Champeon's Home Page</h1>
<p>Hi! Welcome to my Home Page on the World Wide Web!</p>
<p>Here, you can:</p>
<ul>
  <li><a href="me.html">find out more about me</a>
  <li><a href="job.html">learn about my job</a>
  <li><a href="cat.html">see ascii art of my cat</a>
  <li><a href="bm.html">pore over my bookmarks</a>
  <li><a href="resume.html">read my r&eacute;sum&eacute;</a>
</ul>
<hr>
Maintained by: <tt>schampeo@aisg.com</tt>.<br>
<address>Research Triangle Park, NC, USA</address>
Last modified: <em>June 1, 1994</em>
</body>
</html>
```

More complex documents were available as well—documents that took advantage of the entire range of capabilities of HTML, including the various levels of headings, blockquotes, code samples, keyboard input, terminal output, glossaries, and so forth. However, for the most part you could do much of what you needed to do with just a few elements. Of course, most of us didn't need to do that much. The bar was a lot lower, and the designers and typographers hadn't really caught on to the Web.

Presentation of the document's contents was managed by the browser (which might have been a terminal-based program, such as Lynx, or a graphical browser, such as Mosaic) or, in some cases, the end user. In MacMosaic, for example, the user had the ability to set fonts, colors, and sizes for every element provided by HTML, through a complex preferences dialog box. Some users might set their font sizes larger, or use colors to distinguish between different heading levels, or force blockquotes into italics. However, the changes they made to their configuration were applied to all HTML pages. The appearance of the Web was remarkably consistent, as you can imagine. It was also remarkably bland.

The upshot of this was that document authors didn't have much say in the matter when it came to how their documents would be displayed, except in very basic terms (such as whether a chunk of text should be italicized or bolded). Instead, they focused on the document's structure or, if they were really experimental, they tried to make HTML bend to their will, abandoning the intended meaning and purpose of HTML elements such as <pre> or <ul> and using them to affect the visual display of their documents, regardless of what such tinkering did to the underlying semantics.

Needless to say, onlookers were amused (if they knew anything about HTML), inspired (if they knew anything about layout and design), shocked (if they knew anything about semantic markup), or disgusted (if they were using something other than Netscape Navigator 1.1). No matter how you felt about it, the message was clear: The Web needed to provide some way for document authors to control the presentation of their sites, without ruining the semantics of the markup they used to achieve that control. The big question was, how?

Should HTML's existing presentation-related elements be extended to allow for the sorts of tricks people wanted? Should a new language be invented that provided presentation while HTML remained a structural markup language? Or should HTML itself be extended through the addition of new elements? There was some history of this, after all: Marc Andreessen, who had helped bring the world a graphical browser, did so largely by proposing new elements, such as <img>, which didn't exist before 1993 (though it's worth noting that he got some negative feedback on the idea from more experienced markup advocates, who wanted him to use a more generic element name, such as <object>).

As structural markup was gradually abandoned in favor of presentational kludges, the Web was also extended to include a wide variety of new file types and behaviors. No longer was the Web as document-centric as in the early days. Video, sound, animated GIF images, progressive JPEGs, virtual reality, and embedded scripting were promising to blow the Web apart. At bottom, HTML still held things together, like a weave of years of duct tape, Band-Aids, and baling wire.

On the upside, the phenomenal explosion in growth of the Web created entirely new industries and many jobs. On the downside, it left those who had created the Web and all the prior innovations that had led up to it shell-shocked and bitter. All around them, all they could see were ugly examples of how the lessons of the past were being ignored or flouted by a new generation. One of these lessons, learned the hard way in the early days of SGML, was that it's good to keep separate document structure, marked up with tags representing the meaning of every element's contents, from presentation logic, which should be applied to that structure as needed to generate the appropriate output format.

Of course, the Web was just one output format, right? Everything was displayed in the browser; no need to worry about structure or semantics as long as it looked good in the browser, right? Wrong. People don't all have access to the high-end desktop computers and workstations used by web professionals (even more true back then, when early web browsers were only found on high-end UNIX workstations). Some users don't even have sight and don't care about how something looks. People print documents they find on the Web. Nowadays, people expect to be able to access the Web from their ever more powerful handheld computers and cell phones.

The Web is fundamentally about providing information to anyone who wants it, on any platform, in a way that is meaningful and useful to them, regardless of the opinions and aesthetic sensibilities of document authors and designers. So how should we be applying presentation logic to our documents? For that matter, how would we even recognize it if we stumbled across it in a dark alley? What constitutes presentation logic, as opposed to this elusive purely semantic structural markup we keep hearing about?

Identifying Presentation Logic

There are many ways to think about the presentation of information. If you're schooled in the visual arts, typography, or design/layout, you'll probably recognize a lot of the issues we discuss in this section. If not, pay attention. And do your best to think in the abstract. Rather than thinking in terms of a specific page component and how you would style it, think in terms of generic types of presentation characteristics, such as color, typography, and layout.

This sort of thinking may be difficult at first, accustomed as we are to always associating a property with a specific object in the real world. For example, think "green" and you probably immediately think "grass" or something similar. However, the experience will be invaluable to you as you begin to lay down some basic principles for identifying and grouping presentation rules apart from the objects they'll eventually modify.

In addition, don't worry too much just yet about how you're going to encode this presentation information into stylesheets. We'll come to this later when we look at the code behind the abstract in Chapters 4, 5, and 6. For now, just try to think about the fact that structure and content are not, or need not be, inextricably bound up with style, layout, and presentation. You probably already know how presentation varies from browser to browser, due to bugs, shortcomings, and quirks. Now just take that to the next level and consider that it isn't merely a side effect of a software bug; rather, it's the fundamental nature of the medium.

Take any website, preferably not one whose markup you're familiar with, and write down (or type up) your observations about its use of color, typography, and layout. Don't view source—just look at the pages. Try and notice where these uses are consistent (such as the use of a particular typeface and size for navigational elements or a particular color for links) and where they differ (such as different typographical treatments for regular body text as opposed to inline quotations or headlines versus bylines). Be sure to visit several pages within the site, not just the home page, and if the site has multiple sections, visit at least a few of them as well.

Notice when certain stylistic treatments are found together as well. Is there a consistency to the relationships between similar components? If you're looking at a site with multipage stories or documentation, for example, are there any rules that determine how the paragraph immediately following a section header looks? Do all block quotes look the same? Do all links look the same, or do they vary depending on the context? Can you determine the context or contexts in which they differ?

What other effects are noticeable? Does the site use "hover" effects on links? Does it force underlining of links? Are there dynamic HTML components? What activates them? How do they act? By hiding or revealing content, or by exposing navigational or other detail hidden to conserve screen real estate? Are they effective?

Now compare the set of observations you just made with another site of the same type. If you chose a news site for your first analysis, choose another news site for comparison. Do they have a consistent approach toward the things you grouped together as similar? Do the differences between component styles carry over to the other site as well? This isn't to ask if headlines that on one news site were 14 pixels tall and in red Verdana were also 14 pixels tall and in red Verdana on the other. Rather, do the stylistic similarities, differences, and relationships carry over between, for example, headlines, bylines, and body text? If so, are they applied consistently? If not, notice the differences within the sites and between them. If you notice something interesting about the second site, go back and see if you can find similar characteristics in the first site.

While you're comparing your sites, consider the following factors that may have influenced the decisions the site designers made:

- **Branding:** Does the site consistently present its core branding message throughout? Does the site use color, typography, and layout to support and enhance the overall theme, or do local variations (such as flashy animations or garish colors) cause dissonance in the viewer?

- **Audience:** Does the site's choice of typography, color, and layout address the characteristics and needs of its viewers? Does it adequately distinguish between copy (text on the page), navigation, and other types of page content?

- **Variation:** Do different sections of the site use different colors, typography, or layout to help signal to the viewer that he or she is in a different section?

- **Composition:** If you were to remove the specific content and replace it with greeking, or nonsensical content, would the function and purpose of each of the components on the page still be obvious?

- **Typography:** How does the choice of typefaces, sizes, padding and margins, weights, and other factors increase or decrease the legibility of the text?

- **Hierarchy:** Do the relationships between the sizes and placement of textual elements and other page components add to their respective meanings in the context of the page?

- **Harmony:** Are the page components balanced and stable, or do their respective placements create a sense of dynamic movement and action? Is the choice suitable for the content the site is presenting?

If you have a different device (such as a handheld), platform, or browser available, try viewing the site in those other setups. How does the experience differ? Is the site geared toward viewing in very different environments, such as a handheld, or does it simply break down? Are you presented with a completely different arrangement of content, navigation, and so on? Or are you presented with a lean, usable version of the more rich graphical version of the site? Note how the versions are achieved. Do they use the same underlying markup, with the richer site enhancing the experience through technologies not supported by the handheld? Or is the handheld forced to download (and the user endure) a version of the site that assumes high-end graphical desktop browsers and fast pipes?

Try printing the site from a selection of different browsers. How do the printouts vary? Which qualities are preserved, and which are left out or modified in the print version? Can you think of ways in which you would modify the site for print, as opposed to viewing in the browser? What parts of the site would these changes affect? Remember that much of the content on many sites is there for navigation or to provide context within the browsing experience. How much of it can be removed for print? Some content is there for purposes of advertising. Would you remove it from a piece that was meant to be printed? If not, would you change its relationship to the rest of the content? Much of a site's content is *functional*—that is, it provides navigation and other interactivity with goals and targets beyond the current page. When printed, should this distracting and useless (on paper, anyway) stuff simply be hidden? Is it even possible to hide it without destroying the site's branding? Or is the decoration all jumbled in with the functionality and content?

Another consideration is the process by which the documents will be authored, stored, delivered, and possibly transformed into other formats. We hinted at this when we discussed handhelds and printouts, but it's more subtle than simple format differences or browser differences. Depending on the back-end or even client-side software in use, such transformations may be dramatically different from one site to the next. These transformations are, in essence, a form of presentation logic as well. With CSS, however, you're limited to choosing whether an element may be displayed, and changing its position and other stylistic characteristics. With more sophisticated mechanisms (such as XSLT), which are beyond the scope of this book, you can change the actual structure of the document.

Now think about what you've seen on the sites you looked at. Isolate the characteristics related to color, typography, and layout from the specific content of the sites' components. These characteristics are the results of presentation logic. At some point in the process by which the information you see on the page was gathered, marked up, stored, possibly transformed (on either the server side or client side), and rendered, presentation logic was applied to the content in order to effect a specific result.

In subsequent chapters, beginning with Chapter 4, you'll learn how to encode presentation logic using CSS. For now, you'll concentrate on thinking about how to keep these presentation-related aspects separate from the markup in your documents. The next step, now that you've isolated those aspects from the content, is to think about how to create containers for that content to which you can apply the logic.

Identifying Document Components

On the Web, as with many other sophisticated, document-centric environments, markup is the key to identifying specific components within a document. You'll learn in Chapter 3 how to make those components more meaningful and how to choose what to wrap in markup, but for now, you'll focus on the association of presentation logic with markup.

One of the things you'll notice right away when you start viewing source on sites around the Web is that there are a wide variety of approaches toward markup. Some use XHTML's various elements as they're intended to be used, with a high degree of correspondence between the suggested semantics for the element and the apparent meaning of the content being marked up. Others, however, seem to use whatever element comes to mind, either for its familiar display (such as those who use <h6> for very small text such as page footer disclaimers) or for other reasons unrelated to their intended purpose.

As you know, XHTML is a relatively simple vocabulary that was borrowed from HTML and originally intended to mark up scientific reports, technical documentation, and hypertext of any kind. As such, there are headers (as found in outlines and in heavily structured documents), lists, glossaries, anchors, various text- and phrase-related elements, and so forth. As such, XHTML is primarily, though not exclusively, focused on marking up *text*.

In addition to the basic elements and their attributes, there are attributes designed to allow for the unique identification of an element in a document (the id attribute) and to allow the association of arbitrary information with an element (the class and style attributes).

The id attribute dates back to the early days of SGML, when documents were parsed and validated, and it afforded the parser a way to uniquely identify every element in a document, as well as to allow for the reference of those elements by other elements or by the processing software. Each element in a document is referred to as an instance.

In practice, HTML didn't make much use of the id attribute until the introduction of stylesheets, scripting, and other mechanisms that suddenly made uniquely identifying an element far more valuable. (The only other place where unique identifiers were used was in forms, and the attribute used there was name, which still causes confusion today.) You've already seen examples of its use with CSS in Chapter 1's "Ye Olde Cheese Shop" example. You may find documents that have multiple elements having id attributes with the same value, but this isn't valid, so be careful.

The class attribute is relatively new and has many possible uses, but for our purposes it's sufficient to note that not only can many elements have the same value for their class attribute, but also the class attribute's value itself may contain several tokens or names. What this means for us is that there's a way to add to an element's basic semantics as well as group related elements together by assigning their class attributes the same value.

In addition, there are mechanisms by which an element may be identified by what element contains it, or is contained by it, or precedes it in the document, making it possible to associate presentation logic with the greater context in which it is found. This allows a style to be applied not only to single elements or groups of elements, but also to more complex structures (such as you might have in a news story, in which you find headlines, subheadings, and bylines all preceding the body copy of the story itself). This will become clearer to you in Chapter 4 when we discuss the cascade and inheritance of stylesheet rules, and in Chapter 5 when we discuss rule selectors, as well as elsewhere throughout the book.

Instead of the relatively simple, page-centric collections envisioned by the Web's creators, web documents are now often a very complex mix of branding, navigation, related links, abstracts, advertising, and more. With CSS identification mechanisms, we can describe document subcomponents as precisely as we can the overarching document container (the page) itself. This increase in granularity allows us to create styles that are associated with subcomponents rather than with the page as a whole.

For example, in the early days, the document author couldn't specify any text colors. Then, with the introduction of the various attributes of the <body> element, you could specify text and background colors as well as link colors. Later, with the introduction of the <font> element, you could specify colors, faces, and sizes for any text. Now, with CSS, you can specify a wide range of stylistic characteristics to be applied to one element, many elements, the entire document, or what have you, as your needs dictate. You can even specify styles based on an element's position and relationships between elements.

In the following chapter, we discuss the process of analyzing a document or set of documents in terms of the semantics common to their components, but for now it's enough to understand that such analysis is possible and that it's also possible not only to uniquely identify individual elements and groups of related elements, as well as more complex structures, but also to apply presentation logic to them on that basis.

Applying Presentation to Document Components

We'll now present an overview of the ways in which you may manage presentation logic. There are several mechanisms by which you may apply a given style rule to an element:

- You may specify the set of style properties that the element should have as the value of an attribute of that element directly. These are known as *inline* style definitions.

- You may define a stylesheet unique to a given document and that document alone. These are known as *embedded* stylesheets. You saw this technique in the "Ye Olde Cheese Shop" example in Chapter 1.

- You may place your definitions into a file external to the document and then link it in. You're then able to link the same stylesheet to many documents in a given website. These are *external* stylesheets.

You may use one or more of these approaches in the same document. Each approach has its benefits and drawbacks, which we'll cover briefly here. A more detailed examination of these techniques is given in Chapter 6.

Using inline style definitions, you may associate a set of styles with one and only one element (though, as you'll find out in Chapter 4, such styles may also apply to elements contained within that element). This is probably the least powerful, and most wasteful, of all the mechanisms, because it's impossible to reuse the definition within the document and across many documents.

Another drawback to this approach is that unless you have a very good reason to avoid reuse, such styles can increase inordinately the weight of a document due to repetition of property names and the like, even if the values themselves differ. And, of course, the maintenance issues with inline styles are a nightmare. Consider that you must not only update each element using a particular style, but first you must find them and ensure that the element in question *should* be updated. With an embedded or external stylesheet, such updates are one step removed from such a painful search, as you can make the update to the stylesheet and it's automatically propagated to those elements that use the style. We'll talk about this more in subsequent chapters.

The benefit to the inline approach is that you can be very sure how any particular element will be styled, and if reuse isn't important to your application, you may find it appropriate. One other benefit to this approach in current browsers is that it may make it easier to manipulate those styles (and hence, the presentation of the element) from scripts.

Using embedded stylesheet definitions, you define styles specific to a given document. Although not necessarily as specific as inline styles and affording more reuse, as well as a more compact definition, embedded styles can also add to the overall download time of a document because the browser can't cache the definitions but must refetch them every time the document is requested, making the browsing experience more sluggish.

One benefit to this approach, however, is that because the rules and the elements to which they should apply are in the same document, it may be easier to validate the rules against the actual document to which they will apply, checking, for example, whether an element for which there is a unique rule defined actually exists within the document. This is a pretty pathetic benefit, though, given that any reasonably sophisticated validation or consistency-checking software should be able to load any external stylesheet file in order to do such checks. Even embedded scripts should be able to fetch an external file in most modern browsers and base any checking on the combined set of documents and stylesheets. Also, depending on the validator you're using, it may be that you're unable to validate embedded styles at all.

Finally, there are external stylesheets, which are simply style rulesets that have been copied into an external file and referenced by the document using any of a number of different methods. When loaded, the rules defined in the external stylesheet are applied to the document that linked to them, where appropriate. External stylesheets have all of the benefits described previously for embedded stylesheets (reusable across documents and sites, may be more concise and compact than inline styles, and so on), and they may also be cached by the browser, increasing the efficiency of download and, therefore, the user's experience. Being able to use stylesheets across multiple documents makes for a more consistent look and feel as well. Finally, there are many public validation services for CSS that accept a URL for an external stylesheet, making it easy to keep everything correct.

There are also many ways to optimize the management of external stylesheets, though the external stylesheets may be prone to fall out of synchronization with the documents to which they apply, meaning that there may be rules defined in a globally applicable external stylesheet that don't have any targets in a given document within a site. For example, you may have defined a style for blockquotes and stored that rule in a globally applied stylesheet. In some documents, you might not have any blockquotes, so the rule isn't applied.

Optimizing Presentation

Let's go back to the observations you made about the sites you visited earlier. Notice the common characteristics among all of the styles you noted, if any, such as choice of font family, foreground and background color, any special text treatments (such as small capitals), and so on. If on one site, you noticed that all of the type was black on white, Verdana, 14 pixels, but that small caps were used in some places while bold and italics were used consistently in other places, you have an opportunity to optimize the definition of that style. Specifically, all of the elements share a font color, face, and size that can be defined further up in the document hierarchy (as part of the default style for the <body> element, for example), and the special cases—the italics, small caps, and bold—can be defined and applied only to those elements that need them.

As we said before, don't worry about the syntax, which we discuss in later chapters. Just take note of the commonalities among and minor differences between the styles. It won't hurt if you can also identify the sort of content each different presentation was associated with (for example, a byline or a subheading), but it isn't necessary. We go into more detail regarding how to determine and name document semantics in the next chapter.

Now that you've taken notice of similarly presented content, can you make your conclusions global? In other words, is every instance of copy in the document presented in the same font family? Do they all use the same foreground or background color?

If not, what are the exceptions? Are those exceptions predictable, or are they confined to specific areas or components within the document? Of those exceptions, are they meaningful and consistent, or do they look like they may well be accidental? Do those components have a shared purpose or meaning in the document (for example, menu items, advertising slogans, links to related items, and so on)?

Try to list all of the instances in which the document contents appear to have a specific purpose, denoted by a change in their presentation. Then try to list all of the characteristics they share or are mostly common to the whole document, such as font family or foreground color.

Try to think not in terms of each component's qualities (such as a byline being presented using black-on-white, 16 pixel, Verdana small caps) but in terms of a hierarchy of sorts, where those properties mostly common to all components are listed at the top, and minor variations or overriding exceptions are listed at the bottom. Think of them as a tree diagram.

For example, you might say that the entire document uses Verdana, black on white, and that most of the document's text is portrayed at what may well be 12 pixel font. Headlines, on the other hand, though using the same default font family and color, are in 18 pixel, bold font. Subheadings share the headlines qualities, with the exception that they are in 16 pixel, italic font. Bylines share the font color and family but are presented in small caps. Links are blue and underlined. Advertising captions are dark red and in small caps as well. You might also encounter font size specifications that use other units, such as points, which are generally frowned upon for reasons we explain in subsequent chapters, or perhaps using the font size keywords (e.g., x-small, large, and so on). See how these other specifications relate to the overall font size specified for the document body, or how they interact with your personal font size preferences. Adjust the preferred font size in your browser and see what changes and, more important, what doesn't change, in response. This will tell you a lot about how sensitive the document author was to your needs and to those of others.

Keep going through the document, and feel free to refer to other sites if you find yourself running out of examples. There's no score, and you can't fail the test. The trick is to think about styles in terms of their similarities and relationships, as well as their minor and major differences but, more important, in terms of the document and site taken as a whole. It's also helpful, as we've said, to think in terms of the function or meaning of those components that differ. By thinking both "vertically," in terms of slight differences between elements of similar types within a given page, and "horizontally," in terms of similarities of presentation for the same element on different pages or in different contexts, and binding those qualities to the meaning of the elements in question, you can often identify welcome consistencies (or unwelcome inconsistencies, and fix them).

Summary

Congratulations! You now know how to describe styles for web documents in the manner you'll need to use for CSS. All that remains is the syntax and familiarity with a list of properties, their values, and so forth, but that's the easy part. The tricky part, the part that's most difficult to grasp, is how to provide stylesheet definitions in as concise, yet powerful, a manner as possible. And that's what you just did in this chapter. With a few variations and exceptions, such as the techniques required by dynamic HTML, this is how the experts use CSS.

CHAPTER 3

Markup with Meaning

As we've already discussed in this book, one of the core ideas behind the systems of markup that gave rise to the Web is the separation of document structure and semantics from the rules specifying the presentation of the document. By introducing markup elements designed specifically for, or later adapted to the task of, influencing presentation (such as the <b>, <i>, and <font> elements, and various table elements), the Web and HTML lost touch with this original principle.

In this chapter we take a look at how the XHTML markup you write should be affected by this separation concept. Bear in mind that in order to demonstrate some of the original principles of the markup languages that gave rise to both HTML and XHTML, we use some examples in pseudo-SGML and pseudo-XML. If you see unfamiliar tags and attributes in these examples or notice that we're not using complete XHTML documents, but document fragments that illustrate a fundamental concept, don't worry. We'll come back around to XHTML eventually, and what you learn from the non-XHTML examples and incomplete documents will be applicable to your own complete XHTML documents.

Be forewarned that this chapter contains a great deal of discussion of the theoretical underpinnings of the Web, with a focus on fundamentals. If you want to get right into the nuts and bolts of CSS, feel free to skim this chapter, but *do* read the section on document analysis onward. If you don't grasp the fundamentals contained there, your designs will be less powerful and you'll eventually learn all of this stuff the hard way. Or, you won't learn it, and you'll have missed out on a great deal of the power of CSS and XHTML. You may want to revisit this chapter after you've dug into the mechanics a bit; the examples may make more sense and the fundamentals are likely to be much clearer. It's all up to you. People learn in different ways, and we've tried to accommodate all kinds of approaches in this book.

The Roots of Semantic Markup

In this section, we show you how the Web's universal markup language, HTML (and later XML and XHTML), was born of older, more powerful, more specific, and more complex systems designed with broader interests and applications in mind. This section is intended as a reminder of sorts that the Web isn't the be-all and end-all of semantic markup, and that even today we all struggle with some of the limitations imposed on us by the language designers. Hopefully, it will give you some ideas as to the power of XHTML and XML, and expand your perspective regarding how a future Web may take shape, not to mention how to take advantage of the capabilities of today's Web.

Older markup systems, such as SGML, which you encountered in Chapter 1, were often created for a wide array of purposes, data sets, and environments. For example, you might be marking up text for use in an outline-driven multimedia viewer; a search and retrieval system; or a large, long-term storage system. The actual transformations from those markup formats—for example, into print or for viewing in a software application—were treated as having secondary importance. They were usually handled by the custom viewer built specifically for that application or by some filtering software that produced a more mundane print format such as PostScript or RTF. The important thing to realize is that semantic markup was originally intended as a *storage* format; it wasn't meant to be delivered directly to an end user.

The Web, by making the immediate delivery and display of documents possible, has made great strides forward, but in the process it has sacrificed a great deal of the complexity and power of such earlier markup systems. The Web's designers also made a choice to sacrifice specific document semantics in favor of a more general-purpose vocabulary (HTML), which was assumed to cover most cases rather than apply directly to any one custom case.

SGML was intended to provide a platform for the creation and maintenance of *any* type of document in existence, at any level of specificity required, and it included mechanisms for dealing with cross-platform differences, the wide variance between capabilities of different systems and the character sets they supported, and more.

As a result, it was an incredibly powerful idea that was more often partially, rather than completely, implemented. Many popular SGML software packages, such as SoftQuad's Author/Editor (the inspiration for HoTMetaL, an HTML editor), Electronic Book Technologies' DynaText, and others, were often written to serve a particular purpose rather than to implement the wide array of SGML capabilities. In particular, Author/Editor was geared toward the author and editor of SGML documents, whereas DynaText was more of a content management system. Other packages were focused on single-source publishing to multiple media.

These implementations were expensive, prone to incompatibilities with other partial implementations, and had a wide range of different proposed systems for handling transformations and presentation. Usually, these presentation systems took the form of multimedia applications (such as the IETM, or Interactive Electronic Technical Manual, a sort of outline-based document navigator and image viewer) or expensive database search and retrieval tools (such as LexisNexis, a large database of legal decisions and case materials). A generic, powerful, networked presentation management system took a backseat. It's no wonder the Web was seen by many as a more immediate and far easier way to publish information. Early efforts to provide SGML on the Web met with only limited success.

To address the complexity of SGML, a smaller, far simpler subset of SGML was devised: the Extensible Markup Language (XML). As SGML helped to inspire HTML, XML is intended to provide mechanisms for specifying document structure in a semantically meaningful way. And, unlike SGML, XML was designed for use on the Internet and/or the Web, and has the extra advantage of having a generic and powerful language for specifying presentation of documents on the Web: CSS. The benefit is that CSS was designed to work with any markup language that uses elements and attributes in a tree formation (such as XHTML). So XML doesn't need to invent a new purely presentational language; we can simply use CSS. Earlier systems lacked a comprehensive standard for managing presentation.

The popularity and power of a general-purpose SGML document type such as HTML wasn't lost on XML's designers, however, and as a transitional step toward the future, the HTML vocabulary was reimplemented in XML as XHTML, the basis of most of our examples in this book. By making use of a well-known and proven generic document type, XML's creators hope to leverage the knowledge of millions of web authors while tightening down the screws with regard to syntax. As a result, a valid XHTML document may be viewed in any modern browser (and even in most legacy browsers) without much difficulty, and it may also be used by tools designed to interpret and manage XML documents, because it is itself an application of XML. Eventually, the Web's architects expect that we'll all be using XHTML with our own, or with widely adopted, XML formats such as SVG, MathML, RDF, RSS, and others.

There are a few guidelines for ensuring that XHTML documents can be properly handled by legacy browsers. Among these guidelines are the following:

- Empty elements must use a new notation, notation, `/>`, to indicate the end of the tag. For example, always use `<br />` rather than just `<br>`. Include the space just before the / to guarantee backward compatibility with very old browsers.

- Use external rather than embedded stylesheets and scripts wherever possible.

- Don't wrap embedded stylesheets and scripts in comment syntax.

- Avoid line breaks and multiple spaces within attribute values.

- Don't use fragment identifiers (such as `#top`) to refer to named anchors. In XML, this would refer to the element whose `id` value matches the token following the # character. In XHTML, you can use the `id` attribute just as you might have previously used `name`.

- Minimized attributes, such as `"compact"` or `"selected"`, must have a value— for example, `selected="selected"`.

- A character encoding must be specified in both the XML declaration (which you may have to leave off to avoid conflicts with older browsers that simply display it inline) and in a `meta http-equiv` attribute, such as this:

```
<meta http-equiv="Content-Type:" value="text/html; charset=utf-8" />
```

- Language must be specified as attributes to the `<html>` tag, using both the `lang` and `xml:lang` attributes.

Yes, it does seem like XHTML adds a bit more difficulty over old-school HTML. However, bear in mind that most of these guidelines are merely alternative ways of doing what you already do in HTML—just according to a stricter standard. Fortunately, these guidelines become second nature after a very short time (especially if you miss a few of them and get bitten by Internet Explorer 4.0 or some older browser).

Vocabularies

A few words about vocabularies are in order here.

> **NOTE** *Recall that vocabularies (otherwise known as* tagsets *and* document types*) are applications of SGML or XML. Examples include HTML and XHTML, respectively.*

For those web professionals who have only worked in HTML, and whose use of HTML has been largely presentational, the idea of different, more specific vocabularies may seem strange or even incomprehensible. And yet, the power of markup is still rooted in the ability to surround specific content with tags that cast it in its most meaningful light, especially to the relatively unintelligent machines that must *parse,* meaning "read and interpret," that content.

In HTML you would specify an outline by way of header elements (`<h1>`, `<h2>`, and so on), or a list structure by list elements (`<ol>`, `<li>`, and so on), or a glossary by those elements that delimit a term and its definition. However, in more specific vocabularies, you can lend any meaning you want to any content you wish. For example, you could define an element `<catalogitem>` that could contain catalog items, or an element `<album>` that could contain information about an album. In doing so, you can imply not only the specific meaning to be associated with that content ("this is a song title"), but also the larger structure into which that meaning may fit ("song titles belong in song lists that belong in `<album>` elements").

An XHTML document fragment may be easily interpreted by the human eye when displayed in a browser. Obviously, the following example is a song list from an album. Unfortunately, it lacks the capability to tell a computer how to interpret its components in a meaningful way.

```
<table>
<tr>
  <th>Artist</th>
  <th>Album</th>
  <th>Date</th>
  <th>Song List</th>
</tr>
<tr>
  <td>Tom Waits</td>
  <td>swordfishtrombones</td>
  <td>1983</td>
  <td>
    <ol>
      <li>Underground (<i>Waits</i>) 1:58</li>
      <li>Shore Leave (<i>Waits</i>) 4:12</li>
      <li>Dave the Butcher (Instrumental) (<i>Waits</i>) 2:15</li>
      <li>Johnsburg, Illinois (<i>Waits</i>) 1:30</li>
      <li>16 Shells from a Thirty-Ought Six (<i>Waits</i>) 4:30</li>
      <li>Town With No Cheer (<i>Waits</i>) 4:22</li>
      <li>In the Neighborhood (<i>Waits</i>) 3:04</li>
      <li>Just Another Sucker on the Vine (Instrumental) (<i>Waits</i>) 1:42</li>
      <li>Frank's Wild Years (<i>Waits</i>) 1:50</li>
      <li>Swordfishtrombones (<i>Waits</i>) 3:00</li>
      <li>Down, Down, Down (<i>Waits</i>) 2:10</li>
      <li>Soldier's Things (<i>Waits</i>) 3:15</li>
      <li>Gin Soaked Boy (<i>Waits</i>) 2:20</li>
      <li>Trouble's Braids (<i>Waits</i>) 1:18</li>
      <li>Rainbirds (Instrumental) (<i>Waits</i>) 3:05</li>
    </ol>
  </td>
</tr>
</table>
```

The only thing the *parser* (the software that reads and interprets the markup) and, by extension, any manipulation logic you might wish to employ (for example, JavaScript code) "knows" about this chunk of markup is that some of its elements are table headers, others are table cells, and certain of the elements in one cell are an ordered list containing list items. Beyond that, all of the other real information is simply opaque to any effort to pull it out and treat it differently, whether by applying certain styles or simply by using the document as a base for transformation into another.

By contrast, the following document fragment, which makes use of a custom XML vocabulary to describe the same information more meaningfully, regains the power of older technology such as SGML:

```
<album>
  <title>swordfishtrombones</title>
  <artist id="a47362">
    <firstname>Tom</firstname>
    <lastname>Waits</lastname>
  </artist>
  <date type="release" format="year">1983</date>
  <songlist>
    <song><title>Underground</title>
      <lyricist ref=" a47362" /><score ref=" a47362" />
      <length format="MM:SS">1:58</length></song>
    <song><title>Shore Leave</title>
      <lyricist ref=" a47362" /><score ref=" a47362" />
      <length format="MM:SS">4:12</length></song>
    <song type="instrumental">
      <title>Dave the Butcher</title>
      <score ref=" a47362" />
      <length format="MM:SS">2:15</length></song>
    <song><title>Johnsburg, Illinois</title>
      <lyricist ref=" a47362" /><score ref=" a47362" />
      <length format="MM:SS">1:30</length></song>
    <song><title>16 Shells from a Thirty-Ought Six</title>
      <lyricist ref=" a47362" /><score ref=" a47362" />
      <length format="MM:SS">4:30</length></song>
    <song><title>Town With No Cheer</title>
      <lyricist ref=" a47362" /><score ref=" a47362" />
      <length format="MM:SS">4:22</length></song>
    <song><title>In the Neighborhood</title>
      <lyricist ref=" a47362" /><score ref=" a47362" />
      <length format="MM:SS">3:04</length></song>
    <song type="instrumental">
      <title>Just Another Sucker on the Vine</title>
      <score ref=" a47362" />
      <length format="MM:SS">1:42</length></song>
    <song><title>Frank's Wild Years</title>
      <lyricist ref=" a47362" /><score ref=" a47362" />
      <length format="MM:SS">1:50</length></song>
```

```
<song><title>Swordfishtrombone</title>
   <lyricist ref=" a47362" /><score ref=" a47362" />
   <length format="MM:SS">3:00</length></song>
<song><title>Down, Down, Down</title>
   <lyricist ref=" a47362" /><score ref=" a47362" />
   <length format="MM:SS">2:10</length></song>
<song><title>Soldier's Things</title>
   <lyricist ref=" a47362" /><score ref=" a47362" />
   <length format="MM:SS">3:15</length></song>
<song><title>Gin Soaked Boy</title>
   <lyricist ref=" a47362" /><score ref=" a47362" />
   <length format="MM:SS">2:20</length></song>
<song><title>Trouble's Braids</title>
   <lyricist ref=" a47362" /><score ref=" a47362" />
   <length format="MM:SS">1:18</length></song>
<song type="instrumental"><title>Rainbirds</title>
   <score ref=" a47362" />
   <length format="MM:SS">3:05</length></song>
  </songlist>
</album>
```

One of the things you'll notice is that there is a lot of leeway for describing as much, or as little, information as you need. In this case, we've chosen to be verbose, as there is a lot of information to be encoded. You may also notice a bit of redundancy, particularly in the tags describing the songs' lyricist and the author of the score, which in the preceding example are always the same and refer to the artist himself, but which in other songs may refer to different, or even multiple, people. Notice also the use of "empty" elements (such as the <score /> elements) with attributes that contain the relevant information. Finally, you'll notice that we've used attributes to specify other important data that we take for granted while reading, such as the format of the songs' lengths, which may not be evident to a parser.

Of course, parsers themselves aren't "aware" of the meaning of any element or attribute, but high-level logic (such as a JavaScript function or an XSLT stylesheet) can be written that takes advantage of such meaningful names. For example, a parser wouldn't care that we intend "MM:SS" as a value for the format attribute of the <length> element to stand for "minutes and seconds separated by a colon," but a script could apply that format to the data contained within the <length> element in order to arrive at a different measure, such as the total number of seconds in the song. Alternatively, you could supply the format as "seconds" and write a function that converted back from the total number of seconds into a more friendly "minutes and seconds" display.

Although this chapter isn't intended as a tutorial on how you would go about creating your own XML document types and vocabularies for encoding your often highly particular data, it's important to realize that this sort of markup is possible *now* and may be commonly used, for example, as platform-independent transport mechanisms between databases. Those of you who work with databases may recognize in the previous example a common feature of the output from simple queries: They're verbose and often redundant. However, that doesn't have to be the case when you create your own vocabularies. For example, we could represent the same information as in the previous example in a far more compact form:

```
<album title="swordfishtrombones" artist="Tom Waits" releasedate="1983">
  <songlist lyricist="a47362" score="a47362" lengthformat="MM:SS">
    <song title="Underground" length="1:58" />
    <song title="Shore Leave" length="4:12" />
    <song type="instrumental" title="Dave the Butcher" length="2:15" />
    <song title="Johnsburg, Illinois" length="1:30" />
    <song title="16 Shells from a Thirty-Ought Six" length="4:30" />
    <song title="Town With No Cheer" length="4:22" />
    <song title="In the Neighborhood" length="3:04" />
    <song type="instrumental" title="Just Another Sucker on the Vine"
         length="1:42" />
    <song title="Frank's Wild Years" length="1:50" />
    <song title="Swordfishtrombone" length="3:00" />
    <song title="Down, Down, Down" length="2:10" />
    <song title="Soldier's Things" length="3:15"/>
    <song title="Gin Soaked Boy" length="2:20" />
    <song title="Trouble's Braids" length="1:18" />
    <song type="instrumental" title="Rainbirds" length="3:05" />
  </songlist>
</album>
```

You'll notice that all of the information is encoded in attributes or the names of the elements themselves. The length of a song, for example, is now simply assumed to be minutes and seconds, which would have to be encoded into your script or translation software (although, to provide the maximum flexibility, we've supplied the format in an attribute of the <songlist> element).

The downside to this approach is that relatively sophisticated processing must be done to extract the relevant information from the attributes to decide what to display, and where and how to display it. The information we saw easily in the first version of the song list was all contained in elements, not attributes. Text inside elements is shown to the end user, whereas attribute values are not. The result is that if this document were displayed in a browser with an appropriate CSS stylesheet, none of the information would be displayed at all! For this reason, most such solutions that target the Web use semantically meaningful tags that act as *containers* for the data that the author wishes to be displayed.

Future implementations (and a few current ones) may make use of sophisticated transformation languages, such as XSLT (for transforming a document between different XML vocabularies) and XPath (which can be used to base presentation logic on the contents of attributes as well as elements, although that isn't its primary purpose). Currently, these systems, such as Apache's Cocoon, exist only on the server side and deliver plain XHTML to the browser, such as that in the first example. (However, it's possible to use XSLT within Internet Explorer 6.0 and Mozilla, to a certain extent.)

You may be wondering, "What does any of this have to do with CSS?" and you'd be right to do so—we've made a slight digression here. Here are the things to take away from this discussion:

- Documents may be created that encode far more information than is necessary for simple presentation.

- Some of the information so encoded may be used by scripts, on the client side, or by some other application on the server side or elsewhere, or even by CSS (if you use `class` and `id` attributes).

- CSS may be used to specify presentation logic for either custom XML document types (such as the previous examples) or more generic XHTML documents. You're not bound to HTML or XHTML just because you're using CSS.

Defining Your Document Type

Much as HTML and XHTML have rules that define the element and attribute names, and how elements may be positioned relative to one another (for example, "`<p>` elements must be descendants of a `<body>` element"), you can define other custom XML vocabularies with rules too. There are two ways in which you may define these.

The first is based on the original SGML document type definition (DTD) syntax that we mentioned in Chapter 1. This has a few drawbacks, such as the lack of support for specifying the particular data formats a given attribute may contain, the lack of a convenient way to say "this element may only contain x elements of type y," and the fact that a special DTD-aware processor is required in order to *validate* (check the correctness of) any instance of that document type.

The other method, known as *XML Schema*, uses XML syntax to specify the relationships between elements and the attributes they may contain. As a result, this method is far more verbose (as you can imagine from the first XML example in the previous section).

There are only two reasons to document your vocabulary in this manner (whether using DTDs or Schemas). The first is to provide a way by which documents may be validated against the rules set forth therein. The second is to provide a terse and concise framework on which to hang documentation and commentary about why you chose to define the document type in the way you did. A subsidiary reason involves being able to share the document type with others, such as if you're using it to transfer data between applications.

We won't get into the particulars of either of these methods here, as we've got a lot of ground to cover and we're assuming that you'll be working with XHTML more or less exclusively for the time being.

Bringing Arbitrary Document Structures to XHTML

Now that we've tantalized or bored you with all these examples of custom XML vocabularies in action, it's time to point out that the same sort of semantic associations may be given to XHTML elements (though in a more limited capacity) by making use of the attributes id and class, and intelligent naming conventions for the stylesheet rules.

For example, the album we encoded earlier using a custom XML vocabulary may easily be represented in XHTML by substituting the generic elements <span> and <div> with appropriately named id and class attributes, for which you can provide suitable stylesheet rules:

```
<div class="album">
  <span class="title">swordfishtrombones</span>
  <div class="artist" id="a47736">
    <span class="name">Tom Waits</span>
  </div>
  <span class="releasedate">1983</span>
  <div class="songlist">
    <div class="song">
      <span class="title">Underground</span>
      <span class="length">1:58</span></div>
    <div class="song">
      <span class="title">Shore Leave</span>
      <span class="length">4:12</span></div>
    <div class="song instrumental">
      <span class="title">Dave the Butcher</span>
      <span class="length">2:15</span></div>
    <div class="song">
      <span class="title">Johnsburg, Illinois</span>
      <span class="length">1:30</span></div>
    <div class="song">
      <span class="title">16 Shells from a Thirty-Ought Six</span>
      <span class="length">4:30</span></div>
```

```
<div class="song">
  <span class="title">Town With No Cheer</span>
  <span class="length">4:22</span></div>
<div class="song">
  <span class="title">In the Neighborhood</span>
  <span class="length">3:04</span></div>
<div class="song instrumental">
  <span class="title">Just Another Sucker on the Vine</span>
  <span class="length">1:42</span></div>
<div class="song">
  <span class="title">Frank's Wild Years</span>
  <span class="length">1:50</span></div>
<div class="song">
  <span class="title">Swordfishtrombone</span>
  <span class="length">3:00</span></div>
<div class="song">
  <span class="title">Down, Down, Down</span>
  <span class="length">2:10</span></div>
<div class="song">
  <span class="title">Soldier's Things</span>
  <span class="length">3:15</span></div>
<div class="song">
  <span class="title">Gin Soaked Boy</span>
  <span class="length">2:20</span></div>
<div class="song">
  <span class="title">Trouble's Braids</span>
  <span class="length">1:18</span></div>
<div class="song instrumental">
  <span class="title">Rainbirds</span>
  <span class="length">3:05</span></div>
  </div>
</div>
```

There are, of course, obvious disadvantages to using generic elements such as <div> and <span> in the manner we do here:

- By themselves, the elements don't convey any more information about their contents than, say, table cells, paragraph tags, or the usual text/phrase markup.

- In browsers that lack CSS support, the presentation is somewhat underwhelming: All the <div> elements define is that some text should be treated as a block, with a trailing linefeed, and other text, in <span> elements, should be treated like words in a sentence, with no linefeed.

- In some sense, we're subverting the intentions of the designers of XHTML by using XML with a far more limited, generic vocabulary.

- We had to discard some of the information that it wasn't possible to convey or that would have had no effect (such as the lyricist, score, and date formats).

In our defense, there are some real advantages to the use of generic tags with CSS to convey a document's semantics. By so doing, we have

- Isolated the document's structure from its presentation, while tying the semantics to the presentation rules via standards-compliant markup

- Avoided the misuse of semantic markup in a presentational manner (such as using <h2>, a second-level header, to contain information that has little or nothing to do with outlines or reports, or perhaps to achieve a certain weight or font size)

- Added a rich set of semantic information to the document that would have otherwise been lost to even more inappropriate markup (such as tables, or a definition list, or worse)

- Made possible the construction of semantically rich stylesheets, which use class names to signify the type of content to which they should be applied, not just the tag name (which may well be completely inappropriate to the semantics)

- Made it possible to substitute different stylesheets to bring about completely different presentations, whether in reaction to a user's preferences or to suit the capabilities of different browsers and platforms

- Exposed an incredibly rich set of information for use by client-side (or even server-side) scripting and transformations

- Compromised between the pure world of custom XML in the browser with a solution that will work *today* and that still contains enough information to be transformed back into a custom XML vocabulary as the technology matures

However, it should also be noted that by restricting our document markup to the generic <div> and <span> tags, we've actually ignored the existing elements in the XHTML vocabulary that have the basic meaning we're trying to convey. The preceding album is largely a list of songs—XHTML provides list and list item elements, and they should be used when they meet the needs of your document's semantics. The following example is a complete XHTML document that uses specific XHTML elements where necessary but relies on the more generic <div> and <span> elements where no specific element exists in XHTML:

```
<!DOCTYPE html PUBLIC "-//W3C//DTD XHTML 1.0 Transitional//EN"
  "http://www.w3.org/TR/xhtml1/DTD/xhtml1-transitional.dtd">
<html xmlns="http://www.w3.org/1999/xhtml" xml:lang="en" lang="en">
<head>
  <title>Album example</title>
</head>
<body>
<div class="album">
  <span class="title">swordfishtrombones</span>
  <div class="artist" id="a4736">
    <span class="name">Tom Waits</span>
  </div>
  <span class="releasedate">1983</span>
  <ol class="songlist">
    <li class="song"><span class="title">Underground</span>
      <span class="length">1:58</span></li>
    <li class="song"><span class="title">Shore Leave</span>
      <span class="length">4:12</span></li>
    <li class="song instrumental">
      <span class="title">Dave the Butcher</span>
      <span class="length">2:15</span></li>
    <li class="song">
      <span class="title">Johnsburg, Illinois</span>
      <span class="length">1:30</span></li>
    <li class="song">
      <span class="title">16 Shells from a Thirty-Ought Six</span>
      <span class="length">4:30</span></li>
    <li class="song">
      <span class="title">Town With No Cheer</span>
      <span class="length">4:22</span></li>
    <li class="song">
      <span class="title">In the Neighborhood</span>
      <span class="length">3:04</span></li>
    <li class="song instrumental">
      <span class="title">Just Another Sucker on the Vine</span>
      <span class="length">1:42</span></li>
    <li class="song">
      <span class="title">Frank's Wild Years</span>
      <span class="length">1:50</span></li>
    <li class="song">
      <span class="title">Swordfishtrombone</span>
      <span class="length">3:00</span></li>
```

```
    <li class="song">
      <span class="title">Down, Down, Down</span>
      <span class="length">2:10</span></li>
    <li class="song">
      <span class="title">Soldier's Things</span>
      <span class="length">3:15</span></li>
    <li class="song">
      <span class="title">Gin Soaked Boy</span>
      <span class="length">2:20</span></li>
    <li class="song">
      <span class="title">Trouble's Braids</span>
      <span class="length">1:18</span></li>
    <li class="song instrumental">
      <span class="title">Rainbirds</span>
      <span class="length">3:05</span></li>
  </ol>
</div>
</body>
</html>
```

This example has a distinct advantage: By leveraging existing semantics (even their presentational aspects), it may be displayed in a browser with much of its intent intact, as shown in Figure 3-1.

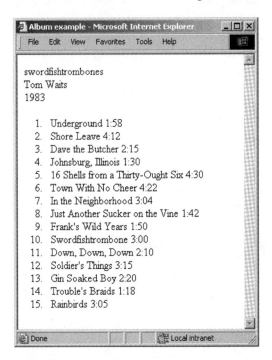

Figure 3-1. An example of semantic markup

The song titles are displayed as a list, the song lengths follow the song titles on the same line, and so forth. However, in contrast to the tabular example that started the chapter off, it now has much more semantic value, both that gained through the use of existing XHTML elements such as <ol> and <li>, and that gained through our marking additional segments as song titles, lengths, and more. With an appropriate CSS stylesheet, such as the one following, the document comes alive. (Again, don't worry too much about understanding the stylesheet yet—all the syntax is covered in Chapter 5. You'll see ways to create interesting and compelling CSS-styled documents in later chapters as well.)

```
div {
  background-color: rgb(204,204,204);
  color: black;
  font-family: Verdana, Helvetica, sans-serif;
  }

div.album {
  font-size: 16px;
  margin: 20px;
  }

div.artist {
  font-style: italic;
  }

span.releasedate {
  font-style: italic;
  margin-left: 20px;
  }

ol.songlist {
  font-size: 14px;
  }

li.song {
  line-height: 2em;
  text-align: left;
  }

li.song[type] {
  font-style: italic;
  }
```

```
span.title {
  color: red;
  display: block;
  font-family: Verdana, Helvetica, Geneva, sans-serif;
  }

li.song > span.title {
  color: #333333;
  display: inline;
  text-align: left;
  }

span.length {
  font-family: "Andale Mono", Courier, monospace;
  font-size: 12px;
  font-style: italic;
  margin: 10px;
  padding: 0px;
  }
```

You may associate the XHTML document, with its relative purity of structure and semantic markup, with the preceding stylesheet simply by adding a `<link>` element pointing to the file in which that stylesheet is stored, as you'll see in Chapter 6. The document is then displayed as shown in Figure 3-2.

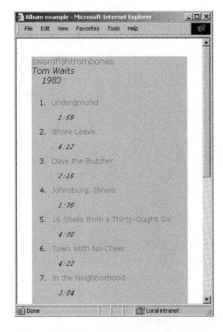

Figure 3-2. An example of styled semantic markup

As a rejoinder to those who would suggest that the song list is, in fact, perfectly appropriate for a tabular display, note that this method allows you to style the content as a table, as a bulleted list, or as an ordered list as required, simply by redefining certain style properties associated with the <ol> element. Again, we'd be subverting the original intent somewhat by turning an <ol> into a table, but it's better than forcing the presentation by using table markup, which is far less flexible than the solution presented here.

You'll learn more about the exact mechanisms and syntax you can use to exploit the advantages listed previously in future chapters. For now, ponder the ways in which you, your company, or your clients can leverage the far more powerful and descriptive approach toward markup discussed previously. In the next section, we'll show you ways in which you can analyze your own data and documents, and come up with a richer understanding of its structures and semantics.

Document Analysis

On the Web, where HTML is the only vocabulary supported by every web browser, the question of document analysis rarely comes up. The only question that authors have to deal with is how to force their documents into HTML so that they'll display properly. However, as you've seen in this chapter, with the generic elements <div> and <span> or the more appropriate list markup, as well as the use of semantically meaningful presentation rules, the barrier of forcing content into inappropriate tags is removed.

Whether you like it or not—and we understand that this may well mean a lot more work for you in the short term as you try to adapt—it's our belief that the advantages of separation will become clear as you move from maintaining tag soup to maintaining well-structured documents with a clear separation of structure and presentation. Every minute you spend up front will be repaid ten- or one hundredfold in future maintenance cost savings.

You've already seen in the examples in the previous section that well-structured and well-defined data can be marked up and presented with very little trouble. What you may have wondered about, however, is how the same can be done with information already in document form, which lacks the well-defined character of simple data such as the title, author, or length of a song.

Well-Defined Document Types

Fortunately, in many industries, common document types have already been or are currently being defined for many purposes, whether dating back to the early days of SGML or of more recent origin. The publishing industry, for example, was an early adopter of SGML and has long been an advocate of it, as have many large corporations and government agencies with lots of documents and publications to manage. Your best bet is to do some research and find out if any efforts are underway. These are usually led or coordinated by industry consortiums, government initiatives, and the like.

Most large public sites and many smaller ones are often a widely varied collection of different types of documents and data formats. This can actually stand as an impediment to the adoption of wide-ranging standards for document structure and semantics, but don't despair. Documents such as the following, with similar format and intent, can be found in any website:

- Marketing materials

- Staff and executive biographies

- Support documentation

- Manuals

- White papers

Much of the markup providing a framework for these documents is fairly regular as well and is often based on templates designed by the original publishers or even used within conventional content management systems. Many of these are designed to allow specific content to be stored in and delivered from databases and wrapped with template markup.

Similarly, many so-called WYSIWYG authoring tools allow for the creation of document templates and even for the splitting up of common elements (such as navigational components, footers, and so forth) to be included at publish time in other documents. Shortly, we'll ask you to identify the existing mechanisms by which your content is managed and created, but for now, let's stick to identifying a few document types (in a loose sense) from among the collection you plan to publish.

Let's say that one of the purposes of your website is to deliver a catalog of items for sale. Each item is likely to have a name, a description, a stock number or price look-up (PLU), a stock status, and other information. In the case of a book sale item, you might also list the author, publisher, page count, ISBN, critical reviews, and so forth. In the case of a piece of software offered for sale, you might also list compatibility information, platform, hardware requirements, and more. Obviously, some of the information will be dependent upon what you're selling.

The point to all this is that you should identify and isolate the components and subcomponents not by the way they will be presented, but by the meaning or purpose of the information.

To use another relatively well-known and common format, let's look at an e-mail message as it might be marked up and displayed. All e-mail messages have headers and a body, and many have an optional "signature" the sender uses to contain a pithy quote or contact information.

Note that there are many ways in which you can choose to break up this information. You could put the signature within the body of the message, or you could give it its own element on the same level as the message body. The headers may be given a container element or not; you may choose to treat certain specific headers (such as From:, To:, Date:, and Subject:) in a common fashion or develop a different presentation for each. You could define an element for quoted text, such as is often found in replies, or you could simply allow the body to contain it as undifferentiated text. What you do depends on your needs—if your visitors are used to mail clients that italicize quoted text or use different colors to distinguish between various levels of replies, obviously you'll need to do more.

If you're creating these documents using data from a database, you may want to assign unique identifiers to given authors, subjects, and more. You may even want to delineate between an author's e-mail address and his name, so as to be able to pick out the e-mail address to use or simply because you want to apply a monospace typeface to it.

```
<div id="abcdef" class="message">
  <div id="headers">
    <span class="from">From:
      <span class="fromname">Steven Champeon</span>
      <span class="fromaddress">schampeo@hesketh.com</span></span><br />
    <span class="date">Date: Wed, 03 Apr 2002 10:40:49 -0500</span><br />
    <span class="subject">Subject: example of marked up email message</span><br />
    <span class="to">To: list@example.com</span><br />
    <span class="organization">hesketh.com/inc.</span><br />
    <span class="url">http://hesketh.com</span><br />
    <span class="genericheader">X-Because-I-Can: because I can.</span><br />
  </div>
  <div id="body">
Hello, world!
  </div>
  <div id="signature">
-- <br />
hesketh.com/inc. raleigh nc 27606
  </div>
</div>
```

Much of the logic that goes into determining how you identify and separate your various information types will depend on the purposes you assign to each component, and how you choose to name your components will depend on the contexts in which you intend to use them. How you choose between <div> and

<span> will be influenced by whether the information needs to be kept together on the same line or it needs to start on its own line (see the discussion of block and inline elements in Chapter 4). The message, for example, might alternatively be marked up as follows:

```
<div id="abcdef" class="message">
  <div id="headers">
    <div class="from">From:
      <span class="fromname">Steven Champeon</span>
      <span class="fromaddress">schampeo@hesketh.com</span></div>
    <div class="date">Date: Wed, 03 Apr 2002 10:40:49 -0500</div>
    <div class="subject">Subject: example of marked up email message</div>
    <div class="to">To: list@example.com</div>
    <div class="organization">Organization: hesketh.com/inc.</div>
    <div class="url">X-URL: http://hesketh.com</div>
    <div class="genericheader">X-Because-I-Can: because I can.</div>
  </div>
  <div id="body">
Hello, world!
  </div>
  <div id="signature">
-- <br />
hesketh.com/inc. raleigh nc usa 27606
  </div>
</div>
```

Another consideration is how you choose to nest your components. This is influenced by how you expect the presentation of elements to affect those elements they're allowed to contain, as you'll see when we discuss inheritance in Chapter 4.

A sample stylesheet for the latter message might look like this:

```
#headers {
  background-color: rgb(224,224,224);
  border: 1px solid rgb(153,153,153);
  color: rgb(0,51,102);
  font-family: Courier, "Andale Mono", monospace;
  font-size: 14px;
  margin-bottom: 10px;
  }

.from {
  font-size: 16px;
  }
```

```
.fromname {
  font-family: "Times New Roman", "New Century Schoolbook", serif;
  font-style: italic;
  }

.fromaddress {
  color: black;
  }

.subject {
  font-size: 16px;
  }

.to {
  color: rgb(51,51,51);
  }

.genericheader {
  color: rgb(51,51,51);
  }

#body {
  background-color: white;
  color: black;
  font-size: 16px;
  }

#signature {
  color: #666666;
  font-family: Courier, monospace;
  }
```

The message then displays as shown in Figure 3-3.

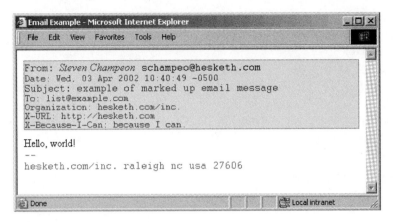

From: *Steven Champeon* schampeo@hesketh.com
Date: Wed, 03 Apr 2002 10:40:49 -0500
Subject: example of marked up email message
To: list@example.com
Organization: hesketh.com/inc.
X-URL: http://hesketh.com
X-Because-I-Can: because I can.

Hello, world!
--
hesketh.com/inc. raleigh nc usa 27606

Figure 3-3. Another example of styled semantic markup

Naturally, your style choices may be different and, we hope, more visually exciting. The preceding stylesheet, though garish, is merely intended to suggest the level to which you can differentiate between properly marked-up elements in terms of the relative importance, prominence, legibility, and other characteristics you wish the final display to take on. A different approach might involve differentiating (using <span> tags) between the name of the header (for example, From:, Subject:) and its contents, and giving them different styles. Another might involve the use of more prominent borders to help differentiate between the headers, the body, and the signature.

Note that the preceding document fragment may well belong in a larger context: either that of a page with navigation or even in a list with a score of other messages presented by thread. In the latter case, you may wish to style and mark up the document differently, so that you can hide irrelevant headers and present the relevant ones in a stacked format, or even as a concise summary below the message that began the thread. You may then want to set the container id to uniquely identify a given message and use a class instead to specify that it should be presented with the "headers" style. The possibilities are endless, particularly if you intend to use a server-side solution to generate the document, or you wish to use client-side scripting to give control over the presentation to the end user.

In addition to semantic reasons for marking up or delivering a document in a certain way, using a particular arrangement or another, there may be practical reasons for doing so as well. For example, you might wish to deliver a dynamic version of your document based on quirks or characteristics of the browser. You might want to present minimal content before the message if the end user is visiting with Lynx or another text-based browser, but deliver a more image-rich version to modern graphical browsers such as Netscape 7, Safari, or Internet Explorer 6.0. Of course, CSS won't help you change the order of elements in your documents—at least not yet—but the use of properly named and identified elements (using either server-side XML and a transformation language such as XSLT, or even the id and class attributes with XML-aware software) can certainly help make it easier to build automated processes that will. And CSS *can* be used to change the order in which those elements are presented to the end user.

OK, enough blue-sky talk. The important thing is that for documents whose entire structure is well known to you, it's easy enough to apply structurally significant markup to their contents. But what about documents whose structure and semantics are in flux, or that are poorly or unevenly defined? Generally speaking, there are two (or three) approaches to the problem of such documents. You can begin at the top, sketching out the basic structure as you find it and using broad strokes; you can begin at the bottom with whatever well-known semantics are available, building smaller known components into larger, more coherent ones; or you can use a mixture of both approaches.

Top-Down Document Analysis

The first approach involves the identification of document-level semantics. We'll use an office memorandum as an example—books on SGML always seem to use this as the archetypical "well-known structured document." The memo has several top-level components:

- Who the memo is from

- Who the memo is addressed to

- What the memo is about

- When the memo was sent

- A salutation

- A body, which might contain several paragraphs

- A closing

- Some information about who dictated the memo and who typed it up

Now, you may be thinking, "But this is almost exactly like the e-mail message example earlier in the chapter!" and you'd be right. But despite certain formal commonalities, they're two different document types and may well deserve to have two different sets of presentation logic. This is where naming these components (using whatever approach seems best, whether it be id and class attribute values mapped to CSS selectors or even tag names in custom XML documents) becomes important. We'll discuss that in the next section.

The memo example is a good one for many reasons, but primarily because it demonstrates a well-known, real-world document type with very strict semantics. Another example that's similarly well known but that doesn't bring to mind the formal aspects of e-mail messages is the press release. Press releases often consist of the following components:

- A title

- A date

- A byline

- A city where the release was posted

- An "executive summary" paragraph

- The body of the press release, which often includes headings and quotations

- A standard blurb describing the company

- Press contact information

- Company contact information

You can see that although the top-level components are well known, it may be that you need to do more research on what each should contain. For example, what goes into the press and company contacts blocks? Do they contain predictable components themselves? If so, is it important that they be styled differently? Often, press release contact blocks contain the following information:

- The name of a person (First name? Last name? Title?)

- The company the person represents (The PR firm? The company about which the release has been written?)

- A physical address for the company

- A phone number (Also a fax number? A telex, for those still living in pre-Internet days?)

- A URL for the company

- An e-mail address (Possibly with a `mailto:` link?)

- Copyright/trademark disclaimers and other legal information

You may wish to style the various subcomponents differently, such as ensuring that the e-mail address and company website lines are always underlined or have hover effects associated with them if they contain a link, or making the phone number larger and in a monospace, nonitalic font to ensure legibility.

This top-down approach to analysis is most useful when the basic components of the document type are apparently well known, but there may be questions remaining about what the subcomponents are and how they're intended to be used. Would a database of press releases be more useful if you could search on the date, press contact, or keywords? If you often use acronyms or terms that require some explanation, perhaps a glossary or other mechanisms should be provided in a standardized format. Formalizing the document type is one way to enable that sort of search or ease of use as a reference. Would building authoring tool templates be easier if the templates' components were formally described? Would content management systems be easier to implement if all of the document types in use within your organization were well known and formalized? Yes. This is true regardless of whether you're using custom XML vocabularies or simply providing some rigor and formality to your XHTML documents.

The point is that the only limit to what you can discover and formalize about any given document type is a practical one: What do you plan to do with the information, should it be styled differently, and is it worth the extra effort to define such documents in a strict, formal way?

You may be surprised at how formal some of the documents in use within your organization really are. Legal documentation, technical manuals, investor relations documents, and securities and exchange filings all have well-known and well-described semantics. In fact, the contents of EDGAR, the U.S. Securities and Exchange Commission's online database of filings and other documents related to publicly traded companies, are all stored in SGML. (Your humble author helped mark up several thousand of them back in the early 1990s, before the Web exploded in popularity.)

You may also, depending on the quality of your office staff and administrators, be deeply saddened by the inconsistency or informality of the documents you use. Often, efforts to put forms into digital systems first require analyses and subsequent overhauls of the paperwork and related processes of entire organizations. It isn't uncommon for such efforts to be so expensive and disruptive that organizations will put off implementing them until pressured to do so by outside authorities, such as accreditation commissions or government regulators. In that case, however, there's hope that such outside forces will bring standards with them that have withstood the test of implementation in other contexts, and so may be more sensible and formal. Or not. But at least you'll have the comfort of knowing you don't suffer alone.

As we've said before, the other important thing to consider is how you plan to nest, or relate, components within a larger context. It may be possible to choose a default set of fonts for use on the entire site and then only vary their weight, size, color, and other effects throughout the rest of the site's subcomponents. In these cases, starting at the top can make the job of the web professional much easier and her presentation rules much more compact (see also the discussion of inheritance and cascade in Chapter 4).

Bottom-Up Document Analysis

What about those documents whose complete top-level structure is unknown, but whose components are well known? What about those cases in which you need to design a presentation ruleset for the pieces of a system that may have multiple "views"—for example, an index view, an individual page view, a view that groups items by category, and so on? The approach to take in these cases is to work with what you know, even if that happens to be the lowest level of the document's semantics.

We actually started to take this approach in our previous discussion of the online catalog. By identifying the individual components common to all catalog entries, it's possible to consider how they could be styled and in what contexts. For example, you may want to make a PLU or stock number less prominent in a single-item display page in which the item could be ordered directly (assuming, for sake of argument, that the stock number is only useful for looking up a part). Alternatively, you may want to highlight the stock number in a tabular display page to make it stand out among the tens and hundreds of other parts in the list. The great thing here is that you can start by identifying that component, or semantic unit, and name it, and then apply different styles to it depending on the context in which it is to be displayed.

The drawback to bottom-up analysis is that it can often take more time and many more iterations to properly and efficiently optimize your rulesets. Because the context in which a rule will be applied isn't yet known, it may well be that many of the presentation rules you've defined will already be inherited from a stylesheet rule further up the chain. You may also consider bottom-up analysis as a way of doing top-down analysis, but without knowing exactly what the top looks like. That is, you may design components knowing they'll fit into a larger page context, but not knowing exactly where, and from there proceed in the usual top-down method.

In summary, bottom-up analysis is sometimes the only option available to you if you have to start working on presentation rules before the larger contexts into which they'll be applied have been defined. One side effect of this type of analysis is that it can require more diligent attention to naming conventions, to which we now turn our attention.

Choosing a Naming Convention

We covered a lot of ground in the earlier sections of this chapter, from SGML through XML to XHTML. You saw examples of vocabularies for custom XML documents (the album), of semantically meaningful class and id attribute values that may be used to identify a given container, and much more. In XHTML, you're mostly limited to the vocabulary defined by HTML 4.0—without a lot of effort, it's not possible to embed instances of your own custom document types into XHTML documents. So, our discussion in this section will focus on naming conventions for id and class attribute values, which then correspond to the selectors in your CSS stylesheets. You'll learn more about the specific syntax required in the next few chapters, but for now it's sufficient to know that stylesheet rules are qualified through the use of names that correspond to id or class values in XHTML elements and to the elements themselves on a broader scale.

Once you've completed your analysis of the structure of your documents, but before it's time to assign permanent names to the elements identified and encode them into stylesheets, it's important to document your findings. There are many ways to go about this, though the simplest solution involves the use of comments within a stylesheet as you create it. You might, for example, insert a comment before a particular rule that explains its purpose and a rationale for the design choices you've made. The biggest challenges you'll face when dealing with naming conventions involve the following factors:

- **Audience:** Who (other than you) will be using these names? Will they be familiar with the contexts from which the names are derived? What sort of documentation do they require?

- **Uniqueness:** Selectors should be unique; otherwise, they may conflict with or interact in unexpected ways with other rules with the same name. How specific should your names be? How much control do you have over their use in context? Are you the only one defining these names?

- **Conflicts:** What software do you run on your site, and does it also use CSS? If so, does it insert document fragments that might contain names that clash with yours? Are you using names that might cause trouble with scripts (such as using the name "links" for the name of a <div>, "body" as the name of a class, and so forth—all of which can cause problems with some implementations)?

- **Precision:** Are the names you assign too generic? Should they be better qualified if only intended for a very specific context? Are they too terse? Might they someday be used in a more general context?

- **Scope:** Are the names you define too specific? Too verbose? Do they add too much weight to the page for their own good? A stylesheet that takes 2 minutes to download because it contains the entire change history, rationale, documentation, and a few ASCII art pictures of the box model is probably a bit much, as are names such as `styleToBeAppliedToTheCurrencySymbolBeforePricesInACatalogListing`, when `currency` might be just as effective.

- **Purpose:** Are the names you've chosen meant to apply to document components that will be used by scripts? Do they work well within the contexts of those environments, or will web professionals have to come up with workarounds or special handling logic to deal with incompatibilities between your environment and theirs?

- **Cultural:** Are there cultural/corporate characteristics of your names that might present problems for the future in terms of a name change within the organization? If someone were to view source on your pages, would that person be offended? Does that person even speak the same language?

- **Other concerns:** If you're creating custom XML vocabularies meant for long-term storage and translation before delivery to a browser or other device, will your names be easy to map to those required by the final output format? If you're using a special storage solution such as an object-oriented XML database, will the names work well there?

- **Legal characters:** As a general principle, `id` and `class` names can contain only alphanumeric characters, and they must never start with a number or contain spaces. The CSS Recommendation permits the use of the hyphen (-) and underscore (_), but these characters are known to cause problems in some browsers and are best avoided.

Documenting your naming conventions may be as simple, as we've mentioned, as comments in the stylesheet or as complex as a full set of documentation explaining the rationale for your choices, the process by which such conventions should be applied during document and template creation, and more. If you've created a custom vocabulary, you may need to document this in the DTD or schema, as well as within the stylesheet.

If you're using XSLT or some other transformation language, you may need to document the naming convention several times or show the relationships between the storage format (whether document repository, object database, relational database, or flat files), the transformation rules (whether XSLT or some other software package with XML support), the output format (whether another custom XML document, XHTML, legacy HTML, or another format), and the associated files, such as CSS stylesheets, JavaScript files, and so forth.

At any rate, once you've documented your naming convention and presentation rules, it's time to integrate them into your website. Depending on the complexity of your environment, this may be as simple as using the documentation as an aid when creating flat XHTML files and scripts, working with production folks to ensure the creation of the proper templates for use with authoring tools, or working with web professionals to implement your document's structure and corresponding naming conventions into a content management system or other document repository.

Integrating Structure with Presentation Logic

In Chapter 2, we first tackled the various ways in which you can associate presentation with a document: inline, embedded, and external. In this section, we'll assume you're using external stylesheets for the sake of reuse and global applicability. (The details of using these various techniques are covered in Chapter 6.)

Without going into the syntactical details of stylesheet rules, which are covered far more extensively in Chapter 5, it's important to note that you may define them in several ways:

- For specific elements based on their tag names (for example, you may define a rule to be applied to all `<span>` or `<div>` elements)

- For specific elements based in their `id` attribute (which must be unique, effectively limiting the ruleset/element relationship to a one-to-one mapping)

- For specific elements based on their `class` attribute (which allows you to define a single class that may be applied to a variety of elements)

There are other combinations, such as rules that only apply to an element that is contained within another element or that follows a specific element, but we'll leave those until Chapter 5.

The various combinations are relevant because, despite the guideline that suggests you should keep your presentation rules separate from your document structure, it isn't possible to completely divorce your knowledge of the structure of a document from your encoding of presentation rules (and vice versa, to a more limited extent). And that's just fine: The guideline is there to discourage you from *embedding* style rules into the document directly, not from building them without knowledge of the documents to which they're supposed to apply.

From the standpoint of defining document structure, this means that you must be aware of the vagaries of your presentation so that the documents will be structured in a way that best takes advantage of your styles. There's bound to be a bit of give and take as you work on these separate pieces of the whole puzzle, so expect a certain amount of iteration and testing. In a situation in which you're designing a pure XML vocabulary to be transformed into XHTML or some other format, it's important to prevent the corruption of that "pure" view of the data with assumptions about a particular rendering environment. An example of this as applied to naming conventions in XHTML would be not to name your navigation bar style after the side of the screen on which it was first placed. "leftNav" sounds fine for a navigation bar that always appears on the left side of the screen on a graphical browser, but what if you decide to move it to the right side? What if in a different browser, such as a handheld, it appeared across the top of the display? Try to keep such context-dependent, nonsemantic judgments from tainting your naming convention. Use terms that will remain meaningful even after a change in design or in audience.

One important detail that you shouldn't miss is that you may find that for a given chunk of document structure (as determined by the semantics you've applied via `id` or `class` attributes) there may not be any special or different presentation rule. Don't get caught up in the mistaken belief that just because some piece of a document has been marked as having special semantic value, it has to also be presented differently. Your application and audience will determine whether this is necessary or important.

For example, the following document fragment contains a wide array of semantic markup, which may well be useful for manipulation by a script or server-side process, and which may be usefully styled to differentiate between the various components, their purpose, and their relative placement and importance in the overall document context:

```
<div class="newsitem">
<h1 class="headline">
<span class="company">FooCo</span> Announces New Metasyntactic Variable</h1>
<h2 class="subhead">&#8220;boo&#8221; added to foo, bar, baz</h2>
<div class="date">April 1, 2002</div>
<div class="byline">by <span class="author">Gilles Deleuze</span>,
<span class="location">Paris</span></div>
<p class="bodytext">
<span class="company">FooCo, Ltd.</span> is proud to announce the release,
after years  of product development, market research, testing and quality
assurance, not to mention the consumption of an inordinate number of
<span class="product">Cheez Doodles&#8482;</span>, the availability of
Yet Another Metasyntactic Variable, known as
<span class="product">&#8220;boo&#8221;</span>.
</p>
<p class="bodytext">&#8220;boo&#8221; may be used immediately by the legions
of programmers who have desperately needed a new metasyntactic variable to
represent a value beyond the traditional, but limiting, triune of foo, bar,
```

```
and baz. Although trinitarian relationships are among the most stable, as is
evidenced by the popularity of the stool, the French slogan &#8220;Liberty,
Fraternity, and Equality&#8221;, and the habit common to graduate scholars of
titling their papers in the form &#8220;Subject, Subject, and Subject: An
Epistleatory Niceness&#8221;; sometimes the situation demands a fourth, such
as in golf or bridge, or when securing sheets to a bed.</p>
<p class="bodytext">It is to rectify these demanding, post-modern challenges
that we introduce &#8220;boo&#8221;. For more information, please see our web
site at <a class="http://example.com">http://example.com</a>.
<span class="disclaimer">If you can read this, you're too close. Cheez Doodles
are a trademark of <span class="company">Wise Foods, Inc.</span></p>
</div>
```

Just because the document contains semantic markup that allows for the identification of companies, products, and the various structural elements of the fragment, this doesn't necessarily imply that their presentation should be altered in any significant way.

On the other hand, some presentation-oriented markup in your documents may be just fine, on the assumption that you don't really care all that much about its semantics. Imagine a discussion of typography in mass-market paperbacks, or a discussion on the use of unusual emphasis to convey subtle issues of tone in written speech in a college writing seminar, using this little demonstration:

```
<blockquote><p>Franny took advantage of the slight pause that followed to
 straighten her back a trifle, as though, for some reason, good posture, or better
 posture, might come in handy at any moment.</p>
<p>"It <i>scares</i> me a little bit, but it doesn't <i>pet</i>rify me. Let's get
that straight. It doesn't <i>pet</i>rify me. Because you forgot one thing, buddy.
When you first felt the urge, the <i>call</i>, to say the prayer, you didn't
immediately start searching the four corners of the world for a master.
You <i>came home</i>."</p></blockquote>
```

Now, some would argue that instead of the purely presentational <i>, we should use the more abstract <em>, and this argument has its merits. But the point is that it isn't always necessary to use semantically charged markup to convey the presentational character of certain content. In the preceding example, we're reproducing the text of a quote, in the printed version of which Zooey's response to Franny appears in italics. If you're trying to reproduce the meaning, rather than the presentation, you might want to use <em>. It's up to you to determine what level of specificity your document's presentation demands.

Summary

Semantic document markup is a powerful idea with a long history compared to the Web (which it helped to inspire, but which quickly went astray). Through the use of observant document analysis techniques, whether top-down or bottom-up, it's possible to develop a keen understanding of the meaning and purpose of the components of your document. These understandings may be encoded in custom vocabularies using SGML or XML, or simply written up in a design or rationale document. Such documents are important, especially for large teams or for content that may be maintained by someone other than the original author, as they allow for the transmission of the naming conventions you've chosen to use. Your vocabularies may be as verbose or concise as the application demands. You may use a transitional approach, using XHTML and attributes more commonly meant for linking styles and structure, and concentrate on those aspects of your documents' semantics that have a consequence for their presentation. Even then, it isn't necessary to have a one-to-one mapping between semantic components and presentational ones, as some markup may well be purely presentational.

CHAPTER 4

Fundamentals

BEFORE YOU WRITE any CSS you need to know how a browser will apply it to your XHTML. There are fundamentals behind this, basic forces that make things happen, similar to gravity being the basic force that applied an apple to Newton. The fundamental concepts for CSS are *block* and *inline, inheritance* and *cascade,* and the *box model.*

CSS rules themselves will be detailed in Chapter 5, and attaching them to your markup will be covered in Chapter 6. But to establish the fundamentals for these chapters it's necessary to show you some CSS now. You'll be able to read the basic meaning in these simple rulesets without knowing the fine points of their syntax.

Some of the examples may not display as illustrated in your browser because some browsers have shortcomings. These are handled later in Chapter 10. For now we'll use concise CSS to express the fundamentals cleanly.

Block and Inline

Because you know XHTML, you probably know about *block* and *inline* elements, but it's worth a quick refresher to clear away any confusion that might cause you to misapply CSS.

Simply put, block-level elements always start a new line for themselves, and any content that follows them also starts on a new line. Familiar block elements are `<p>` and `<h1>`. Block-level elements may contain other block-level elements as well as inline elements.

Inline elements follow each other like the letters in this sentence, only beginning a new line when they have run out of space on the previous one. They do not force the following element to begin a new line. Familiar inline elements are `<em>`, `<img>`, and `<a>`. Inline elements may only contain other inline elements.

Styles may be applied to any of the elements of your XHTML markup, block or inline. You can also style a section of your XHTML that isn't already framed by an existing element. You tag the section by using `<div>` or `<span>` as desired. The `<div>` element is for block-level use, and `<span>` is for inline use. You can also individualize these tags with the `id` and `class` attributes. In this way you have the option of applying styles to all `<div>` and `<span>` elements or only to particular ones.

To give you a quick taste of how these elements are applied in the XHTML, here's an example (Figure 4-1 shows the result):

```
<body>
  <div id="content">
    <h1>Fox</h1>
    <p>The quick brown <span class="animal">fox</span> jumped over the
    lazy <span class="animal">dog</span>.</p>
    <p>This typical sentence rests the mind while exercising the
      <span class="machine">keyboard</span>.</p>
  </div>
</body>
```

Fox

The quick brown fox jumped over the lazy dog.

This typical sentence rests the mind while exercising the keyboard.

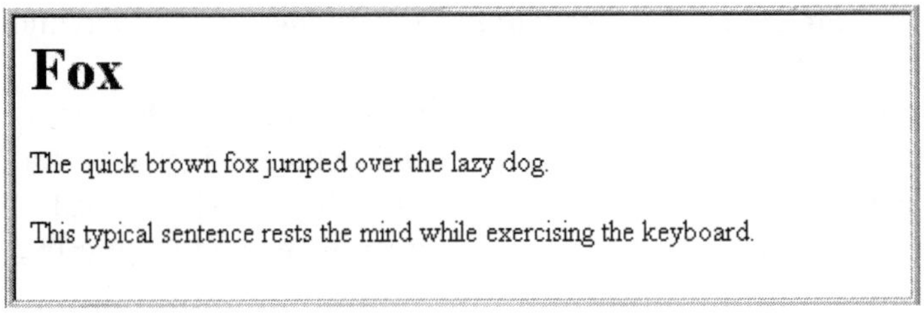

Figure 4-1. Unstyled, as seen by the browser

Without any styles declared, the <div> and <span> elements have no effect on how a browser displays the XHTML. With CSS you can add visual styles to the containing <div> to create a layout (Figure 4-2 shows the result):

```
div {
  padding: 20px;
  margin: 0px auto;
  background: #ccc;
  border: 5px solid #000;
  width: 50%;
  }
```

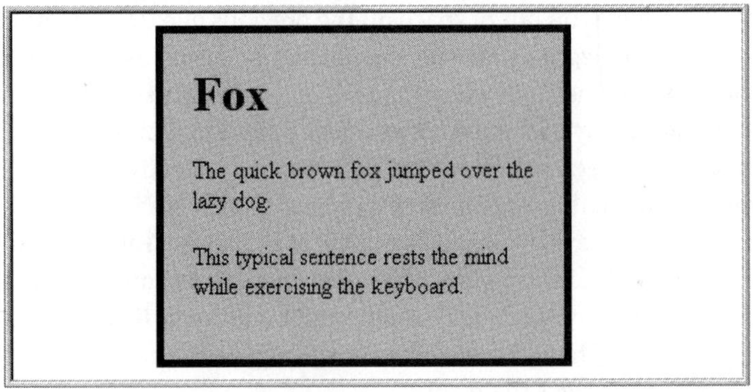

Fox

The quick brown fox jumped over the lazy dog.

This typical sentence rests the mind while exercising the keyboard.

Figure 4-2. Figure 4-1, with styles

Let's modify the XHTML a little. Wrap each phrase within its own `<div>` element instead of using a single container, and apply the identical style. By using the same style for a sequential series of `<div>` elements, a descending series of boxes will be created on the page (Figure 4-3 shows the result).

```
<body>
  <div>
    <h1>Fox</h1>
  </div>
  <div>
    <p>The quick brown fox jumped over the lazy dog.</p>
  </div>
  <div>
    <p>This typical sentence rests the mind while exercising the keyboard.</p>
  </div>
</body>
```

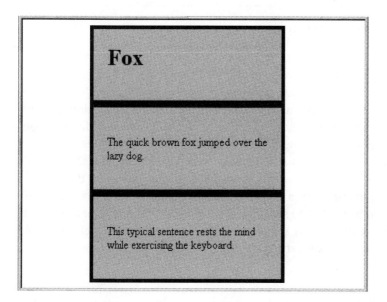

Figure 4-3. Styled with sequential `<div>`*s*

As block elements can contain other block elements, you can also nest these styles. Here we reduce the XHTML's content to allow the example to fit on the page and apply the same styles as before (Figure 4-4 shows the result):

```
<body>
  <div><div><div>
    <h1>Fox</h1>
  </div></div></div>
</body>
```

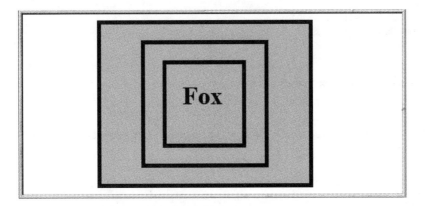

Figure 4-4. Styled with nested <div>*s*

You can do quite a bit with <div> elements. Chapter 8 is dedicated to showing you how to arrange <div>s into layouts.

The <span> element can be used to attach styles to a desired section without creating a line break. Commonly, this is done to create classes outside the scope of XHTML's writing-based elements such as headings and paragraphs. These classes can be anything you wish. In the next example we've created the classes "animal" and "machine" so that we can apply distinguishing styles for these genres in the document. <span> tags are placed around instances of genre, and then rulesets are added to the CSS to style these <span>s (see Figure 4-5 for the result). (The styles here are uninspired, we admit. In the real world of the Web, we would illustrate this better with color styles.)

```
<body>
  <div id="content">
    <h1>Fox</h1>
    <p>The quick brown <span class="animal">fox</span> jumped over the lazy
      <span class="animal">dog</span>.</p>
    <p>This typical sentence rests the mind while exercising the
      <span class="machine">keyboard</span>.</p>
  </div>
</body>
```

```
.animal {
  font-variant:small-caps;
  }
.machine {
  font-variant:small-caps;
  text-decoration:underline
  }
```

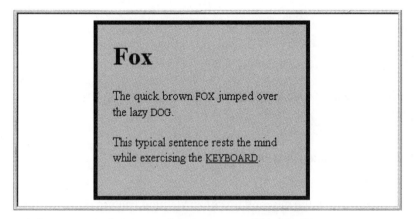

Figure 4-5. Styling with inserted `<span>`*s and classes*

Although this is useful for emphasis, it also comes with cautions. You have to insert the appropriate `<span>` tag in your XHTML for each item you wish to style. Also, because the extra meaning will only be communicated to CSS-capable browsers, it's inappropriate to use for critical information. CSS is for enhancements to your XHTML message, not the message itself.

Inheritance and Cascade

It's entirely possible, and even likely, that a single element will have more than one style applied to it. *Inheritance* and *cascade* describe how styles are applied through one another without conflict.

Inheritance

Inheritance works in a manner that you're already familiar with from XHTML:

```
<body>
  <h1>Very Brief Example</h1>
  <p>Now <em>that's</em> a <strong>jumping fox!</strong></p>
</body>
```

In this example, <body> is the *ancestor* of <h1>, <p>, <em>, and <strong>; all of the elements <body> contains. Similarly, <h1>, <p>, <em>, and <strong> are all *descendants* of <body>.

Also, <body> is the *parent* of <h1> and <p>, while <p> is the *parent* of <em> and <strong>. Note that although a parent can have more than one child, no child can have more than one parent. Children of the same parent are called *siblings*. Figure 4-6 illustrates this concept.

```
<body>

<h1>Very Brief Example</h1>

<p>Now <em>that's</em> a <strong>jumping fox!</strong></p>

</body>
```

Figure 4-6. Inheritance shown by shading

Due to inheritance, all the descendants of an element will use the same font style and color as their common ancestor, unless you override this by adding further styles to descendants. For example, if you declare white text for the <body> element, all of the text contained within <body> will be white, including all of it within the descendant elements. The style is inherited right through the lineage. However, if you declare a further style of light gray text for <p>, then all text within the <p> element, and within its descendants, will be light gray. The text within <h1> will remain white, as <h1> is a sibling of <p>, not a descendant, and inherits its color from their parent, <body>. To wit (Figure 4-7 shows the result):

```
body {
    background:#000;
    color:#fff;
    }
p {
    color:#c0c0c0;
    }
```

Figure 4-7. A display of inheritance

There are exceptions to this inheritance, but these will make sense to you. For example, the background property is not inherited. By default a background is always transparent, so the background specified in an ancestor element will show through descendant elements. In this way background appears to be inherited, at least at first.

Imagine if background *was* inherited, and you'll see why this exception was made. If you had used a background image in <body>, it would be repeated in every descendant, creating a fractured collage instead of your single background image for the whole page. To fix that you'd have to write declarations for each descendant to use a transparent background. That's a lot of typing, which is directly opposed to the intent of inheritance.

Cascade

Much of the power of CSS is in the ability to cascade a number of different stylesheets into one result. A page may have more than one stylesheet because the browser may provide one of its own, the user may provide one and, of course, you, the author of the web page, may provide one. In fact, as author you may provide a number of stylesheets, taking advantage of cascade to give you more options.

When there are multiple stylesheets, the browser will give the sheets greatest weight in descending order: author, user, browser. There are exceptions, but this is the general method. An author-declared style will override a user-declared style, and both author and user styles will override a browser-declared style.

The browser's stylesheet is one you're already familiar with. Make any unstyled XHTML document and load it in your browser. Likely you're now looking at black Times New Roman font on a white background, with the links picked out in bright blue. Dull, isn't it? But there *is* a stylesheet in use. Headings appear large and bold, and <em> text is italicized. All this, even the white background, is specified by the browser stylesheet. The plain XHTML only supplies characters and tags. Basic style comes from the browser.

You change this by creating your own stylesheet, which can be as simple as a new font family and color for the <body> tag. Your styles will be inherited throughout the page. For every element, the browser consults all declarations that apply from all stylesheets. If any stylesheet doesn't have a specific style for any element, then the inherited value will be used. The browser applies the rule of greatest weight to these collected styles.

So although the user or browser may have a specific font family and color declared for an element such as <p>, the inherited style for <p> from your stylesheet will take precedence. Properties of elements that aren't styled by you or the user will retain the browser's default style. In the case in which only the font family and color for <body> were altered, the document's headings will retain their larger relative size, and the <em> text will remain italicized, as specified by the browser stylesheet.

Overriding Author Styles

As mentioned, a user may also create a stylesheet. Because of the relative weights of stylesheets, any author-styled page will be presented to the user with the author's choices, and any page without author styles will receive the improvements of the user's stylesheet over the browser's default.

However, the user also has the option of adding the `!important` declaration to a style so that it takes precedence over an author-defined style. There is a very good reason for this. A user's styles may not be just aesthetic improvements, but may be for personal access needs such as high contrast and large text. The syntax is very simple:

```
p {font-size: 25px;}
```

becomes

```
p {font-size: 25px !important;}
```

Note that the `!important` declaration will only apply to the style it is with. In the following rule, only the font size carries the increased weight in the cascade, not the font family or color:

```
p {
    font-size: 25px !important;
    font-family: verdana, arial, helvetica, sans-serif;
    color: #000;
    }
```

> **NOTE** *In CSS1, the page author had the option of adding the* `!important` *declaration to any rule, which would then override an* `!important` *declaration in the corresponding rule in a user's stylesheet.*
>
> *This order of precedence was reversed in CSS2 to recognize the crucial purpose that the user's* `!important` *declaration can be serving. This is a rare instance in which CSS2 contradicts CSS1. You should keep this exception in mind and be reluctant to use the* `!important` *declaration in your author stylesheets. It's very likely that if a user declares something is important, it is.*

Author Stylesheet Precedence

Cascade also decides precedence when you, as page author, have provided more than one stylesheet. For example, a complex business website may require stylistically distinct but related subsections representing the different divisions within the company. You can simplify and organize your styling task by creating a set of stylesheets that separate the distinct and related style in a similar manner. A global stylesheet can be created for the styles common to all documents, and then there can be individual stylesheets for further styles unique to site subsections. A single page might be styled by three stylesheets:

- corporate.css

- marketing.css

- specialOffers.css

In this case the corporate.css file would be for the global styles suited to the corporate identity and would be referenced by all documents. Documents specifically produced for the marketing department would also refer to the marketing.css file to add or change some styles as suited to that branch of the corporation. Marketing documents that carry promotions could additionally refer to a specialOffers.css file to add or change styles as appropriate to that subfunction, and which can now be shared with other departments such as sales to provide function continuity for clients.

The browser will know what stylesheet precedence you intend by the order in which you list them in the head of the XHTML document. Each stylesheet will outweigh a preceding stylesheet, so for the preceding example the global stylesheet would come first and the most specific specialOffers stylesheet would be last.

```
<head>
  <title>Labor Day Sale</title>
  <link rel="stylesheet" href="css/corporate.css" type="text/css"
        media="screen" />
  <link rel="Stylesheet" href="css/marketing.css" type="text/css"
        media="screen" />
  <link rel="Stylesheet" href="css/specialOffers.css" type="text/css"
        media="screen" />
</head>
```

The Box Model

The CSS *box model* is a visual layout tool. You may create a box around any section of your document by containing it within a <div> tag. A box has a number of properties that you can manipulate. Figure 4-8 illustrates these properties.

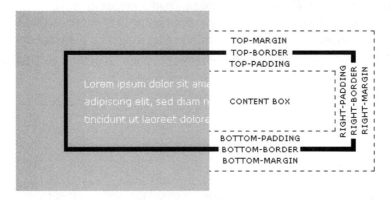

Figure 4-8. The box model

The content box wraps only around your content. You may set the width and height of this, or let the browser decide its dimensions based on the content size, the viewport size (normally the window of your browser), or a number of other factors that depend on the complexity of your layout. In other words, it may be fluid or rigid about its size, although it will always be rectangular or square.

You may push the outer edge of the box out from the content by adding padding. Padding can be added as one size all the way around or as individual sizes for the top, right, bottom, and left sides.

A border may be added around this padding. The outer edge of the box is now the outer edge of the border. CSS allows you to style the width, type, and color of the border, all the way around or as individual sides again. The common border types are solid, dotted, dashed, and none.

A margin may be added around the border to push the border away from outside elements. This too extends the outer edge of the box and may be applied all the way around or as individual sides.

You may also decide to use only margin or border or padding; using any one doesn't require the use of the others. But note that however much padding or border or margin you add, the internal content area is still sized by your width and height declarations. The outer edges of the box are a result of the sum of the content area and any padding, border, and margin declared.

```
#box {
  width: 300px
  padding: 10px;
  border: 1px solid #000;
  margin: 20px;
  }
```

For the preceding box the total width, outer edge to outer edge, will be 20px + 1px + 10px + 300px + 10px + 1px + 20px, or 362 pixels. This may be nonintuitive at first, so take your time with the concept. The declared width of 300px doesn't measure across the outer edges or across the visible borders; it only applies to the content area.

When a background color or tiled image is applied to a box, it fills the area within the outer edge, excluding margins. When there is a border, the background treatment will be applied as far as the outside edge of that border, so it will be the visible background in the gaps of a dashed or dotted border.

There is also an important exception in margin behavior to be aware of. Whenever box elements are stacked vertically by the normal flow, the touching top and bottom margins overlap or, in the terminology of the CSS specification, they *collapse*. Hence the distance between the adjacent borders of these boxes isn't the sum of the two margins, but is instead only the size of the greater margin, as shown in Figure 4-9.

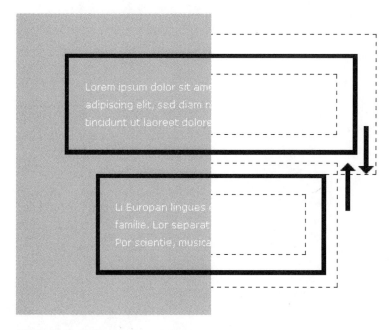

Figure 4-9. Collapsing margins

Margins of boxes that touch at left and right sides don't collapse, but act as expected. The distance between side borders of adjacent boxes will be the sum of their touching margins.

These are the basic qualities of the box model. They're quite straightforward, but they do require an amount of visualization because most of the time you can't see the padding and margins—you just see their effects on your page. In Chapter 8 we go into detail with box style rules and show how sets of boxes can be combined for page layout.

Summary

In this chapter we covered the fundamental concepts behind CSS. The block and inline elements of XHTML were reviewed in the light of how CSS styles are applied, cascade and inheritance were shown to be the path used by style rules to affect individual elements, and the box model was introduced as a primary visual layout tool. Having set these basics in place, we can now discuss the types of CSS rules and their syntax.

CHAPTER 5

Rules

THIS CHAPTER IS YOUR introduction to the actual code that makes a stylesheet. An XHTML document is styled by specifying a list of rules that target selections of your markup. In this chapter we'll discuss what makes a rule, what values can be applied with rules, and the different ways rules can select precisely the markup you wish to style.

Rule Structure

Every rule follows a specific format. A simple example is as follows:

```
body {margin: 0px}
```

There are two main parts, the *selector* and the *declaration*. The selector names the element or elements in the XHTML that this rule styles: <body>. The declaration expresses the desired styling: {margin: 0px}.

The declaration itself has two parts, the *property* and the *value*. The property is the property of the XHTML element that you wish to style: margin. The value is the value you are applying to that property: 0px.

So with this rule, the <body> element is declared to have its margins set to 0 pixels. A rule may also have multiple declarations. These are separated by semicolons.

```
body {margin: 0px; padding: 0px; font-family: sans-serif}
```

The <body> element now has three properties styled. Margins and paddings have been set to 0, and fonts will be the browser's default sans serif type.

Stylesheets are typically written with line breaks between declarations for legibility. The browser ignores any white space in a stylesheet, so you can use spaces and tabs as you prefer.

```
body {
  margin: 0px;
  padding: 0px;
  font-family: sans-serif;
  }
```

You'll notice that I added a semicolon after the last declaration and put the closing curly brace on the next line. That's just my own writing style—it's not a requirement of CSS syntax. I do it to make adding and deleting declarations quick work. When I'm busy, it's far too easy to add a declaration and forget to add the separating semicolon to the preceding one. This can result in time lost trying to figure why things suddenly don't play right in the browser.

The CSS syntax isn't too strict, which allows for personal formats. All parts of a rule must be included and be in the correct order, but the white space, line breaks, and final semicolon are up to you.

Shorthand

CSS allows a number of ways to express the same thing, to aid either brevity or legibility as you desire. For example, the following three rules all express the same style.

Rule 1:

```
body {margin: 0px}
```

Rule 2:

```
body {margin: 0px 0px 0px 0px}
```

Rule 3:

```
body {
    margin-top: 0px;
    margin-right: 0px;
    margin-bottom: 0px;
    margin-left: 0px;
    }
```

All three rules create zero body margin. The first version is the simplest statement; whatever value is placed in it will be applied to all four margins, which is the number of margins all elements have. In the second version, each margin value is stated individually. They apply in a clockwise rotation starting from top: top-right-bottom-left. The third version is the longest form of this rule, not shorthand. This is seldom seen but is the easiest to read when you're new to CSS. Each property and value declaration is stated separately.

In the full version you may mix the order with no ill effect:

```
body {
  margin-bottom: 0px;
  margin-left: 0px;
  margin-top: 0px;
  margin-right: 0px;
  }
```

You may also style only individual properties and skip the others. The browser's default will be applied for missing styles:

```
body {
  margin-right: 0px;
  margin-bottom: 0px;
  }
```

There is also a shorthand method that has only two apparent values:

```
body {margin: 0px 0px}
```

This short form reflects symmetry common in design. The first value applies to the top and bottom margins, and the second applies to the right and left margins.

And there is a shorthand method that has only three apparent values:

```
body {margin: 0px 0px 0px}
```

This short form reflects side-to-side symmetry. The first value applies to the top margin, the second applies to the right and left margins, and the third applies to the bottom margin.

Personally, I use the form `0px 0px 0px 0px` when I'm building a new design, even when all values are initially the same. It simply saves typing, as I need only alter one or two digits to adjust individual properties when I'm experimenting with proportions. Your mileage may vary, of course. Everyone tends to evolve his or her own opinion of what's easiest.

Different properties may have different methods of shorthand available. Typically you'll see a border expressed in this way:

```
div {border: 5px solid #ccc}
```

What that means becomes clear in the longer form:

```
div {
  border-width: 5px;
  border-style: solid;
  border-color: #ccc;
  }
```

Note that this longer form is itself composed of three shorthand properties, and the longest form would be as follows:

```
div {
  border-top-width: 5px;
  border-right-width: 5px;
  border-bottom-width: 5px;
  border-left-width: 5px;
  border-top-style: solid;
  border-right-style: solid;
  border-bottom-style: solid;
  border-left-style: solid;
  border-top-color: #ccc;
  border-right-color: #ccc;
  border-bottom-color: #ccc;
  border-left-color: #ccc;
  }
```

No matter the complexity or brevity of a rule, it always follows the same structure of `selector {property: value}`. It's a left to right statement of what element is being styled, what property of that element is being styled, and finally, what the value for that property is.

For the rest of this chapter we'll take a closer look at values and selectors for rules. Further detail on individual properties is given in Chapters 7 and 8.

Values

The CSS specifications provide a broad range of values. Not all of them apply to screen browsers because styles may also be declared for other media types, such as `print` and `aural`. In this section we cover common value types for `screen` so you'll have a functional knowledge of your choices in color and size.

Color

The color values will be familiar to you from XHTML. You have 16 keywords (aqua, black, blue, fuchsia, gray, green, lime, maroon, navy, olive, purple, red, silver, teal, white, and yellow), and you have RGB hexadecimal colors, which range from #000000 (black) through #ffffff (white).

CSS also allows shorthand for hexadecimal value whenever the value pairs carry the same digits. Hence, the rich blue #3300ff becomes #30f. It's a small thing, but one I'm grateful for at the end of each long day.

In addition, RGB values may be expressed in percentage and decimal forms. This is less common, but it may suit people coming from a graphic arts background. Pure red, which is #ff0000 in hexadecimal, can be expressed as rgb(100%,0%,0%) and rgb(255,0,0).

Size

Primarily you'll use percent (%), pixels (px), or ems (em) to express any length measurement.

Pixels are an absolute value, so if you declare that an item is 100px, then it will be 100px of the user's display. Percentage and ems, however, are relative. They tell the browser to calculate a property's size based on different things depending on the property involved.

For instance, you may declare a content box's width in percentage so that it will be sized in relation to browser window size, which can vary from user to user:

```
div {width: 50%}
```

The browser will calculate the size as a percentage of the parent element's width. A solitary box is usually descendant of <html> and <body>, which are often unstyled, leaving this box to become half the width of the page. If you place this box within another simple 50% wide box, then the inner box would be half the width of the outer box, which itself is half the width of the page.

Inheritance also applies when using percentage for font sizing. If font size is declared to be 20px for body and then 80% for paragraphs, then paragraph fonts will be calculated and displayed as 16px.

Ems are similar to percentages in that they're calculated. An em is the height of the character box of the default text of the user's system, or the height of the ancestor font-size declaration in your CSS when you supply one.

```
h1 {font-size: 1.5em}
```

If font size for body has been declared as 20px, this rule would display main headings as 30px. So 1.5em would be the same as writing 150%.

There is an exception to normal inheritance to be aware of with ems. For properties other than font-size, an em value will reference its own rule's font size, not the system default or rule ancestor. In the following example, the left margin of the heading is set to twice the heading's font size, which is itself 1.5 times the system default or rule ancestor.

```
h1 {
  font-size: 1.5em;
  margin: 0 0 0 2em;
  }
```

If there was a body font size of 20px declared previous to this, the calculation for this heading's left margin would be

```
2 x 1.5 x 20px = 60px
```

Percentage has its own quirk. Had the margin been set in percentage rather than ems, then the margin value would relate instead to the element's containing block. In the following example, the left margin of the heading would be 2% of the width of the box it is in, and if there is no box, then it would be 2% of the `<html>` width.

```
h1 {
  font-size: 1.5em;
  margin: 0 0 0 2%;
  }
```

Font size may also be declared by a series of keywords, such as `small`, `medium`, and `large`. Several size units are available for fonts, and some have issues regarding browser support and the accessibility of your pages. Chapter 7 discusses this in some detail to help you make an informed choice.

Selectors

As stated in the beginning of this chapter, a selector is the part of a style rule that states what element of your XHTML the rule applies to. This is the most basic form of selector:

```
p {margin: 20px}
```

This selector's target is `<p>` elements, and the rule states they'll have 20px margins all the way around.

You may group selectors as a comma-separated list to apply styles common to several elements concisely when this can't be achieved through normal inheritance. In the following example, three heading types are given shared font and color to distinguish them from those of their ancestor, and rules for individual sizing follow. Grouping in this way saves only two lines of code over repeating the styles in three rules, but it also makes clear at a glance that these headings have both shared and distinct styles among them.

```
h1, h2, h3 {
  font-family: serif;
  color: #33f;
  }
h1 {
  font-size: 2.5em;
  }
h2 {
  font-size: 2.0em;
  }
h3 {
  font-size: 1.5em;
  }
```

Simple selectors such as these that refer to XHTML elements are called *type selectors*. The CSS specs provide a broad range of selector methods beyond this basic one, but not all are well supported by our browsers yet. For the rest of this section we'll concentrate on the methods that are in common use today.

Contextual Selection

Contextual selectors target not all instances of an element, but only the instances that occur in a particular relation to another element.

Descendant Selector

This selector's target is elements that are descendant of another element. Both elements are stated in the selector and they're separated by a space, not a comma. The first is the ancestor element and the second is the descendant:

```
p em {text-decoration: underline;}
```

This example targets emphasized text within paragraphs, and only within paragraphs. It will not apply to any unemphasized text within paragraphs, nor will it apply to any emphasized text that is outside of paragraphs, such as in the heading. The selector tells the browser first that it's only about paragraphs, and then that it's only about emphasized text within those paragraphs. Figure 5-1 shows the result.

```
<body>
<h3>Yet <em>More</em> About Foxes</h3>
<p>That <em>quick</em> brown fox <strong><em>really</em>
ran circles around the dog this time</strong>.</p>
</body>
```

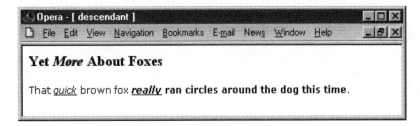

Figure 5-1. Descendant selector

Child Selector

This selector's target is the child of an element:

```
p > em {text-decoration: underline;}
```

This example targets emphasized text within paragraphs, and only within paragraphs, but only when the emphasized text is a child. This is more specific than descendant, so it wouldn't include "grandchildren" emphasized text that occur within other children of a paragraph. Figure 5-2 shows the result.

```
<body>
<h3>Yet <em>More</em> About Foxes</h3>
<p>That <em>quick</em> brown fox <strong><em>really</em>
ran circles around the dog this time</strong>.</p>
</body>
```

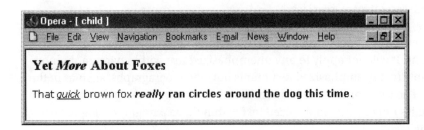

Figure 5-2. Child selector

Adjacent Sibling Selector

This selector's subject is the following sibling of an element:

```
h2 + h3 {margin-top: 10px}
```

This example targets <h3>, but only when <h3> and an <h2> have the same parent, *and* when <h3> immediately follows the <h2>.

"Whatever for?" you may ask. The example fragment, h2 + h3 {margin-top: 10px}, is a good example. Headings often have larger margins than paragraphs. Although the top and bottom margins around your <h2> and <h3> may look fine when both headings are surrounded by paragraphs, when placed together their margins may cause too great a gap between them.

```
h2 {
  margin-top: 30px;
  margin-bottom: 20px;
  }
h3 {
  margin-top: 30px;
  margin-bottom: 20px;
  }
p {
  margin-top: 20px;
  margin-bottom: 20px;
  }
```

Because upper and lower margins collapse into each other, in this example either heading is followed by regular text after a 20px interval. But whenever <h3> follows an <h2>, it follows at an interval 50% larger. This may be unwanted, and an adjacent sibling selector can let you fine-tune your typography for these instances.

Attribute Selectors

These selectors are wonderfully specific and have four basic variants. You can create rules that target attribute names or attribute values. The following two elements have typical attributes:

```
<a href="http://www.w3.org/" title="The W3C">the source</a>
<img src="../img/early_phone.gif" title="Figure 1" alt="Early systems were not
much better than tin cans and a string." />
```

href, title, src, and alt are all attributes and can be targeted by attribute selectors in either broad or narrow terms depending on the variant used. An example of each follows. Note the gently increasing complexity within the [ ] and that it reflects greater specificity of the selector.

```
img[title] {border: 2px solid #000}
```

The preceding rule styles any <img> with a title attribute.

```
img[title="Figure"] {border: 2px solid #000}
```

The preceding rule styles any <img> with the title attribute "Figure", and only this *exact* title, since the symbol = signifies an exact match. The prior XHTML example isn't a match in this case, and the style wouldn't apply.

```
img[title~="Figure"] {border: 2px solid #000}
```

The preceding rule (note the additional ~) styles any <img> with a title attribute that includes Figure in a space-separated list of words. This rule will target our example.

```
*[lang|="en"] {color: #ccc}
```

This rule styles any element with a lang attribute that begins with "en" in a hyphen-separated list. This attribute selector variant is primarily used to target language subcodes, such as en, en-uk, and en-us. However, the bar may be used to create a selector to target any hyphen-separated list of attribute values that you may be faced with.

Class Selectors

This is where things get interesting. The class selector is a form of attribute selector, and one that sees heavy use in current CSS practice. By adding a class attribute to any element of your XHTML, you can target that element. In its simplest form, the markup could look like this:

```
<p class="warning">Beware of the Grue.</p>
```

And the relevant style rule would be this:

```
p.warning {color: #f00}
```

Now all paragraphs with this class attribute value will have red text. You can also style all elements with the class attribute value "warning", not just paragraphs, by restating the rule as follows:

```
.warning {color: #f00}
```

Nor do you have to stop there. You can apply this rule to sections of your markup without being restrictive to using regular elements. You can supply the <div> and <span> elements, discussed in Chapter 4, as targets. These elements have no meaning outside of CSS, and they're similar in function except that <div> is a block element and <span> is inline. Typical forms would be as follows:

```
<div class="warning"><p>Beware of the Grue.</p></div>

<p><span class="warning">Beware</span> of the Grue.</p>
```

Due to this flexibility, class selectors are a powerful tool, and it follows that you can overuse them. Remember that browsers that don't use your stylesheet won't receive the extra information you meant to communicate. You need to distinguish between enhancement and core message. So before you rely on a <div> or a <span> to style a selection, ask yourself if there's an existing element that can do the job. The last example would be better expressed as follows:

```
<p><em class="warning">Beware</em> of the Grue.</p>
```

Now your warning will be emphasized in any browser without CSS support, and you're free to add further style for more capable browsers, such as removing the italics that most CSS browsers apply for <em> and using bold red letters instead:

```
.warning {
  color: #f00;
  font-weight: bold;
  font-style: normal;
  }
```

It's worth taking some care when you invent a class name. By using a generic but still meaningful name, you'll avoid having names that don't make sense when you revise a design at later date. Had we named the previous class redText, the name would make sense today but not later if it changes to yellow. By naming the class simply with its function, warning, we've communicated the meaning without describing the form.

Class selectors may also be used to target subsets of elements with more than one class attribute value. In the following example, each element has an attribute with a space-separated list of values:

```
<p class="foreign car">1</p>
<p class="foreign car parts">2</p>
<p class="foreign car drivers">3</p>
<p class="foreign motorcycle parts">4</p>
```

If the following style is declared, then all of the previous paragraphs will be in the color blue:

```
p.foreign {color: #00f}
```

By using multiple values in a class selector, you can target subsets of these multiple value class attributes. The syntax simply requires that each selector's value be preceded by a period (.). This next rule styles only the first three paragraphs of the example, because only these have both "foreign" and "car" in their classes:

```
p.foreign.car {color: #00f}
```

The fourth paragraph isn't styled because it doesn't have "car" in its class. Similarly, the selector `p.foreign.car.used` wouldn't style any of the previous paragraphs because none of their class attributes include the value `used`.

ID Selectors

The ID selector is very similar to the class selector, but with an important difference. The rule will only be applied once, as each ID attribute in a document must be unique. This selector is most commonly used to style individual layout boxes, such as for main content or menu, but they also may be suited to styling singular items such as your copyright notice or your page's title.

In syntax they're differentiated from class selectors by using # instead of . :

```
#mainText {
  padding: 10px;
  margin: 40px 40px 20px 40px;
  border: 1px solid #000;
  }
```

This example would typically be used in conjunction with the XHTML tags `<div id="mainText"></div>` to create a primary content box for a layout.

> **NOTE** *Pause time! In many ways the preceding sections on rules, values, and selectors will be your core knowledge of CSS. Now would be a good time to pause to ensure things sink in or to have a second reading. Proceed with the following section after you familiarize yourself with these sections.*

Pseudo-Classes and Pseudo-Elements

These allow you to target portions of your XHTML that aren't specifically tagged, hence the "pseudo" prefix.

Pseudo-classes deal with element characteristics, and *pseudo-elements* deal with structure that exists within your document but isn't labeled as an element. It's difficult to visualize these in the abstract, so let's go straight into examples.

Pseudo-Classes

The following sections describe two pseudo-class types: the first-child pseudo-class and the anchor pseudo-class.

First-Child Pseudo-Class

This pseudo-class targets an element that is the first child of a parent. For example, you may wish to style the first paragraph within each of your layout <div>s distinctly, perhaps with an indentation or with italics. Because these paragraphs are children of the <div> element, this selector allows you to target them without having to add any class attributes to your XHTML. This first example styles any first-child elements that are paragraphs:

```
p:first-child {font-style: italic}
```

This will style the first-child paragraphs within <div>s, but it will also style all first-child paragraphs that occur outside of <div>s in your document. To be absolutely precise, use child selector notation with the appropriate element included:

```
div > p:first-child {font-style: italic}
```

By using this first-child pseudo-class within a descendant selector, we can clear up a problem created by our example: We made a paragraph italicized, and italics are often used by browsers to express the <em> tag. The following rule selects all emphasized text within all first-child paragraphs and provides correction:

```
div > p:first-child em {font-weight: bold}
```

You should note an important limitation of this technique. To be targeted, a paragraph must be the first child of the <div> element. If a heading or other element precedes the first paragraph, then the paragraph won't receive the style.

Anchor Pseudo-Class

This pseudo-class is a set of rules that target the different states of a link:

```
a:link {color: #00f}
a:visited {color: #0f0}
a:hover {color: #c0f}
a:active {color: #f00}
```

The link can be an ordinary link such as <a href="http://www.w3c.org/">. There doesn't need to be any classes in the markup because the browser already understands that these states exist. Note that because these states can occur at the same time, you must use their order to indicate which takes precedence. hover follows link and visited in our example so that the color will change as you mouse over the link, whether or not it has been previously visited.

You may also combine these pseudo-classes with other selectors to be more specific. Adding a class selector to the rule allows you to apply a distinct color for links that lead outside of your website.

```
a.external:link {color: #93f}
```

Such links would require classes assigned in the XHTML:

```
<a class="external" href="http://www.w3c.org/">.
```

By adding a contextual selector to the rule, you can apply a particular style for images that are also links:

```
a:link img {border-color: #00f}
```

> **NOTE**   *In this section we've grouped together what the W3C considers to be two types of pseudo-classes in order to provide a well-rounded example.*
>
> *The CSS2 specification considers* :link *and* :visited *to be* link pseudo-classes, *and* :active *and* :hover *are joined by* :focus *to form the* dynamic pseudo classes. *The difference is that the link pseudo-classes are meant to be used only with hyperlinks, whereas the dynamic pseudo-classes may be applied to any element.*
>
> *However, our current browsers don't yet recognize* :active *and* :hover *when applied to elements other than hyperlinks, so for current practical purposes we can make a single group of* anchor pseudo-classes. *The distinction in the W3C specification will become useful in the future when we move beyond the monitor/mouse interface.*
>
> :focus *is similarly limited in that our browsers currently only recognize it in relation to forms. In this case it's the state when the form is ready to accept your keyboard input.*

Pseudo-Elements

Pseudo-elements are similar to the first-child pseudo-class in that they refer to structural position within your document. They're considered pseudo-*elements* because although their behavior is as if the targeted markup was tagged, it isn't. The first-child pseudo-class is considered akin to classes because it applies to an existing element. As in the previous section, this will make more sense with examples.

First-Line Pseudo-Element

This pseudo-element allows a way to express the typographic convention of emphasizing the first line of a paragraph, but it may be applied to any block-level element. Its rule form is the same as that of pseudo-classes:

```
p:first-line {
  color: #ff0;
  font-size: 400%;
  }
```

The first-line pseudo-element has a restricted set of properties to choose from. For quick reference, these are as follows:

- background

- clear

- color

- font

- letter-spacing

- line-height

- text-decoration

- text-shadow

- text-transform

- vertical-align

- word-spacing

First-Letter Pseudo-Element

This pseudo-element allows a way to express the typographic convention of emphasizing the first letter of a paragraph, but it may be applied to any block-level element. Its rule form is also the same as that of pseudo-classes:

```
p:first-letter {font-size: 150%}
```

The first-letter pseudo-element is restricted to the following properties:

- background

- border

- clear

- color

- float

- font

- `line-height`

- `margin`

- `padding`

- `text-decoration`

- `text-shadow`

- `text-transform`

- `vertical-align`

You may use both `:first-letter` and `:first-line` pseudo-elements. Because `:first-letter` is within `:first-line`, it will inherit the values of `:first-line`. If any of the same properties are set in `:first-letter`, then their values will override the inherited value.

Stylesheet Order

Now that we have a lot of rules, we should say something about ordering them on the page. Syntactically, there isn't much to worry about. A CSS file requires no headers or trailers; you just write down your rules.

Precedence does matter. A style later in the stylesheet will override an earlier style when they select the same element. Beyond this, the order of your rules is only a question of clarity. It's good form to break your rules into sections so that you can find things quickly. Precisely what method you use is up to you, but we'll make a few suggestions.

One method is to begin with elements, listing them either by generality or alphabetically. Either way, `<body>` will be first, which is helpful to anyone trying to visualize what you're doing by reading your CSS. Follow this with classes and selectors as individual groups, also each ordered alphabetically. This allows basic and detailed layout styles to be quickly read together, and it saves you reading a whole sheet through to assure there isn't a related rule hiding somewhere in a haphazard order. Also, for highly styled sites it can be helpful to have a typography section that is separate from layout. Comments may be inserted by using the following comment syntax:

```
/*This is the form for your comments within a stylesheet. The browser will not
read anything within these boundaries.*/
```

Summary

With this chapter you can begin writing your own CSS. You can now read a rule, create a rule to target precisely what you wish to be styled in your XHTML, and express a style for that target. You now know enough to get into trouble. Chapters 7 and 8 go into further detail on styling typography and layout, but before that we need to discuss the many ways that CSS may be attached to your XHTML in Chapter 6.

Attaching CSS to Your Markup

YOU'VE NOW BEEN introduced to most of the basics of developing web pages with CSS, including intelligent markup practices, CSS rule structure, and CSS fundamentals such as the box model. You've also learned about the separation of structure and presentation, which is the conceptual underpinning that explains both the how and the why of CSS as a presentation language for well-structured XHTML markup. In this chapter, we'll explore how CSS and XHTML can be kept separate but brought together for the display of web pages.

In the XHTML and CSS samples in the previous chapters, you saw various techniques for attaching CSS to HTML markup. Indeed, in Chapter 2 you were introduced to these three methods: inline, embedded, and external. In this chapter we'll show you the proper syntax for each, with examples, and discuss when and why you should or shouldn't use it.

Inline Styles

Using inline styles is the simplest method of attaching styles to HTML elements. You may already be familiar with the basic mechanism of inline styles, which use the style attribute of an HTML element, like so:

```
<h1 style="color: red">Your one-stop hurdy gurdy site</h1>
```

Note that the value of the style attribute is a CSS style declaration: "color: red". Except for this syntax, using the style attribute is just like using other HTML attributes. Consider the following snippet of HTML, which sets the page's background color to white:

```
<body bgcolor="#ffffff">The document contents go here.</body>
```

Using inline styles, you would accomplish the same thing like this:

```
<body style="background-color: #ffffff">The document contents go here.</body>
```

The style attribute is quite a bit more powerful than this, though, because it allows you to define as many style properties as you like, all of which will be applied to the element and its children according to the rules of the inheritance, as discussed in Chapter 4. Consider the following:

```
<h1 style="color: red; background: white; font-family: sans-serif;
font-size: 1.5em; margin: 0 0 .5em 0; padding: 0; ">Your one-stop hurdy gurdy
site</h1>
```

Clearly, the `style` attribute gives a lot of control over presentation to the web professional, especially because it can be applied to nearly all HTML page elements. The `style` attribute is also an easy concept to grasp and implement for HTML authors unfamiliar with CSS, as it functions so similarly to legacy HTML elements with their attributes, such as the `<font>` element:

```
<font face="sans-serif" color="red">A red sans-serif sentence!</font>
```

The `style` attribute is a definite improvement over such markup abuses, but it still has its problems. Chiefly, using inline styles with the `style` attribute severely limits the reusability of your CSS styles. In fact, it renders your styles completely unreusable, even within the same document. Not only is this an inconvenience to you as you craft your pages, because you have to specify the same rule over and over again for elements that you want styled in the same way, but also it results in markup bloat as it inflates the file size of your web pages, slows down page downloads, and increases page rendering time.

In addition, the `style` attribute has been deprecated in the XHTML Recommendation, meaning that although its use is still valid, it's marked for elimination in a future version of XHTML. The reasons for this are complicated and have been hotly debated, but it comes down to the question of whether the `style` attribute is appropriate within XHTML markup, which is supposed to be a purely structural markup language. You may want to consider phasing out the use of the `style` attribute in your markup to conform to the W3C vision of CSS and markup.

One significant benefit of using inline styles is that the styles defined with the `style` attribute are easily accessible in scripts, because they appear as properties of the `style` object property of the object that represents the HTML element to which the styles apply. For instance, consider the following example:

```
<a style="color: #cc0000;" href="#"
onclick="if (this.style) {alert(this.style.color)}; return false;">link</a>
```

In modern browsers with adequate support for the DOM, the link as previously defined will result in a pop-up alert box announcing the link's color as #cc0000. When styles are applied to an element in any way other than inline via the `style` attribute, the `style` properties are much more difficult to access in scripts. There are ways to work around these difficulties, although methods differ from browser to browser, and none provides the ease of accessing style properties directly via the `style` object as is made possible with the use of inline styles.

As we explore the benefits of embedded and external stylesheets, the downsides of inline styles will become more apparent.

Embedded Stylesheets

Embedded stylesheets provide all the presentation power that inline styles provide, but they also allow you to take advantage of many of the more significant benefits of CSS. Before we get to that, however, let's take a look at the mechanism you'll use to add embedded stylesheets to your HTML documents, namely the <style> element. This element allows authors to put stylesheet rules in the head of the document—any number of <style> elements may appear in the <head> section of an HTML document. Embedded stylesheets look like this:

```
<head>
  <title>Embedded Stylesheet Example</title>
  <style type="text/css">
    body {
      background-color: yellow;
      color: red;
      }
    a {
      color: brown;
      }
  </style>
</head>
```

As you can see, your CSS style rules are simply placed within the start and end <style> tags. Any number of style rules can appear in one <style> element.

The <style> element has five possible attributes, one of which is required and four of which are optional: type (required), media, title, lang, and dir. The attributes lang and dir are global HTML attributes of little relevance to the <style> element. The dir attribute, with possible values LTR (left to right) and RTL (right to left), is used to override the document's base text directionality, and the lang attribute is used to override the default document's base language.

The type attribute, which takes a Multipurpose Internet Mail Extension (MIME) type as its value, is required. In nearly all cases, you'll use the value "text/css". As defined by the W3C, the type attribute has no default value, though in practice you'll find if you don't provide a value for type, browsers will assume the value "text/css". This is because the type attribute is a forward-looking mechanism for specifying any number of style language types. Because there are currently no other style languages supported by the major browsers, "text/css" is the effective default. Because of this, you may be tempted to leave out the type attribute, but don't. Not only will your documents not validate if your `<style>` elements lack the `type` attribute, but also they may not function properly in the future as new browser releases add support for alternate style languages.

The `media` attribute is optional and used to specify the destination medium for the styles contained within the `<style>` element to which the attribute applies. It may be a single media descriptor or a comma-separated list of descriptors. Table 6-1 describes the possible values for the `media` attribute.

Table 6-1. Possible Values for the media Attribute

Value	Description
screen	Intended for nonpaged computer screens
tty	Intended for media using a fixed-pitch character grid, such as teletypes, terminals, or portable devices with limited display capabilities
tv	Intended for television-type devices (low resolution, color, limited scrollability)
projection	Intended for projectors
handheld	Intended for handheld devices (small screen, monochrome, bitmapped graphics, limited bandwidth)
print	Intended for paged, opaque material, and for documents viewed onscreen in Print Preview mode
braille	Intended for Braille tactile feedback devices
embossed	Intended for paged Braille printers
aural	Intended for speech synthesizers
all	Intended for all devices

Because this book deals with using CSS to influence presentation of documents on the Web, nearly all examples you see will leave the `media` attribute unspecified, which according to the W3C's recommendation should be the same as specifying "screen" but which you'll find in practice find to be implemented in browsers as the same as specifying "all." (Even the W3C seems inconsistent on this matter. Its own examples imply that "all" should be the default value, and the default value for the `media` attribute of the CSS `@import` directive is specified as "all.") As support for CSS broadens, developing stylesheets for various types of devices will become commonplace. In that scenario, the `media` attribute is an invaluable tool, as it provides each device with the directions on which stylesheets to disregard and which to apply.

One use of the media attribute in fairly common use today is to provide a stylesheet for printing. For instance, you might want to keep site navigation links from appearing when the page is printed, or you may want to make sure your page prints out with simple black text on white background, even though onscreen you specify more interesting colors:

```
<head>
  <title>Embedded Stylesheet Example</title>
  <style media="all" type="text/css">
    body {
      background-color: yellow;
      color: red;
      }
    a {
      color: brown;
      }
  </style>

  <style type="text/css" media="print">
    body {
      background-color: white;
      color: black;
      }
    #nav {
      display: none;
      }
  </style>
</head>
```

The title attribute of the <style> element is optional and has no default value. It's used to provide metainformation about the element to which it applies. For elements such as images or links, this metainformation may be presented to the user by the browser in the form of pop-up tool tips or other such interfaces. For embedded stylesheets, there's currently little to be gained by specifying a value for the title attribute, although in a document with multiple embedded stylesheets you might find it useful to give each stylesheet a meaningful title for easier comprehension.

Pros and Cons of Embedded Stylesheets

The main advantage of embedded stylesheets over inline styles is reusability. Whereas inline styles only apply to a single element (and its children via inheritance), embedded style rules can be written to apply to multiple elements.

Remember our previous example using inline styles to define the presentational aspects of a header:

```
<h1 style="color: red; background: white; font-family: sans-serif;
font-size: 1.5em; margin: 0 0 .5em 0; padding: 0; ">Your one-stop hurdy gurdy
site</h1>
```

If multiple `<h1>` elements appeared in the document, each would need to have an identical `style` attribute value to ensure consistency of presentation unless, of course, the style definitions were moved into an embedded stylesheet, as follows:

```
<head>
  <title>Hurdy Gurdy Online</title>
  <style type="text/css">
    h1 {
       color: red;
       background: white;
       font-family: sans-serif;
       font-size: 1.5em;
       margin: 0 0 .5em 0;
       padding: 0;
       }
  </style>
</head>
```

As you learned in Chapter 5, the preceding rule uses a type selector to apply the style definitions to all `<h1>` elements in the document.

You can maximize reuse and efficiency by allowing style properties that you want to share between various elements to be inherited from a parent element. For instance, if the entire document is intended to be in `sans-serif` typeface, the following rule for the `<body>` element saves you from having to specify the `font-family` property in other rules:

```
<head>
  <title>Hurdy Gurdy Online</title>
  <style type="text/css">
    body {
      font-family: sans-serif;
      }

    h1 {
      color: red;
      background: white;
      font-size: 1.5em;
```

```
      margin: 0 0 .5em 0;
      padding: 0;
      }
   </style>
</head>
```

When you want style properties to be shared across sibling elements that don't inherit from one another, grouping selectors can increase efficiency quite a bit:

```
<head>
   <title>Hurdy Gurdy Online</title>
   <style type=""text/css">
     body {
        font-family: sans-serif;
        }

     h1, h2, h3, h4, h5, h6 {
        color: red;
        background: white;
        margin: 0 0 .5em 0;
        padding: 0;
        }

     h1 {
        font-size: 1.5em;
        }
     h2 {
        font-size: 1.4em;
        }
   </style>
</head>
```

In addition to the ease of reuse and general efficiency, embedded stylesheets offer another minor benefit. Because with embedded styles all your rules are contained within the HTML document to which they apply, editing and maintenance is eased slightly, as it's easier to cross-reference styles against the markup to which they apply.

On the other hand, if the same rules exist in multiple embedded stylesheets in multiple documents across a website, you must edit each document to make sitewide changes.

One problem with the use of embedded stylesheets in XHTML documents is that because the style rules appear within the document itself, they're bound by the formatting rules of XHTML. That means you can't use a & or < character in a rule without escaping it, and escaping those characters will prevent the rule from working on non-XML HTML parsers, which means most browsers in use today. Luckily these characters are fairly rare in CSS, and you may use embedded stylesheets that don't contain them without a problem. If your rules must contain & or <, it's recommended that you place the rules in an external stylesheet, which we cover in the next section.

Another problem with embedded stylesheets and XHTML is that the old trick of nesting rules within HTML comment tags creates invalid XHTML markup. You may have seen this trick in use before—it looks something like this:

```
<style type="text/css">
  <!--
  a {color: red}
  -->
</style>
```

The HTML comment tags are intended to hide the contents of the `style` attribute from older browsers that don't support CSS or the `<style>` element, browsers that would display the style rules as page content were they not hidden within the HTML comments. Because this isn't valid XHTML, however, it's recommended that you use external stylesheets if legacy browsers are a concern.

One final and significant downside to embedded stylesheets is that because they're contained within the document itself, they add to the file size of the page and therefore slow the download and rendering of the document. As you'll learn in the next section, external stylesheets solve this and other problems, and afford you the fullest power of CSS.

External Stylesheets

External stylesheets offer all the ease of reuse and efficiency of embedded stylesheets, and then some. Not only do external stylesheets allow reuse of rules within a specific document, but also they allow the stylesheet itself to be shared across multiple documents. Using external stylesheets allows you to maintain a single stylesheet for an entire website.

In addition, external stylesheets are downloaded once by the browser and then cached so that subsequent pages using the same stylesheet don't require the download of the stylesheet. This can result in significant bandwidth savings, as the browser needs to download the stylesheet only once, and then it can retrieve just the markup for other pages on the site.

There are two primary methods for attaching stylesheets to XHTML documents: the `<link>` element and the `@import` directive. Each has its appropriate uses.

External Stylesheets Using the <link> Element

The principal and most widely supported method for attaching external style-sheets to an HTML document is the <link> element, which is used like this:

```
<link rel="stylesheet" href="stylesheet.css" type="text/css" />
```

The <link> element, which must appear in the <head> section of an HTML document, is used for quite a few things other than just stylesheets, such as linking related web pages together. However, many of its other uses aren't currently implemented in the major browsers, and because those uses aren't directly related to our conversation, we won't spend much time on them. In short, the <link> element is used to express a relationship between documents, including an HTML document and a stylesheet.

When you use the <link> element to attach an external stylesheet to an HTML document, there are three required attributes: href, rel, and type. In addition to these attributes, the title attribute plays a special role in defining persistent and preferred stylesheets, which we discuss in detail at the end of this chapter, and the media attribute specifies the destination medium for the styles contained within the linked stylesheet. See the earlier "Embedded Stylesheets" section for coverage of the media attribute, including acceptable values. Its use is identical for both the <style> and the <link> elements.

The href attribute value must be a Uniform Resource Identifier (URI), which indicates the location of the stylesheet. In the preceding example, the <link> element with an href value of "stylesheet.css" will attach the external stylesheet entitled stylesheet.css that resides in the same directory as the containing document. In most cases you'll want to use a relative URI for an external stylesheet that is to be shared across multiple documents in a site. For instance, if you store a stylesheet in a directory named "inc" found at the root of your site's files structure, the following href attribute value can be used in any document on your site and will always reference the stylesheet correctly, no matter where the containing XHTML document appears in the directory tree:

```
<link rel="stylesheet" href="/inc/stylesheet.css" type="text/css" />
```

The rel attribute of the <link> element plays an important role, as it informs the browser or Internet device what relationship the document indicated by the href attribute has to the document containing the <link> element. There are two acceptable (case-insensitive) values: "stylesheet" and "alternate stylesheet". We discuss alternate stylesheets with persistent and preferred stylesheets at the end of the chapter, so for now we'll just look at linked documents using the value "stylesheet".

The `type` attribute is the same as the `type` attribute for the `<style>` element (discussed previously in this chapter), and it's used to indicate the MIME type of the stylesheet. As in the case of the `<style>` element, in this book there will appear only one value: `"text/css"`. In the future, if and when multiple style languages are supported for styling HTML documents, the `type` attribute will indicate which language is in use.

It's worth noting that external stylesheets shouldn't contain any HTML. It's a common error of web authors unfamiliar with CSS to wrap style rules with `<style>` tags even in an external file, which is incorrect and may generate errors and/or keep the stylesheet from functioning properly.

The recommended file extension for external stylesheets is `.css`, although they can end with any extension of your choosing, provided that the web server hosting the documents is configured to serve documents that have that extension with the `"text/css"` MIME type header.

External Stylesheets Using the @import Directive

In addition to the `<link>` element, external stylesheets can be included in a document by way of the `@import` directive. Unlike `<link>`, which is an HTML element, `@import` is actually a part of CSS. This means that it must be used within an existing stylesheet, be it an embedded stylesheet, an external stylesheet linked with the `<link>` element, or another external stylesheet included with the `@import` directive.

You can use multiple `@import` rules within a stylesheet, but they must all appear at the top of the stylesheet before any other rules are specified. `@import` rules that appear after other rules in the stylesheet should be ignored, although some browsers still incorrectly honor them. The following is an example of a stylesheet imported into an embedded stylesheet:

```
<head>
  <title>Hurdy Gurdy Online</title>
  <style type="text/css">
    @import url(stylesheet.css);
    body {
      font-family: sans-serif;
      }
  </style>
</head>
```

Any rules that appear after the `@import` rule will take precedence in the cascade over the rules from within the imported stylesheet. For instance, in the preceding example, if the imported stylesheet `stylesheet.css` contained a rule like so:

```
body {
  font-family: serif;
  }
```

the rule that follows the import rule would take precedence and body text would take a sans serif typeface.

In addition to the url argument, which informs the browser of the location of the stylesheet to be imported (and which must be a valid URI, just as the href attribute of the HTML <link> element must be), an optional media argument may be passed to the @import directive. As you might have guessed, the media argument, which may be a single value or a comma-separated list, has the same effect as the media attribute of the <link> and <style> elements: It specifies the destination medium for the styles contained within the stylesheet. The default value (both as specified by the W3C and as implemented by browser makers) is "all". See the earlier coverage of the media attribute for the <style> element, including acceptable values. Excluding syntax, the media argument of the @import rule functions identically. The following are examples of passing media arguments to the @import rule:

```
<style type="text/css" media="all">
  @import url("printstylesheet.css") print;
  a {
    color: red;
    }
</style>
```

The following applies the file stylesheet.css to screen renderings of the document and applies printstylesheet.css to print renderings:

```
<style type="text/css" media="all">
  @import url("stylesheet.css") screen;
  @import url("printstylesheet.css") print;
</style>
```

The following applies the file stylesheet.css to both print and screen renderings of the document:

```
<style type="text/css" media="all">
  @import url("stylesheet.css") print, screen;
</style>
```

Notice in the previous examples that the media attribute of the <style> element has the value "all". In cases in which stylesheets are imported with specified media types, the containing stylesheet, whether it's a <style> element using @import or a `<link>` element, should have a `media` attribute value of `"all"` to ensure that the imported stylesheets reach their intended media-device destinations.

The `@import` directive is a powerful tool. It allows you to create complex webs of stylesheets as needed for multiple devices and for efficient sharing of basic style rules across many pages or even multiple sites. Sadly, it isn't supported by all browsers that support CSS. However, this has an added benefit: As we detail in Chapter 10, by using `@import` to import external stylesheets you can hide more complex style rules from legacy browsers such as Netscape Navigator 4, which has trouble with a wide range of CSS properties. By using `@import`, style rules that may not be properly handled by Netscape Navigator 4 can be effectively hidden from that browser, which simply ignores the `@import` directive.

Alternate, Persistent, and Preferred Stylesheets

Alternate stylesheets are a useful mechanism for providing multiple stylesheets for a single document. Unfortunately, support for alternate stylesheets isn't broad, although the Mozilla browser and Netscape 6+ have implemented them quite well. Because alternate stylesheets are so useful, and because future versions of other major browsers should provide better support for them, it's useful to detail how they function.

First, what syntax designates these types of stylesheets? They are all external stylesheets that are imported using the `<link>` element, with the considerations outlined in Table 6-2.

Table 6-2. Stylesheet Types and Their Attributes

Stylesheet Type	`<link>` Element's rel Attribute Value	`<link>` Element's title Attribute
Alternate	`"alternate stylesheet"`	Must be included
Persistent	`"stylesheet"`	Must not be included
Preferred	`"stylesheet"`	Must be included

In a browser or other Internet device that supports alternate stylesheets, the user is offered a choice of which of the preferred and alternate stylesheets available should be used to render the page. How this choice is made is left to the browser manufacturer, but ideally it would be a choice available in the software's menus.

Alternate stylesheets must have a `title` attribute specified in the `<link>` element. That title will be used by the browser when offering a choice between stylesheets. An alternate stylesheet isn't used to style the page unless the user chooses it.

The *preferred stylesheet* is used to style the markup when the page is first loaded by the browser. There should be only one preferred stylesheet listed in any one document. If more than one exists, the browser will use the first preferred stylesheet, and it may or may not treat any others as alternate stylesheets.

Persistent stylesheets are always used in conjunction with whichever preferred stylesheet and alternate stylesheet is currently used to style the page. Remember, persistent stylesheets can't have a title value set using the title attribute of the <link> element. It's a common error to give a title to a stylesheet that's intended to be persistent, but doing so causes the browser to interpret it as a preferred stylesheet. Because there can be only one preferred stylesheet to a document, the browser may then ignore other stylesheets with the title attribute. As a general rule, if you don't intend to offer your site visitors alternate stylesheets, do *not* use the title attribute in stylesheet <link> elements.

In the following example, the file basic.css is a persistent stylesheet and would contain style definitions that are to be used all the time. The file default.css is the preferred stylesheet, because the value of the rel attribute is "stylesheet", just like that for basic.css, but it has the title attribute set to "default". The files medium.css and large.css are alternate stylesheets, as their rel attribute indicates. Their titles ("medium type" and "large type") serve as clues to what alternate stylesheets would be quite useful for, were they supported broadly: providing alternate stylesheets to aid people with visual disabilities.

```
<head>
  <title>Hurdy Gurdy Online</title>
  <link rel="stylesheet" href="basic.css" type="text/css" />
  <link rel="stylesheet" href="default.css" type="text/css" title="default" />
  <link rel="alternate stylesheet" href="medium.css" type="text/css"
    title="medium type" />
  <link rel="alternate stylesheet" href="large.css" type="text/css"
    title="large type" />
</head>
```

In the preceding example, the file basic.css might contain rules that specify things such as color and layout. The file default.css might contain rules that set the page's font size such as is suitable for the average reader, whereas the files medium.css and large.css might contain much larger font size rules, allowing people to adjust the text size of the page to suit their needs.

Summary

CSS provides many different mechanisms for attaching style rules to HTML markup, from the very specific and easy-to-use inline style; to reusable embedded stylesheets; to external stylesheets, which provide the maximum benefits to both the author and the user. Each mechanism has its place, although it's certainly ideal to use external stylesheets whenever possible, as they provide the most complete separation of structure and presentation available to web professionals.

Now that you've learned all the basics—and some of the not-so-basics—of CSS, you're ready to move on to the nitty-gritty of CSS design. In the next chapter you'll discover how stylesheets offer an incredible level of control over the typography of your HTML documents.

CHAPTER 7

Typography

TYPOGRAPHY IS ABOUT the design of text, which covers a very wide range of things: books, posters, and websites are all textual. Typography goes beyond the letters on screen or paper: It's also concerned with the space around the text, the way it sits on a page or screen, and the size and proportions of those mediums. In this chapter we're sticking closely to the core typographic concerns for the Web. You'll learn how to use type intelligently and to set text so that it works for you.

The typographer's job is to make things clear and to make things work—to make sure that the text is legible and that the underlying structures in the author's manuscript (such as headings, chapters, and sections) are accurately reflected in the final work.

Typography on the Web

Typography on the Web is different from typography in print in many ways, and although the principles hold across the media, the ways in which those principles are applied differ. Things that are "free" in print, such as resolution and a stable page size, are all but impossible on the Web, and things that are "free" on the Web, such as color, interaction, and rich media, are expensive or impossible in print. If you play to the strengths of the Web, then there's no reason why web typography can't be as effective as print typography.

You've already seen how limited user and author control of presentation was before CSS. The typographic possibilities offered by CSS are, by comparison to <font>, vast. In fact, the more advanced CSS selectors begin to take CSS to a level where things impossible in print page layout applications are possible on the Web. CSS covers all the basic typographic options well: The author has control over type, size, color, interlinear space, and space above and below blocks of text. This control can be exerted over block-level elements, such as <p>, as well as inline elements, such as <em> and <strong>. The property inheritance offered by CSS means that you can cascade typographic decisions through a document, only overriding when you need to. In short, it's powerful stuff.

Type Basics

First, some definitions of terms. A *typeface* is a set of characters drawn from the same design. Times and Arial are typefaces. Strictly speaking, Times Regular and Times Bold are different typefaces, but they're part of the same typeface family. The term *font* is often used interchangeably with typeface, but it shouldn't really be. A font is a software implementation of a typeface; it's a collection of every character available in that typeface. Although everyone has something called Times installed on their computer, the implementations differ. If you're on a PC, you've got a different piece of code from the Times on a Mac. Beyond platform, you have format (Postscript Type 1, TrueType, OpenType, and the UNIX bitmap formats), version (1.0 and so on), and even name (Monotype.com and Andale Mono are the same typeface). Even though the font files are different, the type-face—the design—is the same.

In metal typesetting (the way most printing happened until the 1960s), a character was called a *printing type* and was a piece of metal with a reversed image of the character in relief on its face. The character was cast on the body of the type, and the size of the type referred to the size of metal body of the type, not the size of the character. This way of thinking about type has persisted into digital type and, although a type's body has no real equivalent on screen, digital type is still sized according to this notional body. font-size: 12px doesn't refer to the distance between the top of the ascenders and the bottom of the descenders (see Figure 7-1); it refers to the size of this invisible, imaginary body.

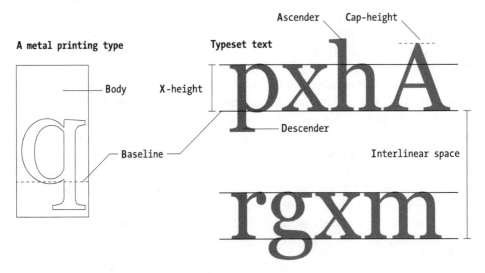

Figure 7-1. Common typographic terms

Type has a *baseline*, which is an imaginary line that the bottoms of charac-ters sit on. With metal type the baseline was at a predetermined standard height, which meant that different typefaces cast at the same body size would line up with one another neatly. The same applies in digital type; the baseline is what allows text of different sizes and in different typefaces to align. Although the baseline is an imaginary line, the same way that the body of digital type is imaginary, it has a concrete result: You can see where the baseline is, unlike the body. The *cap height* of the type is the imaginary line on which the tops of capital letters sit.

The distance between the baseline and the top of the lowercase letters is called the *x-height*. X-height is also a convenient way to refer to the imaginary line that cuts across the top of a line of text, in the same way that the baseline runs below it. The x-height is where visual alignment with the top of lines of text happens. The space between lines is called *interlinear space*. The best way to measure it is from baseline to baseline.

Interlinear space is often called *leading,* a name that originally referred to the process of increasing the space between lines of metal type, by putting thin strips of lead in between the lines. With digital typography you aren't limited to just adding space, and there aren't any physical type bodies anymore to put the lead between. Interlinear space is a much clearer term—in fact, it was the industry term before desktop publishing (DTP) came along and, for some reason, resurrected the old term.

Typographers and printers have traditionally referred to numbers in two ways: figures and numerals. Figures are usually used to refer to Arabic numbers (1, 2, 3, and so on) and numerals to Roman numbers (I, II, III, and so on). There are two kinds of figures: ranging and nonranging. *Ranging figures* are all the same height—that of a capital letter. *Nonranging figures* are different heights. Ranging figures are also called *lining figures,* and nonranging figures are also called *nonlining* and *old-style figures*. In Figure 7-2, ranging figures are the lower line.

1234567890

1234567890

Figure 7-2. Ranging and nonranging figures

When body text is referred to in this chapter, what's meant is the main text—the text that is read. Elements of typography concerned with the main text form a subsection of typography called *text typography*. Elements concerned with large-scale type manipulation, type-as-image, such as advertising typography, form a subsection known as *display typography*. CSS is good for text typography and not so good for display typography, although you can apply everything you'll learn in this chapter to display typography.

When it comes to dealing with blocks of text (paragraphs and pages), typographers often refer to the "color" of the block. They aren't referring to the actual color of ink used to print the text; rather, they're referring to the visual effect of the whole block, where the text type and the white space around it become a solid object. In Figure 7-3, the block on the left has a much more even color than the block on the right. The spaces between the words of the block on the right vary, and the result is ugly gaps between the words and "rivers of white" where gaps line up across lines. The ideal is evenly colored blocks. The other main factor affecting the evenness of a block is the interlinear space.

Lorem ipsum dolor sit amet, consectetuer adipiscing elit, sed diam nonummy nibh euismod tincidunt ut laoreet dolore magna aliquam erat volutpat. Ut wisi enim ad minim veniam, quis nostrud exercitation

Lorem ipsum dolor sit amet, consectetuer adipiscing elit, sed diam nonummy nibh euismod tincidunt ut laoreet dolore magna aliquam erat volutpat. Ut wisi enim ad minim veniam, quis nostrud exercitation

Figure 7-3. The effect of word space on the color of a text block

Figure 7-4 shows too-dark and too-light blocks caused by too little and too much interlinear space.

Lorem ipsum dolor sit amet, consectetuer adipiscing elit, sed diam nonummy nibh euismod tincidunt ut laoreet dolore magna aliquam erat volutpat. Ut wisi enim ad minim veniam, quis nostrud exercitation ulliam corper suscipit lobortis nisl ut aliquip ex ea commodo consequat. Duis autem

Lorem ipsum dolor sit amet, consectetuer adipiscing elit, sed diam nonummy nibh euismod tincidunt ut laoreet dolore magna aliquam erat volutpat. Ut wisi enim ad minim veniam, quis nostrud exercitation

Figure 7-4. The effect of interlinear space on the color of a text block

Specifying Type

CSS provides several ways to specify how your type looks. We'll cover how they work in this section. We're also going to describe CSS shorthand properties for type, which allow us to replace several declarations with one. (Recall the shorthand properties for margins and borders that you saw in Chapter 5.)

In print, when you talk about type you're usually talking about a particular typeface and its size, weight, and what the interlinear space should be. CSS is no different. The CSS properties `font-family`, `font-size`, `font-weight`, and `line-height` are responsible for these aspects of the type. The following CSS rule says that all paragraphs should be set in bold 12px Arial, with 15px interlinear space.

```
p {
  font-family: Arial;
  font-size: 12px;
  font-weight: bold;
  line-height: 15px;
}
```

That's pretty easy to understand, but we'll expand on each of these properties here. There are a few other simple properties that control how type looks: font-style controls whether your type is italicized or not, and text-decoration controls details such as underlining. A quick modification to the last rule gives us bold, italic, underlined 12px Arial, with 15px interlinear space:

```
p {
  font-family: Arial;
  font-size: 12px;
  font-weight: bold;
  line-height: 15px;
  font-style: italic;
  text-decoration: underline;
}
```

In the sections that follow, we'll walk through the properties.

font-family

The font-family property specifies which typeface the browser should use. In its simplest form, all that it needs is a single name. Because typefaces live in font files on the client and not everyone has the same typefaces, sometimes you may specify a typeface that not everyone using your site has. font-family provides a mechanism for dealing with this: It accepts a comma-separated list of names, and it will try each in turn until it succeeds in matching an installed font. CSS also provides a list of generic typeface families that you can use. If one of these generic families is the last item in a list, then, if all else has failed, you have some degree of assurance that you'll get a serifed typeface and not a sans-serif. It's a good idea to get into the habit of finishing font-family declarations with a generic family.

Some of you may be wondering about *serif* and *sans-serif*. Simply put, serifs are the sharp ends of strokes on typefaces, such as Times. Sans-serif typefaces don't have any serifs. The illustrations in Table 7-1 should make the distinctions clear.

Table 7-1. The Generic font-family *Values*

Sample	Name	Description
Serif	serif	Serifed typefaces, such as Times or New Century Schoolbook.
Sans-serif	sans-serif	Typefaces without serifs, such as Arial or Helvetica.
Cursive	cursive	Typefaces that look like calligraphic writing, such as Zapf Chancery or Caflisch Script.
Fantasy	fantasy	Typefaces that don't fit into any other category. IE 5 for Mac (IE5/Mac) defaults fantasy to Comic Sans, and the CSS1 specification gives "Wild West" wood type (the ornate poster letters) as an example.
Monospace	monospace	Typefaces in which all the letters occupy the same amount of horizontal space, such as Courier or Andale Mono.

When you use font names that contain white space, you need to enclose them in quotes. Here's an example:

```
font-family: "New Century Schoolbook", "Times New Roman", Times, serif;
```

In all these cases, you're specifying a typeface's name, so you need to get the spelling right.

font-size

The font-size property controls the size of your type. As you saw earlier on in the chapter, type isn't sized according to the distance between the top of the ascender and the bottom of the descender; rather, it's sized according to the invisible "body" of the type.

In addition to that confusion, other factors affect how big type looks. The x-height of typefaces varies a lot, and type with a smaller x-height looks smaller than type with a larger x-height. For example, compare Times and Georgia in Figure 7-5.

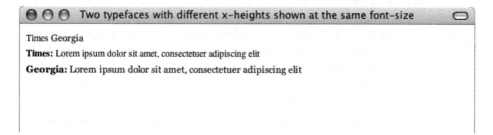

Figure 7-5. Two typefaces with different x-heights shown at the same font-size

As you can see, despite both fonts being declared as 12px, Times looks a lot smaller than Georgia because it has a smaller x-height. Another result of Times's small x-height is that its characters are narrower than Georgia's.

font-size accepts a value in one of the units that CSS understands, which we covered in Chapter 5. The physical units (pt, cm, inch, and so on) are only useful for print stylesheets. It's best to stick to CSS's relative units for screen work: px, em, and %.

> **NOTE**   *Yes, CSS considers pixels to be a relative unit. Don't worry about it—it only means that a 1200dpi laser printer isn't supposed to think that 12px text should really be rendered at 12 of the printer's pixels (or letters 1/100 of an inch high).*

In addition to accepting lengths, there's also a set of absolute size keywords for use with font-size, although they're absolute only in name—there's a lot of ambiguity about how big they should actually be. These sizes equate roughly with the <font size="n"> you may be used to. There are recommended scaling factors between the values for working out the final size, but the two CSS specifications recommend different factors (1.5 in CSS1 and 1.2 in CSS2). This, together with the unpredictability of the result, rules out their use unless your layout doesn't need any more precision than this system provides.

```
font-size: xx-small;
font-size: x-small;
font-size: small;
```

```
font-size: medium; /* roughly equivalent to <font size="3"> */
font-size: large;
font-size: x-large;
font-size: xx-large;
```

There are two `font-size`-specific keywords (very similar to the previous keyword values). `smaller` and `larger` make your type smaller or larger than their parent element's type. The browser should use the absolute size keywords we just covered to decide what the final size of the adjusted type should be. For example, making `medium` type larger will result in `large` type. If your type's parent element wasn't sized using an absolute size keyword, then the browser is supposed to "lock on" to a keyword value if the parent's size is close to one of the keywords.

The most interesting possibilities for `font-size` are offered by relative units. The usual relative length units are available, and the "Relative Units: Describing the Relationships Between Elements" section at the end of this chapter revolves around relative units. Getting to grips with `em` is a very good idea—it can quickly transform your site's CSS maintainability. The normal relative CSS units (`em` and %) work, as discussed in Chapter 5. These are usually the best units to go for, with `px` coming in third.

line-height

Interlinear space is controlled with the `line-height` property. The `line-height` property is possibly the greatest single contribution that CSS has made to web typography. Before `line-height`, we were stuck with the browser maker's standards for interlinear space, which, as far as reading large amounts of text goes, were awful. The default is for the tightly set text shown in Figure 7-6.

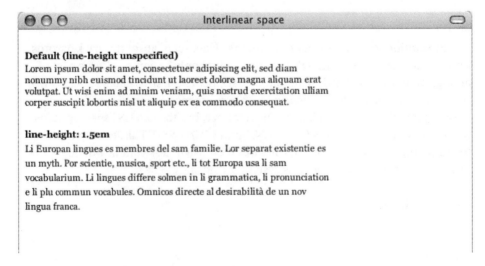

Figure 7-6. Interlinear space

If the interlinear space is set too tightly or too loosely, the reader will often "double" (i.e., reread the line he or she just finished reading). A good rule of thumb for body text is to set interlinear space to 1.5 times the type size. As the measure (the width of your text column) increases, you may well need to increase the interlinear space of text in that column. In general use, 1.5 will work very well. We go into more detail on measure later in the chapter.

You'll need to consider larger text, such as headings and pull quotes, differently. Larger text often will look best set quite tightly with a small interlinear space. You should experiment until you find a value that works and looks right for your needs.

CSS doesn't think about interlinear space as being from baseline to baseline. It considers what it calls leading and half-leading. Basically, it works out the difference between the font-size and the line-height, then it adds (or subtracts) half to the top and half to the bottom to produce the final line box, as shown in Figure 7-7.

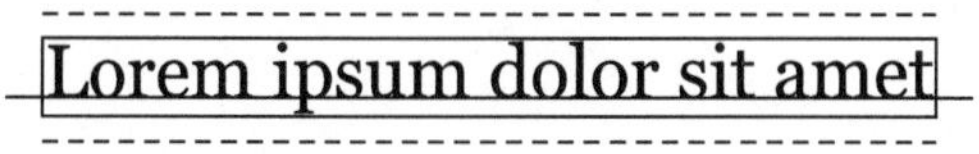

Figure 7-7. A line of type showing the extra space above and below caused by adding interlinear space

If the preceding text had a font-size of 12px and a line-height of 14px, then 1px of space would be added above and 1px would be added below. If the line-height was 15px (a better value under the circumstances), then that extra pixel has to go either above or below. Mozilla and Netscape 6+ put the extra pixel below; IE5/Mac puts it above.

You can use any of the standard CSS units to specify line-height, as well as numeric values. Numeric values are used as relative multipliers, exactly like the other CSS relative units. For example, line-height: 2; will give you 24px interlinear space if your type has a font-size of 12px. line-height specified using relative values is always based on that element's font-size.

Let's look at some examples:

```
body {
  font: 12px Georgia;
}
h1 {
  font-size: 1em;
  line-height: 1.5;
```

```
    font-weight: bold;
    margin: 1em 0 0 0;
}
p {
    margin: 0;
}
p.one {
    font-size: 1em;
    line-height: 1.5em;
}
p.two {
    font-size: 1em;
    line-height: 1em;
}
<body>
    <h1>Size: 1em, line-height: 1.5em</h1>
    <p class="one">Lorem ipsum...</p>
    <h1>Size: 1.2em, line-height: 1.5em</h1>
    <p class="two">Lorem ipsum...</p>
</body>
```

Figure 7-8 shows the results.

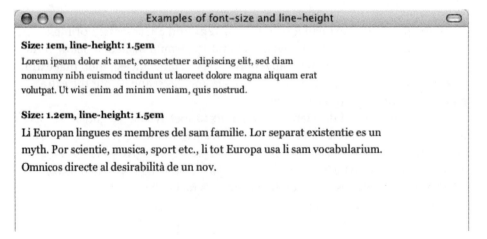

Figure 7-8. Examples of font-size *and* line-height

font-weight

You have two ways to specify font-weight in CSS, one absolute and one relative. The absolute method is easy: Specify either bold or normal weight:

```
font-weight: bold;
font-weight: normal;
```

The relative method uses the keywords `bolder` and `lighter` to make your type change weight. The only things to watch out for are making bold type bolder and normal type lighter, which don't work.

```
font-weight: bolder;
font-weight: lighter;
```

font-style

The `font-style` property controls the italicization of text.

There are actually two ways of creating a typeface that slopes like an italic. The first is to redraw the whole typeface as an italic (for type-spotters, these *true italics* tend to have single-story *a*s). Their most important aspect is that they were drawn from scratch to be italics. The other way is to simply slope the characters in an existing typeface by about 15 degrees. These are known as *oblique typefaces.* Figure 7-9 compares a line of characters in an oblique typeface to the true italic of the same typeface.

A line of assorted characters
A line of assorted characters

Figure 7-9. Oblique (top) and italic type

The declaration `font-style: italic` attempts to use the true italic variant of the current typeface specified by font family. If there isn't one, it falls back to an oblique typeface, which will be created for you if it isn't already there. A `font-style: oblique` declaration will give a real or created oblique typeface. The declaration `font-style: normal` will cancel out any italics currently in force and give you an upright typeface.

font-variant

The `font-variant` property controls whether a small-capitals variant of the current typeface should be used. Small capitals are, simply, capital letters that are the same size as lowercase letters: SMALL CAPS compared to ALL CAPS.

This property accepts two values: small-caps and normal. The first switches small caps on, and the second cancels it. Browser support isn't bad: IE 5 for Windows (IE5/Windows) renders it incorrectly (with all-capitals instead), Safari 1.1 and Netscape Navigator 4 (NN4) ignore it, but all the other big browsers get it right.

The big problem with this is that the CSS specification says that only lower-case letters should be made into small caps, and one of the main typographic uses of small caps is for abbreviations and acronyms (such as IBM or NATO). This is the nub of the problem: Using lowercase letters for abbreviations (and for acronyms that haven't been around long enough to lose their capitals) makes it difficult to identify them as being an acronym. There are HTML tags for these situations (<acronym> and <abbr>), but browser support is patchy (even among non-CSS user agents such as Lynx).

The other problem with font-variant is that it's not likely that real small caps, as opposed to scaled normal capitals, will be available reliably. Scaled normal capitals are smaller, but they don't have the correct proportions. This is usually a bigger problem in print, where the difference is very noticeable, but the usual browser-generated small caps are bigger than lowercase letters and quite hard to distinguish from normal caps unless there are some normal caps nearby to compare against.

If you want to use small caps in text, then it's likely you're aiming for typographic sophistication and subtlety. Browsers ignoring or misrendering font-variant will ruin that. Essentially, font-variant is problematic and worth avoiding.

text-decoration

The text-decoration property allows you to decorate text, for example with underlines. It accepts the following values: none, underline, overline, and line-through. You can use combinations of more than one value in a declaration to get several decorations at once. However, you shouldn't combine none with any other values, as it overrides and cancels them out.

```
text-decoration: underline;
text-decoration: overline;
text-decoration: line-through;
text-decoration: underline overline line-through;
```

Figure 7-10 shows the effects.

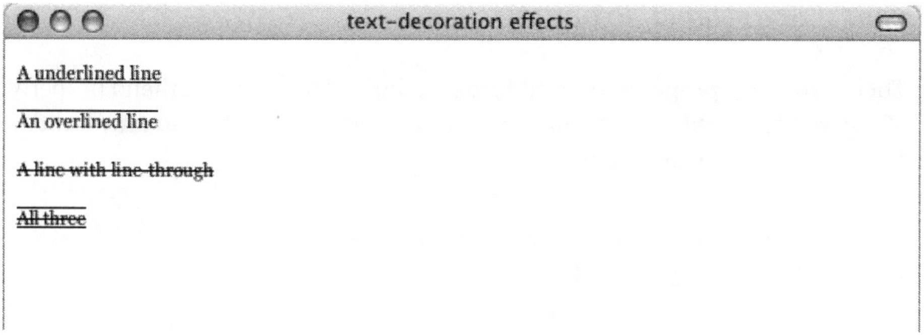

```
┌─────────────────────────────────────────────────────────────────────┐
│  ● ● ●              text-decoration effects                    ⬭      │
├─────────────────────────────────────────────────────────────────────┤
│  A underlined line                                                    │
│                                                                       │
│  An overlined line                                                    │
│                                                                       │
│  A line with line-through                                             │
│                                                                       │
│  All three                                                            │
│                                                                       │
└─────────────────────────────────────────────────────────────────────┘
```

Figure 7-10. text-decoration *effects*

Underlines (and other lines) are a typographic oddity. They were used with typewriters as a substitute for italics, and they're still used by people who mark up manuscripts by hand to mean "Italicize this." Underlines are very crude graphic devices, and there are usually much better ways to communicate the change in meaning they represent, for example by using italics and changes in color. The exception to this is with hyperlinks, where the use of underline has become the standard, so much so that underlining nonhyperlinks can be confusing to the reader.

You can affect whether links display with underlines or not using text-decoration. There's more about that in the "Formatting Links" section later in this chapter.

The other possibilities have even less typographic precedent. This isn't to say you shouldn't use them—just be careful to use them in such a way that your readers can understand what they mean. We've seen line-through used to show edits in text, so that people can see how revisions had been made. Overlines, particularly, become confusing when used with tightly set text, because they start to look like underlines of the line above.

text-transform

The text-transform property allows you to change the case of text without having to rewrite it. It accepts four values: capitalize, uppercase, lowercase, and none. capitalize forces the first letter of each word to be a capital letter, and uppercase and lowercase do exactly as their names imply: force all the letters to be either capitals or lowercase. none simply cancels any values of text-transform in force. This is simple enough that we'll forgo an illustration and just provide a sample line of code (taken from the CSS specification):

```
h1 { text-transform: uppercase; }
```

The property is well supported—only NN4 ignores it.

font: Shorthand Property

There's one final property we need to look at here. The font: shorthand property allows you to combine all the font- properties and line-height into one declaration. It's also a fairly intuitive way to do it:

```
font: bold italic 12px/15px Verdana, sans-serif;
font: 1em/1.5em Georgia, serif;
```

If you've ever come across a typographic layout with type details, you'll probably get the basic gist of the previous declarations.

The format of the font: declaration is pretty simple. It first takes values for each of font-style, font-weight, and font-variant. If one of these values isn't explicitly mentioned, then it's set to normal. This is the best way to set values to normal. The order of these first values doesn't matter, because each value is a different string. After these, a value for font-size is given. If you want to declare an explicit line-height value, then follow the font-size value with a slash and then the line-height value. The last set of values should be a font-family declaration.

There are a couple of catches with this, which primarily relate to browser bugs. IE5/Mac doesn't respect a font: declaration that makes a heading unbold. This was fixed in IE5.1/Mac. Netscape 6/7 and Mozilla don't like you to declare font-style or font-weight as normal, even though it's perfectly legal CSS. Odd things happen if you do.

Despite this, the font: property can save lines and lines of code and make your font-related declarations easier to understand. Figure 7-11 shows an example of the use of the font: shorthand property.

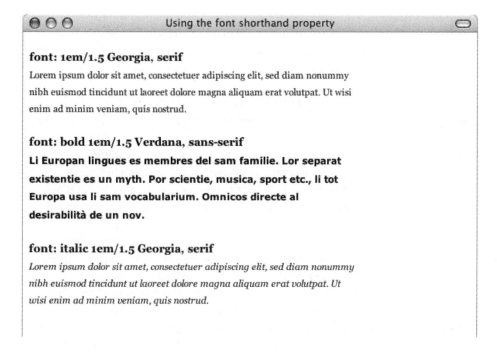

Figure 7-11. Using the font: *shorthand property*

Color and Type

Color in typography needs to be approached with some care. It's very easy to make text hard to read by making it a color with little contrast from the background. Fortunately, the CSS behind it is very simple. The vast majority of this section is concerned with choosing and using colors with type.

To recap from Chapter 5, the CSS property for the color of type is the color property, as you would expect. You set the background of either a block (for a block-level element) or the relevant part of a line (for an inline element) with the background-color property.

The primary use of color in text typography has traditionally been for differentiating elements, often headings. Differentiating with color is mainly an exercise in creating contrast between the thing that is being differentiated and its surroundings. This means the background as well as the surrounding text. Red and black have traditionally been paired in print, because both colors are strong and contrast with white and each other.

In continuous text, contrast is still the critical factor, but there are other concerns too. The choice of background is important. Most novels aren't printed on high-white paper; rather, they're printed on off-white paper. This is because the contrast between the high-white paper and black ink is too harsh and becomes fatiguing. Essentially, there can be too much contrast. There are two ways to deal with this onscreen. One is to use a slightly colored background, and the other is to use nonblack type. Setting your type in a very dark gray actually makes a significant difference to the harshness of black-on-white type (for example, rgb(30,30,30) or #333333), even though it's hard to pin down exactly what it is that's different.

The main things to remember with color and text type are that there needs to be sufficient contrast between the text and the background, and that text darker than its background is likely to be easier to read, especially for long periods of time. You need to carefully think through how you differentiate things. There are other kinds of contrast besides color—contrasts in size and weight—so you may well find that some text needs less obvious color changes to make it stand out than others, or that using color means that size and/or weight changes can be reduced without reducing how much the type stands out.

Another excellent use of color changes is to suggest relationships between elements. For example, with a visited link, you need the change in state from unvisited to visited to be clear to the user, but you'll also want to suggest that both are part of the same kind of element: the link. Another example is when a site wants to use a background color in a main text column that is related to the strong foreground color it uses for the space around its menus. In the first case, a darker shade of the unvisited link color would be appropriate, and in the second, a lighter shade of the strong color would work.

The red, green, blue (RGB) color model doesn't provide an easy way to change colors based on those kinds of criteria. RGB color really isn't intuitive, but there is a color model that is intuitive: the hue, lightness, saturation (HLS) model. HLS is also called HSB and HSV (hue, saturation, brightness and hue, saturation, value). In HLS, *hue* controls the kind of color you get (red, orange, green), *lightness* controls how bright a color is (zero lightness always equals black, full lightness always equals white), and *saturation* controls how strong a color is (the lower the value, the more washed out the result; no saturation gives grayscale). In HSB and HSV, *brightness* and *value* are synonyms, but they aren't the same as *lightness*. Brightness or value of 100% doesn't give white; it gives maximum color brightness, which is the same as 50% lightness.

Adjusting one value at a time will give a series of colors that are related to each other, even if they have different hues, or lightnesses (or saturation), depending on which value you adjusted to make your series. If you wanted to build a palette using varying shades of red for headings so that you could avoid size or weight changes between headings, this would be the way to build them.

HLS values aren't yet directly supported in CSS (although they're proposed for CSS3), so some software is needed to create and change their values into RGB values (either rgb(x,x,x) or hex). Adobe GoLive and Macromedia Dreamweaver both offer this, as do most paint or photo-editing packages.

Measure

Measure is the typographic term for the width of a column of text. The measure of a column affects the way it reads as much as the way it looks, so the fact that it's possible to resize columns of text on the fly in a web page doesn't always make it a good thing to do, in either visual or legibility terms. No matter what legibility research disagrees about (whether serif or sans-serif text is more legible, for example), the research says this with some certainty: There is such a thing as a line that's too long or too short. The optimum seems to be about 50 to 70 characters per line in print, and this translates to screen as well.

The first problem with measure is that, as you saw at the beginning of the chapter, different typefaces have characters with different widths, so a measure that produces 65 characters per line in one typeface will give a different number of characters per line in another. For example, in a measure of 33em, Georgia averages 67 characters per line, whereas Times averages 86.

There are a couple of other significant issues with CSS and measure. The first is the issue of layout composition in browser windows of varying sizes. The other is the issue of specifying a measure accurately. The first issue won't go away if you use a liquid layout. If you fix your measure, then your text column won't shrink and expand, and your layout won't be as liquid as it was. You need to make decisions about those kind of tradeoffs carefully, but you do need readable text.

The issue of accuracy is a much simpler issue in CSS. Although working out what a good measure is when your type size is fixed is easy, working it out when your type size can change (either because you use the user's defaults or because you provide user control over it) is impossible using absolute units. Relative units, however, make it much easier. The em is based on the current type size, so a width set to a certain number of ems will shrink and expand (in pixel terms) as your type does. A measure of 33em will always fit an average of 67 characters using Georgia, no matter whether the font size of the text is 12px or 24px.

Table 7-2 lists some common typefaces and the measure needed to get around 65 characters per line. Figure 7-12 shows different measures.

Table 7-2. Typefaces and the Measures Needed for About 65 Characters per Line

Typeface	Measure	Characters per Line
Arial	30em	64
Verdana	35em	64
Times	27em	66
Georgia	33em	67
Palatino	30em	65

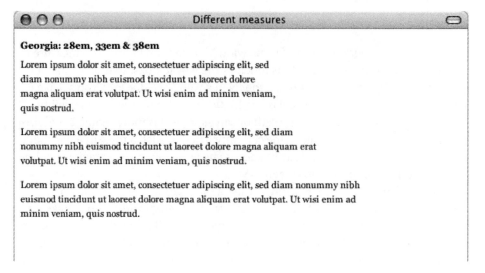

Figure 7-12. Different measures

Influencing Line Breaks

You have several ways to influence where a line will break. The first is how long the line is, which we covered in the previous section. The second is the use of <br /> elements to force a line break. The third is for the browser to respect where the author has made line breaks in the code, for example using <pre> blocks.

The CSS property white-space controls how the browser deals with white space characters (spaces, tabs, and returns) in the code. The default setting, normal, causes the browser to ignore runs of spaces and the other white space characters in text. If you have several returns in the code of what ought to be a single line, the browser won't recognize them and you'll get a single line.

The other two values for white-space, pre and nowrap, cause the browser to respect white space in your code or to never break the text of a particular element into lines, respectively:

```
body {
  font: 12px/1.5em Georgia, serif;
}
h1 {
  font: bold 12px/1.5em Georgia, serif;
  margin: 0.75em 0 0 0;
}
p {
  white-space: normal;
  margin: 0;
}
```

```
div.pre p {
  white-space: pre;
}
div.nowrap p {
  white-space: nowrap;
}
<body>
<div>
  <h1>white-space: normal</h1>
  <p>Lorem ipsum dolor sit amet, consectetuer adipiscing elit,
  sed diam nonummy nibh euismod tincidunt ut laoreet dolore
  magna aliquam erat volutpat.
  Ut wisi enim ad minim veniam, quis nostrud.</p>
</div>
<div class="pre">
  <h1>white-space: pre</h1>
  <p>Lorem ipsum dolor sit amet, consectetuer adipiscing elit,
  sed diam nonummy nibh euismod tincidunt ut laoreet dolore
  magna aliquam erat volutpat.
  Ut wisi enim ad minim veniam, quis nostrud.</p>
</div>
<div class="nowrap">
  <h1>white-space: nowrap</h1>
  <p>Lorem ipsum dolor sit amet, consectetuer adipiscing elit,
  sed diam nonummy nibh euismod tincidunt ut laoreet dolore
  magna aliquam erat volutpat.
  Ut wisi enim ad minim veniam, quis nostrud.</p>
</div>
<div class="pre">
  <h1>white-space: pre</h1>
  <p>Lorem ipsum dolor sit amet, consectetuer adipiscing elit,
sed diam nonummy nibh euismod tincidunt ut laoreet dolore
magna aliquam erat volutpat.
Ut wisi enim ad minim veniam, quis nostrud.</p>
</div>
</body>
```

Figure 7-13 shows the effect of the different values of white-space.

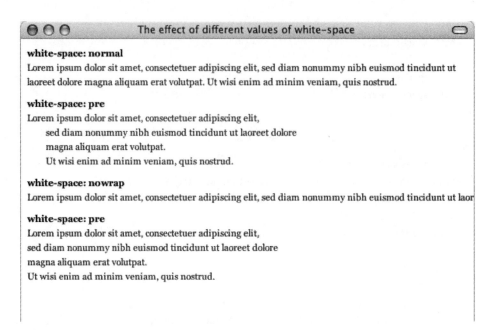

Figure 7-13. The effect of different values of white-space

The thing to remember, as illustrated in Figure 7-13, is that respecting white space in the code means all the white space—tabs and runs of spaces too—so indenting your code (for readability, say) will give you indented text in the browser.

> **CAUTION** *IE 6 supports the* white-space *property only when it's in Standards mode. If it's in Quirks mode, it will ignore* white-space. *NN4 supports* pre, *but not* nowrap.

There are some semantic problems with using white-space to alter line-breaking behavior. An element that doesn't normally have the pre value associated with it will be treated as if it had white-space: normal set in a browser that doesn't understand CSS. If you were to set, say, poetry using hard returns in the code and white-space: pre to force the browser to render them, then in a speech browser your poem would likely become experimental prose.

These issues aren't so problematic when it comes to normal paragraphs. If you were to control your line breaks in a paragraph using white-space: pre, then in a non-CSS browser all you'd lose would be the line breaks and none of the semantics. Your paragraph would still be a paragraph. However, the editing and maintenance cost associated with this is enormous. If you spend hours sorting out perfect line-endings for your text and then add or take away a word somewhere, you'll ruin at least a paragraph's worth of line endings. Every edit is followed by the cost of reworking your line endings, no matter how trivial.

white-space: nowrap, on the other hand, won't cause you any problems with editing, but a paragraph with white-space: nowrap set will render as one line, even if it contains the complete works of Tolstoy.
 elements will cause line breaks in paragraphs so afflicted, but you're back to the problem of editing requirements.

In short, unless you're doing something that would normally require the <pre> tag, then avoid white-space. If you're doing something that would normally require the <pre> tag, then use the <pre> tag. In short, then, avoid white-space.

Type Blocks

Once you move from characters and lines of text to paragraphs, you begin to deal with the issues of blocks of type. How these blocks relate to each other is critical, because it's at this level of detail that logical and visual hierarchies of information must be communicated. The way that the spaces between paragraphs in continuous text, as well as headings and paragraphs, work was one of the biggest problems web typography had before CSS, because the prescribed options available were crude at best. This section aims to teach you enough about typography at a block level to make your text work, both visually and functionally, and to teach you how to achieve this with CSS.

The main task you face when dealing with blocks of type is to make the relationships between them clear. For example, if your most important headings look less important than your third-level headings, then your users are going to be confused and have a hard time figuring out what's what. Equally, if your users can't tell where one paragraph ends and another begins, then you've also got problems. In a good design you'll be able to tell what the most important thing on a page is and where paragraphs begin and end, and you'll be able to differentiate between paragraphs of different types (for example, body text and marginal notes). You can use space, indentation, color, and many other properties to achieve this.

Paragraphs in Continuous Text

In continuous text, where there's a lot of text in one stream (an article, for example), you need to make sure that the reader can distinguish between paragraphs, and you also need to make sure that you don't separate them to the degree that they begin to look like separate objects instead of part of the same text flow.

There are two main approaches to working with paragraphs: indentation and extra vertical space.

With indentation it's common to indent the first line of a paragraph, without adding extra space above the paragraph. The first paragraph in a sequence, however, is normally not indented. Indentation is the norm in book typography; a good indent is usually around one line space—the value of line-height. However, you may need to vary this if your interlinear space is significantly different. If you choose to add extra vertical space, then it's common to not indent the first lines of the paragraphs, as shown in Figure 7-14.

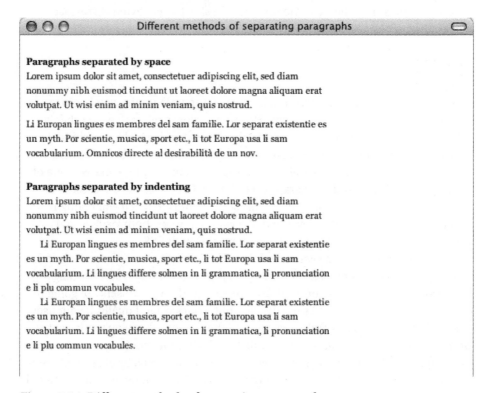

Figure 7-14. Different methods of separating paragraphs

The other major variable that you need to look at is the justification (or alignment) of the text—whether it's set ranged-left, ranged-right, centered, or justified. In the ranged-left setting, the left edge of the text column is straight and the right is ragged. Ranged-right is the reverse of ranged-left. The centered setting centers each line in the column, leaving both edges ragged. The justified setting keeps both left and right edges straight by varying the space between words as necessary. The ranged-left setting is also called ragged-right, left-aligned, and unjustified (the ranged-right setting has other names like this).

The main problem with justification (which is essentially the process of deciding where and how to break lines) in web browsers is that no browsers make intelligent decisions about line breaking. To compound this, there's no way to influence line breaks without resorting to <br /> tags, using the white-space property, or using the <pre> element.

Many people regard the justified setting, where left and right margins are straight, as the most legible in print, and there are arguments for and against this. However, on screen the justified setting is usually much less legible than ranged-left for the simple reason that browsers don't hyphenate, and hyphenation is essential if you want to get a decent justified setting. To keep the right margin straight, the browser has to introduce extra space between words, and often lots of space, which makes reading difficult. The ranged-left setting, in contrast, uses equal space between words, with the right edge left ragged. The default value for justification gives you ranged-left text, so it's not normally necessary to specify it.

The CSS properties responsible for text indents and justification are text-indent and text-align, respectively. The text-indent property just needs a length value, and text-align takes one of four possible values: left, right, center, or justify. NN4 doesn't accept justify. If you want to use indentation, don't forget to override the default margins on <p> or you'll get extra space anyway. The following code produces the output illustrated previously:

```
body {
   font-size: 12px;
}
h1 {
   font: bold 1em/1.5em Georgia, serif;
   margin: 0;
   padding: 0;
}
div {
   margin: 2em 0 0 5em;
   width: 33em;
   font: 1em/1.5em Georgia, serif;
}
div.space p {
   margin: 0.5em 0 0 0;
   padding: 0;
}
div.space p.first {
   margin: 0;
}
div.indent p {
   margin: 0;
   padding: 0;
   text-indent: 1.5em;
```

```
}
div.indent p.first {
   text-indent: 0;
}
<div class="space">
   <h1>Paragraphs separated by space</h1>
   <p class="first">Lorem ipsum dolor sit amet...</p>
   <p>Li Europan lingues es membres del sam familie...</p>
</div>
<div class="indent">
   <h1>Paragraphs separated by indenting</h1>
   <p class="first">Lorem ipsum dolor sit amet...</p>
   <p>Li Europan lingues es membres del sam familie...</p>
   <p>Li Europan lingues es membres del sam familie...</p>
</div>
```

The alternative to the previous, more complex markup is to use CSS2's adjacent selectors, as in the following example, which will produce an identical result to the previous, more complex code in a browser that understands the selector. In IE 6, which doesn't understand the selector, it will simply follow the rules in the p selector and produce a half-line gap between the paragraphs.

```
p {
margin: 0 0 0.75em 0;
padding: 0;
text-indent: 0em;
}
p+p {
text-indent: 1.5em;
margin: 0;
}
<h1>Paragraphs separated by indenting</h1>
<p>Lorem ipsum dolor sit amet...</p>
<p>Li Europan lingues es membres del sam familie...</p>
<p>Li Europan lingues es membres del sam familie...</p>
```

Separating paragraphs with space is simply a matter of adjusting the margins and/or padding on the paragraphs. You can specify whatever value you want, so the main question becomes *how much space?*

When it comes to separating paragraphs with extra space, a whole line space is normally far too much; the gap becomes a gaping hole. But if the space between two paragraphs isn't detectably bigger than the space between lines, then your paragraphs will appear to be one homogenous lump. This tendency is made worse when the last line in a paragraph is a full (or nearly full) line. Whether a space works is largely dependent on the measure of the text, with a longer measure needing a larger space. Try a quarter or half of the value of line-height to start with, and modify it based on how well you think it works. Although working in quarter-line increments may seem overly precise, it's not: A quarter of a line is actually quite a large space. With 1.5em interlinear space, working in increments of 0.25em (⅙ of a line space) is a good way to find out what works. When you're experimenting, always try to use several paragraphs of several lines—and certainly more than in the next example, which is short because of space restrictions. Figure 7-15 shows paragraphs separated by a space, which grows by ⅙ of a line at a time.

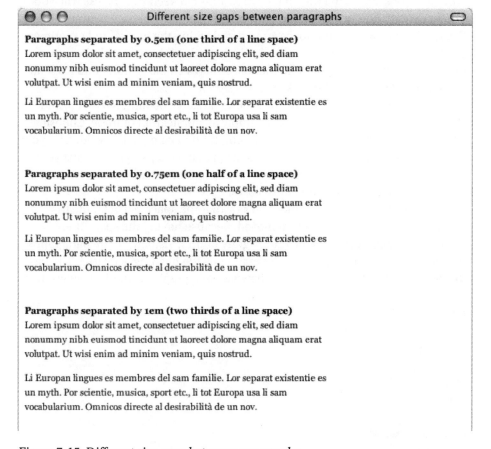

Figure 7-15. Different size gaps between paragraphs

The Space Between Blocks

The critical thing to remember about separating blocks of type with space is that paragraphs and headings are just block-level elements in CSS and follow the box model, as described in Chapter 4. There's a big catch related to this: Paragraph and heading margins collapse exactly the same way that more obviously block-like blocks do. It also means that you use the properties `padding` and `margin` to specify space around text blocks.

Designing the space between blocks of type is a balancing act. Things that don't belong to each other (such as headings) need to look like they don't belong to each other, and things that do belong to each other (such as paragraphs) need to look like they belong to each other, but not like they're a single object. With short paragraphs, for example, too much space between them will begin to make them look like list items or a publicity blurb from a brochure, rather than paragraphs that are part of a single text stream.

Adding to your task is the fact that all the space—horizontal and vertical—around a block affects the way that relationships between your blocks will work. There's no easy rule to govern how you should manage the space between blocks. You need to be aware of the space around and within the blocks, and experiment until you find combinations that work. The best idea is to start with the critical bits, such as interlinear space and the spaces between paragraphs, and work up through headings to whole blocks of text.

The CSS itself is relatively simple. You've already encountered `margin` and `padding`, and space between blocks is simply an application of these. Choosing whether to use one (and which one) or both, is often going to be decided for you: The rest of your layout (and factors such as margin collapsing) will affect your decision. All things being equal, it won't really matter which you use, because the visual effect will be identical in most cases.

In the last couple of examples you saw that the space between the first paragraph and the heading was removed, because having the space there is unnecessary and having the heading tightly bound, visually, to the paragraphs following it makes it clear to which paragraphs the heading is related. The following excerpt (from the first space between paragraphs examples) shows that:

```
div.space p {
  margin: 0.5em 0 0 0;
  padding: 0;
}
div.space p.first {
  margin: 0;
}
<div class="space">
  <h1>Paragraphs separated by space</h1>
  <p class="first">Lorem ipsum dolor sit amet...</p>
</div>
```

There are other situations in which you would want to adjust the space between two text elements. One such situation is when a heading is immediately followed by another heading (usually a subordinate heading). The subordinate heading normally needs a similar amount of space before it to the main heading, as shown in Figure 7-16.

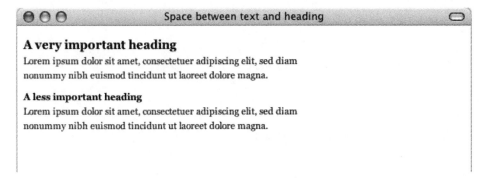

Figure 7-16. Space between text and heading

However, when a subordinate heading immediately follows the main heading, the amount of space it would usually require after text is too much, and it looks wrong after the main heading, as shown in Figure 7-17.

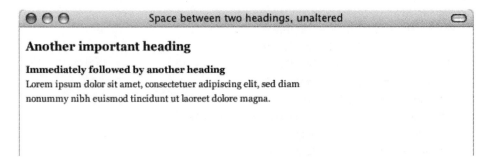

Figure 7-17. Space between two headings, unaltered

The solution is to reduce the amount of space between the two, as shown in Figure 7-18.

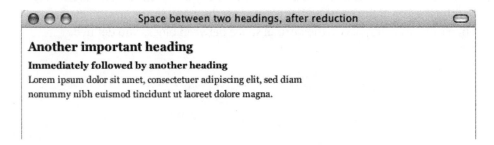

Figure 7-18. Space between two headings, after reduction

All three examples were produced from this code:

```
body {
  font: 12px/1.5em Georgia, serif;
}
h1 {
  font: bold 1.25em/1.5em Georgia, serif;
  margin: 0.8em 0 0 0;
}
h2 {
  font: bold 1em/1.5em Georgia, serif;
  margin: 0.75em 0 0 0;
}
p {
  margin: 0 0 0.75em 0;
  width: 33em;
}
h2.post-h1 {
  margin: 0.25em 0 0 0;
}
<body>
  <h1>A very important heading</h1>
  <p>Lorem ipsum dolor sit amet...</p>
  <h2>A less important heading</h2>
  <p>Lorem ipsum dolor sit amet...</p>
  <h1>Another important heading</h1>
  <h2>Immediately followed by another heading</h2>
  <p>Lorem ipsum dolor sit amet...</p>
  <h1>Another important heading</h1>
  <h2 class="post-h1">Immediately followed by another heading</h2>
  <p>Lorem ipsum dolor sit amet...</p>
</body>
```

As with paragraph indentation, an easier solution is to use CSS2 adjacent selectors. The following CSS makes it unnecessary to use classes on the headings and, as before, if the browser doesn't support the selector nothing drastic happens, the user simply gets the normal space between blocks you defined:

```
h1 + h2 {
  margin: 0.25em 0 0 0;
}
```

Above or Below?

You may well be tempted to add a bit of space above a paragraph and a bit of space below, until things look "about right." This isn't the best policy for several reasons.

The primary reason is that this will inevitably come back and bite you. If you have specified extra space above and below your type block, then there will come a point at which you introduce a new kind of block—say a heading, quotation, or reference—and the space you want to get around that block isn't possible because of a bit of extra space around a paragraph style, which you can't change without changing headings . . . and so on, ad nauseam. Although collapsing margins will sometimes produce the result you want, most often there will be situations in which you want less margin than there is already (margins collapse to the largest) or no margin at all.

Another good reason is the difficulty you may have in working out how much space there was supposed to be between paragraphs compared with how much there actually is. A system where you stick to just space above, or just space below, eliminates uncertainties and ought to make integrating new kinds of block into your design later on a lot easier. The best choice is usually to have extra space above a block. The space around any one block then doesn't affect the space around following blocks, and this is usually the behavior you want. In exceptional situations you use a slightly altered style, or more tightly constructed selectors, as you would for other exceptional behavior, such as removing paragraph space immediately after a heading.

Headings

Headings can be a thorny issue. They play a vital role in making content easy to navigate and understand, but they're often, in design terms, just slapped together. The heading structures available in plain HTML are visually quite crude. However, through CSS, it's possible to make headings that provide clarity in the navigation and integrate design elements together. There are three big issues to take into account:

- Can you tell the headings apart?

- Can you tell what the order of importance of the headings is?

- Will the headings work with your text?

The typographic options available to you with headings are, as always: type, weight, size, space, and color. You usually need to use only one or two of these variables; if you start changing all of them at once, then each heading will most likely lose any sense of coherence or sequence. If your headings have visual characteristics in common—if they look related to each other—then your readers stand a much better chance of being able to usefully pick out what's happening with your headings.

There are several things to note about the way that headings do and don't have to look. For example, headings don't have to be in bold, and they don't have to all be different sizes either. The key is making your headings distinct from your body text. The next few examples show some possibilities, but they by no means represent an exhaustive list.

All the examples use the following markup, and their rulesets are listed after each one:

```
<body>
    <h1>The most important heading</h1>
    <p>Lorem ipsum dolor sit amet...</p>
    <h2>A less important heading</h2>
    <p>Li Europan lingues es membres del sam familie...</p>
</body>
```

The result of this first example, below, is shown in Figure 7-19.

```
ody {
    font: 12px/1.5em Georgia, serif;
}
h1 {
    font: bold 1em/1.5em Georgia, serif;
    margin: 1.25em 0 0 0;
}
h2 {
    font: italic 1em/1.5em Georgia, serif;
    margin: 1.25em 0 0 0;
}
p {
    margin: 0;
    width: 33em;
}
```

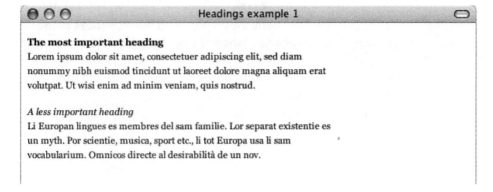

Figure 7-19. Headings example 1

The result of this second example is shown in Figure 7-20.

```css
body {
  font: 12px/1.5em Georgia, serif;
}
h1 {
  font: bold 1.5em/1em Verdana, sans-serif;
  margin: 1.25em 0 0 0;
}
h2 {
  font: 1.5em/1em Verdana, sans-serif;
  margin: 1.25em 0 0 0;
}
p {
  margin: 0;
  width: 33em;
}
```

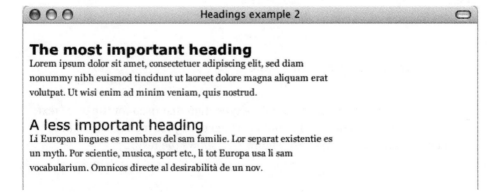

Figure 7-20. Headings example 2

This example is almost identical to the previous example, except that the heading type is 1.2em instead of 1.5em. This has pushed the screen size of the normal sans-serif type down to the point where the strokes are only 1px wide, and it's much harder to tell the second heading from the body text. Also worth noting is that in the first example it's much harder to tell the normal sans-serif from the bold. Figure 7-21 shows the result.

```
body {
    font: 12px/1.5em Georgia, serif;
}
h1 {
    font: bold 1.2em/1.25em Verdana, sans-serif;
    margin: 1.25em 0 0 0;
}
h2 {
    font: 1.2em/1.25em Verdana, sans-serif;
    margin: 1.25em 0 0 0;
}
p {
    margin: 0;
    width: 33em;
}
```

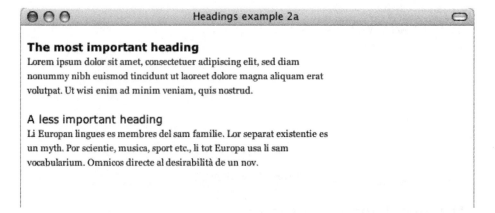

Figure 7-21. Headings example 2a

This example uses a larger size of the type than that used for the body text. The size difference is enough that bold isn't necessary for readers to tell the heading apart from the body text. Figure 7-22 shows the result.

```
body {
    font: 12px/1.5em Georgia, serif;
}
```

```
h1 {
  font: 1.5em/1em Georgia, serif;
  margin: 0.5em 0 0.25em 0;
}
p {
  margin: 0;
  width: 33em;
}
```

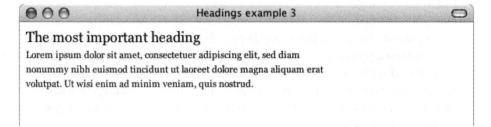

Figure 7-22. Headings example 3

This example uses outdented (aka hanging indent) italic at the same size as the text. The outdenting has the advantage of being very easy to pick out against the left edge of text. Figure 7-23 shows the result.

```
body {
  font: 12px/1.5em Georgia, serif;
}
h1 {
  font: italic 1em/1.5em Georgia, serif;
  margin: 0.75em 0 0 0;
}
p {
  margin: 0 0 0 1em;
  width: 33em;
}
```

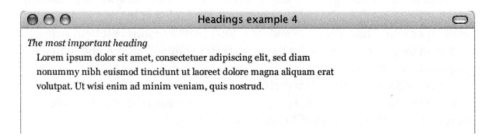

Figure 7-23. Headings example 4

On a structural note, please don't use styled paragraphs to represent headings. WYSIWYG editors can make it very easy to do this, even without your noticing. Also, please don't jump around the headings just to get a different default size or weight—that's what the CSS is for. On a contradictory note, NN4 forces all headings to have a certain amount of vertical space around them, and on the Mac it forces headings to be bold too, so you may need to balance these two issues if you code for NN4.

Lists

The purpose of a list is simple: to present a collection of items. The formatting of lists, however, presents some relatively complex design decisions. You have to decide how to separate out the items, whether to use some kind of visual cue for this, and how you should differentiate the list from its surroundings. If you're coding for NN4, look to the end of this section for information on the problems it has with lists and CSS.

If you choose some kind of visual cue or marker to visually separate items, then there are a variety of possibilities, only some of which will be appropriate for a particular situation.

There are two main kinds of cues in lists: specific cues and nonspecific cues, which essentially map to ordered (numbered) and unordered (bulleted) lists: <ol> and <ul>. CSS provides both types, so the primary guide to which to use has to be what the list is doing. Specific cues enforce some kind of sequence on a list, whether that's an order for doing things in or an order of importance, whether you like it or not. Nonspecific cues, on the other hand, don't enforce a sequence, but they do still allow list items to be picked out accurately. In technical documents, ordered lists are used only when the order is important, if the order in which the parts of a task are performed dictates the success or failure of the task, for example. The nature of the list may be such that you don't need any cues at all to tell the reader that it's a list or help the reader find each item.

In CSS it's the <li> element itself that's styled. If you were to set the display property on an <li> element to inline or block, then it would stop acting like a list item and no longer generate a marker or incrementing counters (<li>s have display: list-item set by default). You can also set the display property on another element to list-item and it will start to behave like a list item. It's also possible to make <ol>s appear as <ul>s, which subverts the meaning of the tags and is, generally speaking, a bad idea. <ol> and <ul> don't actually control list item styling, although they do contain the list items, so their padding, borders, and margins impact the whole list.

Three CSS properties, list-style-position, list-style-image, and list-style-type, and one shorthand property, list-style, are related to lists. We cover all of these properties in the next few sections.

list-style-position

If you're dealing with cues such as numbers or bullets, then the next question is where to put them. The default is to put the marker outside the content box, but it's also possible to put the marker inside the content box generated by the list item, as shown in Figure 7-24.

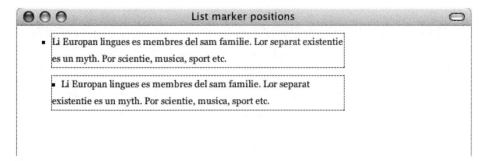

Figure 7-24. List marker positions

When the marker is outside the list item's content box, it has no effect on the layout, much the same as an absolutely positioned box. The CSS to control this is very simple: Set list-style-position to either inside or outside. The default is outside.

```
li {
  list-style-position: inside;
}
```

> **CAUTION** *If the list item happens to be flush with the left edge of the page and has* list-style-position: outside, *then the marker will disappear off the side of the page!*

The list-style- properties are inherited and only affect display: list-item elements (only ‹li›s by default), so you can simply style ‹ul› instead of ‹li› and the properties will be inherited by the ‹li›s, which generally makes for simpler CSS:

```
ul {
  list-style-position: outside;
}
```

By and large the best option is to have the marker outside the content box of the item. This gives clear separation of the marker, making it easy to pick out (more of a problem with lists using an alphabetical numbering scheme). If the marker is hung outside the list item's content box, then it becomes possible to align the left edge of the list item (not the marker) with the left edge of the surrounding text. The HTML default is to indent the list items. Figure 7-25 shows both options.

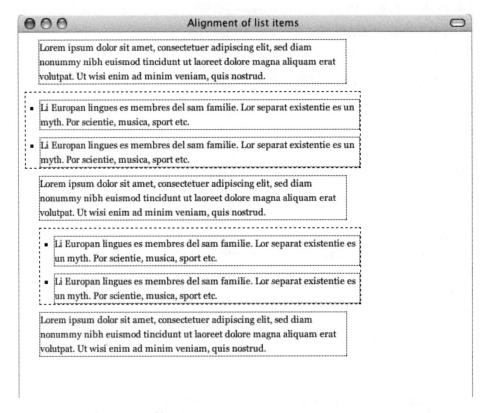

Figure 7-25. Alignment of list items

While the CSS specification is ambiguous about precisely where the marker should be when `outside` is specified, most browsers render it a little bit outside the main content box. You can't control the marker's position with CSS.

Marker Clipping in Internet Explorer

It's worth talking about a problem IE has with lists here. You can see from the example that padding has been used on the `<ul>` whose `<li>`s align with the main column edge, instead of controlling the margin. This is because IE clips any list markers that extend beyond the padding edge of a <ul> or <ol>. This is shown nicely in Figure 7-26 (with both IE and Firebird shown for comparison).

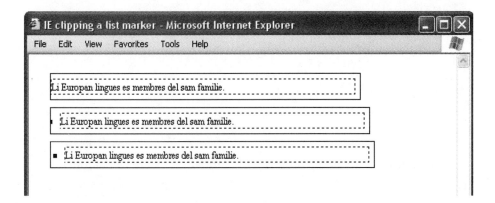

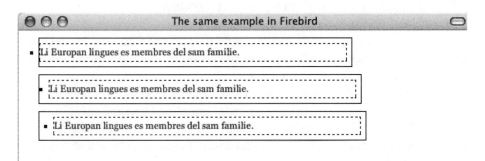

Figure 7-26. A list marker being clipped in IE (top) and displayed correctly in Firebird (bottom)

Figure 7-26 shows three lists, each with one item, and was generated by the following code, which sets the padding and margins on <li>s to 0 for the sake of the example. What's accomplished with the <ul>'s left padding could also be accomplished with left margin set on the <li>s.

```
ul {
  list-style-type: square;
  list-style-position: outside;
  width: 33em;
  padding: 0.5em;
  border: 1px solid black;
  margin: 0.75em 0 0 1.5em;
}
ul.one {
  padding-left: 0;
}
```

```
ul.two {
  padding-left: 1em;
}
ul.three {
  padding-left: 1.5em;
}
li {
  padding: 0;
  margin: 0;
  border: 1px dashed black;
}
```

Once you know about the problem, it's normally trivial to work around it.

list-style-type and list-style-image

list-style-type and list-style-image control the types of cues used for the list, with the first offering a preset range of markers and the second offering the ability to use an image in place of a marker.

list-style-type is straightforward. There's a fairly wide selection of values to choose from, offering nonspecific markers for unordered lists and specific markers for ordered lists. The specific markers come in the various numbering schemes you'd expect: European-Arabic (1, 2, 3, and so on), Roman (i, ii, iii, and so on), and alphabetic (a through z):

```
/* nonspecific markers */
list-style-type: disc;        /* solid circle   */
list-style-type: circle;      /* outline circle */
list-style-type: square;      /* solid square   */

/* specific markers */
list-style-type: decimal;     /* European-Arabic numerals (1,2,3,4...)    */
list-style-type: lower-roman; /* Lowercase roman (i,ii,iii,iv...)   */
list-style-type: upper-roman; /* Uppercase roman (I,II,III,IV...)   */
list-style-type: lower-alpha; /* Lowercase alphabetic (a,b,c,d...) */
list-style-type: upper-alpha; /* Uppercase alphabetic (A,B,C,D...) */

/* special case */
list-style-type: none;        /* no marker */
```

The default for <ul>s is list-style-type: disc; for <ol>s the default is list-style-type: decimal. To use an image for the marker, use list-style-image. It takes a URL as its value in the form you've seen in @import rules: url(list-marker.png). If the browser supports it and the image is available, then the image will be displayed instead of the normal list marker; otherwise, the browser will fall back to list-style-type. This example specifies a list with square markers outside the content box and a list with a simple image for a marker:

```
p {
  margin: 0 0 0 1.5em;
  padding: 0;
  border: 1px dotted black;
}
ul {
  list-style-type: square;
  list-style-position: outside;
  padding: 0;
  border: 1px solid black;
  margin: 0;
}
li {
  margin: 0 0 0 1.5em;
  padding: 0;
}
ul.image {
  list-style-image: url("square.gif");
}
<p>Lorem ipsum dolor sit amet...</p>
<ul>
   <li>Li Europan lingues es membres del sam familie...</li>
   <li>Li Europan lingues es membres del sam familie...</li>
</ul>
<ul class="image">
   <li>Li Europan lingues es membres del sam familie...</li>
   <li>Li Europan lingues es membres del sam familie...</li>
</ul>
```

Figure 7-27 shows the result.

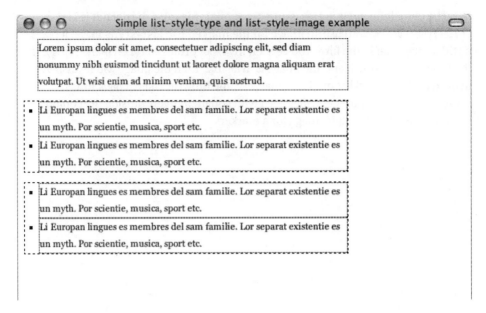

Figure 7-27. Simple list-style-type *and* list-style-image *example*

list-style Shorthand Property

There's a list-style shorthand property, which is very similar to the font: short-hand property. With it you can specify the marker type, image, and position together.

```
ul { list-style: disc outside; }
```

The syntax is very straightforward: a value for list-style-image, followed by a value for list-style-type, and then a value for list-style-position. All the values are optional and can be used in any order.

```
ul { list-style: disc; }
ul { list-style: url(pretty_disc.png) disc outside; }
ul { list-style: url(pretty_disc.png) outside; }
```

Greater Control

There will, of course, be times when you need more specific control over individual <li> elements. You'll often want to put some space between list items, especially if you're separating paragraphs with extra space. Deal with the basic formatting decisions in a <ul> style, and then style <li> to add the extras. If you need to change the way that <li> is styled (for example, if you have <ol>s and <ul>s), then using contextual selectors with your ruleset (of the form ul li { /*styles*/ }) is normally enough to catch the differences without resorting to class or id attributes in your markup. The following ruleset is from the second list in Figure 7-25:

```
ul {
  list-style-type: square;
  list-style-position: outside;
  margin: 0.75em 0 0 1em;
  padding: 0 0 0 1.5em;
  width: 33em;
  border: 1px dotted black;
}
li {
  margin: 0.75em 0 0 0;
}
```

Netscape Navigator 4 Problems

NN4's support for lists in CSS is seriously flawed. Not only are several of the properties unsupported, but also setting some others will cause the list to be rendered incorrectly. Table 7-3 shows what isn't supported.

Table 7-3. Summary of NN4 Problems with CSS Lists

Problem	Notes
list-style-image is unsupported.	If you also specified list-style-type in your ruleset, you'll get that marker.
list-style-position is unsupported.	You're stuck with the default: outside. Having this property present doesn't break anything, though.
Setting margin-left, margin-right, padding-left, or padding-right on a \<ul\> or \<ol\> element causes the list-style-type to be forgotten and reset to the default: disc for \<ul\> and decimal for \<ol\>.	margin-top, margin-bottom, and corresponding padding properties don't trigger this. If you've set list-style-type to none, it still gets reset to disc.

147

Table 7-3. Summary of NN4 Problems with CSS Lists (continued)

Problem	Notes
Setting margins or padding on an `<li>` element produces bizarre results.	Applying `margin-top` or `padding-top` to an `<li>` element doesn't work and causes the cumulative inter-item margin to be applied above the first `<li>` only. Applying `margin-bottom` or `padding-bottom` causes the list item content to be displaced downward from the marker, leaving the marker floating above the content. Setting left or right margins or padding causes the marker to disappear altogether.
Styling an `<li>` element directly only styles the marker.	This concerns inline properties such as color and font. A workaround is to enclose the whole `<li>` content in a `<span>` element and style that.

Inline Boxes

Inline boxes are the other major kind of box in CSS. All your text is laid out using inline boxes once you get past the gross characteristics you've specified by styling paragraphs and `<div>`s. A paragraph will probably contain several inline boxes, starting with one for each line. If your paragraph has no inline elements in it, then that's it, but if it has some—`<strong>`, for instance—then they get their own inline boxes and things get more complicated. Figure 7-28 shows a simple paragraph with one box per line.

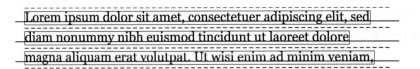

Figure 7-28. Line boxes within a `<p>` block

The block-level element, which is `<p>` in this example, has a series of line boxes made from the contents of `<p>`, but they aren't associated with inline elements such as `<strong>`. CSS calls these boxes *anonymous inline boxes*. The solid box represents the inline boxes, the dashed line represents the total line box height (from the `line-height` property), and the long, solid line represents the baselines of the line boxes, as shown in Figure 7-29.

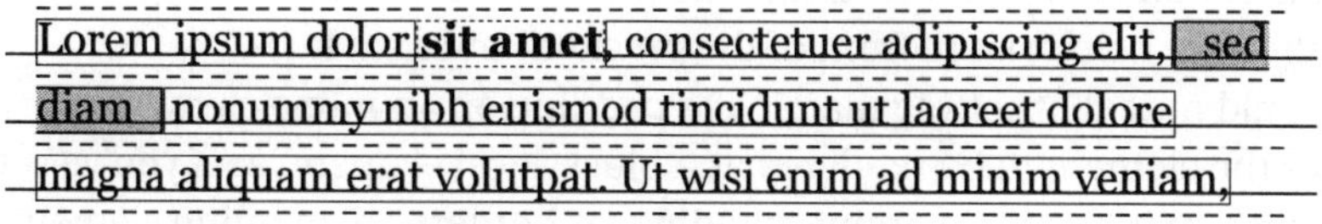

Figure 7-29. Inline boxes within line boxes

The dotted line around the bold text represents a `<strong>` element, and the box around "sed diam" represents a `<span>` element. You can see how the first line box is made of four inline boxes: an anonymous box, the `<strong>` box, another anonymous box, and then the `<span>` box. The `<span>` was styled with this:

```
span {
  padding: 0 0.5em 0 0.5em;
  background-color: rgb(210,210,210);
  border: 1px solid black;
}
```

The gaps at the left and right of the span are caused by the padding set on the element. What's interesting is the way the span's inline box reacts to its contents being split across two lines. Essentially it's split into two boxes, which we'll call A and B. Note that the padding isn't applied to the right edge of box A or to the left edge of box B. Margin, padding, and border properties (which are all perfectly allowable) shouldn't be applied to the edges of the splits, although they are in IE 6. They apply only to the actual beginning and end of the element's content. If the example span had been split across three lines instead, then the padding and border ought to apply as shown in Figure 7-30.

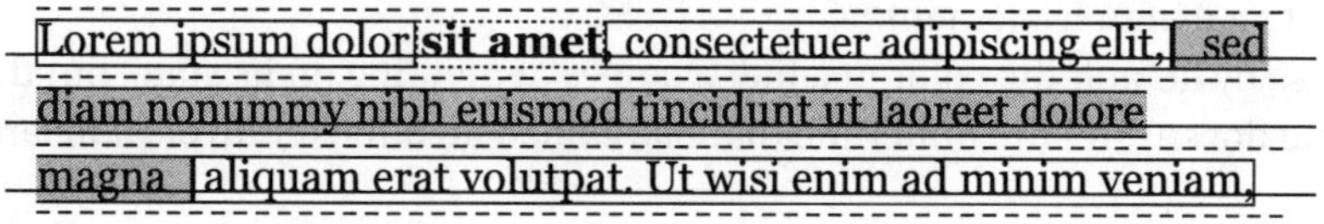

Figure 7-30. Inline boxes breaking across lines

Any vertical borders, margins, or padding that would be pushed outside the line box don't increase its height; they spill over above and below the line box. The exact behavior when this happens varies across browsers. In IE6/Windows and Mozilla/Netscape 6+, things that spill above sit on top of the previous line, whereas things that spill below sit under the next line. In IE5/Mac, things that spill out (above or below) sit in front of the previous and next lines.

You should note that setting margins or padding on an inline element in NN4 causes the element to be rendered as a block-level element, as if you've set `display: block` on it. Setting margins, padding, or borders on an inline element works fine in IE 6, but has no effect in IE5/Windows.

The typography associated with inline formatting is concerned with differentiating little meanings within the text: emphasis and quotation, for example. This is subtler than block-level typography and needs a correspondingly subtle hand. You can specify that the HTML element `<em>` use type that is 2 pixels bigger than the norm, but you can almost certainly also differentiate `<em>` from its surroundings with the use of italic, bold, or color (usually not in combination). In the majority of texts, hyperlinks will be the most inline typography you have to worry about, and there's a section on those coming up in this chapter, but sometimes you'll have to deal with a much wider range of inline elements. It's important to know what you have to deal with so that your solutions to each of the inline tasks don't clash with each other.

Formatting Links

Links are the original web typographic irritant, because (among other things) they change their appearance dynamically, something traditional typography was never equipped to deal with. Tim Berners-Lee thought that links should be underlined, which isn't a bad idea. Underlining is rare in print, and so it wasn't weighed down with associations. He also decided that links should be blue, which, debatably, isn't quite so clever. There have been raging arguments about the "correct" link color. This is one of the rare occurrences when using two variables (color and underlining) to differentiate an element actually works: One variable (color) tells you it's different from surrounding text and gives you state information (visited and unvisited), and the other variable (underlining) indicates that it's a dynamic element.

Because by default the color of a link changes depending on its state, but the underlining doesn't, it's the underline that has gained an almost universal meaning: link.

TIP *Because underlining is rare and has become associated with links, it's usually a good idea to avoid using it for anything other than links.*

There are three states exclusive to links: link, which is the basic, unvisited, and inactive state; visited; and active. There's also a fourth state, hover, which other elements can have too. hover is the state when the user's mouse is hovering over a link. In the sections that follow we look in detail at each of these states.

The element used for linking is the <a> tag. The first thing to remember is that the <a> tag does more than provide links: It can also act as an anchor for links. CSS recognizes the distinction and, as you saw in Chapter 5, provides several pseudo-classes to access them. Traditionally, <a>s used as anchors had no graphical effect on their content. If you directly style the <a> tag, you may discover unexpected side effects elsewhere. An <h1> element whose text you nested inside an <a name> tag for internal page navigation would turn the same shade of red as your links, for example. The four states are accessed in CSS using the pseudo-classes :link, :visited, :hover, and :active.

Each state can have a different typographic treatment. Whether each state needs a different treatment is another matter. The main consideration is the job the link is doing. A sitewide navigation menu and links within body text will probably need different treatments. You might not want your sitewide menu to have a different treatment once visited, but you'll almost certainly want visited body text links to be different. We go through some of the possibilities and considerations in the next sections.

The one major gotcha to watch for with pseudo-classes relates to the way that the cascade determines which selectors match which elements. The lower an item comes in a stylesheet, the more important it is. Also, because you can apply only one selector of a particular importance to an element, if more than one equally important selector matches, then whichever is lower in the stylesheet will win. In the next example, all three a selectors have equal importance. While a link is unvisited, mousing over a link will match the a:hover rule, which will override the a:link rule, giving your link an underline. Once you've visited a link, then a:link no longer matches, and a:visited matches instead. Now, when you mouse over the link, the a:hover can't override the a:visited rule because it doesn't "win" the battle of the selectors; you won't get any underlining on a visited link. If you were to reverse a:visited and a:hover, then a:hover would win, and visited links would get underlining when they're moused over too.

```
a:link {
    color: rgb(210,0,0);
    text-decoration: none;
}
a:hover {
    text-decoration: underline
}
/* a:visited trumps a:hover because of document order priority */
```

```
a:visited {
  color: rgb(175,0,0);
  text-decoration: none;
}
```

The Default Link State

The default state of your links is critical. The important thing isn't that your links are blue and underlined, but that they're clearly recognizable and their nature is made apparent.

Color works very well for links. Certain people, notably Jakob Nielsen, argue for strictly following the blue-underlined link convention. However, others argue that because red is a color naturally associated with grabbing attention, it should be used for links instead of blue. There's something valuable in both points of view, but they should be taken as guidelines.

Generalizing both of these views provides a useful approach: We should establish and follow consistently link-formatting conventions within sites that make use of color that contrasts with our text. Of course, there are sites that deliberately make the default state of their links pretty much indistinguishable from their text. If part of their reason for being is "play and exploration," this may well be an approach that their users enjoy. If the site in question is an e-commerce site, though, this isn't a good idea.

If you do choose to rely solely on underlining to differentiate your links, ensure that you enforce this with a text-decoration declaration. Not everyone surfs with underlining of links on by default.

The Visited State

Visited links usually need to be differentiated from unvisited links. This helps users remember where they've been, and often where they've come from. However, there are circumstances in which you don't want to treat visited links differently—perhaps in a sitewide navigation menu, for example, which just wants to sit quietly and be available when it's needed. These decisions depend on the context in which the links appear.

In general, if you want to differentiate visited links from unvisited links and the surrounding text, use a darker shade of your default link color. This has the advantage of retaining a graphic connection with the original link, while also becoming less visually important.

The Hover State

When the user hovers the cursor over a link, without clicking it, the hover state is entered. Hover is a very good way of clearly indicating that some text really is a link. A good application of this state is to toggle the link's underlining—bare links gain an underline briefly, and underlined ones lose it. This helps to reinforce that the link is an active thing as well as invoke the links-are-underlined convention. Whatever method you choose, the point should always be to confirm to the user that the link is an interactive element and that it's responding to them. It's important to note that :hover doesn't work in NN4.

The Active State

Links are only active while you're clicking them. As often as not, an extra level of visual coding in this state won't really enhance your site. If you do feel that you need to use this state then, given that it only applies when activating a link, a style that concretely demonstrates this may well be what you want—a change in background color for the link or something similarly dramatic.

Other Link Possibilities

You can do other things with links that can make a significant difference in their utility. Most sites, for example, have links that point to internal pages and links that point to external pages. Differentiating these kinds of links makes a lot of sense. Very often, sites use small graphics to indicate this, but there's no reason why it can't be done more elegantly with simple typography. If you have a link style that uses a color to denote links, then italicizing the external links will mark them as different but maintain their "linkness."

Some sites give written clues to the occurrence of links—for example, "To find out more, visit the official fan site." Even without the underline, it's not hard to guess where the link is. Such links will still work effectively without being bold and colored and underlined. A more subtle approach could work well, but only if you're sure of (or have control of) the editorial policy regarding links. If you can't guarantee that 100% of the links you want to treat in a particular way are going to be verbally signposted in that way, then it's not worth risking stray links getting visually lost.

If your different classes of links (navigation bar links and links within the main text, perhaps) are contained within different structures (container <div>s, for example), then it's often a relatively easy matter to discriminate between them with selectors. Most often a simple descendant selector will do:

```
div#navbar a:link { /* rules */ }
div#content a:link { /* rules */ }
```

In other circumstances (say, when differentiating internal and external links within the main body of a page), you may well have to add classes (or maybe even IDs in some situations) to your links or to parent elements closer to the text.

```
a.className:link { /* rules */ }
a#specialLink:link { /* rules */ }
p.externalLinks a:link { /* rules */ }
```

There are a lot of possibilities for both the problems and their solutions, so it's always good to experiment.

Superior and Inferior Text

There are many things in text that need to be picked out from their surroundings, but that also must not interrupt their surroundings. Good examples of this are the verse numbers in the Bible and references to footnotes in text. The usual tactic is to use smaller type for these references and lift them slightly above or slightly below the normal flow of text. When numbers (figures) are treated in this way, they're usually referred to as either *superior* or *inferior* figures. With text this is often called *superscript* or *subscript*. Fundamentally they're the same thing. The advantage of this tactic is that readers are familiar with it.

It may well not be enough to simply specify that the text should be "superior" or "inferior." You need to give thought to the type you're using. Georgia, for example, has nonranging figures, and the kind of variance in size, say between a 1 and an 8, will produce poor visual results. It's worth switching to a sans-serif font with ranging figures (such as Verdana or Arial) if you want very small figures. (For a discussion of ranging and non-ranging figures, see the "Type Basics" section of this chapter.)

You've already seen how line boxes are made from one or more inline boxes. If you pop your reference inside a <span> element, then it gets its own inline box in the line that you can slide up and down within the line (see Figure 7-31).

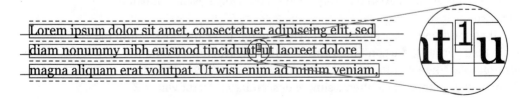

Figure 7-31. Positioning inline boxes vertically within a line box

This is done with the `vertical-align` property, which affects only inline elements (and table cells; see Chapter 9 for more information). It takes one of several possible values:

- `baseline`: Simply aligns the baseline of the inline element with the main baseline

- `sub`: Moves the element's baseline to the position the browser thinks is correct for subscript

- `super`: Moves the element's baseline to the position the browser thinks is correct for superscript

There are several other values that `vertical-align` can take, but their implementation differs enough between platforms that it's worth avoiding them and sticking with the preceding three, which should be more than enough for what you want to do.

Note that setting `vertical-align` to `sub` or `super` doesn't change the `font-size` of the element. You should be aware of HTML's `<sub>` and `<sup>` elements, which indicate sub- and superscript (but likewise don't alter `font-size`) and are perfectly valid HTML. There's no reason why you shouldn't use them over an anonymous element such as `<span>`. Often you'll want superior or inferior elements for references, when it makes sense to directly style the `<a>`. The only markup argument against them is that they're style elements like `<b>` or `<i>`, and so tie their presentation into your content, which isn't always a good thing. They are, however, supported by NN4, which ignores `vertical-align`.

The sizing of the superior or inferior elements is crucial. Be aware that you can't go below 8px without seriously undermining the legibility of the type, even if they're figures. If you're using letters, then going below 9px will cause you real problems. You should note that we're not talking about specifying sizes in `px` here; we're talking about the size of the character bitmaps output to the screen because of whatever units you were using. If you're sizing using relative units, then be sure to test with the size that you're scaling from set down to smaller sizes, to ensure that your just-so superior figures don't become an unusable mess if the user overrides your type size. If you use relative units for the rest of your text, but absolute sizes for references, beware of your relatively-sized text being considerably different in size from your references.

If you have more than one set of superior or inferior elements (for example, the notes and verse system found in most Bibles), then you'll want to pay attention to making sure that they can be told apart. Color is likely to be the best option at small sizes because it doesn't involve using another set of bitmaps, as italic or bold would. At larger sizes, switching from serif to sans-serif or to italic will probably prove effective. Another option is to switch from figures to letters. This kind of styling is difficult to get right; experimentation is essential.

```
p {
  font: 12px/1.5em Georgia, serif;
}
a.reference:link {
  font: 9px/1em verdana, sans-serif;
  vertical-align: super;
}
```

Figure 7-32 shows various relatively-sized examples of superior and inferior text.

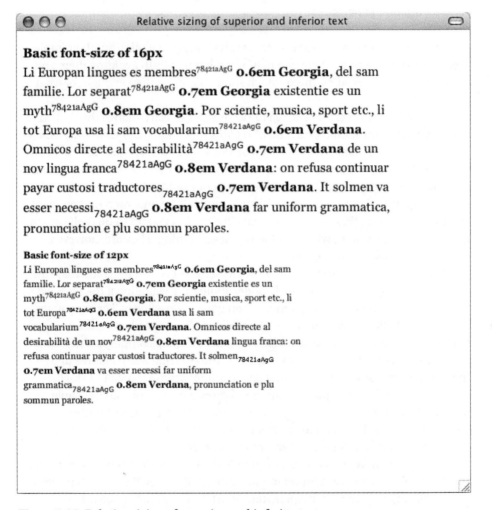

Figure 7-32. Relative sizing of superior and inferior text

Relative Units: Describing the Relationships Between Elements

As you've seen throughout this chapter, the job of specifying sizes and position of the various elements that make up the text of a page—text, headings, and links—generally becomes an exercise in establishing visual relationships between those elements. No matter whether you specify in absolute or relative units, this remains true. If you had specified body text to be 12px in size and headings to be 16px, and then you changed the body text to be 16px, it's unlikely that you would leave the headings as they were. The visual relationship that gave the elements their meaning (headings being more important than body text, to put it crudely) would be damaged.

Using relative units and inheritance together enables these relationships to be preserved automatically as the size of a common ancestor changes. The implications reach far wider than the way that type is specified. You can apply the same techniques to boxes. You saw this earlier when we covered measure, which we specified using the width property. With measure we tied the width of a block containing text to the size of the text within it. There's no reason why you can't then tie that block's height or (through careful construction of rulesets and markup) make good use of inheritance to tie all a page's elements together, so that it's possible to scale, or allow user control over, entire pages from a single point. The result is that you can build a page that doesn't depend on overriding the user's preferences to look the way that you intended. This ability to retain proportions is a fantastic step forward. Proportions are one of the most basic design elements. The Golden Section isn't a list of approved rectangles, after all—it's a ratio of height to width that allows an infinite number of good-looking rectangles to be made.

```
body { font-size: 12px; }
p { font-size: 1em; }
h1 { font-size: 1.5em; }
<body>
   <h1>A heading</h1>
   <p>Some body text</p>
</body>
```

Because the heading and paragraph share the same parent, they automatically share the same base font-size, inherited from <body>. Because their own font-size properties are set using ems, they'll always be directly related by the same proportion.

There are, of course, limitations to this technique. Although the internal proportions of type remain constant as it changes in size, the way that type reacts to its surroundings does change, and so the design needs to change to reflect that.

This is really only a problem when you're working on a very large or very small scale with a design that originally worked somewhere in the middle of the extremes. Though it's unlikely that you'll have a design that begins to look awful at a certain size—there isn't enough space on screen for that—you'll have to consider what happens when small sizes of type scale up or down, because the bitmaps drawn on screen vary greatly at small sizes (as you saw in the superior and inferior text example earlier). This isn't a warning against this technique—it's merely a warning that extensive testing is always a good thing.

The other thing to watch out for is nested relative sizes. You need to be careful where and how you set relative sizes. For example, take the rule div { font-size: 1.5em; }. If you were to nest a <div> within another <div>, any children of that inner <div> would inherit a size of 2.25em (or 1.5em * 1.5em), which is probably not what you wanted.

Practicalities

As you already know, ems are calculated with respect to the font-size of an element. Things start to get more complex at this point because only the font-size of an element is calculated with respect to its parent. All the element's other properties (margin, padding, line-height, and so on) are calculated with respect to that element's own font-size. That means that in the following ruleset and markup sample, the margins of each element will not be the same:

```
p {
  font-size: 1em;
  margin: 0 0 0 2em;
}
h1 {
  font-size: 1.5em;
  margin: 0 0 0 2em;
}
<div>
  <h1>A heading</h1>
  <p>Some body text</p>
</div>
```

Figure 7-33 shows the result.

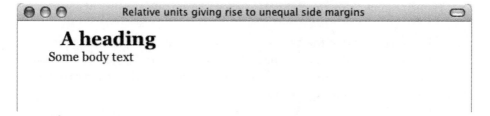

Figure 7-33. Relative units giving rise to unequal side margins

A lot of the time that isn't the behavior that you want, but at other times (with measure, for example), it is. The solution is, first of all, to think carefully about what you want to do visually. Second, you should make sure that your markup is good markup. Clear markup is often vital to using relative units to their full potential. In the preceding example, the way to get a straight left margin is to avoid using margins on the paragraph and heading elements, and instead use margins or padding on their common parent. Making good use of relative units requires more discipline than just specifying in absolute units.

```
div {
   padding: 0 0 0 2em;
}
p {
   font-size: 1em;
   margin: 0;
}
h1 {
   font-size: 1.5em;
   margin: 0;
}
<div>
   <h1>A heading</h1>
   <p>Some body text</p>
</div>
```

Figure 7-34 shows the result of using padding on a parent element.

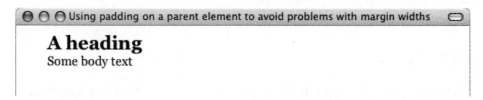

Figure 7-34. Using padding on a parent element to avoid problems with margin widths

Here are some fairly simple strategies for making effective use of ems:

- Pick an element as the basis for your visual relationships. Arrange your ruleset so that this element has a `font-size` of 1em. Normally this would be the body text, but anything else would work provided it serves to help you keep what's going on clear.

- Use sensible units—0.565em is never likely to produce exact, scalable, and cross-platform results.

- Write well-thought-out markup (see Chapters 2 and 3 for pointers).

- Make good use of ancestor elements and inheritance to provide some of the visual formatting of text elements.

- Plan, refine, and, above all, experiment.

There are things to watch out for, primarily at small sizes. Precise changes to type set at small sizes, perhaps in a legal notice at the bottom of a page, can be a pain. Relative units may not always be able to provide the changes because of the resolution of the screen: 0.8em of 12px equals 8.6px, and browsers can't render fractions of a pixel. These fractions need to be rounded. The usual conventions would make 0.8em of 12px equals 9px. 0.7em of 12px equals 8.4px, but rounding would make it 8px. These two examples show that a slight difference in specified size can become a significant difference in result size. Often you can overcome these problems with some fairly simple math, but they can prove infuriating.

Pixels, Scaling, and Internet Explorer

It's worth pointing out that IE doesn't allow for text sized in `px` to be scaled using the text zoom feature. This is an accessibility problem, especially if you've gone to the trouble of building your site entirely with `ems` or `%` from a `px`-based `font-size` value on `<body>` precisely so that people can scale the text if they have a visual impairment (or just want bigger text) while preserving your carefully-sized design for everyone else. If you want to allow users to scale your design in IE, then it's a fully-relative design or bust, I'm afraid.

Summary

Text is the underpinning of the Web—people read the Web. Good typography is essential to making the users' experience as easy and useful as possible. The ability of good typography to pick out meaning, signpost information, and provide ways for readers to navigate within a document makes it valuable. Typography doesn't have to be flashy, showy, or overstated to do its job, and in fact these things don't normally help at all. Typography is about making information, structure, and meaning clear. The visual and typographic possibilities open to the web typographer are now essentially the same as those open to the print typographer, thanks to CSS. A web typographer, working with a knowledge of the constraints and opportunities of the medium, can bring the same kind of functionality to text on the Web as their traditional counterpart can to print.

Boxes, Boxes, Boxes

CSS BOXES ARE YOUR layout bread and butter. The box model outlined in Chapter 4 is an extremely flexible and well-thought-out tool. With it you can create the fancy layouts that web design is famous for.

However, boxes can also be the number one CSS trouble source for a developer. Sometimes this is because the developer has a marginal understanding of what boxes can and can't do, and sometimes the trouble is browser bugs. This chapter's sole purpose is to give you a solid understanding of how layout boxes work, alone and in combinations. Rogue browser issues will be covered in Chapter 10, after the foundational knowledge of correct box behavior has been set in place.

The examples in this chapter use simple, correct CSS to ensure clarity in what can be very new concepts. No concessions have been made for the shortcomings of any browser. For this reason, some of the rulesets presented here may not display exactly as illustrated in your browser. In order to start at the beginning, we need to start with correct behavior.

First we discuss the base mechanisms that place a box on the screen. Then we go through a series of box layouts, building from simple beginnings into reasonably complex layouts, using different box types, and noting how they react alone and with each other. We don't cover all layouts, partly because all layouts haven't been discovered yet, but mainly because our purpose here is to teach how boxes interact so that you can create your own combinations. We finish up the chapter with a discussion of layout strategies for applying your new techniques. Note that you can find further, increasingly advanced examples of box layouts in Chapter 12.

> **CAUTION** *If you're an experienced developer, you'll already be familiar with controlling layout by using table tags. Forget it. Forget all of it. Put tables out of your mind and learn boxes fresh, because comparing the two will cause you great confusion. Boxes simply don't act anything like table cells. So clear your mind to ease your way in this chapter. And if you're a new developer who hasn't used tables for layout yet, then please forget that I just mentioned it, OK? Table layout was an unfortunate hack that's no longer necessary now that we have browsers with CSS support. Tables are for displaying tabular data, not for page layout.*

Flow

Document flow is pretty simple, and it's the root concept of CSS layout. All elements sit in the flow, and all position properties describe their element's position in relation to the flow. Flow is what allows web layout to be a fluid medium that works on any screen.

It's very simple: A lone element will be placed in the top-left corner of the screen. As more elements are added, they're placed to each preceding element's right, until there's no more space, and then they move below to begin again at the left, exactly like the word-wrap of text, which is inside the flow too. Everything is. Flow is the universal force of web layout.

Your design choices are made with concern for flow just as an architect's design choices are made with concern for gravity.

CSS boxes are boxes in that they have four corners, but that is all. It's important to understand that they aren't necessarily rigid; neither are they fixed upon a grid. Boxes have entirely malleable shapes, and they interact with one another within the document flow. You have a broad variety of rules available to specify sizes and relationships to flow. By beginning with simple rules, you can build a vocabulary of box layouts that allows you to create complex designs that will act reliably in the flexible medium of the Web.

Position

To begin, let's take this very simple XHTML and CSS example:

```
<body>
<div class="wee">1</div>
<div class="wee">2</div>
<div class="wee">3</div>
<div class="wee">4</div>
</body>

body {
  margin: 0px;
  padding: 0px;
  color: #000;
  background-color: #ccc;
}
.wee {
  padding: 10px;
  margin: 5px;
  background-color: #fff;
  border: 1px solid #000;
}
```

That ruleset does *not* produce Figure 8-1.

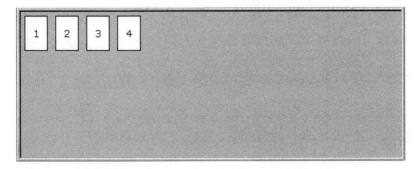

Figure 8-1. What our boxes don't do

It produces Figure 8-2.

Figure 8-2. What our boxes actually do

That's because a ‹div› is a block-level element, so each box begins its own line. Flow is working perfectly, doing what it can with block-level elements, stacking them down the screen. Forgive us if you think that's obvious, but we've lost count of the number of times someone starting CSS has expected the first result and not the second, so it's best to make this aspect clear.

These simple ‹div›s span the browser window because there's nothing to stop them from doing so. Width hasn't been declared, and margin is simply 5px. They expand to fill the available space of the window.

If some text is placed between the ‹div›*s like so:*

```
<body>
  <div class="wee">1</div>
  The quick brown fox jumped over the lazy dog.
  <div class="wee">2</div>
```

```
  <div class="wee">3</div>
  <div class="wee">4</div>
</body>
```

the result is what's shown in Figure 8-3.

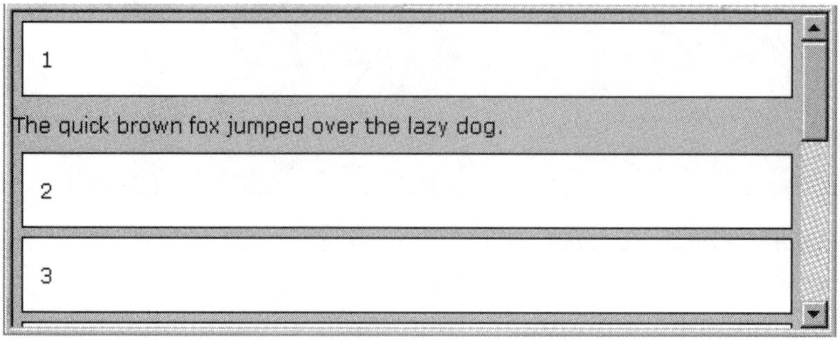

Figure 8-3. Text between the `<div>`*s*

If the same `<div>`s were shortened, say by declaring `width: 20%`

```
.wee {
  padding: 10px;
  margin: 5px;
  background-color: #fff;
  border: 1px solid #000;
  width: 20%;
}
```

you would see the result shown in Figure 8-4.

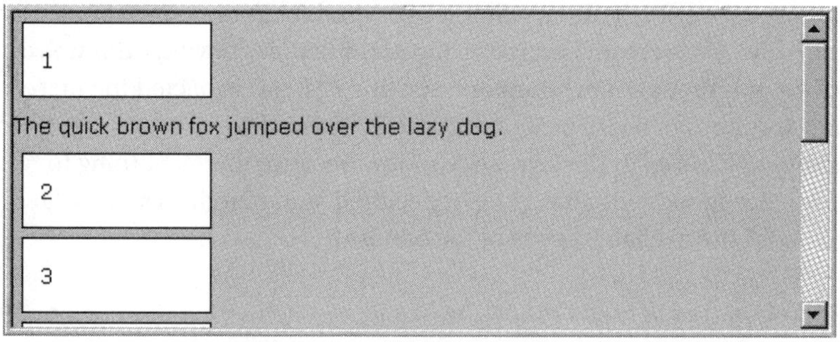

Figure 8-4. Text between shortened `<div>`*s*

The shortened `<div>`s will also run down the page, and there will be nothing beside them. Block-level elements start their own line, and any content that follows also starts its own line, so the text remains between.

The plain boxes that follow this normal flow behavior are referred to as *statically positioned*. It's unnecessary to include this declaration in your ruleset because it's the default value. However, you did include it, you would write it as follows:

```
.wee {
  position: static;
  padding: 10px;
  margin: 5px;
  background-color: #fff;
  border: 1px solid #000;
  width: 20%;
}
```

An element may also be positioned as relative, absolute, or fixed. Each of these values describes a different positioning behavior than the default behavior of static flow. To demonstrate, we'll keep the XHTML the same, apart from one change: The first <div> will be given a new class to apply a new position value to. The rest of the <div>s will remain static to show normal flow for comparison.

```
<body>
  <div class="different">1</div>
  <div class="wee">2</div>
  <div class="wee">3</div>
  <div class="wee">4</div>
</body>
```

Relative Position

Relative positioning does two things. It offsets the box from where it would have been placed as a static box, and it also preserves the space left behind. By "preserves," we mean the other elements in the flow react as if the box is still in the position it was offset from (see Figure 8-5).

```
.different {
  position: relative;
  top: 25px;
  right: 25px;
  padding: 10px;
  margin: 5px;
  background-color: #fff;
  border: 1px solid #000;
  width: 20%;
}
```

Figure 8-5. Relative positioning of the first <div>

The offset value is inserted where declared by the property. Hence top: 25px means that 25 pixels are inserted above the <div> to push it down from the static position, and right: 25px pushes the <div> 25 pixels to the left. Similarly, a bottom value would push up, and left would push right. This sounds a little back-to-front, but the property is stating where the value is inserted, not the direction in which the element is moved. For example, using bottom and left would give the following results (see Figure 8-6):

```
.different {
    position: relative;
    bottom: 25px;
    left: 25px;
    padding: 10px;
    margin: 5px;
    background-color: #fff;
    border: 1px solid #000;
    width: 20%;
}
```

Figure 8-6. More relative positioning of the first <div>

Absolute Position

Absolute positioning completely removes the <div> from the document flow. It's positioned in relation to its containing block, and other elements act as if it isn't there.

The containing block of an absolutely positioned <div> is its nearest ancestral element with a position *other* than static. Where there is no such ancestral element, as is often the case, the containing block is the root element of your document, meaning the <html> element rather than the <body> element; hence the <body> margins don't affect the placement of an absolutely positioned <div>.

Keep in mind that *statically positioned* is the term for plain <div>s following normal flow behavior, and it doesn't mean they're fixed to anything. *Absolute* and *fixed* positioned <div>s, however, *do* display fixed behaviors, but they aren't *static* in name.

```
.different {
  position: absolute;
  top: 25px;
  right: 25px;
  padding: 10px;
  margin: 5px;
  background-color: #fff;
  border: 1px solid #000;
  width: 20%;
}
```

Figures 8-7 and 8-8 illustrate absolute positioning of the first <div>.

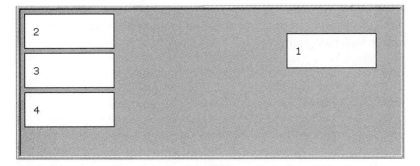

Figure 8-7. Absolute positioning of the first <div>

```
.different {
  position: absolute;
  bottom: 25px;
  left: 25px;
  padding: 10px;
  margin: 5px;
  background-color: #fff;
  border: 1px solid #000;
  width: 20%;
}
```

Figure 8-8. More absolute positioning of the first `<div>`

Fixed Position

Fixed position is absolute position with a difference: The containing block is now the viewport, not the `<html>`. This means that as you scroll a document, the `<div>` stays put on the screen.

To have this example make practical sense, let's replace the three static `<div>`s with some long paragraphs:

```
<body>
<div class="different">1</div>
<p>Lorem ipsum dolor sit amet, consectetuer adipiscing elit, sed diam nonummy
nibh euismod tincidunt ut laoreet dolore magna aliquam erat volutpat. Ut wisi
enim ad minim veniam, quis nostrud exercitation ulliam corper suscipit lobortis
nisl ut aliquip ex ea commodo consequat. Duis autem veleum iriure dolor in
hendrerit in vulputate velit esse molestie consequat, vel willum lunombro dolore
eu feugiat nulla facilisis at vero eros et accumsan et iusto odio dignissim qui
blandit praesent luptatum zzril delenit augue duis dolore te feugait nulla
facilisi. </p>
<p>Li Europan lingues es membres del sam familie. Lor separat existentie es un
myth. Por scientie, musica, sport etc., li tot Europa usa li sam vocabularium.
```

Li lingues differe solmen in li grammatica, li pronunciation e li plu commun
vocabules. Omnicos directe al desirabilitá de un nov lingua franca: on refusa
continuar payar custosi traductores. It solmen va esser necessi far uniform
grammatica, pronunciation e plu sommun paroles. </p>
<p>Ma quande lingues coalesce, li grammatica del resultant lingue es plu simplic e
regulari quam ti del coalescent lingues. Li nov lingua franca va esser plu simplic
e regulari quam li existent Europan lingues. It va esser tam simplic quam
Occidental: in fact, it va esser Occidental. A un Angleso it va semblar un
simplificat Angles, quam un skeptic Cambridge amico dit me que Occidental es. </p>
</body>

The CSS is as before, but with a fixed position declared for the box. A hefty
margin has been added to the paragraphs so that they clear this box, which they
can't "see" because a fixed box is an absolute type and is thus removed from the
flow (see Figures 8-9 through 8-11).

```
p {
  margin-left: 30%;
}
.different {
  position: fixed;
  top: 0px;
  left: 0px;
  padding: 10px;
  margin: 5px;
  background-color: #fff;
  border: 1px solid #000;
  width: 20%;
}
```

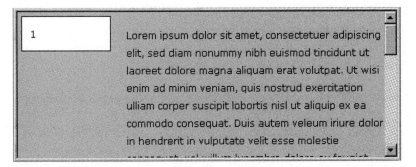

Figure 8-9. Scrolling . . .

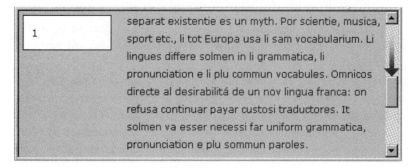

Figure 8-10. . . . scrolling . . .

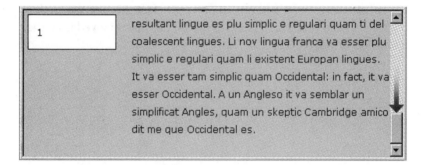

Figure 8-11. . . . scrolled. Yet the <div> *stays put.*

Float

float is a property itself, not a value of the position property.

Floated elements are taken out of normal flow, but not removed from it entirely, and the other elements remain aware of the floated element. A floated element literally "floats" up in the flow, and then over in whichever direction is stated in the property. A paragraph following a floated box will have its words wrap around it (see Figure 8-12).

```
<body>
<div class="wee">1</div>
<p>Lorem ipsum dolor sit amet, consectetuer adipiscing elit, sed diam nonummy
nibh euismod tincidunt ut laoreet dolore magna aliquam erat volutpat. Ut wisi
enim ad minim veniam, quis nostrud exercitation ulliam corper suscipit lobortis
nisl ut aliquip ex ea commodo consequat. Duis autem veleum iriure dolor in
hendrerit in vulputate velit esse molestie consequat, vel willum lunombro dolore
eu feugiat nulla facilisis at vero eros et accumsan et iusto odio dignissim qui
blandit praesent luptatum zzril delenit augue duis dolore te feugait nulla
facilisi.</p>
</body>
```

```
.wee {
  float: left;
  padding: 10px;
  margin: 5px;
  background-color: #fff;
  border: 1px solid #000;
  width: 20%;
}
p {
  margin: 5px;
  padding: 10px;
}
```

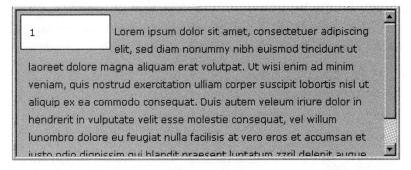

Figure 8-12. Text wrapping around a floated <div>

There is something to watch out for, however. Only the content of this paragraph is wrapped around our box. Any border, background image, or background color will extend under the box, as these aspects will always form a rectangle around their content (see Figure 8-13).

```
.wee {
  float: left;
  padding: 10px;
  margin: 5px;
  background-color: #fff;
  border: 1px solid #000;
  width: 20%;
}
p {
  margin: 5px;
  padding: 10px;
  background-color: #fff;
}
```

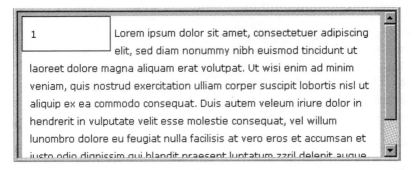

Figure 8-13. The text background doesn't wrap, but forms a rectangle.

If this wrapping behavior isn't a desired effect, then you have the option of applying the clear property to the following element, for either the left or right side, or for both. Once cleared, the words will now appear below the preceding floated element (see Figure 8-14).

```
.wee {
    float: left;
    padding: 10px;
    margin: 5px;
    background-color: #fff;
    border: 1px solid #000;
    width: 20%;
}
p {
    clear: left;
    margin: 5px;
    padding: 10px;
}
```

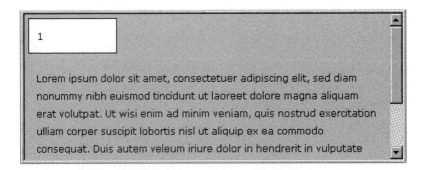

Figure 8-14. The clear property applied to text

When a floated box follows text in the XHTML document, it acts as a normal block element and starts its own line. The text doesn't wrap around it (see Figure 8-15). The following floating element can rise no higher than the natural bottom of its preceding element.

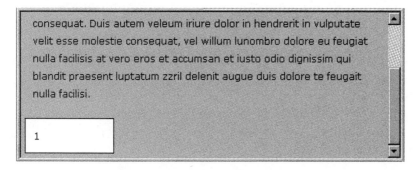

Figure 8-15. No wrap for a following <div>

Now let's use a series of floated boxes. To all of these we'll apply the same class, floating left:

```
<body>
  <div class="wee">1</div>
  <div class="wee">2</div>
  <div class="wee">3</div>
  <div class="wee">4</div>
</body>

.wee {
  float: left;
  padding: 10px;
  margin: 5px;
  background-color: #fff;
  border: 1px solid #000;
  width: 15%;
}
```

Figure 8-16 shows the result.

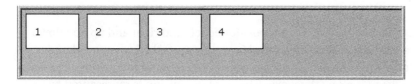

Figure 8-16. Float left

The first box floats as high as it can and then to the left. Each following box is placed as high as the preceding box and no higher, and as far left as margins will allow. If we change the float value to right

```
.wee {
  float: right;
  padding: 10px;
  margin: 5px;
  background-color: #fff;
  border: 1px solid #000;
  width: 15%;
}
```

we get the result shown in Figure 8-17.

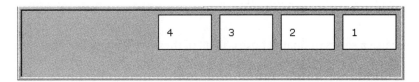

Figure 8-17. Float right

Notice how the fourth <div> is on the left? That's because the first box now floats as high as it can and then to the right, *then* the second box is placed as high as the preceding box, and as far right as the margins will allow. The third and fourth boxes follow in the same way. Layout in this manner takes the linear order of your XHTML and inverts it against the convention of left-to-right reading. Not all information will be flexible enough to mean the same both forward and backward, so a caution is in order for applying a series of right floats.

Before we leave the basic float property, do note that all of our floated boxes have a declared width. This wasn't optional convenience. The CSS specification requires an explicit width for a floated box. This can be set using the width property or considered understood by the intrinsic width that exists for a replaced element such as <img> or <object>.

Z-Index

CSS lets you declare how <div>s are positioned left and right and up and down on a screen, and it also lets you control how they're stacked when overlapping. In geometry, positioning left or right is commonly referred to as along the x-axis, and up and down is along the y-axis. The third dimension is represented by a z-axis; in our case, the apparent position between your eyes and the screen.

Setting the *z-index* declares what element will be on top in an overlap. The basic idea is pretty straightforward: An element with a larger number will be closer to you than an element with a smaller number.

In the following example, each <div> is absolutely positioned with reference to the top-left corner of the containing element, in this case <html>, which matches our viewport. The <div> background colors are alternated for visibility. No z-index has been set yet.

```
<body>
    <div id="one">1</div>
    <div id="two">2</div>
    <div id="three">3</div>
    <div id="four">4</div>
</body>

#one {
    position: absolute;
    top: 10px;
    left: 10px;
    padding: 10px;
    background-color: #fff;
    border: 1px solid #000;
    width: 20%;
}
#two {
    position: absolute;
    top: 40px;
    left: 40px;
    padding: 10px;
    background-color: #ccc;
    border: 1px solid #000;
    width: 20%;
}
#three {
    position: absolute;
    top: 70px;
    left: 70px;
    padding: 10px;
    background-color: #fff;
    border: 1px solid #000;
    width: 20%;
}
#four {
```

```
        position: absolute;
        top: 100px;
        left: 100px;
        padding: 10px;
        background-color: #ccc;
        border: 1px solid #000;
        width: 20%;
}
```

Figure 8-18 shows the result.

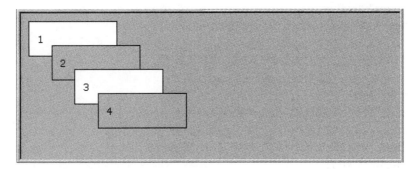

Figure 8-18. One example of default overlap

Because no individual z-index was set, and because all of these boxes belong to the same containing element, they've been stacked one on top of the other in the order in which they appear in the XHTML. Think of it as laying playing cards on a table.

Now, on *my* browser that's how it looks, and it's likely that it looks like this on *your* browser too. But it should be mentioned that this time the CSS specification has left the default interpretation open to the browser makers. A browser maker may decide that the first box should be on top and following boxes should appear underneath. So anytime you're going to have overlapping elements, make sure you declare their z-indexes in order to retain control.

If you give two boxes the same z-index, they'll follow the browser maker's default as above. If you declare a positive z-index for one box and none for the other, the box with the z-index will be on top, regardless of the order in which the boxes appear in the document. If you declare a negative index for one box and none for the other, the box with the z-index will be positioned below the others, regardless of document order.

However, *don't* use negative z-index values. It's useful, valid CSS, but Mozilla-based browsers will place that box behind the canvas, where no one will ever see it.

So to keep things easy for yourself, remember to always declare the z-index of overlapping boxes and never use negative z-index values. With these caveats in mind, let's proceed to apply values:

```css
#one {
  position: absolute;
  top: 10px;
  left: 10px;
  z-index: 4;
  padding: 10px;
  background-color: #fff;
  border: 1px solid #000;
  width: 20%;
}
#two {
  position: absolute;
  top: 40px;
  left: 40px;
  z-index: 3;
  padding: 10px;
  background-color: #ccc;
  border: 1px solid #000;
  width: 20%;
}
#three {
  position: absolute;
  top: 70px;
  left: 70px;
  z-index: 2;
  padding: 10px;
  background-color: #fff;
  border: 1px solid #000;
  width: 20%;
}
#four {
  position: absolute;
  top: 100px;
  left: 100px;
  z-index: 1;
  padding: 10px;
  background-color: #ccc;
  border: 1px solid #000;
  width: 20%;
}
```

Figure 8-19 shows the result.

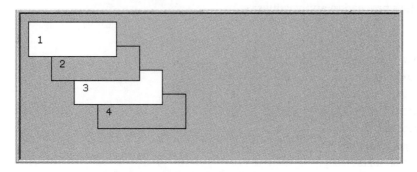

Figure 8-19. Overlap controlled by z-index

Next, we've done the same thing but have given the second <div> a very large z-index value. This doesn't place the box any "closer" than it would be if the value were only one digit larger than all the other z-indexes. The visual result is the same whether you use 5 or 300, but a large figure is useful when you wish to set a z-index value that you'll be unlikely to accidentally trump while adjusting other z-indexes in a complex layout.

```
#one {
    position: absolute;
    top: 10px;
    left: 10px;
    z-index: 4;
    padding: 10px;
    background-color: #fff;
    border: 1px solid #000;
    width: 20%;
}
#two {
    position: absolute;
    top: 40px;
    left: 40px;
    z-index: 300;
    padding: 10px;
    background-color: #ccc;
    border: 1px solid #000;
    width: 20%;
}
```

```
#three {
  position: absolute;
  top: 70px;
  left: 70px;
  z-index: 2;
  padding: 10px;
  background-color: #fff;
  border: 1px solid #000;
  width: 20%;
}
#four {
  position: absolute;
  top: 100px;
  left: 100px;
  z-index: 1;
  padding: 10px;
  background-color: #ccc;
  border: 1px solid #000;
  width: 20%;
}
```

Figure 8-20 shows the result.

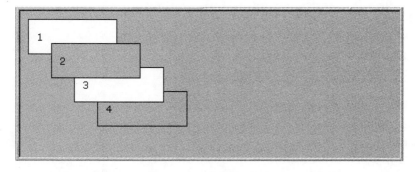

Figure 8-20. Further overlap controlled by z-index

The preceding examples show how the z-index works when all the <div>s have the same containing element. Things change a little when different containing elements are involved. An individual <div>'s z-index relates to its siblings. Where children of different parents overlap, it's not their own z-index values that decide which is on top, but those of their parents.

Let's nest the boxes into two parent-child sets:

```
<body>
  <div id="one">1<div id="two">2</div></div>
  <div id="four">4<div id="three">3</div></div>
</body>
```

Because absolute positioning relates to the containing element, we've adjusted these values for the children to keep them in place, but we've left all widths at 20% so you can see easily which boxes are the children.

```
#one {
  position: absolute;
  top: 10px;
  left: 10px;
  z-index: 1;
  padding: 10px;
  background-color: #fff;
  border: 1px solid #000;
  width: 20%;
}
#two {
  position: absolute;
  top: 30px;
  left: 30px;
  z-index: 300;
  padding: 10px;
  background-color: #ccc;
  border: 1px solid #000;
  width: 20%;
}
#three {
  position: absolute;
  top: -30px;
  left: -30px;
  z-index: 3;
  padding: 10px;
  background-color: #fff;
  border: 1px solid #000;
  width: 20%;
}
#four {
  position: absolute;
  top: 100px;
  left: 100px;
  z-index: 4;
```

```
    padding: 10px;
    background-color: #ccc;
    border: 1px solid #000;
    width: 20%;
}
```

Figure 8-21 shows the result.

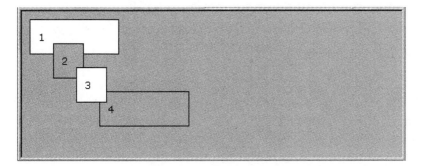

Figure 8-21. Complex overlap controlled by z-index

Box 2 has a z-index of 300 and box 3 has a z-index of 3, yet box 3 is on top. That's because box 2 and box 3 aren't siblings. The z-indexes that decide the overlap sequence here are those of their parents, which *are* siblings. In this case, box 4 (the parent of box 3) has a greater z-index than box 1 (the parent of box 2).

Z-index is a fairly simple concept, but getting it to work in a fairly complex layout can sometimes be confusing, so we've taken some time explaining this one. If things aren't turning out on the page the way you expect, then reexamine the ancestral sequence of your design. There's a good chance you're applying your desired z-index to the wrong <div>.

Had enough theory? We have. Let's combine it into page layouts.

Box Sets

This section covers a few common web page layouts, from a simple, single box through combinations of columns and rows. The intention is to show a number of possible desirable techniques, not to show the "best" or only way to achieve these layouts. As in the previous section, the rulesets may not give the same result on your browser, because this is how the layouts *should* work. How they *actually* work is covered in Chapter 10.

Note that we use the terms "columns" and "rows" because that's what the boxes look like, not because there's any such distinction in the markup, as there is for tables. All the browser sees is positioned boxes.

Centered

Figure 8-22 shows a basic centered box—not much is happening here.

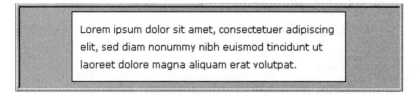

Lorem ipsum dolor sit amet, consectetuer adipiscing
elit, sed diam nonummy nibh euismod tincidunt ut
laoreet dolore magna aliquam erat volutpat.

Figure 8-22. A simple centered box

The box has a set width that is less than the window, and its right and left
margins are set to auto to center it.

```
<body>
  <div id="content">
    Lorem ipsum dolor sit amet, consectetuer adipiscing elit, sed
    diam nonummy nibh euismod tincidunt ut laoreet dolore magna
    aliquam erat volutpat.
  </div>
</body>

body {
  margin: 0px;
  padding: 0px;
  font-family: verdana, arial, helvetica, sans-serif;
  font-size: 12px;
  line-height: 22px;
  color: #000;
  background-color: #ccc;
}
#content {
  padding: 10px;
  margin-top: 5px;
  margin-bottom: 5px;
  margin-right: auto;
  margin-left: auto;
  background-color: #fff;
  border: 1px solid #000;
  width: 70%;
}
```

Two Rows

This layout is also very simple, as shown in Figure 8-23.

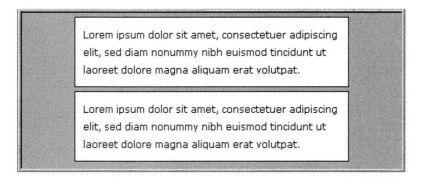

Figure 8-23. Two rows

The two rows consist of one box on top of the next as a result of the normal flow behavior of static boxes. Both boxes use exactly the same styling, and they're centered with auto side margins.

```
<body>
<div id="content">
Lorem ipsum dolor sit amet, consectetuer adipiscing elit, sed diam nonummy nibh
euismod tincidunt ut laoreet dolore magna aliquam erat volutpat.
</div>
<div id="content2">
Lorem ipsum dolor sit amet, consectetuer adipiscing elit, sed diam nonummy nibh
euismod tincidunt ut laoreet dolore magna aliquam erat volutpat.
</div>
</body>
body {
  margin: 0px;
  padding: 0px;
  font-family: verdana, arial, helvetica, sans-serif;
  font-size: 12px;
  line-height: 22px;
  color: black;
  background-color: #ccc;
}
#content {
  padding: 10px;
  margin-top: 5px;
```

```
      margin-bottom: 5px;
      margin-right: auto;
      margin-left: auto;
      background-color: #fff;
      border: 1px solid #000;
      width: 70%;
   }
#content2 {
      padding: 10px;
      margin-top: 5px;
      margin-bottom: 5px;
      margin-right: auto;
      margin-left: auto;
      background-color: #fff;
      border: 1px solid #000;
      width: 70%;
   }
```

Two Columns

You would typically use this layout for content with a menu along one side, as shown in Figure 8-24.

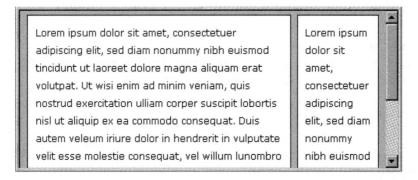

Figure 8-24. Two columns

The simple content box on the left has been given a fluid width by setting the side margins only. Its right margin is set in pixels to assure a fixed gap, and then an absolutely positioned box of fixed pixel width is set in this gap. An absolutely positioned box is useful in this application because it gives the developer more choices in presentational order. Because an absolute box is out of the document flow, the menu information may be placed either first or last in the

XHTML's linear structure, allowing the developer to optimize for aural and text browsers.

```
<body>
<div id="menu">
Lorem ipsum dolor sit amet, consectetuer adipiscing elit, sed diam nonummy nibh
euismod tincidunt ut laoreet dolore magna aliquam erat volutpat.
</div>
<div id="content">
Lorem ipsum dolor sit amet, consectetuer adipiscing elit, sed diam nonummy nibh
euismod tincidunt ut laoreet dolore magna aliquam erat volutpat. Ut wisi enim ad
minim veniam, quis nostrud exercitation ulliam corper suscipit lobortis nisl ut
aliquip ex ea commodo consequat. Duis autem veleum iriure dolor in hendrerit in
vulputate velit esse molestie consequat, vel willum lunombro dolore eu feugiat
nulla facilisis at vero eros et accumsan et iusto odio dignissim qui blandit
praesent luptatum zzril delenit augue duis dolore te feugait nulla facilisi.
</div>
</body>
```

```
body {
    margin: 0px;
    padding: 0px;
    font-family: verdana, arial, helvetica, sans-serif;
    font-size: 12px;
    line-height: 22px;
    color: #000;
    background-color: #ccc;
}
#content {
    padding: 10px;
    margin: 5px 122px 5px 5px;
    background-color: #fff;
    border: 1px solid #000;
}
#menu {
    position: absolute;
    top: 0px;
    right: 0px;
    padding: 10px;
    margin: 5px;
    background-color: #fff;
    border: 1px solid #000;
    width: 90px;
}
```

The next version is the same layout but with percentage values for the width of the menu box and for the horizontal margins and padding. By using percentages, a proportional visual effect is preserved across different size screens. In this case the sidebar will remain at 25% of total screen width, as shown in Figure 8-25.

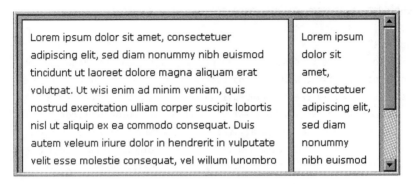

Figure 8-25. Two columns using percentage values

There is a tradeoff for this visual flexibility, though. At the illustrated width of 500px, 25% is barely wide enough to be readable. On a smaller screen it would be too narrow. By using a pixel width, narrow menu boxes can't end up too small.

```
body {
    margin: 0px;
    padding: 0px;
    font-family: verdana, arial, helvetica, sans-serif;
    font-size: 12px;
    line-height: 22px;
    color: #000;
    background-color: #ccc;
}
#content {
    padding: 10px 2% 10px 2%;
    margin: 5px 26% 5px 2%;
    background-color: #fff;
    border: 1px solid #000;
}
#menu {
    position: absolute;
    top: 0px;
    right: 0px;
```

```
    padding: 10px 2% 10px 2%;
    margin: 5px 2% 5px 1%;
    background-color: #fff;
    border: 1px solid #000;
    width: 18%;
}
```

Three Columns

This is a very common form for Web documents at the moment: body text bracketed by a pair of sidebars for links and commentary. Figure 8-26 illustrates this form.

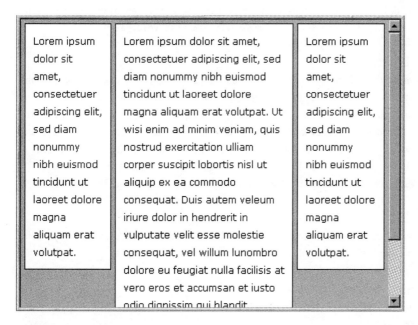

Figure 8-26. Three columns

In this example, the center box is a static box in normal flow with fixed side margins to leave space for absolutely positioned side columns, each of fixed width. As browser-window size varies, the large center box contracts or expands. It's a robust layout that retains its arrangement across screen sizes and has two absolutes that can accept content originating from anywhere in the XHTML sequence.

Note that the side boxes end before the middle box does. The height of each box is set by its content. You can declare a fixed or relative height for a box, but that invites trouble. A fixed height of, say, 600px, risks creating a box that won't be tall enough for its content when the screen is narrow. If you declare a relative height in percentage, then that relates to the containing block.

This may sound good if you consider that the containing box is the document body and would always be at least as high as the highest box, but there's a problem with that. The specifications state that, to calculate height based on the containing block, the containing block itself must have an explicit height. This is impractical to set because we need it to expand with the content. The specifications go on to say that, when there is no explicit height for the containing block, the browser will interpret the percentage height as height: auto, which brings us back to square one with a default box height set by the box content.

Hence there is no way to declare, "Have all boxes share the height of the longest box." The individual boxes will have individual heights.

```
<div id="left">
Lorem ipsum dolor sit amet, consectetuer adipiscing elit, sed diam nonummy nibh
euismod tincidunt ut laoreet dolore magna aliquam erat volutpat.
</div>
<div id="middle">
Lorem ipsum dolor sit amet, consectetuer adipiscing elit, sed diam nonummy nibh
euismod tincidunt ut laoreet dolore magna aliquam erat volutpat. Ut wisi enim ad
minim veniam, quis nostrud exercitation ulliam corper suscipit lobortis nisl ut
aliquip ex ea commodo consequat. Duis autem veleum iriure dolor in hendrerit in
vulputate velit esse molestie consequat, vel willum lunombro dolore eu feugiat
nulla facilisis at vero eros et accumsan et iusto odio dignissim qui blandit
praesent luptatum zzril delenit augue duis dolore te feugait nulla facilisi.
</div>
<div id="right">
Lorem ipsum dolor sit amet, consectetuer adipiscing elit, sed diam nonummy nibh
euismod tincidunt ut laoreet dolore magna aliquam erat volutpat.
</div>
body { margin: 0px; padding: 0px;
    font-family: verdana, arial, helvetica, sans-serif;
    font-size: 12px;
    line-height: 22px;
    color: #000;
    background-color: #ccc;

}
#left {
    position: absolute;
    top: 0px;
    left: 0px;
    margin: 5px;
    padding: 10px;
```

```
  border: 1px solid #000;
  background-color: #fff;
  width: 90px;
}
#middle {
  margin: 5px 122px 5px 122px;
  padding: 10px;
  border: 1px solid #000;
  background-color: #fff;
}
#right {
  position: absolute;
  top: 0px;
  right: 0px;
  margin: 5px;
  padding: 10px;
  border: 1px solid #000;
  background-color: #fff;
  width: 90px;
}
```

Figure 8-27 shows the same layout with less content in the middle box for comparison.

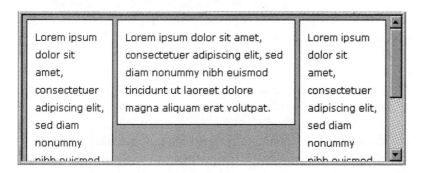

Figure 8-27. Box length reflects box content

Three Columns Plus Top Row

An additional top box (see Figure 8-28) allows a title to span all the columns for more emphasis, or it could be used to contain a logo and possibly a global navigation bar.

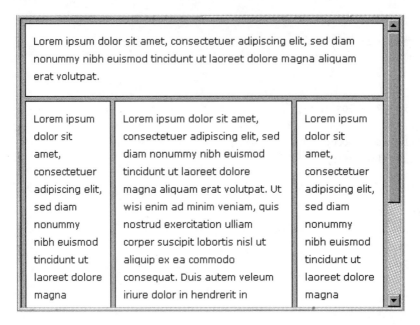

Figure 8-28. Three columns plus top row

The top box and the middle box in this case are both static boxes set in normal flow, just as in the earlier two-row example. The middle box also has large fixed margins to provide spaces for the pair of absolute box side columns, as was done for the three-column example. These absolute boxes have top margin values set to equal the vertical sum of the top box's height, padding, borders, and margins, in order to clear the top box and begin at the same height as the middle box.

This layout is essentially two normal boxes forming a T-shape, with a pair of absolute boxes set in the blank side areas. Because there are two types of boxes below the spanning top box, two techniques were used to accommodate it.

Note that both the top box height and the side columns' top margins are fixed in pixels. Because the side columns are absolute and thus out of the flow, there's no way to give them a relative top margin that can relate to a varying top box height. Because of the top box's fixed height, we have to take care that it's tall enough that its content won't cause overflow, either from a large font size added in a restyle or by the content being wrapped on a narrow screen.

```
<body>
<div id="top">
Lorem ipsum dolor sit amet, consectetuer adipiscing elit, sed diam nonummy nibh
euismod tincidunt ut laoreet dolore magna aliquam erat volutpat.
</div>
<div id="left">
Lorem ipsum dolor sit amet, consectetuer adipiscing elit, sed diam nonummy nibh
```

euismod tincidunt ut laoreet dolore magna aliquam erat volutpat.
</div>
<div id="middle">
Lorem ipsum dolor sit amet, consectetuer adipiscing elit, sed diam nonummy nibh
euismod tincidunt ut laoreet dolore magna aliquam erat volutpat. Ut wisi enim ad
minim veniam, quis nostrud exercitation ulliam corper suscipit lobortis nisl ut
aliquip ex ea commodo consequat. Duis autem veleum iriure dolor in hendrerit in
vulputate velit esse molestie consequat, vel willum lunombro dolore eu feugiat
nulla facilisis at vero eros et accumsan et iusto odio dignissim qui blandit
praesent luptatum zzril delenit augue duis dolore te feugait nulla facilisi.
</div>
<div id="right">
Lorem ipsum dolor sit amet, consectetuer adipiscing elit, sed diam nonummy nibh
euismod tincidunt ut laoreet dolore magna aliquam erat volutpat.
</div>
</body>

```
body {
    margin: 0px;
    padding: 0px;
    font-family: verdana, arial, helvetica, sans-serif;
    font-size: 12px;
    line-height: 22px;
    color: black;
    background-color: #ccc;
}
#top {
    margin: 5px;
    padding: 10px;
    background-color: #fff;
    border: 1px solid #000;
    height: 70px;
}
#left {
    position: absolute;
    top: 97px;
    left: 0px;
    margin: 5px;
    padding: 10px;
    background-color: #fff;
    border: 1px solid #000;
    width: 90px;
}
```

```
#middle {
  margin: 0px 122px 5px 122px;
  padding: 10px;
  background-color: #fff;
  border: 1px solid #000;
}
#right {
  position: absolute;
  top: 97px;
  right: 0px;
  margin: 5px;
  padding: 10px;
  background-color: #fff;
  border: 1px solid #000;
  width: 90px;
}
```

Three Columns Plus Top and Bottom Rows

Because we're building with regular complexity in each example, you may be expecting this layout to be the preceding layout plus a window-wide box across the bottom. It's not. You can't do that.

Well, you *can* do it, but not reliably. The problem is that the absolutely positioned side boxes we're using are out of the flow. A spanning bottom box will be vertically positioned by the margin between it and the middle box in normal flow. If the absolute side boxes then become longer than the middle box due to varied content or different screen widths, they'll overlap the ends of the wide bottom box, leaving us with a mess.

We can't use an absolutely positioned bottom box either, as the column boxes will vary in length with screen size—there's no way to figure out where "bottom" is other than by remaining in the flow so other boxes can be sensed. Because the sides are absolutes and can't be sensed, that leaves only the middle box, and the bottom box is limited in width just as the middle box is to clear the absolutes.

So, the only reliable option is to have three normal boxes forming a T, with a pair of absolute side columns in the gaps:

```
<body>
<div id="top">
Lorem ipsum dolor sit amet, consectetuer adipiscing elit, sed diam nonummy nibh
euismod tincidunt ut laoreet dolore magna aliquam erat volutpat.
</div>
```

```
<div id="left">
Lorem ipsum dolor sit amet, consectetuer adipiscing elit, sed diam nonummy nibh
euismod tincidunt ut laoreet dolore magna aliquam erat volutpat.
</div>
<div id="middle">
Lorem ipsum dolor sit amet, consectetuer adipiscing elit, sed diam nonummy nibh
euismod tincidunt ut laoreet dolore magna aliquam erat volutpat. Ut wisi enim ad
minim veniam, quis nostrud exercitation ulliam corper suscipit lobortis nisl ut
</div>
<div id="right">
Lorem ipsum dolor sit amet, consectetuer adipiscing elit, sed diam nonummy nibh
euismod tincidunt ut laoreet dolore magna aliquam erat volutpat.
</div>
<div id="bottom">
Lorem ipsum dolor sit amet,
</div>
</body>
body {
    margin: 0px;
    padding: 0px;
    font-family: verdana, arial, helvetica, sans-serif;
    font-size: 12px;
    line-height: 22px;
    color: #000;
    background-color: #ccc;
}
#top {
    margin: 5px;
    padding: 10px;
    background-color: #fff;
    border: 1px solid #000;
    height: 70px;
}
#left {
    position: absolute;
    top: 97px;
    left: 0px;
    margin: 5px;
    padding: 10px;
    background-color: #fff;
    border: 1px solid #000;
    width: 90px;
}
```

```
#middle {
  margin: 0px 122px 5px 122px;
  padding: 10px;
  background-color: #fff;
  border: 1px solid #000;
}
#right {
  position: absolute;
  top: 97px;
  right: 0px;
  margin: 5px;
  padding: 10px;
  background-color: #fff;
  border: 1px solid #000;
  width: 90px;
}
#bottom {
  margin: 5px 122px 5px 122px;
  padding: 10px;
  background-color: #fff;
   border: 1px solid #000;
}
```

Figure 8-29 shows the result.

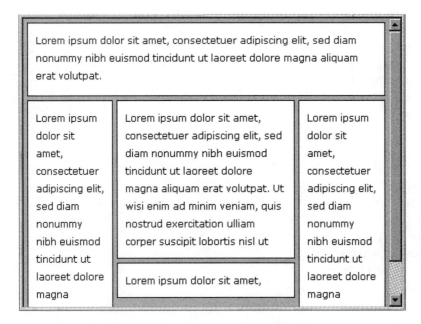

Figure 8-29. Three columns plus top and bottom rows

Next let's step back from spreading outward with additional boxes and add a little visual density instead.

Nested

A nested box like the one shown in Figure 8-30 is handy to separate portions of text.

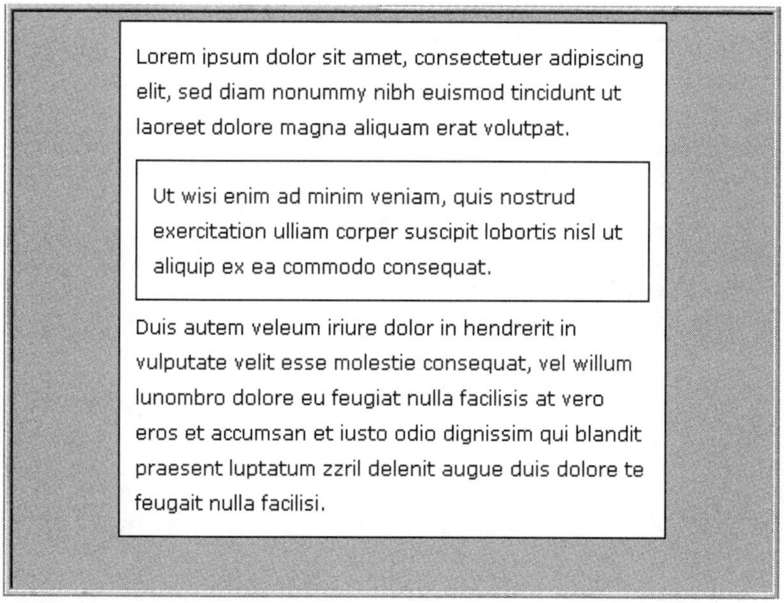

Figure 8-30. Nested box

Because it's a style that's likely to be reused, we've made it a class rather than an id. The ruleset is straightforward, with only margin, padding, and border values being created. The box takes its position from normal flow, its width from the space available within the parent element's padding, and its height from its own content. We've set its side margins to 0 so that its borders line up with the text edges of the greater body.

```
<body>
<div id="content">
Lorem ipsum dolor sit amet, consectetuer adipiscing elit, sed diam nonummy nibh
euismod tincidunt ut laoreet dolore magna aliquam erat volutpat.
<div class="innerBox">
Ut wisi enim ad minim veniam, quis nostrud exercitation ulliam corper suscipit
lobortis nisl ut aliquip ex ea commodo consequat.
</div>
```

Duis autem veleum iriure dolor in hendrerit in vulputate velit esse molestie consequat, vel willum lunombro dolore eu feugiat nulla facilisis at vero eros et accumsan et iusto odio dignissim qui blandit praesent luptatum zzril delenit augue duis dolore te feugait nulla facilisi.

```
</div>
</body>
body {
  margin: 0px;
  padding: 0px;
  font-family: verdana, arial, helvetica, sans-serif;
  font-size: 12px;
  line-height: 22px;
  color: black;
  background-color: #ccc;
}
.innerBox {
  padding: 10px;
  margin: 10px 0px 5px 0px;
  border: 1px solid #000;
}
#content {
  padding: 10px;
  margin-top: 5px;
  margin-bottom: 5px;
  margin-right: auto;
  margin-left: auto;
  background-color: #fff;
  border: 1px solid #000;
  width: 70%;
}
```

Bottom Again

Akin to using nested boxes for setting off text, it's common to have a navigation bar or copyright information at the bottom of a page, as shown in Figure 8-31. This can be neatly separated with a dedicated box, which in turn has a distinct ID selector that allows quick restyling of a sitewide element.

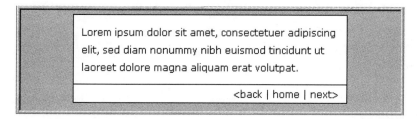

Figure 8-31. Dedicated bottom box

Here we've used a static box that matches the one above it, set the margins between them to 0, and then eliminated the top border of the bottom box. The single-pixel dividing line is actually the bottom border of the top box. You can just as easily reverse things and use the top border of the bottom box as the divider.

```
<body>
<div id="content">
Lorem ipsum dolor sit amet, consectetuer adipiscing elit, sed diam nonummy nibh
euismod tincidunt ut laoreet dolore magna aliquam erat volutpat.
</div>
<div id="navBar">
&lt;back | home | next&gt;
</div>
</body>
body {
    margin: 0px;
    padding: 0px;
    font-family: verdana, arial, helvetica, sans-serif;
    font-size: 12px;
    line-height: 22px;
    color: black;
    background-color: #ccc;
  }
#content {
    padding: 10px;
    margin-top: 5px;
    margin-bottom: 0px;
    margin-right: auto;
    margin-left: auto;
    background-color: #fff;
    border: 1px solid #000;
    width: 70%;
}
```

```
#navBar {
  padding: 0px 10px 0px 10px;
  margin-top: 0px;
  margin-bottom: 5px;
  margin-right: auto;
  margin-left: auto;
  background-color: #fff;
  border-top: 0px;
  border-bottom: 1px solid #000;
  border-left: 1px solid #000;
  border-right: 1px solid #000;
  width: 70%;
  text-align: right;
}
```

Background Images

One of the nice things about CSS is the ability to put background images in any individual box, not just in the whole body (see Figure 8-32). Because these images are linked from the stylesheet and not the XHTML, you should limit their use to decorative elements suited to your screen presentation. Any images that convey key information should remain in your XHTML.

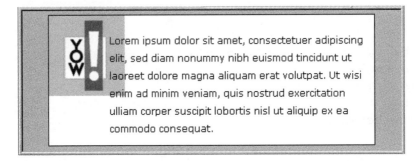

Figure 8-32. Background image

A background image doesn't interfere with a <div>'s content in any way. It's as innocuous as background color, which it's related to. In this example we need to adjust the box padding to align the content with the background image:

```
#content {
  padding: 20px 10px 10px 80px;
  margin-top: 5px;
  margin-bottom: 5px;
```

```
    margin-right: auto;
    margin-left: auto;
    background-color: #fff;
    border: 1px solid #000;
    width: 70%;
    background-image: url(../img/fun.gif);
    background-repeat: no-repeat;
    background-position: top left;
}
```

Notice that the preceding rule that states no-repeat. By default, a background image is repeated for a wallpaper effect. You may also declare that the image only be repeated horizontally or vertically. This

```
background-repeat: repeat-x;
```

will repeat the image horizontally, and this

```
background-repeat: repeat-y;
```

will repeat the image vertically.

You can also control where a background image is placed within a box. In the example we've specified background-position: top left.

For this property there are two values that act in combination. One handles vertical with top, center, or bottom, and the other handles horizontal with left, center, or right. You can use them together in either order, and you can use shorthand single declarations:

- top is the same as top center

- right is the same as right center

- bottom is the same as bottom center

- left is the same as left center

- center is the same as center center

You may also use percentage figures instead of words. 0% is the top-left corner, and 100% 100% is the bottom-right. And if that's not enough, you may use distance measures such as px, em, pt, and cm. The em unit is handy when aligning images with text blocks; pt and cm are best used in stylesheets for printing. You may also combine percentage and distance units when that better suits your needs.

It's a very flexible system, and there's still more. You can also declare whether a background image scrolls with the document or stays fixed in place with the viewport as the document scrolls past, by using either of these two rules:

```
background-attachment: scroll;
background-attachment: fixed;
```

scroll is the normal behavior you'll be accustomed to, and because it's the default behavior, you needn't specify it. But fixed is quite different, and you should think ahead if you wish to use it.

For fixed, the background image remains fixed relative to the viewport as you scroll the document. When such an image is used in short boxes on a long page, your reader can scroll into a position where the image has become invisible because the box edge has scrolled past it. The image will only be visible while within the confines of its box, and where it passes these edges it effectively slips behind all other backgrounds.

All of the background properties may also be combined into one shorthand ruleset. The preceding example would be expressed as follows:

```
background: url(../img/fun.gif) #fff top left no-repeat;
```

Cleanliness

Although CSS positioning uses a box model, you don't have to show it off. Consider Figure 8-33.

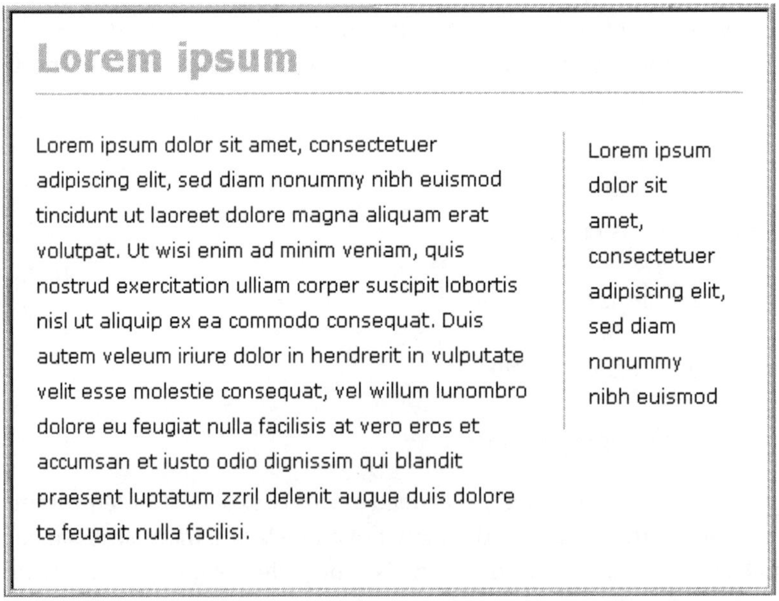

Figure 8-33. Boxes below the surface

For this example I first wrote a three-box layout without any box background colors or borders declared. The body color supplied a unified background for the entire page, while the contents retained distinction through margins and padding. Next I added a thin bottom border to the top box for a single fine line right across the page beneath the title, and then I set the top box's left padding to 0 so the title would start directly above this border.

I then experimented with a dividing line between the content and sidebar boxes. I tried both a right border of the content box and a left border of the sidebar, to see if I preferred a line that ran the remaining length of the page or one that only ran alongside the shorter sidebar content. I also exchanged both top padding and top margin of the sidebar box to see if I preferred having the vertical divider touch the horizontal one or start somewhat below. This time I decided I liked having it start at the same height as the main content text, but slightly above the beginning of the sidebar text.

But I used neither top padding nor top margin to achieve this in the end. Instead I used the absolute positioning in combination with the font's line-height. Why? Well, why not? There are so many variables in CSS that you usually have a number of ways to achieve any given layout idea.

In short, I just played around with it as ideas came to me. Which is what I hope you'll do because that's the best way to get familiar with all the options. By using your editor as a sketchpad to adjust and change variables, while you click the Refresh button on your browser to see what happens, you'll help yourself get past the hesitant abstraction stage of layout and into a comfortable fluency with it.

```html
<body>
<div id="top">
<h1>Lorem ipsum</h1>
</div>
<div id="content">
Lorem ipsum dolor sit amet, consectetuer adipiscing elit, sed diam nonummy nibh
euismod tincidunt ut laoreet dolore magna aliquam erat volutpat. Ut wisi enim ad
minim veniam, quis nostrud exercitation ulliam corper suscipit lobortis nisl ut
aliquip ex ea commodo consequat. Duis autem veleum iriure dolor in hendrerit in
vulputate velit esse molestie consequat, vel willum lunombro dolore eu feugiat
nulla facilisis at vero eros et accumsan et iusto odio dignissim qui blandit
praesent luptatum zzril delenit augue duis dolore te feugait nulla facilisi.
</div>
<div id="sidebar">
Lorem ipsum dolor sit amet, consectetuer adipiscing elit, sed diam nonummy
nibh euismod
</div>
</body>
body {
  margin: 0px;
  padding: 0px;
  font-family: verdana, arial, helvetica, sans-serif;
```

```
    font-size: 12px;
    line-height: 22px;
    color: #000;
    background-color: #fff;
}
#top {
    margin: 5px 15px 0px 15px;
    padding: 10px 10px 10px 0px;
    color: #ccc;
    border-bottom: 1px solid #ccc;
    height: 25px;
}
#content {
    margin: 0px 122px 0px 5px;
    padding: 20px 10px 20px 10px;
}
#sidebar {
    position: absolute;
    top: 75px;
    right: 0px;
    margin: 0px 0px 5px 0px;
    padding: 0px 10px 10px 15px;
    width: 90px;
    border-left: 1px solid #ccc;
}
```

Thinking About Design

> *"Design is an art of planning. A problem is presented, a conceptual blueprint is formed in response, a solution is achieved. Style is a matter of appearance— the way something looks or feels."*

—*Paula Scher,* Make It Bigger

Web developers have been saying "the Web is not print" for years. Believe it. We're creating layouts for a fluid medium. CSS is specifically written for this task. The different capabilities of different rulesets can help you decide which to use in implementing a design, and they can also provide guidance when you're beginning afresh. In this section we cover some of the considerations that shape a plan so you'll have a starting point for your own designs.

Blank Page

When you're starting from scratch with no preset design requirement, look to your content. The XHTML document that you'll be styling already has a simple design in order to make linear sense. Because you mean to enhance the document message, you can use the existing structure to inform your CSS layout choices. First identify the basic elements of that structure and start by assigning layout <div>s to these.

A typical web page may have general content accompanied by global navigation. Simple enough. Wrap both sections in <div>s with id names that describe the content type, such as "MainContent" and "Menu." These would be ids and not classes because they're distinct elements that occur only once in the page; classes are for styles that will be reused on a number of elements. Names that describe the content type should be selected, not visual styles such as "Sidebar" or "RedBox," because the layout may be changed at a later date and such names would no longer make sense.

Now you have two boxes. Where do you put them on the page? If the global navigation in the XHTML follows the content, then you already have an order that you can use as-is or change, depending on the box type assigned.

A pair of plain static boxes will match the top-down order of the XHTML. But what if you wish to have the global navigation on top or on the sides?

You can set the widths of a pair of floats to create two columns, and the top-down order will become right-left or left-right depending on which way you choose to float. This is also where the out-of-flow nature of an absolute comes in handy. You can create a layout that deviates from the XHTML order by placing the global navigation in an absolute box and then set a margin of the content box to provide a space for it.

Fixed boxes are also out of the flow. If your global navigation is short enough that you're assured it won't be longer than a small browser window size, then you can create a sidebar for it that will stay visible while the visitor scrolls down the content. You could also make this menu <div> into a top or bottom horizontal bar that will stay visible as the visitor scrolls, as long as you set the z-index to ensure that it will always be on top of the other page content.

So you have plenty of choices. Once you identify which sections of the XHTML make distinct message divisions, these become the building blocks that you apply your positioning rules to. The way you wish to arrange these elements for the screen will suggest which box types to select to make it happen.

Preset Design

It's not uncommon to have a layout pre-assigned, either by yourself, or by an art director, or by being tasked to convert an old table layout to CSS.

In the last case there's usually more work to be done than just creating a stylesheet, so be cautious here. CSS is entirely capable of mimicking table layouts, but developer stress can arise because many pages that had been laid out with tables also ignored the structural intent of other tags as well. You know that CSS is part of a unified approach to creating accessible cross-platform web pages—an approach that begins with appropriate tags and document structure in the XHTML. Many old table pages are an irreverent tag soup, so you'll have to make clear to your client that to enjoy the full benefits of CSS, you must be assigned the likely expensive task of cleaning up all past sins. CSS layout isn't a simple window dressing or paint job in these cases.

Once proper XHTML is assured, the approach to any pre-assigned design becomes a question of how to create that layout with boxes in a flow. To illustrate the method, let's reconsider the example in the "Three Columns Plus Top Row" section of this chapter. There is no single "right" way to create this generic layout, but the characteristics of the different box types can quickly guide you to a combination that suits your needs.

Our example is essentially one box over three. Immediately it's clear that we can't create this solely from static `<div>`s, as these are block elements that would always form four boxes down the page. Relative positioning is similarly impractical, as is fixed, which produces unscrollable boxes.

We could achieve the one-box-over-three layout with four absolutely positioned boxes, as they'll sit right where we put them. Is there any reason not to?

A compromise stems from their advantage. Absolutes are easy to place anywhere on the screen because they're independent of flow and other boxes. This also makes it difficult to use them in a combination that can flex as content and screen size varies. No box would be able to sense and accommodate a change in size of another. With absolutes, this layout would be entirely rigid, which is quite the opposite of the intent of the medium and would require us to change the positioning rules every time any content is changed.

Floats present a more interesting possibility. Through a careful combination of widths we can create an entirely flexible one-box-over-three layout. The top box would be set to a width near 100% to leave no space for a box alongside. The lower three would be sized so that their total widths and margins don't exceed 100%, so that they'll share the space below the first box. Unlike the original "Three Columns Plus Top Row" example, there would be no need to set a height limit for the top box, as this entirely floated layout can expand as it needs.

Now, what are the disadvantages? Foremost with floats is that anytime the total widths of our trio add up to more than 100%, the third box will be moved below all the other boxes. For most designs this would be considered a catastrophic failure, and it can happen more easily than you might expect.

Unexpected wide content and narrow screens can trigger it, and so can an attempt at a visually precise layout. Notice that the original example has equal margins throughout. The eye is quite sharp, and discrepancies of only a few pixels would be noticed and spoil this effect. With floats, it becomes impossible to be this precise.

First, you'll find that you're restricted to setting all widths and side margins in percentages because other units aren't relative to the screen. On narrower screens, the larger equivalent percentage values of other units will create a total width exceeding 100%, and that third box will end up below.

Now, say you choose 2% margins in a combination of 2+20+2+52+2+20+2 to equal 100% total width on all screens. Two problems emerge.

That 2% margin is relative to the varying screen width. How will you create matching top margins? You have no way to specify these as 2% of screen width; you can only set them in absolute values or in values relative to screen height. As window sizes vary, your side and top margins will vary with each other, almost never being exactly the same.

Second, and quite unintuitively, a 100% total width for a layout with three boxes across will fail in most browsers by being too tight, and the third box will end up below again. Why? Probably because the browser's method for converting your % widths into the screen's pixels needed to round up a figure or two during the addition, resulting in more pixels than are actually available.

If you compensate for this by using a 99% or 98% total width, you'll now have a rather noticeable extra space on one side: 1% of an 800px screen is 8px. So although you can make three floated boxes work alongside one another, you'll be unable to make their outermost edges equal distances from the window edges or have them line up with the outside edges of the top box above.

This isn't to say that floats are bad—just that they're inappropriate to mimic our "Three Columns Plus Top Row" example. In a looser design, akin to the "Cleanliness" example, you may well have a page that can absorb this kind of variance without any ill effect. It simply depends on what your requirements are.

The "Three Columns Plus Top Row" example itself uses a combination of static and absolute boxes. This was in order to fulfill specific requirements I had when making a demonstration in the early days of CSS popularity. I wanted a complex layout that reflected the familiar precision of the printed grid that developers had been mimicking with table tags, and I wanted this layout to be quite robust so beginners could modify it easily without becoming frustrated.

Floats could have been used to make the general layout, but the result would not have had the grid-like precision desired. Also, developers new to the concept of flow would be really startled when minor modifications caused the last box to be spat down below the rest. Arguably this would be because they were trying to run before they could walk, but CSS in those days was fighting an initial reputation of being "too hard" or "unready." So I needed something that looked good, looked familiar, and would handle beginner experiments without coming apart.

Hence the T-shape of static boxes with an added pair of absolutes. It's robust, fluid overall, and the paired absolutes can take contain information from anywhere in the XHTML's order. The compromises are the fixed top-box height and the fixed sidebar widths. Because this type of layout commonly frames a simple title or logo across the top, and menu links down the sides, I decided this box construction would suit my purposes.

Which box types you use in your designs will depend on your precise requirements. To begin, consider how your layout relates to flow and what box types can achieve that. Then consider the advantages and disadvantages of the possible combinations to arrive at one design that meets your needs.

Summary

That's the basics of boxes. We covered the different positioning methods individually, then combined them into a few typical layouts, and discussed making your own designs.

CSS is a remarkably well-thought-out specification that gives us an extensive toolset for a very new fluid medium. We can create complex screen presentations that viewers and clients have come to expect without compromising the XHTML document for other media types. It's all good, rather exciting, but there's a considerable bump in our path: Popular browsers often make a real mess of perfectly valid box layouts.

CHAPTER 9

Styling Tables with CSS

TABLES, BY WHICH we mean tables of information and not layout tables, have always been a thorny typographic issue. Table design is just plain hard. Table design on the Web has its advantages (fewer problems with page size) and disadvantages (more problems with horizontal and vertical alignment, type size, and table size). Table design with CSS suffers from additional problems: There are quite a few implementation problems, and NN4 supports none of it (so if you have to develop for total NN4 parity, you might as well stop reading).

If you have to deal with real tables, then the advantages of CSS are immediate: fine-grained control, with the ability to adjust borders and padding on a per-cell, -row, or -column basis if you need to, plus the usual typographic benefits CSS gives you.

We won't go into depth about table design here; rather, we'll just identify the basic graphic variables you can control with CSS and give you enough advice to get you started toward creating good tables. It's perfectly possible to make very good tables on the Web—it's just a little more involved than you might like it to be.

The cells in the rows and columns that make up tables can largely be dealt with as you would any other kind of text block. The tricky part of dealing with tables is handling what goes between cells and the text that links cells, such as row or column headings. For the sake of simplicity, we use these distinctions and split the discussion into three sections: general advice; backgrounds; and gaps, borders, and separators.

General Advice

Tables mainly cause a problem for people when they can't establish where row and column boundaries are, so they then can't figure out what constitutes a particular row or column. It then becomes difficult for them to find their way around and difficult to cross-reference to column and row headings, as well as confusing when cell contents appear to run into one another. The main things you need to consider are the width and height of your table, how your rows and columns hang together visually, and how the rows and columns are kept separate from other rows and columns.

Caveats

There are a couple of things it's useful to talk about before we get much further: padding and margins on tables and cells. Simply put, you can have margins on <table>s, but not on cells (<td>, <th>), and you can have padding on cells, but not on tables. Space around a table is controlled, like any other block box, by margin. Space inside a <table> is controlled by a different property, which we'll come to later (much like the cellspacing HTML attribute). Space outside cells is controlled by the <table> instead, but space inside cells is controlled by padding, rather than a single attribute such as cellpadding. This gives you much greater control over space inside cells than HTML tables gave you. You can adjust the space on a per-side, per-cell basis as you require. Figure 9-1 illustrates the difference between the HTML and CSS table models.

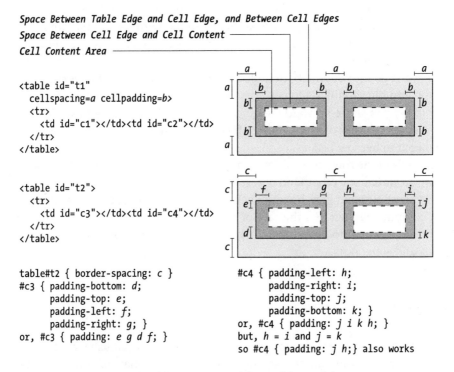

Figure 9-1. Comparison of the HTML and CSS table models

Width and Height

Dealing with the width and height issues in a table is critical to getting it to look right and work well. Too wide and the table can look entirely out of place, or even push the right side far enough out that people don't notice it's there. Too narrow and the contents can become cramped and unreadable. The context the table appears in is probably the most critical: If it's a table of figures that accompanies a long piece of continuous text, then matching the table width to the measure is the best idea, making exceptions for especially large or awkward tables. If the table is on a page with other tables (scientific results, say), then the priority would be to make the table as readable as possible.

There are no hard-and-fast rules with tables, and they're much too complex and context dependent to go into examples of good and bad tables here. The only rule worth sticking to is that you must give the table enough room to allow its contents to be easily read and navigated. If your design constraints force you into really squishing a table, then it's probably a good idea to think about splitting it into two or more tables.

Height is a much less pressing issue in web tables than in print tables, and for that reason we don't spend much time on it here. Most of the time, the only reason to tinker with the automatic height of table rows is to harmonize their appearance.

CSS provides two methods for working out how wide a table and its columns should be: a quick method that uses the widths of the table, columns, and the first row of cells, and the more involved method that looks at the whole table before it finalizes the table's appearance. Which method is used is controlled using the `table-layout` property on the `<table>` itself. `table-layout` takes the values `fixed` or `auto` (the default).

Specifying Width: Fixed Layout

In fixed-layout mode (`table-layout: fixed`) the browser is supposed to consider only the following things in working out the width of the table:

- The value of width on the `<table>` element

- The value of width on `<col>` elements

- The value of width on table cell elements, but only in the first row, and only if there wasn't a width set for the column the cell is in

If there are any columns which haven't already been considered, because they or the cell in their first row don't have their width set, then the remaining space is divided between them.

The width of the table is then the width of <table> or the sum of the column widths, whichever is larger. This is pretty straightforward, but there are a couple of caveats. First, you can't add more columns in subsequent rows; the first row must have a full complement of table cells. Second, there are differences in the way that browsers deal with cell and column widths. The browser differences are that IE 6 follows the specification, and the other browsers prioritize cell widths over column widths if the cell width is bigger than the column width, and they pay attention to widths specified on cells in subsequent rows. This isn't an enormous problem if you're careful with width declarations, but it can catch you out.

It's useful to be able to specify column width (rather than cell width) because padding on the cells isn't taken into account, the final width of the column will be the width you specified, and the cell width will be that width less the cell's padding, which is almost certainly the behavior you want if you're trying to make the table a particular width without specifying width on the <table> itself. Finally, you must remember to factor in the space between cells and border widths in your table width calculations if you're setting widths on columns.

One final thing to remember is that if you use fixed-size content (such as images) wider than your columns then, once again, browser behavior differs. In theory you can decide what happens by setting the overflow property on the table cells, but in practice only IE honors this, and it does the whole deal: If you have an overflowing image, IE will never make the table cell wider than you asked it to be, and you can hide the excess (overflow: hidden) or allow it to leak out into its surroundings (overflow: visible). IE's default behavior is to hide the excess. In the other browsers the table cell is made wider to accommodate the image.

Specifying Width: Auto Layout

Auto layout doesn't generally differ very much from fixed layout, with the exception that the browser is supposed to spend more time figuring out how to put the table together. The CSS specification doesn't mandate a particular algorithm for calculating table width using the auto method, unlike the fixed method, so there's not an awful lot to say given that in most browsers the two methods produce similar results. IE 6 is noteworthy here because of its closer adherence to the specification. Its correct behavior could be confusing if you've been testing only on another platform.

Specifying Height

Much as with table width, there are several places where you can apply the height property to influence the table height. Apart from <table> itself, there are the cell elements (<td>, <th>), plus the row (<tr>) and rowgroup (<tbody>, <thead>, <tfoot>) elements. Although not all the browsers allow you to style rowgroup elements, all but IE5/Mac and NN4 allow you to style <tr>. The total table height calculation is made by summing the row heights and comparing it to the <table>'s height. The largest wins. A rowgroup taller than its rows divides up the extra space between them. IE5/Mac behaves slightly differently. It will try and reduce row heights to fit into a specified table height, but only while the content allows this. Mozilla 1.0+/Netscape 7 and IE 6 allow rowgroups to be styled.

Hanging Together

The best way to give rows and columns some coherence is to make use of some kind of horizontal (rows) or vertical (columns) alignment. You can do this with cell borders (which we cover later), or you can do it with the edges of the text blocks in the table cells. If your design solution is robust, an awful lot of the time your tables simply won't need borders.

Vertical alignment in a row will, unless the contents of all the table cells occupy one line, mean that you won't want the cell contents to be vertically centered. A better approach is to align cell contents either to the top or bottom of the cell. Figure 9-2 shows this.

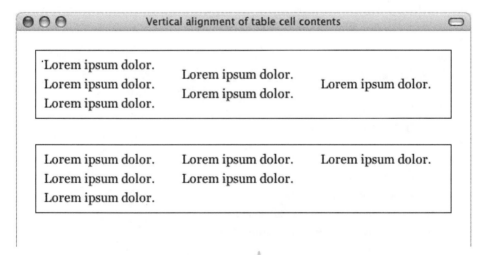

Figure 9-2. Vertical alignment of table cell contents

Vertical alignment within table cells is handled by the vertical-align property you've already encountered. It isn't exactly the same as the vertical-align property you saw when dealing with inline boxes. There are a couple of key differences: Table cells are blocks, not inline boxes, and you can't use all the values of vertical-align you can use on an inline box on a table cell. The valid values for vertical-align on table cells are top, bottom, baseline, and middle.

top, bottom, and middle are all pretty self-explanatory. baseline is a little more complex, but it's also potentially much more powerful. When baseline is specified, the browser is supposed to figure out which of the baselines of the first line in each cell is farthest from the top and then align all the first-line baselines to that farthest one. This is best explained by the following code and Figure 9-3.

```
table {
   font: 1em/1.5em Georgia, serif;
   border: 1px solid black;
   margin: 1em 1em 0 1em;
}
td {
   width: 10em;
   line-height: 1.5em;
   padding: 0.25em;
   border: 1px dashed black;
}
table.type1 td {
   vertical-align: top;
}
table.type2 td {
   vertical-align: baseline;
}
td.two {
   line-height: 2.5em;
}
td.three {
   line-height: 2em;
}
<table class="type1">
   <tr>
      <td>Lorem ipsum dolor</td>
      <td class="two">Lorem ipsum dolor</td>
      <td class="three">Lorem ipsum dolor</td>
   </tr>
</table>
<table class="type2">
   <tr>
      <td>Lorem ipsum dolor</td>
      <td class="two">Lorem ipsum dolor</td>
      <td class="three">Lorem ipsum dolor</td>
   </tr>
</table>
```

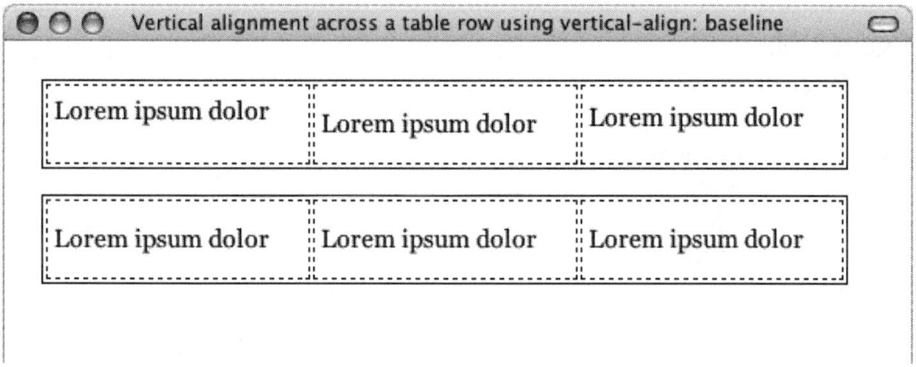

Figure 9-3. Vertical alignment across a table row using vertical-align: baseline

In Figure 9-3, you can see that in the first table each cell is on its own baseline, and none of them align. In the second table, with vertical-align: baseline specified, the cell baselines align with the baseline of the deepest cell. Things get a bit more complex if you've tagged content in the cell—<p>s, for example. The CSS specification says that browsers should use the farthest-down first-line box and work it out from there, and technically that means that they should include margins and padding from any block-level elements inside the cells. Only Opera 7 gets this absolutely right. All the major browsers (except NN4) get block-level elements with differing padding right, but differing margins cause a problem, and each browser gets it wrong slightly differently. The key, then, is to ensure that one of two things happens with your markup: either that no top margins are used by any elements that are the first child of a <td>, and then <td>s with text and <td>s with elements can be happily mixed; or that all <td>s in a row are uniform, with all <td>s containing only elements (with the same top margins) or all <td>s containing only text. Taking the CSS from the example shown in Figure 9-3, plus the following additional rules, and applying them to the following markup covers the permutations. Figures 9-4 through 9-6 show them in Firebird 0.7, IE 6, and Opera 7.

```
p {
  margin: 1em 0 0 0;
  padding: 0;
  border: 1px dotted black;
}
p.extraSpace {
  margin: 1.5em 0 0 0;
}
p.lessSpace {
  margin: 0.5em 0 0 0;
}
```

```
table.type3 p {
  margin: 0;
  padding: 0.75em 0;
}
table.type3 td.two p {
  padding: 0.5em 0;
}
table.type3 td.three p {
  padding: 1em 0;
}
<table class="type2">
  <tr>
    <td>Lorem ipsum dolor</td>
    <td class="two"><p>Lorem ipsum dolor</p></td>
    <td class="three">Lorem ipsum dolor</td>
  </tr>
</table>
<table class="type2">
  <tr>
    <td><p>Lorem ipsum dolor</p></td>
    <td class="two"><p>Lorem ipsum dolor</p></td>
    <td class="three"><p>Lorem ipsum dolor</p></td>
  </tr>
</table>
<table class="type2">
  <tr>
    <td><p>Lorem ipsum dolor</p></td>
    <td class="two"><p>Lorem ipsum dolor</p></td>
    <td class="three"><p class="extraSpace">Lorem ipsum dolor</p></td>
  </tr>
</table>
<table class="type2">
  <tr>
    <td><p>Lorem ipsum dolor</p></td>
    <td class="two"><p>Lorem ipsum dolor</p></td>
    <td class="three"><p class="lessSpace">Lorem ipsum dolor</p></td>
  </tr>
</table>
<table class="type3">
  <tr>
    <td><p>Lorem ipsum dolor</p></td>
    <td class="two"><p>Lorem ipsum dolor</p></td>
    <td class="three"><p>Lorem ipsum dolor</p></td>
  </tr>
</table>
```

```
<table class="type3">
  <tr>
    <td><p>Lorem ipsum dolor</p></td>
    <td class="two"><p>Lorem ipsum dolor</p></td>
    <td class="three">Lorem ipsum dolor</td>
  </tr>
</table>
```

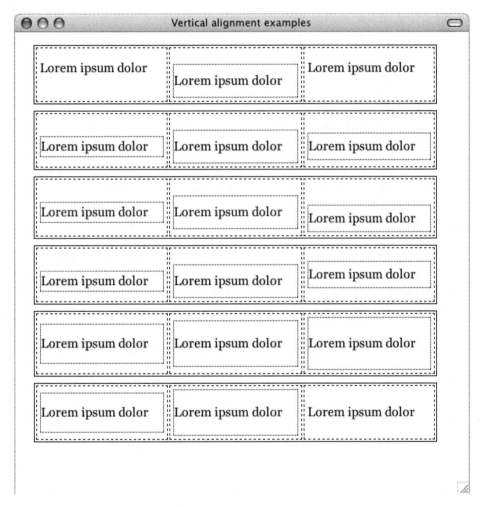

Figure 9-4. Vertical alignment examples in Firebird 0.7

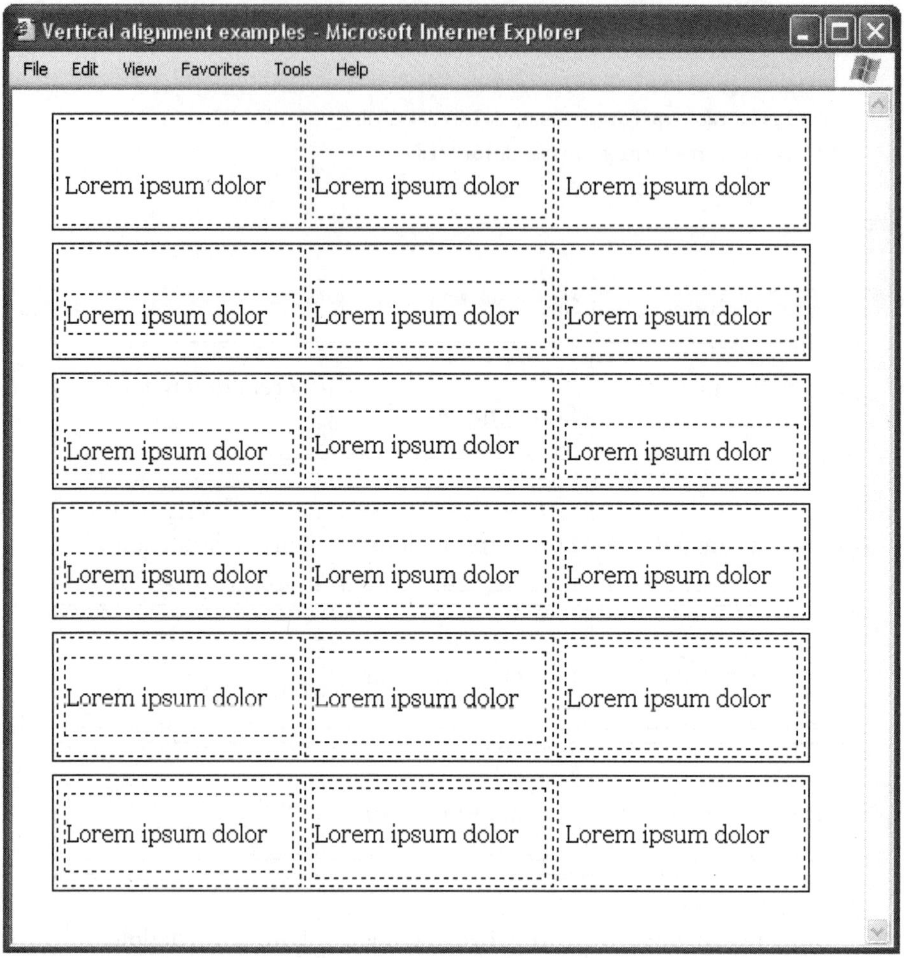

Figure 9-5. Vertical alignment examples in IE 6

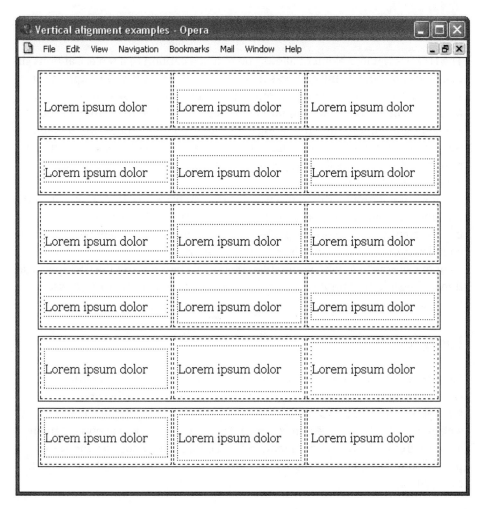

Figure 9-6. Vertical alignment examples in Opera 7

The last piece of general advice about tables is about horizontal alignment of columns. Much as with vertical alignment within rows, establishing a clear visual edge for a column can allow for easier navigation and use of a table, by which we mean contents left- or right-aligned in a cell. Even if a table has borders, establishing a clear edge to a column can help you locate things in the column more easily, especially if its contents vary widely in width. This is as simple as specifying the text-align property for <td>s, and it behaves exactly as it does on a <p>.

Captions

The HTML <caption> element allows you to add a caption to a table. Captions sit in a block box outside the <table>'s margins. HTML 4 says that the caption can sit above, below, out to the left, or out to the right of the <table>'s block box, but most implementations only support above and below, and those that do support left and right differ in their rendering. CSS 2 allowed for all the HTML possibilities, but as a result of the implementation problems, the W3C removed left and right from CSS 2.1. The CSS property that controls this is caption-side, which accepts the values top and bottom.

Implementation of this varies widely between browsers. IE 6 ignores it, and the browsers that do support it deal with the interaction between table and caption differently (and incorrectly). We won't give any examples here because of the complexity of the issues and the relative unimportance of the topic, but if you want to use <caption> with your tables, then you'd best consult the CSS specification and experiment until you get results that are acceptable across browsers.

Backgrounds

Setting backgrounds on various parts of your table is as simple as setting background, or background-color, in a style rule applied to whichever part of the table you want. The HTML table model allows for explicitly defined columns, as well as ways to group rows and columns. The CSS table model allows for styling all those things. As with a lot of table-related CSS, browser support for this is patchy, so we'll explain the theory but provide only simple examples that work everywhere.

Table Layers

The core of the CSS table visual formatting model is tied up with boxes and layers. You already know about boxes, and table boxes are just the same, with the exception that internal table boxes (cells and rows) don't have margins. Layers come into it when you start to look at the different kinds of boxes in the table model, most obviously the table box itself and cell boxes. In addition to these, CSS says that each row of cells is contained in a box, as is each column, group of rows, and group of columns. The cells are grouped into a layer, as are the rows and the rowgroups. In fact, all the different table box types get their own layer. These layers are laid one on top of the other, much as if each were drawn on tracing paper, and so backgrounds (and borders) set in one layer only show through to the surface if nothing obscures them in the layers above. The order of the layers is (from the top down) cells (<td>, <th>), rows (<tr>), rowgroups (<tbody>, <thead>, <tfoot>), columns (<col>), column groups (<colgroup>), and the table itself.

Because of the varying browser support, we're going to provide only a simple example with table cells blocking out the background set on the table, as shown in Figure 9-7.

```
table {
  font: 1em/1.5em Georgia, serif;
  background-color: rgb(230,230,230);
  border: 1px solid black;
  margin: 1em;
  border-collapse: separated;
}
td {
  vertical-align: baseline;
  padding: 0 0.5em;
  border: 1px dashed black;
}
td.background {
  background-color: rgb(200,200,200);
}
<table>
  <tr>
    <td>Lorem ipsum dolor</td>
    <td>Lorem ipsum dolor</td>
    <td>Lorem ipsum dolor</td>
  </tr>
  <tr>
    <td>Lorem ipsum dolor</td>
    <td class="background">Lorem ipsum dolor</td>
    <td>Lorem ipsum dolor</td>
  </tr>
  <tr>
    <td class="background">Lorem ipsum dolor</td>
    <td>Lorem ipsum dolor</td>
    <td class="background">Lorem ipsum dolor</td>
  </tr>
</table>
```

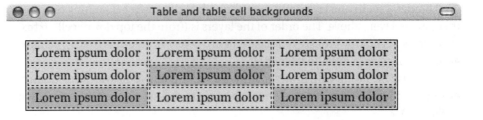

Figure 9-7. Table and table cell backgrounds

Rows and Columns

Briefly running through the more complex end of the table box spectrum, we come to rows, columns, and groups of both. In the CSS table formatting model, you can style <tr> and <col>, as well as the grouping elements <tbody>, <thead>, <tfoot>, and <colgroup>. The only styling you can do is to background, border, and things that will be inherited, such as font. The ability to hang styles off these elements is nice, but you'll find it almost as easy to use the element as a component in contextual selectors, giving you essentially the same end result, but without the cross-platform worries. Using a class on alternate <tr>s is a good way to specify an alternating dark-light row pattern, for example. The exceptions to this are columns and column groups, which aren't table cell ancestors and so can't be used in contextual selectors.

Separators: Gaps and Borders

The best way to differentiate and bring out the various parts of a table is by making good use of the separation between cells, and between rows and columns. This means both gaps between, and borders on, cells, rows, and columns.

When you design a table, one of the key questions is how to visually separate rows and columns. There are a couple of major factors to keep in mind: the complexity of the cell contents and the design of the rest of the page or site. If the contents of your cells are fairly simple—numbers or a single paragraph of text, for example—then you probably don't need to use cell borders. A sensible amount of space between cells will give you all the visual separation you need, and if you've established a clear visual edge to your cells and vertically aligned the rows, then those will create as clear a border as an actual 1px line. If your cell content is more complex—several paragraphs per cell, or paragraphs and lists, for example—then you're likely to at least need borders between the rows or it will be hard to tell where one cell ends and another begins. Of course, there may be aesthetic reasons that push you toward a particular approach to keep the tables within the site's design. Tables are visually complex, with space within and without the table interacting to affect how the table works. You're going to need to experiment to get the best results.

The CSS Table Border Model

Of critical importance to both gaps and borders between cells is the way that the browser handles what's called the *border model*. There are two ways to handle table borders in CSS: separated borders or collapsed borders. The essential difference between the two approaches is that with separated borders you specify borders around cells, and with collapsed borders you specify borders between cells. Which model is used is controlled by the border-collapse property, which takes the values collapse and separate. The following code and Figure 9-8 show this.

```
table {
  font: 1em/1.5em Georgia, serif;
  border: 1px solid black;
  margin: 1em;
}
td {
  width: 10em;
  vertical-align: baseline;
  padding: 0 0.5em;
  border: 1px dashed black;
}
table.separate {
  border-collapse: separate;
}
table.collapsed {
  border-collapse: collapse;
}
<table class="separate">
  <tr>
    <td>Lorem ipsum dolor</td>
    <td>Lorem ipsum dolor</td>
    <td>Lorem ipsum dolor</td>
  </tr>
  <tr>
    <td>Lorem ipsum dolor</td>
    <td>Lorem ipsum dolor</td>
    <td>Lorem ipsum dolor</td>
  </tr>
</table>
```

```
<table class="collapsed">
  <tr>
    <td>Lorem ipsum dolor</td>
    <td>Lorem ipsum dolor</td>
    <td>Lorem ipsum dolor</td>
  </tr>
  <tr>
    <td>Lorem ipsum dolor</td>
    <td>Lorem ipsum dolor</td>
    <td>Lorem ipsum dolor</td>
  </tr>
</table>
```

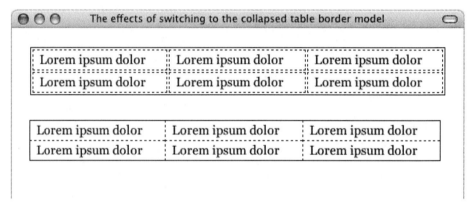

Figure 9-8. The effects of switching to the collapsed table border model

It's a significant effect, and collapsed borders mean that you don't have to carefully specify border-right and border-top (for example) to create a single border between cells. Unfortunately, although IE 6, Mozilla 1.0, Netscape 7, and Opera 5 get this right, IE5/Mac and Safari 1.1 don't. (Later versions of Safari will support border-collapse.) Mimicking collapsed borders requires some careful thought, and we cover it further a little later on in this chapter.

The separated borders model uses another property, border-spacing, to control the space between cell borders (remember that you can't specify margin on <td>s). It takes a length as its value. The next code sample and Figure 9-9 illustrate this.

```
table {
  font: 1em/1.5em Georgia, serif;
  border: 1px solid black;
  margin: 1em;

  border-collapse: separate;
}
td {
  width: 9em;
  vertical-align: baseline;
  padding: 0 0.5em;
  border: 1px dashed black;
}
table.nospace {
  border-spacing: 0;
}
table.space {
  border-spacing: 0.5em;
}
<table class="nospace">
  <tr>
    <td>Lorem ipsum dolor</td>
    <td>Lorem ipsum dolor</td>
    <td>Lorem ipsum dolor</td>
  </tr>
  <tr>
    <td>Lorem ipsum dolor</td>
    <td>Lorem ipsum dolor</td>
    <td>Lorem ipsum dolor</td>
  </tr>
</table>
<table class="space">
  <tr>
    <td>Lorem ipsum dolor</td>
    <td>Lorem ipsum dolor</td>
    <td>Lorem ipsum dolor</td>
  </tr>
  <tr>
    <td>Lorem ipsum dolor</td>
    <td>Lorem ipsum dolor</td>
    <td>Lorem ipsum dolor</td>
  </tr>
</table>
```

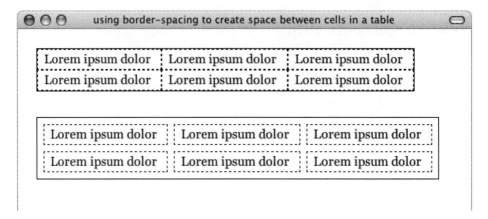

Figure 9-9. Using border-spacing *to create space between cells in a table*

Unfortunately, IE5/Mac and IE 6 don't support border-spacing, so you'd need to use <table>'s cellspacing attribute to control it.

Collapsed Borders

The main thing to realize about tables with collapsed borders is that there are rules governing how conflicts between borders are resolved (what happens when two adjacent table cells have different borders set). Failure to understand this is likely to result in tables with cell borders you didn't want. The following example code and Figure 9-10 show this in action.

```
table {
  font: 1em/1.5em Georgia, serif;
  border-style: none hidden;
  margin: 1em 0 0 0;
  border-collapse: collapse;
}
td {
  width: 6em;
  vertical-align: baseline;
  padding: 0 0.5em;
  border: 1px dashed black;
}
tbody {
  border: 2px solid black;
}
tr {
  border: 1px solid black;
}
```

```
colgroup {
  border: 4px solid black;
  border-style: none solid;
}
col#col1 {
  border-color: black;
  border-width: 1px;
  border-style: none solid;
}
<table>
  <colgroup>
    <col id="col1"/>
    <col />
  </colgroup>
  <colgroup>
    <col />
    <col />
    <col />
  </colgroup>
  <tbody>
    <tr>
      <td>Lorem ipsum</td>
      <td>Lorem ipsum</td>
      <td>Lorem ipsum</td>
      <td>Lorem ipsum</td>
      <td>Lorem ipsum</td>
    </tr>
    <tr>
      <td>Lorem ipsum</td>
      <td>Lorem ipsum</td>
      <td>Lorem ipsum</td>
      <td>Lorem ipsum</td>
      <td>Lorem ipsum</td>
    </tr>
    <tr>
      <td>Lorem ipsum</td>
      <td>Lorem ipsum</td>
      <td>Lorem ipsum</td>
      <td>Lorem ipsum</td>
      <td>Lorem ipsum</td>
    </tr>
  </tbody>
  <tbody>
```

```
  <tr>
    <td>Lorem ipsum</td>
    <td>Lorem ipsum</td>
    <td>Lorem ipsum</td>
    <td>Lorem ipsum</td>
    <td>Lorem ipsum</td>
  </tr>
  <tr>
    <td>Lorem ipsum</td>
    <td>Lorem ipsum</td>
    <td>Lorem ipsum</td>
    <td>Lorem ipsum</td>
    <td>Lorem ipsum</td>
  </tr>
  <tr>
    <td>Lorem ipsum</td>
    <td>Lorem ipsum</td>
    <td>Lorem ipsum</td>
    <td>Lorem ipsum</td>
    <td>Lorem ipsum</td>
  </tr>
  </tbody>
</table>
```

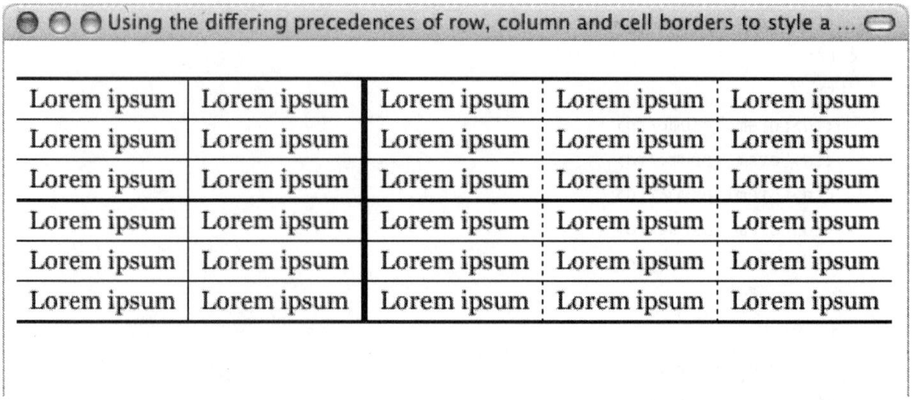

Figure 9-10. Using the differing precedences of row, column, and cell borders to style a table

As you can see from Figure 9-10, there are several different border styles in the table. The example also introduces something new: borders on columns and rows.

In the collapsed borders model it's possible for table rows (`<tr>`), rowgroups (`<thead>`, `<tbody>`, `<tfoot>`), columns (`<col>`), and column groups (`<colgroup>`) to have borders. One of the primary advantages this gives is the ability to specify borders without having to style table cells: to bring out structural groupings within the table without needing complex markup and selectors. You need to remember that row and column boxes have borders on all four sides, so a full border on a row will give you borders between the row and its neighbors (or the table edge) and at the left and right edges of the table. IE 6 and Safari 1.1 don't support borders on rows, rowgroups, columns, or column groups, whereas Netscape 7, Mozilla 1.0, and Opera 5 do.

Border Conflicts

The general rule of thumb is that borders with more visual heft take priority (the specification says "more eye-catching"). The way this works is that several factors are balanced: the border's style, its width, and its place in the table's visual layers. Border width has the most weight, followed by border style, and then the border's place in the table's layers. Table 9-1 shows how this works, with most important at the top and the least important at the bottom.

Table 9-1. Border Conflict Resolution

Property	Notes
`border-style: hidden`	This is the trump: It overrides any conflicting border.
`border-width`	Larger values are more important.
`border-style`	The values, from greatest to least importance, are as follows: `double`, `solid`, `dashed`, `dotted`, `ridge`, `outset`, `groove`, `inset`.
Table layer	The layers, from greatest to least importance, are as follows: cell, row, rowgroup, column, column group, table.
`border-style: none`	This is the least important. Everything overrides it.

There's a problem with collapsed borders, which is that the browsers that support them don't agree about how to resolve conflicts between adjoining layers and adjoining cells when they're of equal importance. Because of this it's only a problem if conflicting borders differ in color.

Separated Borders

Separated borders are a good deal simpler than collapsed borders—there aren't any conflicts to resolve. There are two properties that relate to separated borders, both of which are nice and straightforward. The first is the border-spacing property, which specifies how much space there should be between cells; it's the equivalent of the HTML cellspacing attribute on <table>s. The second is the empty-cells property, which controls whether cells with no content (<td></td>, or cells that were simply omitted from the markup) should have their borders and backgrounds shown. Both properties apply only to <table> elements and won't have any effect if applied to another element (such as <tr>s or <td>s). Figure 9-11 shows the effect of these two properties.

```
table {
    font: 1em/1.5em Georgia, serif;
    border: 1px solid black;
    margin: 1em;
    border-collapse: separated;
}
td {
    background-color: gray;
    vertical-align: baseline;
    padding: 0 0.5em;
    border: 1px dashed black;
}
table.show {
    empty-cells: show;
    border-spacing: 1em;
}
table.hide {
    empty-cells: hide;
    border-spacing: 0.5em;
}
<table class="show">
    <tr>
        <td>Lorem ipsum dolor</td>
        <td>Lorem ipsum dolor</td>
        <td>Lorem ipsum dolor</td>
    </tr>
    <tr>
        <td>Lorem ipsum dolor</td>
        <td></td>
        <td>Lorem ipsum dolor</td>
    </tr>
```

```
  <tr>
    <td></td>
    <td>Lorem ipsum dolor</td>
    <td></td>
  </tr>
</table>
<table class="hide">
  <tr>
    <td>Lorem ipsum dolor</td>
    <td>Lorem ipsum dolor</td>
    <td>Lorem ipsum dolor</td>
  </tr>
  <tr>
    <td>Lorem ipsum dolor</td>
    <td></td>
    <td>Lorem ipsum dolor</td>
  </tr>
  <tr>
    <td></td>
    <td>Lorem ipsum dolor</td>
    <td></td>
  </tr>
</table>
```

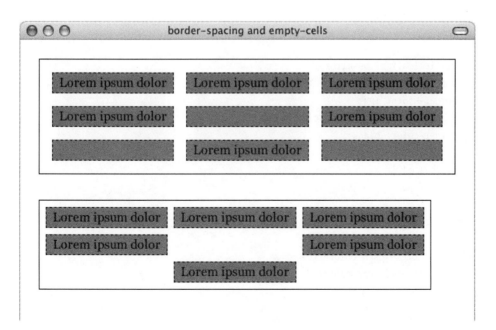

Figure 9-11. border-spacing *and* empty-cells

It's important to note that Mozilla/Netscape 6.2+ support both properties, Opera 5+ and Safari 1+ support `border-spacing` only, and IE5/Mac and IE 6 support neither. IE 6 will always hide a cell's borders when nothing is in it (i.e., nothing or plain white space), but it won't ever hide the background. Opera 5+ behaves in the same way.

Mimicking Collapsed Borders with Separated Borders

If you want to make a table that works in IE 6 but looks like it's using the collapsed borders model, with borders between rows and columns rather than around cells, then you need to mimic the effect of collapsed borders.

Mimicking collapsed borders is, by and large, fairly straightforward. The key is to set borders on only two sides of the table cells and set borders only on the other two sides of the table itself, as in the following example, shown with and without `border-spacing: 0` in Figure 9-12. It's also necessary to use the HTML `cellspacing` attribute on your table to make IE 6 behave itself.

```
table {
    font: 1em/1.5em Georgia, serif;
    border-width: 1px;
    border-style: solid solid none none;
    border-color: black;
    margin: 1em;
    border-collapse: separated;
    border-spacing: 0;
}
td {
    vertical-align: baseline;
    padding: 0 0.5em;
    border-width: 1px;
    border-style: none none solid solid;
    border-color: black;
}
table.spaced {
    border-spacing: 0.5em;
}
<table class="spaced" cellspacing="0">
    <tr>
        <td>Lorem ipsum dolor</td>
        <td>Lorem ipsum dolor</td>
        <td>Lorem ipsum dolor</td>
    </tr>
```

```
<tr>
  <td>Lorem ipsum dolor</td>
  <td>Lorem ipsum dolor</td>
  <td>Lorem ipsum dolor</td>
</tr>
<tr>
  <td>Lorem ipsum dolor</td>
  <td>Lorem ipsum dolor</td>
  <td>Lorem ipsum dolor</td>
</tr>
</table>
<table cellspacing="0">
  <tr>
    <td>Lorem ipsum dolor</td>
    <td>Lorem ipsum dolor</td>
    <td>Lorem ipsum dolor</td>
  </tr>
  <tr>
    <td>Lorem ipsum dolor</td>
    <td>Lorem ipsum dolor</td>
    <td>Lorem ipsum dolor</td>
  </tr>
  <tr>
    <td>Lorem ipsum dolor</td>
    <td>Lorem ipsum dolor</td>
    <td>Lorem ipsum dolor</td>
  </tr>
</table>
```

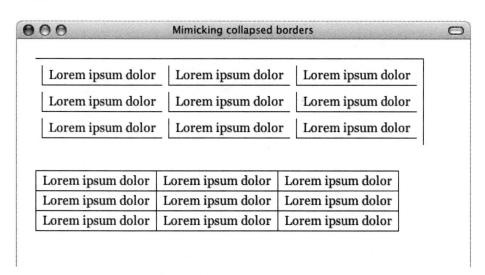

Figure 9-12. Mimicking collapsed borders

The trick is that you're setting borders on only two sides of the cells and using table borders set on the opposite sides of the table to mask the empty sides of the cells. More complex effects can be achieved by using <tr>s and <tbody>s (not to mention <th> and the other row-grouping elements) in contextual selectors, and once classes on rows, rowgroups, and cells are brought in, you can do just about anything you want—it just requires extra work in the markup and the CSS.

Summary

Tables are complex things, both in design and markup terms. When tabular information needs to be presented, it needs to be well presented—to work, graphically and functionally. In this chapter, you've seen the control over tables CSS affords, along with how to exercise that control, with a little bit of what makes for good tables thrown in as well.

CHAPTER 10

Cross-Browser CSS

THE REASON *WHY* browsers have buggy CSS support isn't the issue here.

Buggy browsers are a fact. Minor bugs are only human, but there are a number of bad bugs in popular browsers that make learning CSS difficult. Once you've read any new concept, you need to apply it in order to learn, and with CSS your new code runs straight into a number of browser issues. This is why CSS often involves an initial 2 weeks of stress and despair for many developers. There's just too much to know before your first few layouts succeed.

This book's purpose is to help with that initial learning period. In this chapter we cover places where major browsers commonly misstep and how you can write valid, sensible code that compensates.

Before that, however, a brief history is useful to put things in perspective.

The Name Game

Generalizing about browsers incurs some generalizing about names. On the Net you'll see phrases such as "version 5 browsers" in relation to CSS, but what does that mean?

In the early days, there was a period of stability with two major graphical browsers, Internet Explorer (IE) and Netscape Navigator. The competition between these two, and the generally similar capabilities of both at the same version number, created an association between version numbers and standards capability. This is a convenient coincidence (with a little push from marketing sometimes, perhaps), and browser version numbers aren't directly tied to capability or to a release year.

But a casual association exists, so it will be helpful to new developers if we make some sweeping generalizations to bring them up to speed. This is neither a rigorous nor a complete history; this is just a recap relevant to CSS on popular browsers.

With their respective version 4s, IE and Netscape Navigator dominated the market, and neither browser was much good with CSS. You may think of this as the "Dark Age."

IE got serious about CSS with version 5 for the Mac platform. Sadly, development ceased with version 5.2.3. IE for Windows has gone through major releases 5, 5.5, and 6, each with improved CSS capability. Microsoft is currently stating that version 6 will be its last stand-alone browser. It's important to note that the Mac and Windows IE browsers have been entirely separate projects, and each has different CSS issues.

For Netscape Navigator, there was no version 5. Development of this browser changed track and Netscape 6 was an AOL adaptation of the Mozilla 0.6 open-source browser, giving Netscape its first serious CSS support. Netscape 6.1 was based on Mozilla 0.9, and Netscape 7 was based on Mozilla 1.0. The Netscape and Mozilla browsers differ in detail, but their CSS capability is shared. In the first edition of this book we simplified this by referring to both by the better-known Netscape name, as chances were that anyone who knew Mozilla would also know that Netscape was AOL's version. Since then, Mozilla has become a popular browser itself and Netscape has gone out of development as AOL adjusts itself to a difficult economy. Mozilla browsers across the Mac, Windows, and Linux platforms use the same version number, and each has the same CSS capability.

Opera's version numbering roughly follows that of IE and Netscape. With version 5, Opera had good CSS support and was established as a competitor. Like Mozilla, individual Opera versions have mostly identical CSS capability across Mac, Windows, and Linux. Currently, Windows and Linux have version 7 available; Mac is still using version 6.

Apple has also recently entered the browser market with Safari for OS X. Being brand new, it has modern CSS capability and no earlier versions to watch out for. Because it's an Apple product and there's little other choice for a completely modern browser for Mac, Safari should be considered a major browser immediately. It's essentially assured to be popular.

So what does "version 5 browsers" mean? Essentially any current or near-current version of the previously mentioned browsers—any version that's newer than the time when IE 4 and Netscape Navigator 4 ruled the Web. These browsers are considered to have "modern" CSS support.

The last generalization we'd like to make is that Mozilla and Opera users tend to upgrade to the most current version quickly. This is likely because both browsers have established themselves primarily with web-savvy users. Conversely, IE and Netscape are vastly better known to the general public, which includes a great many people who are reluctant to upgrade from a version they've become familiar with. So although it may be very rare to find Opera 5 or Mozilla 0.6 in your ref logs, you'll most assuredly find IE 5, for both Mac and Windows.

Now, what about version 4 browsers? This is where the fun begins. The problem isn't that these early browsers had no CSS support, but that they had badly broken CSS support.

Crossing the Great Divide

The support of CSS in version 4 browsers creates a sharp dividing line for developers. Much of what is discussed in CSS today presumes that your audience is using at least a version 5 browser. Most people are, but a few are still using older versions.

Browser vendors have improved their CSS support with every release since the version 4 era, but the old releases don't expire, so developers need to code with old browsers in mind. This isn't difficult when all browsers have correct standards implementation. The theory is that as standards evolve, developers will use modern methods to enhance web pages for modern browsers, while older browsers will show a site in the simpler form of their simpler capabilities, and nothing breaks. The W3C has been very careful to make evolving standards work this way, and all browsers are required to ignore markup and rulesets that they don't recognize.

But the version 4 browsers didn't just have limited CSS ability; they had vastly flawed ability. They actually made a hash of perfectly valid code, effectively blocking a website's content from their user.

At the time, developers compromised. Lacking proper methods to make layout, they used a creative hack involving table tags, which in turn made a hash for anything that wasn't a graphics-capable browser. But in those days, IE or Netscape Navigator on a home computer was by far the most common way to view the Web, and enormous sums were spent by companies vying to join the great dot-com boom. Standards and alternative devices were essentially ignored in this gold rush, and bad code became normal practice.

When the more capable version 5 browsers arrived, developers could finally use CSS to create layouts and not serve hash to alternative devices. Except a very large part of the audience were still using version 4 browsers, and these users were estimated to continue doing so until at least 2004. This put developers in a spot. We couldn't wait—the Web was expanding well beyond access through just two browsers on home computers, but at the same time a major slice of the audience was used to seeing perfectly good layout in their version 4 browsers, thanks to the table hack. We couldn't just switch to CSS and serve these people broken pages. What to do?

Three techniques developed to deal with this difficult situation. Which you use will depend on your target audience. They're arguably compromises, but they're a darn sight more attractive than the previous one, and they also look ahead instead of locking themselves to the past.

NOTE *Minor digression: May we say it like it is? Although it's correct to use generic terms such as "version 4 browsers," what we're really referring to today is Netscape Navigator version 4. This was an enormously popular browser, and it still has a large installed user base in libraries, schools, and businesses. Netscape Navigator 4 is the primary old browser with buggy CSS support that developers are still coding for, almost without exception. Your pages may never be viewed by another version 4 browser.*

In recognition of Netscape Navigator 4's yeoman service, from here on we'll refer to it directly. Let it be understood that much of this information also embraces equivalent, and all but extinct, browsers of that era. The techniques of this section could possibly be best thought of as "Being Nice to Netscape 4."

@import

The first method is to avoid Netscape Navigator 4 (hereafter referred to as NN4). On a noncommercial site or one with a tech-savvy audience that upgrades, you may choose to simply hide your CSS from old browsers with poor support. Because you're creating device-independent XHTML, all of your content will remain available to the few version 4 browsers—it will simply be unstyled.

We also strongly recommend avoiding NN4 in this way while you're still learning CSS. There's already quite enough to keep track of while getting used to making layouts that work for modern browsers. It's best if you become comfortable with regular CSS before you start dealing with the rather difficult NN4. If that describes your situation, then skip the second and third techniques for now and go directly to the section "Our Modern World" after you finish reading this section. The second and third techniques will be right here when you feel ready to take on NN4.

Hiding your CSS from NN4 is quite simple. It doesn't recognize the @import method of linking stylesheets. Use it in the XHTML to attach your stylesheet, and NN4 won't be able to embarrass itself on your CSS. NN4 will instead display only the XHTML, entirely intact, unconfused, and very, very plain:

```
<style type="text/css" media="all">@import url("/main.css");</style>
```

Note that this syntax uses both url( ) and quotes together. Either alone is correct and will block NN4, but together they'll also block IE4.5/Mac. This was a similarly poor browser, and it's quite rare today, but it was also the default browser on a lot of new Macs at the time. As a result, it does show up now and again, and chances are that the person still using it will be from the middle management of a client you're trying to impress. So you may as well deal with it along with NN4. Serve both browsers safe, plain XHTML.

Now, it's entirely possible that serving plain XHTML to NN4 will be unsatisfactory for you. A person using NN4 is used to seeing colorful, highly designed websites, and for all they know, your site really *is* plain, not just in her browser. If you choose to have minimal consideration for NN4, you may wish to add an explanatory notice for those users.

Browser Upgrade Notice

In February 2001, the Web Standards Project (WaSP, http://www.webstandards.org/) launched a Browser Upgrade Campaign (BUC). The reason for this is obvious now, though it was less obvious then. We had modern CSS-capable browsers, we had a world in need of device-independent code, and yet we were being held back because people are slow to upgrade. Developers were in a bind.

The WaSP's solution was to combine the @import link with a message. NN4 would render the plain XHTML with this message displayed across the top of the page. A modern browser would render the page fully styled, and without the message.

Right after <body>, this markup was inserted:

```
<h1 class="ahem">
  This site will look much better in a browser that supports <a
  href="http://www.webstandards.org/upgrade/" title="Download a browser that
  complies with Web standards.">web standards</a>, but it is accessible to any
  browser or Internet device.
</h1>
```

In the imported stylesheet, the following rule hid the message from modern browsers:

```
.ahem {
  display: none;
}
```

The link within the upgrade message led to a WaSP page that explained why you were there and what the campaign was about, and it provided links to the latest versions of the most popular browsers.

The BUC was a smart move, and we're grateful to the WaSP for publicizing and hosting the method. It helped a lot of people realize that a browser upgrade wasn't just a change of chrome, and it helped a lot of developers move on to modern markup. However, there were a number of issues, and after 2 years and considerable internal debate, the WaSP closed down the campaign, and the preceding link now leads to a page that explains the history of the campaign and why it's time to move on.

Briefly, a big reason was that most people who could upgrade from NN4 had already done so by 2003. The remaining NN4 users were generally stuck with the browser because it was an institution-wide installation in libraries, schools, and businesses; it wasn't something they could change themselves. Another problem was that several developers had somehow thought it was OK to block any older browser and redirect it. Rather than use CSS and JavaScript as sensibly layered enhancements over their XHTML, and so serve to each browser what each was capable of reading, these developers simply blocked all people without the very latest browsers and directed them to the WaSP upgrade campaign page. These users would then complain loudly to the hapless WaSP for supposedly hijacking their browser.

At the end of the day it had become clear that the campaign had achieved all it could and was instead becoming a source of very wrong publicity for what standards are about, so the WaSP withdrew the method.

Your Own Notice

You may still wish to make NN4 users aware that your pages are available fully styled in better browsers. In that case, you could use the WaSP method to place a notice that links to an explanatory page of your own.

Be aware that some versions of NN4 on some platforms will fail to display the notice if a <div> is used to apply the class, so instead use an element such as <h1> or <p>, as is done in the example.

We also suggest an improvement to the WaSP method. Instead of a text notice, use a worded image without an alt attribute. Text-only browsers, aural browsers, and search engines have no use for the NN4-specific message. By using an image without an alt, you'll avoid causing confusion for these users. For the image itself, do be sure to keep it plain so people won't think it's an irrelevant banner advertisement, and use a shape uncommon to banners so that any user's banner-blocking software won't block it.

Cascade

If you have commercial clients or a general-access website, then you possibly won't wish to serve plain pages to NN4. Be aware that it can be a lot of work catering to this fading browser, and you should go through the ref logs with your client to reach agreement on whether the extra cost is worthwhile. NN4 has highly limited CSS capability, but it does have some, and with clever work you can create a good compromise layout for it, although it won't be as complex as you can create for a modern browser.

CSS is designed to serve styles appropriate to different browser types. NN4 isn't a unique type as intended by the W3C, but the cascade function can let us treat it as one:

```
<link rel="Stylesheet" href="css/basic.css" type="text/css" media="screen" />
<style type="text/css" media="all">@import url("css/advanced.css");</style>
```

With the preceding lines in the XHTML, we have a handy trick whereby NN4 retrieves basic site styles from the linked basic.css file and is shielded from advanced styles of the imported advanced.css. A modern browser will retrieve both stylesheets and combine them.

By placing the `@import` link second, elements that are styled by both stylesheets will take their style from the advanced sheet. This allows you to tailor individual elements to look best for either the basic layout or the advanced layout, and it allows you to serve quite different rules when NN4 accepts a style, but in a botched manner. We'll go into that in detail later in this section.

NN4 doesn't handle CSS layout well at all, so layout will be the most noticeable difference between the basic and advanced stylesheets in this method. NN4 will derive its layout primarily from your XHTML document's linear structure, just like a text browser or aural browser does. However, it need not look plain. The typography, colors, and proportions of the page can still be controlled and allow you to make a linear layout that is attractive and recognizably similar to your full CSS version. What you're creating is two "looks" that are related to preserve the visual identity of your site. That's a design challenge, but well, that's what you do for a living.

Let's go into the details.

The Basic Stylesheet

First you need to decide how much you want to do to accommodate your remaining NN4 audience. In theory the desire is to build a modern site that also looks acceptably similar in NN4. The operative word is "acceptable." If you have the time or the mandate to get the last ounce of style from NN4, then I highly recommend you dig into Internet resources for more detail. There are charts, articles, and discussions across the Net that detail the nuances of NN4's quirky CSS support. This browser can have quite a bit squeezed out of it, but the effort required climbs sharply while the gains decrease. In this section we cover only the basic compromises made to style for NN4. The idea is to achieve a strong result on a limited time budget and to illustrate the basic capabilities and limits of this browser.

NN4 can be quite problematic. Just about everything printed about it, *including what we write here,* can turn out to act differently in some lesser-used sub-version, and there were many, many sub-versions of NN4. This is unfortunate and is highly unsatisfactory for both developer and client. Knowing how to write for NN4 often feels more like an anecdotal lore than a proper science. About all that we can be pleased about is fewer people use NN4 every day, and soon we'll be able to forget it entirely.

But today we're writing for it, and now that the appropriate warnings and disclaimers are out of the way, what do we put in each of the two stylesheets?

Although there are two stylesheets, the basic stylesheet isn't written only for NN4. Modern browsers will read both stylesheets, so the basic stylesheet is meant to contain styles common to both NN4 and modern browsers. The advanced stylesheet will contain the complex <div> positioning information, and because it's placed second in the XHTML, it can also be used to override any rules that we wish to express differently within the more complex layout. This approach saves writing a lot of repeat rules and makes it easier to create recognizably similar pages for the different browsers because all work from common rules in the basic stylesheet.

However, NN4 is not just a rather basic browser, it's also a very buggy browser. Some styles of the basic stylesheet will need to be written strangely to accommodate this.

Inheritance

To begin with, NN4 has poor inheritance support. For example, you would expect to declare a font type and color in the `<body>` rule and then have this become the default style throughout your page, except for where you override it with another declaration.

```
body {
    background : #fff;
    margin : 0;
    padding : 0;
    font-family: verdana, arial, helvetica, sans-serif;
    color: #000;
}
```

NN4 entirely fails to do this. Every element will need to have all of its styles declared directly. But you don't need to write out the same declaration in several rulesets to fix this. Instead you can create a few single rules with multiple selectors specifically for the common declarations. This takes care of the inheritance problem, and it leaves you free to write the remaining rules normally with only styles unique to individual elements.

```
body, div, p, td, ol, ul, li, h1, h2, h3 {
    font-family: verdana, arial, helvetica, sans-serif;
    color: #000;
}
body {
    background : #fff;
    margin : 0;
    padding : 0;
}
```

Caution: Don't place relative typography units within this common ruleset. If you were to add ems as follows, then a normal browser will apply the rule to each instance of selector. So a paragraph within a <div> within the <body> would be 0.7 of 0.7 of 0.7 of the default font. Very small, to say the least. Relative units will have to stay with individual element rules.

```css
body, div, p, td, ol, ul, li, h1, h2, h3 {
    font-family: verdana, arial, helvetica, sans-serif;
    font-size: 0.7em;
    line-height: 1.4em;
    color: #000;
}
body {
    background : #fff;
    margin : 0;
    padding : 0;
}
```

Background Color

The next quirk of NN4 is the background color of a box. If you don't use a border, your background color will appear only behind your content, instead of filling the entire <div>:

```html
<!DOCTYPE html PUBLIC "-//W3C//DTD XHTML 1.0 Transitional//EN"
  "http://www.w3.org/TR/xhtml1/DTD/xhtml1-transitional.dtd">
<html xmlns="http://www.w3.org/1999/xhtml" xml:lang="en" lang="en">
<head>
<title>n4 bg 1</title>
<style type="text/css">
body, p {
  font-family: verdana, arial, helvetica, sans-serif;
  color: #000;
}
body {
  margin: 0px;
  padding: 0px;
  background-color: #fff;
}
p {
  font-size: 0.7em;
  line-height: 1.4em;
}
```

```
#MainText {
  padding: 10px;
  margin: 5px;
  background-color: #ccc;
}
</style>
</head>
<body>
<div id="MainText">
<p>Lorem ipsum dolor sit amet, consectetuer adipiscing elit, sed diam nonummy nibh
euismod tincidunt ut laoreet dolore magna aliquam erat volutpat.</p>
</div>
</body>
</html>
```

Figure 10-1 shows the result.

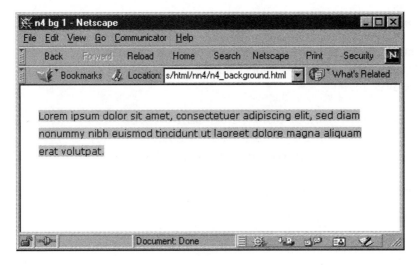

Figure 10-1. Background failure in NN4

Adding a border to the <div> returns the background color to normal, almost
(see Figure 10-2):

```
#MainText {
  padding: 10px;
  margin: 5px;
  background-color: #ccc;
  border: 1px solid #ccc;
}
```

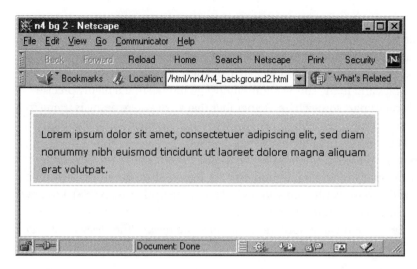

Figure 10-2. Border added to reduce NN4 background failure

That surprise gap is transparent. The result isn't necessarily unattractive, but it may not be what you want. To achieve a box with full background color and no visually separated border, change the border color to match the background color beneath the box (see Figure 10-3):

```
#MainText {
  padding: 10px;
  margin: 5px;
  background-color: #ccc;
  border: 1px solid #fff;
}
```

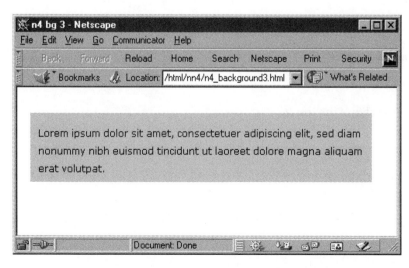

Figure 10-3. Border color changed to minimize effect of NN4 background failure

The remaining problem is that this visual box is a few pixels smaller than the box of your ruleset. It's missing about 4px on all sides due to the invisible border and the gap. This is a small amount, but you'd best be aware of it.

With NN4 it's generally a good idea to avoid designs that are visually tight. The browser's foibles and many sub-versions almost guarantee that a highly precise design will come apart somewhere. Remember that what you're doing is trying to make your page look acceptably similar in NN4—not identical—and give yourself a design that can take a little inconsistency in stride.

Coding for NN4 will sometimes be a measure of your skill, your determination, and your ability to retain hair under stress. Experienced developers won't be surprised by that remark (the browser had a lot of issues other than CSS), but new developers might be, so here's another example of how NN4 can be unexpectedly capricious. Let's take the first borderless example and reverse the <body> and <div> background colors:

```
body, p {
  font-family: verdana, arial, helvetica, sans-serif;
  color: #000;
}
body {
  margin: 0px;
  padding: 0px;
  background-color: #ccc;
}
p {
  font-size: 0.7em;
  line-height: 1.4em;
}
#MainText {
  padding: 10px;
  margin: 5px;
  background-color: #fff;
}
```

Figure 10-4 shows the result.

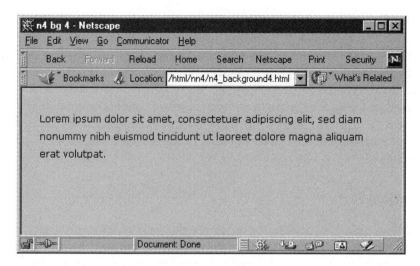

Figure 10-4. Vanishing background in NN4

No background color at all. Why? Who knows. The ugly truth is there are literally hundreds of bugs in NN4. Always test your design carefully in this browser, and never think for a minute that you've seen it all.

Fortunately, that last glitch is merely disturbing, as we've already made it clear you should always use a border, and when you do the missing background color comes right back.

Borders

Now that you're convinced of the benefit of borders, I should add that with NN4 you can't use individual borders. NN4 doesn't recognize any border property more complex than simple border. Your choice is a full border all the way around, or none. More complex properties can be added in the advanced stylesheet.

Background Images

It's likely that you'll want to use a background image on many of your pages. It's also likely that you'll want to use the CSS positioning attributes that were discussed in Chapter 8.

We're sorry to say that these attributes won't work with NN4. NN4 will display a background image, but it will always place it in the upper-left corner. It won't accept other positions, and neither will it fix an image so that it stays put in the viewport as the page scrolls. This isn't a terribly big deal, but it's another limitation to be aware of.

You can still serve advanced positioning information for modern browsers from your advanced stylesheet. This will override the simple information that you supplied for NN4 in the basic stylesheet. And because the advanced stylesheet overrides the information in the basic stylesheet, you also have a further option: You can create two versions of that background image, one for each stylesheet. To fake basic positioning for NN4, you can create a version of your background image with more area above or on the left, colored to match the page background. This will effectively push the intended image out from the upper-left corner by the desired amount.

<div> Positioning

Because NN4 has poor CSS positioning capability, our basic stylesheet will get simple positioning rules. The intent is to have NN4 display the page using the XHTML document structure for order, and have everything wrapped in a single centered box to give you style control for proportions and colors. This single document box can also be broken up into a series of centered boxes, and nesting boxes may be used. These can be accomplished with relatively few cautions, so we recommend them as starting point for positioning with NN4.

More complex styles for modern browsers are applied via the advanced stylesheet. Although NN4 normally ignores rulesets it can't use, it can also crash or refuse to display styles when faced with some <div> positioning information. This is especially true for the box model fix for IE 5 that is introduced later in this chapter (in the "Box Model" section). Keep things simple in the basic stylesheet.

To illustrate simple layout cautions, let's combine two examples from the last chapter and watch them fall apart in NN4. The following markup and ruleset describes a centered box that contains one inner box, plus a bottom centered box for a navigation footer.

```
<!DOCTYPE html PUBLIC "-//W3C//DTD XHTML 1.0 Transitional//EN"
 "http://www.w3.org/TR/xhtml1/DTD/xhtml1-transitional.dtd">
<html xmlns="http://www.w3.org/1999/xhtml" xml:lang="en" lang="en">
<head>
<title>nn4mix</title>
<link rel="stylesheet" type="text/css" href="css/nn4mix.css" />
<meta http-equiv="content-type" content="text/html; charset=iso-8859-1" />
</head>
<body>
<div id="content">
<p>Lorem ipsum dolor sit amet, consectetuer adipiscing elit, sed diam nonummy
nibh euismod tincidunt ut laoreet dolore magna aliquam erat volutpat.</p>
```

```
<div class="innerBox">
<p>Ut wisi enim ad minim veniam, quis nostrud exercitation ulliam corper suscipit
lobortis nisl ut aliquip ex ea commodo consequat.</p>
</div>
<p>Duis autem veleum iriure dolor in hendrerit in vulputate velit esse molestie
consequat, vel willum lunombro dolore eu feugiat</p>
</div>
<div id="navBar">
<p class=nav>&lt;back | home | next&gt;</p>
</div>
</body>
</html>


body { margin: 0px; padding: 0px;
  font-family: verdana, arial, helvetica, sans-serif;
  font-size: 0.7em;
  line-height: 1.4em;
  color: #000;
  background-color: #ccc;
}
#content {
  padding: 10px;
  margin-top: 5px;
  margin-bottom: 0px;
  margin-right: auto;
  margin-left: auto;
  background-color: #fff;
  border: 1px solid #000;
  width: 90%;
}
.innerBox {
  padding: 0px 10px 0px 10px;
  margin: 0px;
  border: 1px solid #000;
}
#navBar {
  padding: 0px 10px 0px 10px;
  margin-top: 0px;
  margin-bottom: 5px;
  margin-right: auto;
  margin-left: auto;
  background-color: #fff;
```

```
    border-top: 0px;
    border-bottom: 1px solid #000;
    border-left: 1px solid #000;
    border-right: 1px solid #000;
    text-align: right;
    width: 90%;
}
.nav {
    margin-top: 0px;
    margin-bottom: 5px;
}
```

Figure 10-5 shows what it looks like in a modern browser.

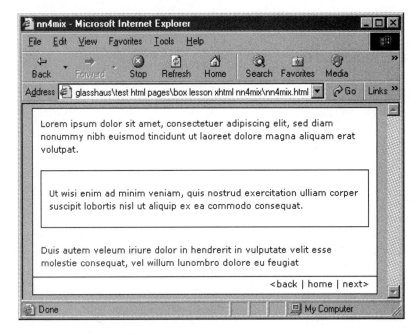

Figure 10-5. Modern browser version

Figure 10-6 shows what it looks like in NN4.

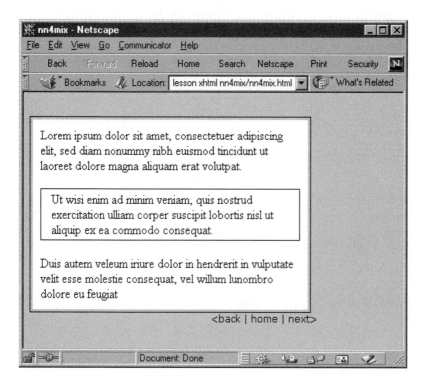

Figure 10-6. NN4 version

Some of these problems are ones we've already discussed, so let's fix those first.

NN4 lacks proper inheritance support, so the common font styles need to be moved into their own rule. The content box also has that annoying border gap, so this time we'll visually remove the border altogether by changing its color to match the body background. The navigation footer has no visible box because as far as NN4 is concerned, we didn't declare a border; in the original, borders were set for only the right, left, and bottom, which are rules NN4 doesn't recognize. We'll change that to a simple border the same color as the body background, just as has been done for the content box. The original border information will now need to be put in an imported advanced stylesheet to override these NN4-specific changes so that modern browsers can continue to display the original intent.

```
body, div, p {
  font-family: verdana, arial, helvetica, sans-serif;
  color: #000;
}
```

```
body {
  margin: 0px;
  padding: 0px;
  background-color: #ccc;
}
p {
  font-size: 0.7em;
  line-height: 1.4em;
}
#content {
  padding: 10px;
  margin-top: 5px;
  margin-bottom: 0px;
  margin-right: auto;
  margin-left: auto;
  background-color: #fff;
  border: 1px solid #ccc;
  width: 90%;
}
.innerBox {
  padding: 0px 10px 0px 10px;
  margin: 0px;
  border: 1px solid #000;
}
#navBar {
  padding: 0px 10px 0px 10px;
  margin-top: 0px;
  margin-bottom: 5px;
  margin-right: auto;
  margin-left: auto;
  background-color: #fff;
  border: 1px solid #ccc;
  text-align: right;
  width: 90%;
}

.nav {
  margin-top: 0px;
  margin-bottom: 5px;
}
```

Okay, next the box centering (see Figure 10-7) needs to be fixed.

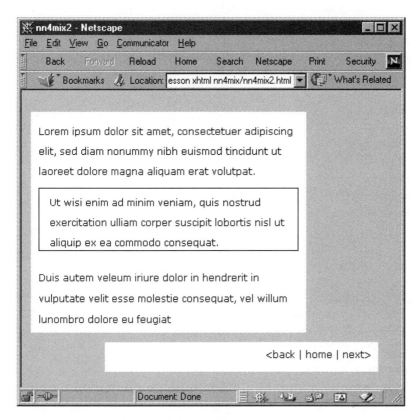

Figure 10-7. Buggy box centering in NN4

NN4 has buggy support for auto margin properties, so we'll change the boxes from being 90% wide with auto margins, to just having side margins of 5% each, something NN4 can understand. While we're at it we'll move the footer up a bit, keeping in mind there are 4px transparent gaps *and* 1px gray borders around both boxes. This second change is NN4-specific, so we'll have to remember to put the correct version in the advanced stylesheet again.

```
body, div, p {
  font-family: verdana, arial, helvetica, sans-serif;
  color: #000;
}
body {
  margin: 0px;
  padding: 0px;
  background-color: #ccc;
}
```

```
p {
  font-size: 0.7em;
  line-height: 1.4em;
}
#content {
  padding: 10px;
  margin-top: 5px;
  margin-bottom: 0px;
  margin-right: 5%;
  margin-left: 5%;
  background-color: #fff;
  border: 1px solid #ccc;
}
.innerBox {
  padding: 0px 10px 0px 10px;
  margin: 0px;
  border: 1px solid #000;
}
#navBar {
  padding: 0px 10px 0px 10px;
  margin-top: -10px;
  margin-bottom: 5px;
  margin-right: 5%;
  margin-left: 5%;
  background-color: #fff;
  border: 1px solid #ccc;
  text-align: right;
}
.nav {
  margin-top: 0px;
  margin-bottom: 5px;
}
```

Figure 10-8 shows the result.

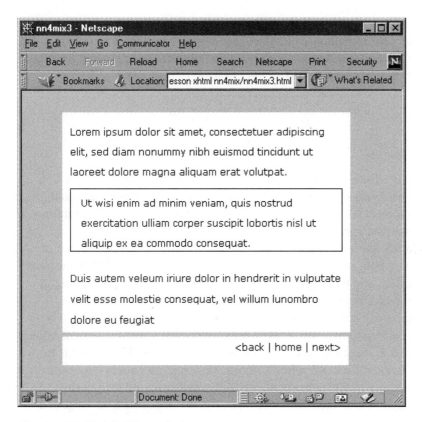

Figure 10-8. Final NN4 variation

Well, that's similar but hardly identical.

One of the many bad things that NN4 does is insert its own default margins in addition to yours, instead of the correct behavior of your margins overriding the browser's. You can fix this by giving the basic.css NN4-specific margin values and then overriding these with the correct values in your advanced stylesheet.

As we said before, it's a question of how much work you want to do to accommodate this marginal browser. If your eyes have started to glaze over with the thought of how much fun it is to write CSS for NN4, we'll repeat that the goal is to make an acceptably styled document for NN4. By using paired stylesheets with enhancing and overriding rulesets, you a have way to present styled documents for NN4 without limiting your layout options for advanced browsers.

Achieving a highly similar result for NN4 can require a long list of overriding rules and explanatory comments in your advanced stylesheet. A layout of any degree of complexity will start to feel like the old balancing act of spinning dinner plates on bamboo sticks. There will be a great deal to keep track of, and even minor future modifications will require you to figure it all out again to avoid upsetting prior dependencies. The time and cost involved has to be considered when deciding what "acceptably similar" will mean for your project, as well as the value of doing so for the remaining NN4 users. This section's purpose is to show that you *can* make an acceptably similar page for NN4 within a limited time frame and to caution that the cost of a detailed effort rises steeply.

Welcome to NN4. It can be quite a challenge.

The Works

You can avoid NN4 and serve it plain XHTML, or you can create a simple CSS layout that works on any browser including NN4, or you can use the paired stylesheets trick to have a simple layout for NN4 and an advanced layout for modern browsers. Can you do more? Yes.

Developers like a challenge. In the last year there have been a number of attempts at making complex modern layouts that also work in NN4. A few have been successful, and this suggests that when sites simply *must* present highly styled documents to all possible browsers, NN4 may still be included.

However, there is a clear caution to be made here: These are advanced layouts by very skilled individuals. These layouts are beyond the scope of this book (even Chapter 12, the projects chapter) insomuch as this book's purpose is to give you a solid foundation to learn from. Normal CSS is already a very large topic with a great many variables, and you need to be well practiced with normal CSS before attempting such bleeding-edge work. We'd be negligent if we suggested otherwise.

But if you want it all, then *yes,* you can do it. Get yourself solid with regular CSS and common browser bugs, and then go on the Net to pick up the latest in NN4 techniques. The WaSP uses such an advanced layout. It's essentially three columns with a top box, a layout that had been considered something of a holy grail for normal CSS only 2 years earlier. To see this made to work for NN4 is remarkable.

Our Modern World

This chapter's primary concern is to discuss the CSS issues of popular browsers, which we can now proceed with after having reached back to embrace the fading NN4.

Our modern world is primarily populated with versions 5 through 6 of IE, Mozilla/Netscape, Opera, and now Safari. Their individual CSS support varies from excellent to awful. Web developers need to provide a bridge between this reality and the W3C specifications because just writing correct code isn't enough to deliver web pages to your audience. This is both unfair and a fact.

This chapter isn't going to cover all browser bugs. There are hundreds (possibly thousands; we certainly haven't found them all). This chapter's intent is to get you past the showstoppers that will keep you from learning how CSS works, plus identify some other common bugs that can cause distress and confusion. Because there are plenty of bugs, the next chapter discusses identifying a bug on your own and what you can do to solve it.

Thinking About It

A bug can be that a browser doesn't interpret a declaration correctly, or that it doesn't recognize the declaration. It's hard to say which is more annoying. Incomplete standards support is so common that it's a contemporary plague. The CSS specifications are the developer's design toolset. When a major browser has incomplete support, the developer has a reduced toolset to create with. When a number of major browsers have individual and different incomplete support, a great many tools are removed from the developer's single toolset. Incomplete standards support by browser vendors is highly irresponsible. Incorrect standards support is hardly any better because it too reduces the toolset, but there's the tiny consolation that at least the browser vendor tried.

Developers have had two responses for dealing with bugs. One is that the CSS specifications are a very large toolset that is capable of a great many things, so there's usually a number of ways to achieve a design and a number of ways to express syntax. When one method doesn't work, another may well do. Although the broad flexibility of CSS was never intended to make up for browser shortcomings, it can effectively do so.

The other response is that developers tend to be creative and stubborn. Developers find, record, and publicize browser shortcomings. Developers find, record, and publicize designs that work despite browser limitations. In other words, developers have been doing the work that browser vendors have failed to, so there's a body of knowledge to help you cope.

And just as there are a number of developers, there are a number of approaches to solving browser shortcomings. We should discuss this.

Workarounds for browser shortcomings aren't necessarily hacks. The old popular table hack for layouts is a hack because this wasn't what table tags were meant to be used for and because this misuse also flew in the face of the intent of web code: The hack screwed up web pages for entirely valid devices. Ideally a workaround is valid code that doesn't present incorrectly in any valid devices. A workaround might lean toward being a hack if the code is being used in a way in which it wasn't meant to be used, but it's arguably not a hack if the code is in fact valid and works correctly for all valid devices.

This definition may sound a little gray, rather than black and white. That's because the lack of proper standards support has forced developers to work in a gray reality. The trick is to do the best you can in a difficult situation. Our guidelines for choosing successful workarounds are that the code is valid and it presents correctly in all valid devices, not just in the invalid browser you're helping out.

The remainder of the silver lining is that not every page has all bugs. You don't need to know them all. Primarily, you need to know some key ones so that you can make your initial layouts work and gain familiarity with CSS behavior. Once you have that, it's unlikely you'll be at a loss when a layout isn't working. You'll be able to judge that the strange behavior isn't your inexperience, but a bug that needs to be fixed.

Common Troubles

By "common trouble" we don't mean trouble common to all browsers, but trouble common to most layouts. These are workarounds and cautions that you should consider part of normal practice.

Box Model

IE5/Windows was one of the first browsers with good CSS support, but it also got the basic box model calculation wrong.

In CSS, your declared width or height sets the content box's size, and then the padding, border, and margin are applied outside of these two declarations. IE5/Windows incorrectly sets the border and padding within your declared width or height, as shown in Figure 10-9. This is an unfortunate error, and Microsoft quickly corrected the problem on all browsers that followed. However, browsers aren't recalled like defective cars, so developers need to provide a workaround anytime a box height or width is declared that includes padding and borders.

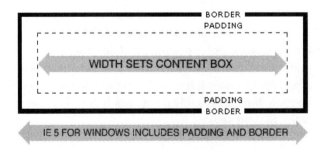

Figure 10-9. IE5/Windows misinterprets the box model

A popular fix is a very sharp bit of work by Tantek Çelik, a browser engineer and contributor to the CSS2 and CSS3 specs (you can see this hack in action in John Simon's project in Chapter 12). Here is a regular width rule, followed by the Tantek Fix version:

```
#box {
   border: 1px solid #000;
   padding: 49px;
   background: #fff;
   width: 300px;
}

#box {
   border: 1px solid #000;
   padding: 49px;
   background: #fff;
   width: 400px;   /* ie5win fix begins */
   voice-family: "\"}\"";
   voice-family: inherit;
   width: 300px;
}
html>body #box {
   width: 300px;   /* ie5win fix ends */
}
```

That's quite a mouthful, isn't it?

Here's what's going on. He's taking advantage of a parsing bug in IE5/Windows to apply an incorrect width that IE5/Windows will display correctly and that is then overridden by the correct width for correct browsers. Then there is a second part, beginning with html>, for browsers that support CSS2 selectors and the CSS box model, but have the same parsing bug as IE5/Windows. This is so they won't be tripped by the incorrect width, which is meant only for IE5/Windows. This part has been called the "Be Nice to Opera Five" rule, but it's equally important for IE5/Windows, as it may otherwise ignore the next rule in your stylesheet. Always use the whole fix.

If you're not sure what it all means, that's OK. Tantek is a browser engineer; he builds browsers for a living. His understanding of browsers and the W3C specifications is considerably deeper than that of a developer. What's key here is that you use the fix exactly as it's written, changing only the three variables to suit your desired box size. We've highlighted them below. The property may be width or height, or any other property you want to display differently in IE5/Windows. The first variable uses the incorrect value for IE, and the next two use the correct value.

```
#box {
  border: 1px solid #000;
  padding: 49px;
  background: #fff;
  width: 400px;   /* ie5win fix begins */
  voice-family: "\"}\"";
  voice-family: inherit;
  width: 300px;
}
html>body #box {
  width: 300px;   /* ie5win fix ends */
}
```

There are other ways to deal with the issue. Obviously, a box without a declared width or height won't need the fix, so if you can get the layout you want by using only content and margins, then you can avoid a lot of unpleasant-looking code.

Another way is to use nested <div>s. Because the declared width or height sets the content box for a correct browser, and for IE5/Windows they set the outside border, a trick can be made using two <div>s to imitate one box. The interior box gets no border or padding and so applies the desired content width or height for either browser. The wrapping box has no declared width or height and carries only the border and margin. The desired padding between the visible border and the visible content box, which is where IE5/Windows causes trouble, is supplied instead by using the margin of the inner box, which IE5/Windows does apply correctly.

```
#box {
  margin: 49px;
  background: #fff;
  width: 300px;
}
#box_wrapper {
  border: 1px solid #000;
  padding: 0;
  background: #fff;
}
```

Many developers prefer this method as cleaner. Others deride it because you now have redundant <div>s in your XHTML, which is arguably putting presentation code where only content should be. We think they both have a point and that IE5/Windows puts us in a compromising position. We leave it to the individual developer to decide which relief is better for her project.

Flash of Unstyled Content

This phenomenon gets its wonderful name from Rob Chandonais, who also supplied the solution.

IE will briefly display some pages without styles. You may not notice it on a fast machine with a fast connection, but on a slow machine with a slow connection it's quite disconcerting. When a page is loaded, it appears unstyled very briefly, and then the styles load. The effect is a flash of light because for a moment the screen displays black text on a white background. This has something to do with how IE loads an imported stylesheet.

Rob discovered that this doesn't occur if you have a linked stylesheet before the @import directive in the head of your document:

```
<link rel="stylesheet" href="css/empty.css" type="text/css" media="screen" />
<style type="text/css" media="all">@import url("css/myStyle.css");</style>
```

If you're already serving two stylesheets to deal with NN4, then you need not worry about this issue. But if you're not, you can still solve the problem by linking to an empty stylesheet that you can use later as an alternate stylesheet or for a media-dependent one such as for print.

Overflow

Overflow is what happens when your content lies partly outside of its box. This may occur if you are using <pre> text or large images in a box of limited height or width, or if you have excess content for a restricted box. There is an overflow property in CSS, but it has almost no support in current browsers, so you can't usefully declare how overflowing content should be displayed. What's worse, current browsers don't have the same default behavior when overflow occurs. Opera and Mozilla let the oversized content escape the box (see Figure 10-10), whereas IE stretches the box to match the content (see Figure 10-11).

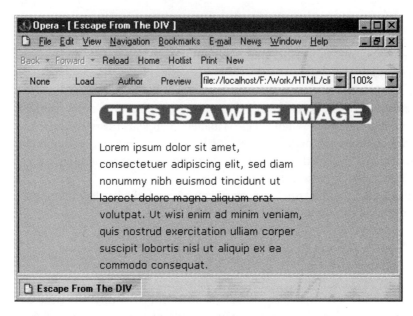

Figure 10-10. Sometimes overflow escapes the box.

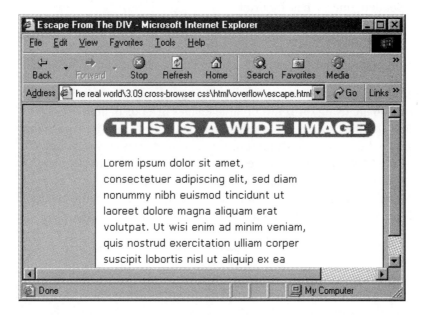

Figure 10-11. Sometimes overflow stretches the box.

Because browsers are inconsistent, the best approach is to avoid overflow altogether.

Obviously, you would test your designs for overflow in small window sizes to consider users surfing from laptops and similar small-screen hardware, but understand that a page's content may be updated over time. Ask yourself what the largest content might be and use that during your test.

A user may also have his default font set quite high for easier reading. In this case, lines of <pre> text will be displayed considerably longer than you had expected. Opera and Mozilla will let the enlarged text flow out of the <div>, where it may still be readable, but IE will widen the <div>, which could cause a floated box on the right to be displaced below. If the box on the right is absolutely positioned, the <div>s could be forced to overlap. Both may be catastrophic failures for your design. If you're framing <pre> text, you may need to use a simpler layout that can allow your content to be read when overflowing.

whitespace Property

IE5/Windows doesn't recognize the whitespace property. Most likely you'll run into this failure when you want to use whitespace: nowrap to disable word wrap or whitespace: pre to preserve formatted content. To get the desired result in IE5/Windows, you'll need to place the old tag <nobr> or <pre> in the XHTML.

It grieves us to say that. The last thing we wish to suggest is that you place any styling information in the XHTML, but in this instance you would need to. We could be poetic and consider this regressive tag use as a last wave farewell to the era we're leaving, except that we've moved on to XHTML, and <nobr> doesn't validate in XHTML.

You're faced with a character-building decision here. You may change your design to avoid the need for whitespace: nowrap, or you may accept that your page won't be displayed correctly in IE5/Windows, or you may accept invalid XHTML. We can only leave this to you and your conscience.

Scroll Bar

There are a couple of quirks to consider with scroll bars. These are aesthetic, but CSS is about style, after all.

When a page has no vertical scroll bar, Opera reserves the space it would have occupied and inserts the background color. This is a small thing, *unless* you are right-aligning a box with high precision in mind. That box won't reach the visible right edge and will instead stop where the viewport edge would have been had a scroll bar been present.

At this point it's best to remember that extreme precision is a holdover from the days of print layout, and it doesn't really fit with a device-independent high-accessibility Web. But you're a web professional and hence tempted by perfection, so we thought we'd best mention this special feature so you don't waste time trying to figure out how to fix it. You can't.

Similarly, Mozilla has an issue here, but with a twist. As far as boxes are concerned, the visible right edge of the viewport is indeed the right edge, whether or not there is a scroll bar present. But a right-aligned <body> background image will slide underneath the scroll bar, referencing where the right edge would be without a scroll bar.

Where this might also annoy you is when you have a center-aligned <body> background image and a center-aligned <div>. When there is a scroll bar, these won't quite line up, because they're referencing different right edges. The difference is only about 5px, but that can be enough throw off the look of your page. When you need to have both aligned together, you'll need to place the background image in the centered <div> instead of the <body>.

Background Image

For the placement and fixing of background images, the language of the W3C specification is a little complex in some instances. The W3C needs to phrase the specifications in broad terms that will stay relevant as the Web develops beyond the software and hardware that we have today. Such language can sometimes cause a developer to spend long hours staring at the screen, trying to figure out just what, exactly, is meant. This is one of those times, and it appears that browser engineers had trouble with this part of the specification too, because browsers react quite differently in one instance of fixed attachment.

Simple background image placement is well supported by browsers except Opera 5. You may place a <body> background image anywhere you like in relation to the viewport, and you may have it stay in place as the page scrolls by using the declaration background-attachment: fixed. However, Opera 5 relates the declared position to your entire page, not to the viewport. So if you specify a fixed placement such as bottom left on a long page, such as with this ruleset:

```
body {
  background-image: url(../img/typical.gif);
  background-repeat: no-repeat;
  background-attachment: fixed;
  background-position: bottom left;
}
```

then an Opera 5 user won't see the image because it's placed at a position below the monitor. And it will stay in that useless virtual position as the page is scrolled because of the background-attachment: fixed declaration.

Fortunately, this was corrected in Opera 6. What's also fortunate is Opera 5 wasn't a widely used browser. Opera gained most of its popularity with version 6, and Opera users in general are quick to upgrade. Most Windows users have already moved on to version 7.

But if you'd rather be certain *all* of your audience with modern browsers sees your fixed body image, then you'll have to limit yourself to placing it along the top of your page, because this is the only area where Opera 5 can agree with IE, Mozilla, and later Operas, as both the initial viewport and a long page have the same top.

Now, things get less simple when you use a fixed background image within a <div>. More simply put, depending on how you view the world, you just can't do it, because there is insufficient agreement between browsers. Different browsers, different interpretations, one bit of CSS:

```
background-repeat: no-repeat;
background-position: bottom left;
background-attachment: fixed;
```

IE will place that image in the bottom left of the <div>, and it will stay there as if you had not specified background-attachment: fixed. Opera 5 and 6 will also place the image in the bottom left of the <div>, and then it will remain fixed in relation to the viewport as you scroll. Mozilla and Opera 7 place the image in relation to the viewport, not the <div>, meaning there is a good chance it's been placed outside your <div> and you won't be able to see it. This is unfortunate.

But do go ahead and use positioned background images within <div> elements *without* the background-attachment: fixed declaration. The support for this is perfect across all the modern browsers.

```
background-repeat: no-repeat;
background-position: bottom left;
```

This will place your background image in the bottom left of the <div> and it will stay there, in all four major browsers, with no trouble at all.

Layout-Specific Troubles

Certain layouts display individual shortcomings of browsers. Here, each trouble-prone layout is discussed in a simple form, but you should keep in mind that any complex layout is built upon these simple ones and will need the same workarounds.

Centering with Opera

It's entirely correct to center a <div> with the following simple rule:

```
margin: 20px auto;
```

However, Opera 5 had trouble with this shorthand. This is easily fixed by using the longer syntax:

```
margin-top: 20px;
margin-bottom: 20px;
margin-right: auto;
margin-left: auto;
```

Centering with Internet Explorer

This one is more fun. The early versions of IE 5 and IE 5.5 for Windows had serious trouble with centering a <div>. The correct method is to simply set right and left margins to auto, as shown in Chapter 8:

```
body { margin: 0px; padding: 0px;
    font-family: verdana, arial, helvetica, sans-serif;
    font-size: 12px;
    line-height: 22px;
    color: black;
    background-color: #ccc;
}
#content {
    padding: 10px;
    margin-top: 5px;
    margin-bottom: 5px;
    margin-right: auto;
    margin-left: auto;
    background-color: #fff;
    border: 1px solid #000;
    width: 70%;
}
```

However, here's what you actually need to do:

```
body { margin: 0px; padding: 0px;
    font-family: verdana, arial, helvetica, sans-serif;
    font-size: 12px;
    line-height: 22px;
    color: black;
    background-color: #ccc;
    text-align: center; /* part 1 of 2 centering hack */
}
#content {
    padding: 10px;
    margin-top: 5px;
    margin-bottom: 5px;
    margin-right: auto;
    margin-left: auto;
    background-color: #fff;
    border: 1px solid #000;
    text-align: left; /* part 2 of 2 centering hack */
    width: 70%;
}
```

Not only is this workaround nonintuitive, but also it has two parts. We don't recommend trying to figure this one out. Instead, we recommend you make a simple centered box CSS template that you can copy and paste this markup from until you memorize it. And you should memorize it—you can expect to be writing for IE5.5/Windows foibles for several more years.

You're likely wondering what happens to any text outside of that centered box, because there is a declared text-align: center for body. Well, it's correctly center-aligned. You'll need to have all text within <div> elements to avoid this trouble when getting simple centered <div>s to work.

Netscape and Margin Top

Netscape 6 ignores the margin-top property for a static box. Sometimes.

We say "sometimes" not because there's a difference between sub-versions of Netscape 6, nor because there are differences between Netscape 6 on the PC and Mac platforms. We say "sometimes" because it doesn't occur with *all* static boxes, although it definitely occurs with *some* static boxes.

If you use a layout like the two- or three-column examples in Chapter 8, the glitch occurs. The static box containing the main content sits up tight against the top of the viewport instead of being spaced by its margin.

```
body {
  margin: 0px;
  padding: 0px;
  font-family: verdana, arial, helvetica, sans-serif;
  font-size: 12px;
  line-height: 22px;
  color: #000;
  background-color: #ccc;
}
#left {
  position: absolute;
  top: 0px;
  left: 0px;
  margin: 5px;
  padding: 10px;
  border: 1px solid #000;
  background-color: #fff;
  width: 90px;
}
#middle {
  margin: 5px 122px 5px 122px;
  padding: 10px;
  border: 1px solid #000;
  background-color: #fff;
}
#right {
  position: absolute;
  top: 0px;
  right: 0px;
  margin: 5px;
  padding: 10px;
  border: 1px solid #000;
  background-color: #fff;
  width: 90px;
}
```

Figure 10-12 shows the result.

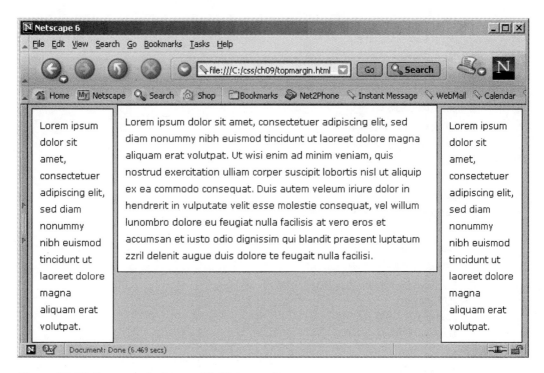

Figure 10-12. Top-margin issue with Netscape 6

Yet in other treatments of the static box, such as the centered example, things sit where they should. How will you know whether your design has an affected static box? Just test your layout in Netscape 6, either PC or Mac; this Mozilla-based browser is consistent across platforms. The fix, however, is so simple you may just want to make it common practice. All you need to do is set the box's top margin to 0px and use the <body> top margin instead:

```
body {
    margin-top: 5px;
    padding: 0px;
    font-family: verdana, arial, helvetica, sans-serif;
    font-size: 12px;
    line-height: 22px;
    color: #000;
    background-color: #ccc;
}
```

```
#left {
  position: absolute;
  top: 0px;
  left: 0px;
  margin: 5px;
  padding: 10px;
  border: 1px solid #000;
  background-color: #fff;
  width: 90px;
}
#middle {
  margin: 0px 122px 5px 122px;
  padding: 10px;
  border: 1px solid #000;
  background-color: #fff;
}
#right {
  position: absolute;
  top: 0px;
  right: 0px;
  margin: 5px;
  padding: 10px;
  border: 1px solid #000;
  background-color: #fff;
  width: 90px;
}
```

Figure 10-13 shows the result.

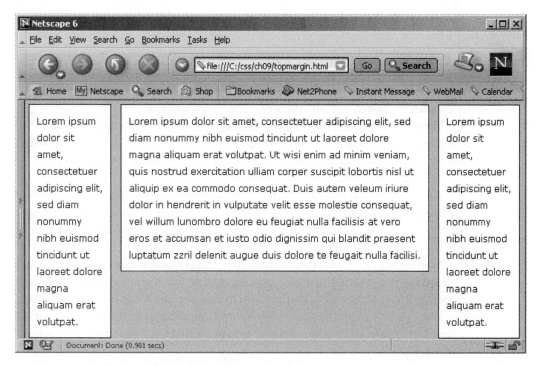

Figure 10-13. Top margin fixed for Netscape 6

The inconsistency of this bug implies that there might be more to learn by investing long nights and much coffee in building test samples. But the browser is otherwise very good with static boxes, and once you know about this issue it's so easy to spot and to fix that most developers are quite happy to apply the fix and save time for inevitable difficult bugs.

Internet Explorer and Floating Boxes

When you float a box left or right, IE 5, 5.5, and 6 for Windows will double your declared side margin between the box and viewport edge. If you're using a large margin, this doubling will be very noticeable and unacceptable. What's particularly odd about this bug is it seems to apply only to the edge of the viewport; if you float a box against another box, the margins work as declared.

As with the Netscape bug, this bug is quickly and simply fixed with substitution. Use a body margin in place of box margin on the affected side.

Content-Related Troubles

Often enough your boxes won't sit in quite the same spot in the different browsers, even after you've dealt with the previously described issues. Things will be just a few pixels off, or the boxes' contents will begin at slightly different heights than declared and desired—small amounts, such as 5px or 10px.

These are bugs, and they're rather tricky ones to see. Sometimes the content's margin is leaking outside of the box and pushes the box down. Sometimes the content's margin slides under the box's padding, making the content begin too high within the box.

Because the amounts are small and most designs aren't tight, the bug may not be noticed by your viewer. You'll notice it when you're comparing your layout in different browsers, side by side. Very often the error is acceptable, although it will be disconcerting for you.

At other times with certain layouts, the error is enough to make your page look wrong. When that's the case, you'll have to decide if you'd rather loosen your design or insert some rather kludgy rules to compensate for these browser slips.

We're going to identify some of these joys and kludges in the sections that follow, but before we do that, we want to suggest that you come back to this section later.

If you're new to layout using CSS, you're probably holding quite a bit in your head right now. It would be best if you skip the next bit and come back after you've had some practice. The following bugs are minor aesthetic nuisances, but they're a little difficult to follow. We fear you may get bogged down trying to remember too many exceptions to rules you've just begun to use. It would be much better to get yourself comfortable with CSS layout first, and then return here when you're ready to track some highly annoying minor bugs.

For Example

If we run a test set of static, floated, and absolute boxes with all else equal, there are some interesting results:

- For a static box, IE5/Windows will begin the text a little higher than all the other browsers. The rest of the browsers will display the text at the desired point.

- For floated boxes and absolutely positioned boxes, IE5/Windows, IE5.5/Windows, and Opera 5 will all begin the text noticeably higher than specified, though by different amounts.

Does it matter? Possibly not. Very possibly your design will be such that a small difference across browsers is visually insignificant. That would be the happiest result. But there will also be times when it does matter. Say you've built a three-column layout that combines a static box flanked by absolutes. Say you've declared the same box padding and text margins in each to get their individual contents to begin in a nice line across the page. And, of course, it will fail to do so in IE5/Windows, IE5.5/Windows, and Opera 5. If you're intent on having these browsers fall in line, then you'd best read the following section to know what's going on.

What's Happening?

Let's magnify things for clarity. Here's our typical example (see Figure 10-14) with some added reference lines and symbolic ovals. BM is the box `margin-top`, BP is the box `padding-top`, and CM is the content's `margin-top`.

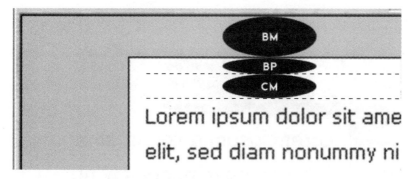

Figure 10-14. Symbolic diagram of box properties

In the static box, IE5/Windows leaks the content `margin-top` outside the box, and it slides *beneath* the box `margin-top`. Oddly enough, if you've got body `margin` as well, it also slides underneath that. Whichever of the three is largest will decide where the box's top actually begins. The lesser two sit beneath the largest, unnoticed.

This leaves the text within the box spaced from the border by only the box padding, as shown in Figure 10-15.

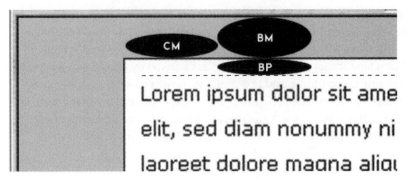

Figure 10-15. Margins overlapping incorrectly

In the floated box and the absolutely positioned box, IE5/Windows and IE5.5/Windows both have the content margin-top properly inside the box, but now it slides beneath the box padding. Again, whichever is largest decides the result and hence how far the text is spaced from the border, as shown in Figure 10-16.

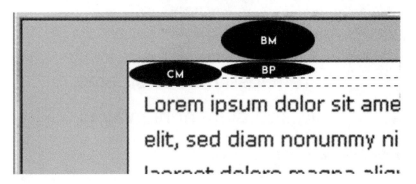

Figure 10-16. Margin and padding overlapping incorrectly

Opera 5 also displays the text high in the floated box and the absolutely positioned box. When you play with the values and measure the results, it becomes clear that the content margin-top is outside the box again and underneath the box margin. Even more interesting is that if you add some body margin to the problem, it pushes the box margin down *into* the box, moving the text down and not the box top. Nice.

This is all very exciting if you like hunting bugs, but it's quite tedious if you're just trying to find a way out of the problem.

What to Do

There is a solution, but we don't recommend it unless you're feeling exceptionally headstrong about this problem. Instead, we suggest you just loosen up your design a bit so you can live with some inconsistency.

However, if you're feeling determined, you can first set your content's top margin to 0 and then add its previous amount to the content's bottom margin to preserve your formatting between paragraphs. Now use box `padding` alone to set the space in the top of your boxes, and use body `margin` to set where the box top begins. Don't set text `margin-top` or box `margin-top`. We call this "The Ugly Fix" and we suggest you put a really descriptive comment in your CSS so you'll remember everything you did the next time you open the stylesheet.

When There Are No Box Margins

When you have a box layout in which the boxes begin right at the top of the page, it appears you've got the same trouble with inconsistent spacing, except Opera 5 suddenly behaves itself.

Why? Well, because the content `margin` isn't really inside or outside the box with Opera; it's simply placed between the text and the first thing it *does* recognize, which in this case is the viewport. So you get the appropriate spacing as a result.

However, you'll still need to use The Ugly Fix for IE5/Windows, because IE5/Windows is placing the content `margin-top` outside the box, where there's supposed to be no margin in this design. This errant content `margin-top` pushes the box's top down, leaving a highly unwanted virtual margin.

You're probably shaking your head as you read this. We agree. We'd apologize, but we don't manufacture browsers. Let's finish on that note.

Is That It?

Gosh no. But it's enough. The intention of this chapter is to get you started and to give you a solid enough footing in known cross-browser issues that your first few layouts don't become a nightmare initiation. There are plenty more browser issues, and real-world CSS layout is young enough that there are still new bugs to be discovered, quite possibly by you. This is why the next chapter is about troubleshooting.

Summary

This was a busy chapter. Let's break it down to make remembering more manageable.

Browsers have bugs, some more than others. In particular, there is a distinct dividing line between the pretty much incapable version 4 browsers and later browsers with slowly improving CSS capabilities. Prior to the dominance of CSS-capable browsers, developers created layout by using a table hack as an interim compromise of limited usefulness.

Writing for the modern Web requires a break from this past practice, but not an abandonment of past browsers. For users either unwilling or unable to upgrade their old browser, we have options, including presenting an acceptably styled document by serving two stylesheets: one with basic styles and one with complex styles that are hidden from the old browsers.

Unfortunately, modern browsers are far from perfect, which makes learning CSS a real chore for developers. To ease this problem, the troubles were broken into three sections:

- The "Common Troubles" show up just about everywhere, so you'd best remember these like you remember phone numbers. We suggest you use whatever memorization method got you through the really boring courses in school.

- The "Layout-Specific Troubles" don't always raise their heads. These are easier to remember by just remembering the layouts they're associated with. You may want to make a generic set of these layouts with the fixes neatly commented. This will give you something to copy and paste from instead of building each new design from scratch.

- The "Content-Related Troubles" should be quite rare unless you're intent on a finicky layout. When you're going down that route, just go back and reread that section until it sticks. These aren't items you want to learn the hard way by figuring them out on your own.

The flexibility of CSS as a design language also allows for a variety of approaches to handling browser bugs. This chapter covered enough of the issue to ensure that you can begin practicing CSS without being stymied and give you a starting point to develop your own strategies from. There are further methods shown by some the different authors of the projects in Chapter 12. Studying their different perspectives on the same issues will help round out your own approach so that coding around browser bugs becomes a routine task, rather than a showstopping problem.

CHAPTER 11

Troubleshooting

CSS ISN'T SIMPLE, because it is powerful. There are plenty of ways to do things wrong so that there can be plenty of ways to do things right. On top of this we have the incomplete, incorrect, and inconsistent standards support of our browsers. A developer needs to look for trouble and be able to fix it.

The first thing to understand is that when a page is displayed incorrectly, you aren't looking at the problem; you're looking at a symptom. The source of the symptom is what you have to find and fix. A symptom may or may not indicate an obvious source, and it may be the result of more than one source. All you know at first is that something is wrong.

Troubleshooting is an organized approach to finding and fixing the source problem. You proceed from the general to the specific, without missing steps, yet as directly as possible. Each step is a test, and each result tells you what step to follow with, until you identify the offending bit of code.

What can make this exercise more fun is that there's a good chance your problematic code is entirely valid, and it isn't being rendered correctly in a particular browser. Because you can't fix the browser, you'll also need a method to decide the best way to alter your code while still satisfying your design, the other browsers, and validity.

In this chapter we first discuss hardware and software for troubleshooting, followed by how to use these to find out what's wrong, and then how to create your own solution to the discovered problem.

Hardware

Obviously, to fix a problem you need to be able to see the buggy browser. This is actually hard to do because some browsers are platform specific. Some are only available for Windows or Mac, and Mac itself is split with the new OS X, which doesn't support all the same browsers as the previous Mac OS 9. What's more, the Windows operating system allows only one version of IE to be installed.

This is a key problem of coding for the Web. With the platform issue the entire tenet of "write once, view everywhere" is mocked by any poor standards support by browser vendors. These failings place an entirely unreasonable workload on the developer, who is supposed to be anyone and everyone, not just fully equipped IT departments. But until all browser vendors create products with full standards compliance and the market has had time to absorb them, cross-browser testing is a necessity. A developer has to pick up the slack somehow, and we present three scenarios for dealing with this.

Update!

As this book goes to press, an important discovery has been made that allows more than one IE to be installed on most Windows operating systems. This greatly reduces the hardware requirement for developers. Please visit two sites that are the most active in this experiment:

```
http://www.insert-title.com/web_design/?page=articles/dev/multi_IE
```

```
http://www.skyzyx.com/archives/000094.php
```

At the time of this writing it appears that IE 5, 5.5, and 6 can be made to coexist on Windows 98, ME, 2000, and XP. Work is continuing on Windows 95 and NT 4. The preceding sites give information on what modifications you must make to these browsers, and they also provide links to preconfigured downloads. By the time you read this, it's reasonable to expect that more will have been learned and the techniques will have spread to other sites.

Thank you, Joe Maddalone and Ryan Parman!

Utopia

Utopia would be a LAN of machines so you can see your layout run on all the current browsers at the same time as you test your markup. I wish I were kidding. Yes, that's a lot of monitors. But this solution is a good one for the professional shop. It's an expense that pays back in speed. The downside is the cost and that it requires a lot of space.

A smaller, if not cheaper, paradise may be had by running multiple operating systems on single machines. There is software available to do this, but I'd rather not name names. With the expense involved, it's better for you to research the competitors' pros and cons thoroughly to decide if their solution is right for you and worth the cost. Having to flip between operating system windows isn't quite as fast as glancing at a row of monitors, but you can also combine the two methods to match the space and budget limitations of your company.

Less Than Utopia

You can approach Utopia for modest expense with only a little compromise in speed; it's not an all-or-nothing situation. This is my own approach, as I needed a solution suited to the income of an individual, not a business.

Most browsers run well on mildly obsolescent computers. This allowed me to reuse my older PCs and Windows operating systems as browser testers, plus I picked up an equivalent PowerMac very cheaply, as they're also obsolescent but just fine for testing web pages. Add Ethernet cards and a hub, and you've got a good chunk of Utopia spread across your desk.

But you might not be able to scrounge all the equipment you need as easily, and you'll need to find other options to fill in missing browsers. In my case, I'm primarily a Windows user so I don't have OS X yet, and it's very expensive to buy a new Mac just to test browsers. So I trade page testing with my Mac friends. They send me screen shots of my pages under OS X, and I send them screens of the various Windows browsers. This is the buddy system, and I recommend it. It not only gives access to a missing platform, but also places two minds on a problem, which can be indispensable.

A downside is that working from screen shots is not as fast as having all the machines in front of you, so it becomes very important to test your layouts early in a project and not test against a missing browser on your last day.

The Struggling Independent

What do you do if you have only one machine and operating system? You network with other struggling independents. It's the extended buddy system. You're hardly alone in this problem, so make contact with others in person and in developer forums, and test layouts for each other.

There is an exceptional forum for CSS questions called CSS-Discuss (http://www.css-discuss.org/). As with any forum, read the rules, consult the aggregated knowledge in the Wiki (http://css-discuss.incutio.com/), and take time to answer questions as well as ask.

The wealth of advice and skill available through this method is enormous, but it can be much slower to troubleshoot your pages this way. If you rely on networking alone, then you'll need to budget more time for debugging a project than you would with the other methods. We suggest that the group advantage should be extended to hosting collections of thoroughly tested layouts to share. Layouts created by modifying a proven base layout will likely have few bugs, if any. By using a distributed approach to a distributed problem, we can reduce a major hurdle for all developers.

In Any Scenario . . .

Whether you have one machine or several, it's useful to know that you can you run several browsers on a single operating system, just not all browsers.

Obviously, you're limited to browsers supported by your operating system. IE is two different browsers of the same name for Mac and Windows, whereas Opera and Mozilla are single browsers adapted to run across Mac, Windows, and Linux. So if you test your layout in one Mozilla or Opera version, then you've tested that version across platforms. This sort of stable cross-platform rendering is very helpful to developers.

The Mac platform itself, however, has been split with the introduction of OS X, which is quite distinct from the preceding OS 9. The Safari browser is available only for OS X, as is Mozilla starting with 1.3. Also, the latest versions of Opera, and Mozilla from 1.0, will only work with a Mac as old as OS 9. The formerly popular OS 8 is becoming less useful to developers, although it's still good for testing the venerable IE Mac.

There's also a question of how many versions of each operating system–compatible browser you may run, because different versions have different CSS capability. IE for Windows is the main problem here, because you can only run one per operating system. Versions 5, 5.5, and 6 have quite different CSS rendering and are all still popular. This oversight by Microsoft forces developers to need three Windows operating systems. IE for Mac allows different versions to coexist.

Other browser vendors have been more considerate. You may run as many versions of Opera and Mozilla and even the old Netscape alongside each other as you wish. You need only be cautioned to install each in distinct directories so that none overwrites an earlier version, and in particular for Mozilla and Netscape, you should create distinct users for each version so that there is no conflict of commonly held bookmarks, settings, or cache. For ease of use, we name both the installation directory and the user with the respective browser's version number.

Browsers are best downloaded from the browser vendors themselves, but when earlier versions are hard to find, consult the archive of the excellent developer community group evolt.org (`http://browsers.evolt.org/`).

Software

There's no need to discuss all the software a developer uses, but there are three items we should emphasize as particularly valuable for troubleshooting.

W3C Validators

The W3C provides us not only with the specifications for our Web, but also with the tools to test that we've written correctly. This is essential software. If you're not already familiar with the W3C validators, then visit them now and read the instructions:

```
http://validator.w3.org/
```

```
http://jigsaw.w3.org/css-validator/
```

Validate your work early, and validate often. It's easier to fix the few mistakes of a stage than all the mistakes of a finished layout, and it's far better to catch a design-changing error in the beginning, before you've spent a great deal of time on refinements.

Although the validators are very good at identifying errors in your XHTML and CSS syntax, an error can sometimes cause them to report subsequent markup and rulesets as errors, even when they're correct. When a validator reports multiple errors, fix the first error and then revalidate. The subsequent errors may disappear or change. Also note that the validators check only for correct syntax, not for your design intent. CSS is quite large enough for you to correctly express a nonsensical design.

To use the validators you need to either upload your files or type in individual file addresses. This can become tedious very quickly, so we suggest you use free bookmarklets (`http://www.tantek.com/favelets/index.html`) created by a generous developer to make using the validators faster for everyone. With these, URL submission is a one-click process. Thank this gentleman when you meet him.

Your Browser

No browser is perfect, but it does matter which you use during your initial construction. If you first build to a browser with good standards support, then you'll have fewer bugs to correct when you test against the others later. If you instead start with a buggy browser, then you'll have a layout tailored to its quirks, which can cause confusion and a great deal more work to achieve a layout that works across all browsers. Make it your first concern to have valid markup and rulesets, and then adjust for individual browser problems.

For example, if you were to build initially to IE5/Windows, there is the issue of its incorrect box model. If you didn't already know about this bug, you would use the wrong width and height values and not realize it, because the layout would look good in IE5/Windows *and* it would pass the W3C validator as valid syntax. Then you'd find your boxes were larger in Opera and Mozilla, and you would likely wonder why those browsers don't get it, because the validator said your code was OK. You'd be started in entirely the wrong direction for troubleshooting, and you could waste a great deal of time before realizing it.

At the moment, the latest versions of Opera and Mozilla have very accurate CSS support compared to other browsers, so we recommend viewing your layout in either of these browsers during initial construction. When you begin cross-browser testing, you may find a browser that doesn't display your layout as these two do. At this point you can be suspicious, though not certain, that what Opera and Mozilla agree on is correct. The next step is to read the relevant W3C specification closely. Once you're certain what the markup or ruleset should be, then use that and find a correcting compromise to address any wrong browser's bug.

It's a primary concern that your work is always correct. The developer's aim is forward compatibility in a Web of expanding devices, not creating pages that will be locked into an incorrect browser's rendering of today. This is the intention and utility of the W3C specifications, and current browser shortcomings make it your challenge.

Please note that we're *not* expressing an overall view of any browser's worth in this section. We're speaking only in terms of correct CSS support, and hence what makes a particular browser a better tool for initial development.

CAUTION *Microsoft has a policy of providing browsers that render more than the W3C specifications. For example, you can solve the IE5/Windows box model issue with an IE expression:*

```
#typicalDiv {
    width : 250px;
    width : expression( navigator.userAgent.match(/MSIE 5/) ? 256 : 250 );
    border: 3px solid #000;
}
```

There is a problem with this. Although it looks good on the surface because it uses an IE expression to fix an IE problem, and although the other browsers ignore markup they don't understand, this isn't W3C markup.

That's a real problem because W3C architects will expand the web specifications by using syntax not already used by the current specifications, and they don't keep track of individual companies' proprietary markup schemes, as that is impractical. At some point, new W3C markup may use some of the preceding syntax, and valid browsers will then trip on IE expressions.

If you're writing for the World Wide Web, you should use only W3C syntax. The preceding syntax is only appropriate in a network that is accessed solely by Microsoft browsers, and such development is outside the scope and spirit of this book. We mention this caution here because developers who test their initial code in IE may well use code appropriate only to IE without knowing that they are and then waste a great deal of time trying to figure out why it doesn't work for other browsers.

A Ruler

Not just any ruler, but any of a number of simple shareware rulers that give you a way to precisely measure distance on your screen. This is a minor piece of software, but it's the only way to be certain just what size a `<div>` or a `margin` is actually being displayed. That can be essential to troubleshooting, and it saves getting fingerprints on your monitor.

Wetware

Now that we've discussed software and hardware, it's time to think about thinking.

When a layout doesn't display correctly, the first thing to determine is if the problem is with the browser or your code. The W3C validator will test your syntax, but not your intention. After your layout passes the validator, test it across different browsers to look for irregularities.

If your layout fails in the newest browsers, and in particular if it works in only one of them, then step back and reread the relevant portions of the W3C specifications and this book. There *is* a chance that you're correct and only one browser supports your desired result, but it's a very slim chance. It's more likely that your use of markup or rulesets is wrong, and this has to be corrected before you can proceed. But once you're sure of your code, and a page still doesn't render correctly for multiple modern browsers, then it's time to share with your peers. It's very likely that you just need a better explanation of how the code is supposed to work, not that you've found a particularly rare browser bug. Post your question to a CSS discussion, describe the issue, and include a link to your validated problem page.

Fortunately, most CSS troubles show up in only one or two browsers. In these cases your valid layout is correct, and you've simply used an item that an individual browser handles badly. At this point, you need to identify the markup or rule that is causing the trouble so that you can fix it.

Finding Trouble

It's important to test a new layout early. If you wait until you've refined a page to perfection, then you can easily become lost among too many possible sources of a problem. Simplify your troubleshooting by testing at three stages during a build so you'll have manageable layers of code to look through:

- Stage 1: Bare layout

- Stage 2: Layout refined with margins, padding, borders, and colors

- Stage 3: Layout filled with actual content

Stage 1: Bare Layout

By a "bare layout" we mean the raw structure of boxes. In particular, when you're new to CSS and browser shortcomings, it's a good idea to test your desired arrangement alone to ensure it's even possible. All that you're testing is that your basic structure works by isolating it from any other trouble sources.

Build your new design with all the <div>s visible and distinct from the background so that you can see conflicts and overlaps. Temporarily use simple margins and padding with distinct sizes in pixels, such as 20px and 10px. With these absolute values it will be easy to see an incorrect display, and when something is wrong a quick measurement will tell you which property is being misapplied. Finally, make all of your content an unstyled faux text such as "Lorem ipsum."

Testing now will show you if your layout choice simply doesn't work, either because you've misunderstood box layout, or you have insufficient browser support yet. If your layout works but with minor discrepancies on some browser, you can use your ruler to measure the difference from correct display. Amounts that match the distinct pixel sizes for margins and padding indicate trouble with those. By changing the size of the individual padding or margins in that area, you can find the one that is troubled.

With a problem isolated, use a method of the section "Fixing Trouble" to form a solution, and then proceed to the next stage of testing.

Stage 2: Add Refinements

Next refine the margins, padding, borders, and colors of the design around the plain content, and then test. If the layout now fails, you'll know it was your new margins or padding that triggered the problem. Make all borders and content box edges visible again by adding these temporary rules to your CSS:

```css
div {
  border: 1px dotted #000;
}
p, ol, li, h2 {
  background: #ccc
}
```

Compare the following two screen shots (Figures 11-1 and 11-2). All that is different is the addition of these two lines to produce the second screen shot.

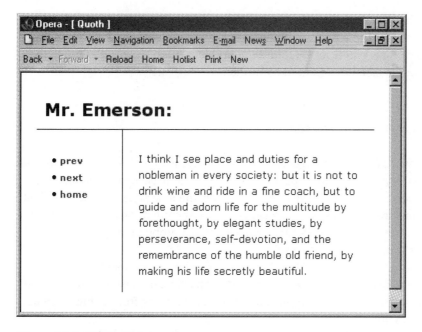

Figure 11-1. Normal view

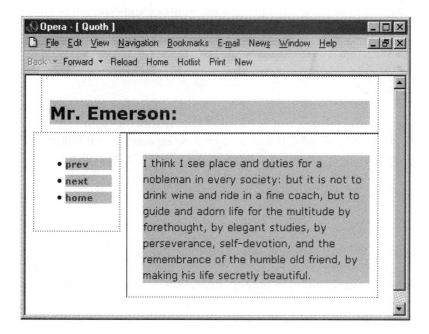

Figure 11-2. Structure exposed

With this visual aid, locate your trouble area and change the values for margins and padding there back to the distinct pixel sizes they were before, testing with each change. When you've found the problem ruleset, use a method in the "Fixing Trouble" section and then continue with stage 3.

Stage 3: Add Real Content

Now apply your CSS to the target XTHML document with real content. Before you add styles, check that special content, such as lists, forms, and tables, is displayed correctly. Once you've done that, apply the final styles and make a final test. With any trouble, isolate a suspicious ruleset or content type by removing it to see if the trouble disappears. Once you've found a problem, use a method in the "Fixing Trouble" section to resolve it.

CSS is often troublesome. A new developer, a developer creating a particularly complex layout, or anyone who is working particularly late at night can use testing in stages to keep the finding half of troubleshooting from being a needle-in-a-haystack affair.

For anyone beset by trouble with a familiar design, an adapted design, or a pre-existing design, it can be enough to simply apply the temporary rules described in stage 2. Very often this will make the trouble visible enough to identify the source by removing or modifying likely rules.

Fixing Trouble

But how do you fix trouble once you've found it? First ensure that your code is correct. Your syntax may be valid, but you may not be expressing your intention correctly. Consult the relevant section of this book and the W3C specifications.

Consult

If you've managed to learn XHTML without getting familiar with W3C documentation yet, then don't put off the experience any longer. You don't need to read the entire CSS specification in order to use CSS, any more than you need to read an entire dictionary in order to speak, but it's vastly helpful to be able to look up items directly in either. The W3C has a "Finding Your Way at W3C" (http://www.w3.org/2002/03/new-to-w3c) page to help new users locate and navigate the structure of their specifications.

Once you've ensured that you're correct, consider how many browsers are showing the problem. If it's all or most of them, then you're likely using an as-yet unsupported section of the specifications. You can do a great deal with CSS at the moment, but there are still sections of the vocabulary that are unavailable to you. You'll have to either use different method to express your design or consider a different design.

There are a number of CSS support charts on the Web (http://devedge. netscape.com/library/xref/2003/css-support/), the most popular likely being Eric Meyer's Mastergrid. These charts are unpleasant to read straight through, of course, but they're very useful when you simply need to confirm support of single items.

If your desired but reluctant design is a layout that you've seen before, then clearly you would view source on an existing version to gain direct enlightenment. But if your design is still hypothetical, or if the inspiring design actually turned out not to be a cross-browser solution either, then get more heads on the problem at a developer forum such as CSS-Discuss (http://www.css-discuss.org/). A lot of the people there like challenges. Either they'll have already considered this design issue themselves, or they'll be keen to figure out how your new idea can be achieved.

More often you'll have a particular issue with a single browser's bug. Most often this bug will be well known. Take the property and browser in question and consult the Web. This can be a quick task if you know where to look, and fortunately other developers have worked together to make this easier by providing and maintaining a resource Wiki (http://css-discuss.incutio.com/) of current CSS solutions and links. You should consider this as valuable as the CSS specifications themselves and become as familiar with looking items up in it.

Re-express

There are also techniques for creating your own solution. CSS is large enough that there are usually a number of ways to express a design. Very often you can get around a browser issue with a change of syntax or a substituted property.

For example, Opera 5 for the PC failed to center <div>s as expected. The rule it wasn't applying was margin: 20px auto. Simply changing the syntax from shorthand to the long form gives an entirely valid solution that works across all browsers. The problem turned out to be not a complete lack of support of the property, just lack of support of one expression of that property.

```
margin-top: 20px;
margin-bottom: 20px;
margin-right: auto;
margin-left: auto;
```

In the case of Netscape 6, it would ignore some <div> margin-top values. Clearly this is a basic property that many designs need, so an alternative method had to be found. A direct method is to simply substitute an adjacent property that can create the same result. Because you can't push the <div> down using its margin-top, push it down by using the body's margin-top instead. This solution is simple, legitimate, and works across all the other browsers.

Filter

There are cases in which simple substitution or syntax changes can't overcome a browser's shortcomings. Sometimes a needed property is entirely unsupported or misapplied, and there's no other property that can take its place. The IE5/Windows box model failure is a classic case in point.

The base idea of the technique is to block a browser from the dangerous rule and feed it an incorrect value that it will display correctly, while also blocking correct browsers from this misinformation. This technique appeared early in CSS development with Tantek Çelik's fix for IE5/Windows's critical box width failure, and developers have since discovered and popularized filters for our other browsers (http://centricle.com/ref/css/filters/).

This is a useful technique when you are stuck, but it comes with a caution. This method makes your code distinctly harder to read. Maintenance time is a real cost to be weighed against the value of the desired property for your design. This should be considered a last-resort method for a particularly valuable result when no other solution can be found. In many cases, a different design can be just as pleasing for your audience and can be achieved without having a code soup.

Reconsider

Suppose one browser shows a small discrepancy in display, like a mis-sized gap between <div>s. Ask yourself if the discrepancy matters. I'm quite serious. Is it actually aesthetically displeasing or jarring? Your audience using that browser doesn't necessarily know it isn't the intended effect; you may only see it clearly because you're comparing browsers alongside. In this light, reconsider the value of finding a solution.

It may well be worthwhile to invest the time in finding a solution for your own educational and for your self-esteem. And it may be foolhardy to do so in view of a deadline or of what you may have to add to your code to provide a fix. Weigh your options.

Life is often about compromise, and with browsers it can be doubly so. Remember that you're a designer and show some flexibility with your talent. Consider if you can successfully loosen things up so that a discrepancy becomes inconsequential to your design. For instance, if you have a small but unwanted gap appearing between <div>s that are meant to touch, you can remove that visual clue by matching the <div> and <body> background colors.

A distinctly human talent is coping with adversity through style. Modifying your design rather than your code should remain an option in your toolset.

Summary

Troubleshooting is a combination of tools and techniques for when things go wrong. This chapter discussed the hardware and software tools you need, then the methodical approach required to find the source problem quickly, followed by methods to solve it. It also discussed deciding if the problem can be solved, as discerning that something is irretrievably broken is also a part of the troubleshooting process. Troubleshooting is essentially about making the unknown known, so that you can make a decision about it.

CSS Design Projects

NOW WE GET to the fun stuff. Here's the part of the book where you take the principles you've learned thus far and apply them to some actual projects. This chapter will walk you through some of the thinking and methodologies of six CSS designers. The projects range from a weblog to a photo gallery to a site for the Buffalo Philharmonic Orchestra. While you examine the projects in this chapter, you may find it handy to follow along with the XHTML/CSS in front of you. Code for each project is available for download from `http://www.friendsofed.com`.

These projects aren't meant to be an exhaustive look at every step of building a CSS-driven site. Rather, they're intended to open up some of the thinking involved in building CSS layouts and highlight potential problem points along the way. The earlier chapters of this book covered in great detail the "how" of CSS design; consider this chapter the "what" of CSS design, as in "What can you do with it?"

You'll get a chance to take a look at the code involved, and in cases where seemingly strange code is used, you'll learn why it's used that way. The designers have run into the same problems you'll eventually come across when you develop with CSS. They've all developed unique ways to solve their respective issues, so reading this chapter is meant to be a way for you to look over the shoulder of an expert, so to speak.

By watching the designers' sites unfold as they break down the problem-solving process, we hope you'll be able to learn from their examples, refer back to their code when facing problems in your own work, and discover new and interesting CSS tricks that you might not have found otherwise.

These projects are a starting point to inspire you. CSS can do so much more than what we can show you in the limited pages of this book, and half the fun is discovering it for yourself.

Fahrner Image Replacement Caveat

There are a few very important points to consider while you read this chapter. Many of the examples make use of a technique called *Fahrner Image Replacement*, or *FIR* as it's commonly known. The FIR technique and syntax will be explained in greater detail in some of the projects, but essentially what it does is allow a designer to replace text items with image-based equivalents. This is desirable from a design point of view because it allows advanced typography and a nicer end result, but there are a few problems with the technique as it's used today.

At the time of this writing, the most popular variant of FIR relies on `display: none;` to hide the text. This breaks in two important ways. First, some screen readers won't read the text aloud, thus rendering it invisible to users with visual impairments. Second, people surfing with images off but CSS on won't see anything but a hole in the layout. This isn't common, but it does happen.

Numerous articles have been written on the subject of FIR, and the technique is evolving. It's hoped that soon there will be a way to selectively serve images without breaking accessibility. FIR isn't that way, so make absolutely sure you use it carefully and for noncritical items only. Better yet, look up some of the other ways to achieve the same effect. These articles are good starting points:

- "Using background-image to Replace Text": `http://www.stopdesign.com/also/articles/replace_text/`

- "In Defense of Fahrner Image Replacement": `http://www.digital-web.com/features/feature_2003-08.shtml`

- "Facts and Opinion About Fahrner Image Replacement": `http://www.alistapart.com/articles/fir/`

Design Projects and Techniques

FIR isn't the only technique on the menu, fortunately! Each designer has a unique approach to CSS, and you may find more than one way to do something. In this section you'll find a list of the projects presented in this chapter and a brief summary of the techniques and tricks employed by the designer.

Weblog: Dave Shea

Weblogs are all the rage these days. Everyone's got one, from your crazy Aunt Mildred to the majority of the candidates in the 2004 U.S. presidential election. Dave guides you through the unique challenges he faced building his popular design weblog, mezzoblue (`http://www.mezzoblue.com`).

Dave covers the following concepts:

- Moving from tables to CSS

- Centering a fixed-width layout

- Understanding Fahrner Image Replacement

- Placing columns within columns and using floats

- Locating a footer below content

Research Institute Site: John Simons

Considering the Web was originally developed for the exchange of research papers between labs, it's only fitting to pay homage with a project for a research institute. John walks you through the development of a site for his fictitious company, BabyGenes.

John covers the following concepts:

- Implementing columnar layouts using absolute positioning

- Hacking around IE 5's buggy box model

- Combining JavaScript and CSS to create dynamic effects

- Degrading gracefully in older browsers

Buffalo Philharmonic Orchestra Site: Michael Switzer

The theater, the opera, and the orchestra—what do they all have in common? Seasonal programs, of course. Michael leads you through the redesign of the Buffalo Philharmonic Orchestra's ('s) site to match the 2003 lineup.

Michael covers the following concepts:

- Centering a fixed-width layout

- Fixing rollover "flashing" images in IE

- Tackling long navigation lists

- Using multicolumn CSS layouts

- Converting table-based layouts

Photo Gallery: Dan Rubin

Image viewers and photo galleries serve a similar purpose: to display a series of images. Image viewers are great for online newspaper stories and magazine articles, as a way to attach a small set of images to the story. Photo galleries generally contain many more photos in an archival format, so they require a slightly different layout technique than image viewers. Dan goes from paper to pixels and touches on important points about considering nongraphical browsers, even for visual projects like his photo gallery.

Dan covers the following concepts:

- Setting goals ahead of time

- Taking ideas from paper to Photoshop to CSS

- Using CSS intuitively to reduce GIF consumption

- Creating JavaScript-free rollovers

- Using class-based "You are here" markers

- Considering nongraphical user agents

- Implementing a screen reader–friendly FIR variant

Image Viewer: Michael Pick

We're all familiar with online image viewers—tiny applications that allow a user to scroll through a list of photos. Michael sees some ways to improve the average image viewer.

Michael covers the following concepts:

- Using absolute positioning

- Using z-index to simulate layering

- Avoiding box model problems with clever padding

- Creating hover effects

- Examining display: none vs. visibility: hidden

- Combining JavaScript with CSS to create dynamic effects

Real Estate Portal: Cornelia Lange

The commercial side of the Web was a large part of the picture in the late 1990s. Although perhaps not as glamorous today as it once was, most web development is still done for a commercial environment. Reduced budgets have made low-cost development a priority; luckily, development times can be dramatically reduced using CSS layouts. Cornelia shows how she used CSS to build Imapa.de, a portal for independent real estate sales.

Cornelia covers the following concepts:

- Considering your audience

- Looking at target browsers and time/cost considerations

- Understanding the "Flash of Unstyled Content" bug in IE and how to avoid it

- Using tables for logical purposes (i.e., tabular data)

- Implementing image maps using CSS positioning

Weblog

by Dave Shea

When I was approached to write this section, I knew immediately which site I would use as my case study. mezzoblue (`http://www.mezzoblue.com`) is my personal portfolio/weblog/publishing empire, and until early August 2003 it was an embarrassing mix of tables and overwrought CSS. The damage had been done earlier in the year when I couldn't figure out how to achieve an effect or two via CSS. The intervening months showed me how it was possible, and ever since I'd been meaning to redo it.

In this section, I'll cover the design, the code, and the foundation of the weblog. I'll explore my conversion from a table-based layout to the same in CSS. I hit a few snags along the way, particularly when I tried to position a set of columns within another set of columns, and I'll show you what I did to get around those.

The Design

The design was originally constructed in Photoshop without any concern about how I would build it. As it turns out, I ended up building the same site two different ways. The old table-built site is still available at `http://www.mezzoblue.com/archives/cssbook/old/` (see Figure 12-1). Load it up and compare against the archived CSS-built test page `http://www.mezzoblue.com/archives/cssbook/new/` (see Figure 12-2). Although they aren't visually identical, the reason for this was less about differences in the technology than it was about taking the opportunity to tweak a few design issues that were bugging me!

Figure 12-1. Screen shot of the original, table-based design: over 126KB including graphics and CSS

Figure 12-2. Screen shot of the CSS-based redesign: slightly under 85KB including graphics and CSS

The Code

As well as working with a prebuilt design, I decided to create my XHTML ahead of time and then apply the design to it afterward. This is the great thing about true separation of content and presentation: You can take a well-conceived document and later design it however you want. Once I'm done with the XHTML, I may make a few minor tweaks afterward to let the document flow better, but hopefully every tweak I make is to further clarify the structure of the document rather than to make an easier job of styling it.

I knew certain things about this design ahead of time. I knew what my main header would be, I knew approximately what my content would be, and I knew that I would have to use a lot of the FIR technique to swap in images where I previously had text. FIR is something I have to plan for a bit more carefully, as it requires a bit of extra code. More on this later.

It's beyond the scope of this chapter to go into the intricacies involved in building every part of this design, but I'll cover some of the basics here. You may want to grab the downloadable code now to follow along with this part of the chapter. A permanent archive of the design, complete with images and the older table version, is available at `http://www.mezzoblue.com/archives/cssbook/`.

The Foundation

Some painters work with an "all-over" method. They build up the entire canvas from a faint, fuzzy background to the intricate foreground detail that eventually completes the piece. The advantage of this method is that, by working the whole canvas at the same time, the painters can stop working at any point and call it complete if they wish.

I approach my CSS with an all-over method that starts with a foundation and then gradually fills in the complex details. mezzoblue required a centered dual-column design with a header and a footer, so I built the basic structure first.

Main Container

To center the content, first I had to wrap a `<div>` around everything else and call it `#container`, which I then centered and gave a width of 840px.

On High Resolution

Why 840px and not a low resolution–friendly number such as 740px? Because I know my audience. Web designers read my site, and it's a really tricky proposition to use any design software with a resolution of less than 1024×768. Even that's pushing it, given the large palettes that clutter Photoshop. A width of 840px is reasonably safe for my audience. Naturally, different audiences require different solutions.

All other elements on the page sit inside the descriptive #container, but how did I center it? Theoretically, I could have assigned both the left-margin and right-margin a value of auto, which would allow them to expand and fill the window (minus the width of #container). In all compliant browsers, this would have allowed me to center #container.

The catch is older versions of IE. You guessed it—the margin trick doesn't work in IE 5. So I had to use text-align: center; applied to the body element to center #container and then add text-align: left; to #container itself so text within it didn't also align to the center. It's easiest to just look at the code that makes this happen:

```
body {
   text-align: center;
}
#container {
   text-align: left;
   margin-left: auto;
   margin-right: auto;
   width: 840px;
}
```

This centering method works fine in all modern browsers. Not too difficult? Glad you're with me so far.

Content and Links

The next problem I had to figure out was how I'd build the two columns to store the weblog text and the sidebar. When the crew at A List Apart redesigned their site in 2001 (http://www.alistapart.com/stories/journey/), they pioneered a technique that floated the main body of the page, leaving a sidebar in the space remaining on the side. This is more or less the exact method I employed on this design, with only a bit of tweaking:

```
#mainContent {
    padding: 0 20px 20px 20px;
    margin: 0 20px 1em 16px;
    border: solid 1px #A5BAF7;
    border-top-color: #B5CAF7;
    border-left-color: #B5CAF7;
    background-color: #C6DBF7;
    float: left;
    min-height: 85em;
    width: 524px;
    voice-family: "\"}\"";
    voice-family:inherit;
    width: 484px;
}
#linkList {
    margin-left: 583px;
}
```

So the main column is given a hard pixel value (with an application of the Tantek hack to make sure IE 5 behaves. See Chapter 10, Cross-Browser CSS, for more information on the topic.) and floats to the left. This is straightforward enough, but the column I'm placing to the right that holds all my links, #linkList, shows up behind the main text column. This is where the large left margin comes into play. Accounting for the width of #mainContent by adjusting the margin, I can make sure #linkList isn't overlapped by it.

The nice thing about doing it this way is that both columns can freely expand to match the height of their content. One is longer than the other? No problem! The effect is further enhanced by the min-height property, but unfortunately for now, IE still doesn't support this one. The design doesn't "break," though; it just means that if #linkList is longer than #mainContent, the paler blue background of #mainContent gets cut off a bit sooner than I'd like. I'm willing to live with that.

Sidebar

Astute readers will have noticed that my two-column layout is technically three columns, because the right side is further cleaved in two. Had I been working with a table-based layout, I would have had to deal with colspans and possibly nested tables. Thankfully, there will be none of that today.

Because the main structure had already set aside the single column on the right, the challenge was then to create the two interior columns. To achieve this effect, I split the link lists into two individual <div>s labeled #firstGroup and #secondGroup.

Both <div>s were assigned a width of just a tad under half that of the main column, and #firstGroup was left in place. #secondGroup ended up beneath it, which is logical because both are block-level elements. So how did I get #secondGroup beside it instead? Like so:

```
#firstGroup {
    width: 120px;
    float: right;
}
#secondGroup {
    width: 120px;
}
```

I kind of cheated, I'll admit it. I actually placed all the content I wanted in the rightmost column into #firstGroup and floated it to the right. The float allowed enough room for #secondGroup. Theoretically, I should have been able to apply float to #firstGroup and position it to the left instead, thus maintaining the "proper" logical order of the document. But in practice, I just wasn't able to find a solution that worked well across all the browsers I tested in.

Sometimes these sorts of hacks are necessary to make sure current browsers render the page properly. Don't be ashamed if you're forced to resort to them, but at least make sure you're aware that restructuring any element of your XHTML document to better facilitate the attached CSS is, purely and simply, a hack. In theory, you should never have to. In practice, sometimes you just can't help it.

Footer

The footer is the last foundational item to tackle. Working with elements below or at the bottom of an element of unspecified or changing height is one of the greatest weaknesses of CSS. Vertically aligning content to the bottom of an element with vertical-align is spotty at best and more or less impossible in some of today's browsers. There is also no way to say something like, "If this element is 200 pixels high, do this. But if it's 600, do *this* instead!"

My site was originally built with tables for this exact reason, as I mentioned at the beginning of the chapter. I just couldn't see a way to place a graphic to the right of the main content area and align it to the bottom, aside from applying it as a background image. That may have worked, but I wanted to place a list of links right underneath it. Not likely. Tables it was.

This is a problem I didn't end up solving, either. I still don't know how to accomplish what I just described. Instead, I've modified my footer design a bit so that it can work as a CSS-based layout.

The main footer area is a box that's positioned exactly like #mainContent—it's been given a width and floated to the left:

```
#footer {
  padding: 10px 20px 10px 20px;
  margin: 0 282px 0 32px;
  width: 484px;
}
#footerBlock > #footer {
  margin: 0 298px 0 16px;
  width: 484px;
}
```

A background image was applied to the right side of the element it sits within, #footerBlock. This is half of what I originally wanted to do, but I compromised on the links. They now sit inside the footer box to the left. You have to be flexible sometimes.

Fahrner Image Replacement

I'm going to skip a few steps and assume that if you've made it this far in the book you'll be able to figure out on your own how to format the text. Once I had the foundation completed, it was time to attend to the images. FIR was heavily used in this design, and items such as the main page header, the project list, and the site content list need some work. At this stage of the design, they remained text, but I replaced them with images (complete with mouseovers).

See Douglas Bowman's article on FIR, "Using background-image to Replace Text" (http://www.stopdesign.com/also/articles/replace_text/), for a brief introduction to the technique. Note that FIR is an accessibility problem, particularly for users who rely on screen readers. Alternatives discussed in Doug's article work around these issues, and it's recommended that you read either his summary or the article titled "In Defense of Fahrner Image Replacement" on Digital Web by yours truly (http://www.digital-web.com/features/feature_2003-08.shtml) before using FIR in your own work.

The simplest explanation of FIR is that if you wrap a block-level element such as a header with a <span> like so:

```
<h2><span>Project List</span></h2>
```

you can then hide the text within the <span>, apply the image to the <h2> as a background image, and set the width and height of the <h2> accordingly.

Because FIR requires the use of two HTML elements, I needed a little extra control of each so that I could place my images using floats. I solved this problem by logically arranging each of the sets of images in lists. My project list, for example, looks like so:

```
<ul>
  <li class="l1"><a href="/"><span>project #1</span></a></li>
  <li class="l2"><a href="/"><span>project #2</span></a></li>
</ul>
```

Semantically speaking, it's not too bad because these elements are, in fact, lists. The extra classes were necessary to give me individual identifiers for each element. A quick look at my CSS file shows that the style necessary to replace the preceding code with an image looks like so:

```
#siteInfo li.li2 a:link, #siteInfo li.li2 a:visited {
  width: 50px;
  height: 16px;
  background: #5F879D url(i/v33nav1-3.gif) top left no-repeat;
  display: block;
}
#siteInfo li.li2 span {
  display: none;
}
```

The other problem at this point was that the links had to be set to display: block; for the width and height to apply properly in some browsers. This is where the <li> came in handy. By floating each <li> to the left, I was able to run the links horizontally, rather than being forced to stack them vertically.

Because I wanted the links on the right side of the screen, I could have floated to the right instead. But that reversed the order of the images so they ran right-to-left, and I didn't want that. So if they're floated to the left, how did I move them back to the right side while keeping them correctly running left-to-right? By strategically padding the <ul> they sat inside:

```
ul#siteInfo {
  padding-left: 509px;
}
```

After applying padding to the left, the <li>s were forced to the right 509px, the width of padding, and I was able to place them precisely where I wanted them.

Summary

Now that I've committed to a fully CSS-based design, I have complete flexibility with my presentation. I can offer up alternative and print stylesheets, I can deploy sitewide changes to my visuals in a matter of seconds by editing one file, and my site loads faster because I managed to shave over 30% off my file size.

And not only that, but valid XHTML is very accessible without much effort, and my site's underlying code can be viewed by any device that supports the standard. Google and other search engines can read all my content, and they like my ordered structure. Even wireless devices and cell phones can get at my site without an interpreter if they're equipped to deal with XHTML.

Did you get all that? All of the advantages of standards-based code with virtually none of the sacrifice. Compare the tabled design to the CSS design. Compare the file sizes. Compare the benefits.

Why didn't I just do this from the start?

Research Institute Site

by John Simons

BabyGenes is the name of a fictitious research institute specializing in genetics. The institute's main focus is investigating how congenital defects in DNA are caused and passed down to children. The main web page for the company (see Figure 12-3) provides a brief description of what it does and provides some recent research findings in the form of "quick facts." (These facts are, of course, completely made up.).

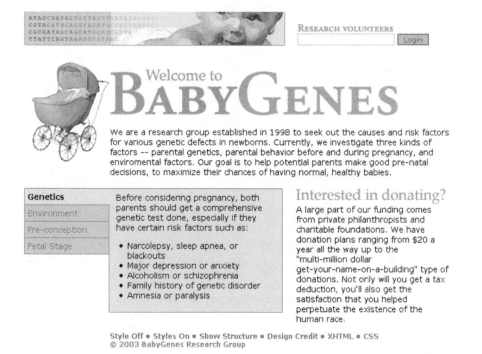

Figure 12-3. The BabyGenes main page

The page is composed of four major sections: the header, the introduction, the sidebar, the pink tabs, and the footer. Each section is fairly independent of the others, so I'll talk about each one in turn. If you're viewing the example in your browser, you can click the Show Structure button at the bottom of the page for an illustration of the CSS boxes.

Header

The image with the baby isn't in a block-level element of its own; rather it's the background to a parent block that has a large amount of padding, as shown in Figure 12-4.

Figure 12-4. The baby image in the header

The markup for the header looks like this:

```
<div id="head">
    <div id="login">
        <div><span>Research Volunteers</span></div>
        <form action="."> ... </form>
    </div>
</div>
```

And the relevant style is as follows:

```
#head {
  height:59px;
  background:url(head.gif) no-repeat;
  padding-left:459px;
}
#login { margin-left:22px; padding-top:17px; }
#login div {
  background:url(login.gif) no-repeat;
  height:21px;
}
#login div span { display:none; }
```

Visually, the end result appears to be two items side by side: the picture of the baby on the left and the login form on the right. But structurally, it's not side by side; it's actually inside/outside. This simulating columns issue comes up a lot in CSS design. Because CSS2 can't do real side-by-side columns (we'll have to wait for CSS3 for that), designers have come up with tricks. The padding-left: 459px makes space for a "fake column," which can then be filled with a float, an absolutely positioned block, or in this case, simply a background image. I set the height of the #head div to guarantee that the whole background image gets displayed.

At this point you might be wondering about IE5.*x*/Windows, which notoriously gets the CSS box model wrong. Because IE5/Windows figures width and height as including padding, some designs that include large amounts of padding may need to employ IE 5–specific hacks to avoid a badly broken layout. In this case, however, I'm not specifying a fixed width on #head, so there is no problem. It's only when you have padding *and* fixed widths or heights that box model issues come into play.

The other thing that's going on here is that text is being replaced with an image. That's what #login div and #login div span are all about. The <span>, which contains the text "Research volunteers," is hidden with display:none. Now the text is gone, but that's okay because the background image login.gif is simply a rendering of the words "Research volunteers." Semantically, there's no difference.

Why bother with this, instead of simply using an <img> tag? Because, for one thing, I want to separate content from style. If I do that, then "style" becomes its own self-contained module, which is easy to change and swap in and out, without ever editing the markup. Imagine, for example, that you have several user-switchable style sheets: each one can have its own version of login.gif, so that maybe one is red, one is italic, and so on.

Another reason is search engine optimization (SEO). When spidering web pages, Google ignores stylesheets and images, and focuses instead on the markup. Having your content present in standard HTML tags such as <h1> makes it accessible to search engines.

Introduction

The introduction section is very similar to the section above it, with an image in the left column and text being replaced with an image. The section is shown in Figure 12-5. Here's the markup:

```
<div id="intro">
  <img src="carriage.gif" />
  <h1>Welcome to BabyGenes</h1>
  <p>We are a research ... </p>
</div>
```

We are a research group established in 1998 to seek out the causes and risk factors for various genetic defects in newborns. Currently, we investigate three kinds of factors -- parental genetics, parental behavior before and during pregnancy, and enviromental factors. Our goal is to help potential parents make good pre-natal decisions, to maximize their chances of having normal, healthy babies.

Figure 12-5. The markup for this block is exactly what you might imagine: an <img>, *an* <h1>, *and a* <p>.

For baby carriage on the left, I *could* have done it exactly as before, with left padding and a background image. But, for the sake of variety, here's an example of how to do it with absolute positioning (notice the addition of an <img> tag in the preceding markup). These are the rules for the introduction section that deal specifically with positioning:

```
  padding:20px 0px 10px 0px;
  position:relative;
}
#intro img {
  position:absolute;
  top:0; left:0;
}
#intro h1 { ... margin-left:151px; ... }
#intro p { margin-left:151px; }
```

The parent block has some top and bottom padding to place the paragraph where it looks pleasing, and the <img> is absolutely positioned flush left. But why do the <h1> and <p> have a left margin? Wouldn't it have been easier to instead put a left padding on #intro? Yes it would have, and normally padding on the parent is equivalent to margin on all the children, but doing it this way works around a bug in IE. If you use left padding on #intro, IE positions the image horizontally relative to the *content box* (the box that is inset by padding) rather than the *outer box* (which includes padding and border). This is incorrect behavior, so you must rewrite your code a bit to cater to the world's dominant web browser.

Now for the absolute positioning. The rules on #intro img say, "Absolutely position this image at (0,0) relative to its parent block." Simple enough, right? The image is taken out of the normal layout flow (because that's what absolute positioning does) and is placed exactly at the upper-left corner of #intro.

There is a small bit of ugliness, though—why does #intro need position: relative? Well, simply stated, when you provide absolute coordinates for an element, that element is positioned relative to its parent element. But here's the confusing part: For the purposes of absolutely positioning, only blocks that have their positioning scheme set to absolute, relative, or fixed count as parents. In other words, when you use absolute positioning, the element is positioned relative to its most direct *positioned* parent.

Relative positioning therefore serves two purposes: It shifts an element relative to itself, and it sets an element as the absolute origin for its children. In this example, I'm "shifting" the #intro block by 0px, which is a useless thing to do, except for the side effect that #intro becomes the origin for #intro img.

Let's look now at the text-image replacement. In the header example, I replaced "Research volunteers" with an image, and I'm going to do the same thing with the BabyGenes title. I could do it the same way as before, but here's a different way. Remember, the markup looks like this:

```
<div id="intro"><h1>Welcome to BabyGenes</h1></div>
```

I can apply this style:

```
#intro h1 {
  background:url(title.gif) no-repeat;
  padding-top:82px;
  margin-left:151px;
  height:0px;
  \height:82px;
  he\ight:0px;
  overflow:hidden;


}
```

The simplicity of this example lies in the fact that I don't need an inner element to hide the text; instead, I just allow 0 height for it. height:0 and overflow:hidden work together to eliminate the contents of the <h1>, while the top padding lets the background image show through.

The drawback of this method is that an IE5/Windows hack becomes necessary. Without it, IE 5 will display a box with 0 height and 0 padding, which means a box of nothing. There are several IE 5 hacks available, including the "initial backslash hack," the "commented backslash hack," and the "Tantek hack." For more information on IE 5 hacks, check out the CSS-Discuss list at http://css-discuss.incutio.com. I'll assume you trust that this is one of them—it relies on the fact that IE 5 can only handle backslashes prepended to the attribute—and it must be copied exactly to work:

```
height:0px;
\height:82px;
he\ight:0px;
```

This gives IE5/Windows a height of 82px, and all other browsers a height of 0.

Sidebar

This section uses the same basic procedure as before: Use padding to carve out the right column (in this case, the sidebar), and then place something in the left margin so it appears to be a column (see Figure 12-6). Except this time I'll *float* the left column into place, rather than using absolute positioning.

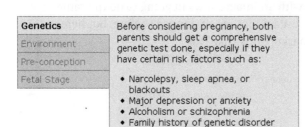

Figure 12-6. A two-column layout. The left item is fixed width and floated left, and the right item has large left padding.

The basic structure looks like this:

```
<div id="tabs">
  <ul id="buttons">
    <li><a href> ... </a></li>
    ...
  </ul>
  <div id="box1" class="infobox">... </div>
  <div id="box2" class="infobox">... </div>
  ...
</div>
<div id="sidebar">
  <div><h2>Interested in supporting us?</h2></div>
  <p>A large part of our funding ... </p>
</div>
```

and this is the style for #sidebar (I explain #tabs in detail in the next section; this just includes its basic outline):

```
#tabs {
  float:left;
  width:455px;
  ...
}
```

```
#sidebar { padding-left:479px; }
#sidebar div {
  height:27px;
  background:url(donate.gif) no-repeat;
}
#sidebar div h2 { display:none; }
```

#sidebar gets a large left padding of 479px to make space for the pink tabs (I could have used margin instead of padding here—because I'm not using a background image it doesn't matter either way). Then #tabs gets a fixed width and is floated to the left. The difference between the sidebar padding and the tabs' width (479px to 455px) will equal the gutter between the two columns (24px).

Note also the rules on #sidebar div and #sidebar div h2. This is the same text-image replacement technique used in the header.

Pink Tabs

The dynamic information box with clickable pink tabs, shown in Figure 12-7, is the most complicated part of the BabyGenes page and therefore deserves some detailed explanation.

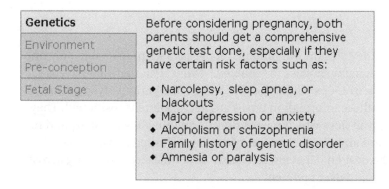

Figure 12-7. Clicking a tab updates the content dynamically by toggling visibility.

The basic layout is two-columned: information boxes on the right and clickable tabs on the left. The columns are implemented the same way as before: the right column has a wide left margin, and tabs fit into place in the empty space. Here's what the markup looks like:

```
<div id="tabs">
  <ul id="buttons">
    <li><a href="#" id="tab1" onclick="selectTab(1); return false;"
      onfocus="blur();">Genetics</a></li>
```

```
    <li><a href="#" id="tab2" onclick="selectTab(2); return false;"
        onfocus="blur();">Environment</a></li>
    <li><a href="#" id="tab3" onclick="selectTab(3); return false;"
        onfocus="blur();">Pre-conception</a></li>
    <li><a href="#" id="tab4" onclick="selectTab(4); return false;"
        onfocus="blur();">Fetal Stage</a></li>
  </ul>
  <div id="box1" class="infobox"> ... </div>
  <div id="box2" class="infobox"> ... </div>
  <div id="box3" class="infobox"> ... </div>
  <div id="box4" class="infobox"> ... </div>
</div>
```

First let's look at the information boxes. This is the style for them:

```
#tabs .infobox {
  margin-left:150px;
  padding:6px 12px;
  border:1px solid #999;
  border-left-width:0px;
  background-color:#FDE9F0;
  display:none;
}
#tabs .enabled { display:block; }
```

You can see they all start out hidden. I'll use JavaScript to enable only one at a time by changing their class to "enabled." Other than that, all I have is a wide left margin of 150px where the tabs will go and various styling information. Notice that these information boxes are *not* absolutely positioned. They remain in the layout flow, which means their containing block will expand to contain them, and anything below the tabs will get pushed down to make room. This is the desired behavior, as I can't count on exact copyfitting across various browsers and user preferences.

The clickable tabs, which are represented as an unordered list in the markup, have several things going on. This is their complete rule set, which is an expanded version of the structural skeleton from the last section:

```
#tabs {
  float:left;
  position:relative;
  width:455px;
  margin-bottom:10px;
  background:url(pixel.gif) repeat-y 149px 0px;
}
```

```
#tabs #buttons {
  position:absolute;
  top:0; left:0;
  width:150px;
  margin:0; padding:0;
  background-color:#ddd;
  color:#888;
  border-top:1px solid #999;
  list-style:none;
}
#tabs #buttons li {
  border-bottom:1px solid #999;
  border-left:1px solid #999;
}
#tabs #buttons a {
  text-decoration:none;
  color:#888;
  display:block;
  border-right:1px solid #999;
  padding:5px;
}
#tabs #buttons a:hover { background-color:#eee; }
```

First, the structure. #tabs is the container element that contains both the tabs and the information boxes. It's fixed width and left floated. Notice the same absolute/relative pair that was used for the baby carriage image: #tabs #buttons gets position:absolute, so #tabs needs to get position:relative. This is fairly counterintuitive, but just remember, when using absolute positioning, you'll always need to have position:relative on one of the parent elements.

There's one hitch: This example doesn't work in Opera (as of version 7.23 for Windows). #tabs #buttons, which should be aligned with the corner of #tabs, is aligned with the top of the page for Opera users. Absolute positioning looks for the most direct *positioned* ancestor as a reference point, and Opera doesn't consider floated elements to be positioned, even if they have position:relative. So if Opera users make up a significant part of your audience, you'll need to take a different approach. Each approach has its own set of tradeoffs.

The rest of the rules deal mostly with getting an unordered list to look like tabs. Margin, padding, and bullets are eliminated; colors are set; and a gray border is added around list items. The anchors (links) are set to display:block so that the link area expands to fill the entire list item, causing the tabs to be clickable all over. A padding of 5px is added to the tabs—it goes on the anchors rather than the list items so that the extra space is included in the clickable area and I don't end up with "dead space" around the edges of the tab.

Now for the trickiest part: getting that vertical line to disappear so the current tab melds with the information box. There are several possible approaches.

One approach would be to give the information box a left border and overlap the tabs on top of the information box by 1px. The problem with this approach is maintaining a proper z-index so that the tabs *always* stay on top of the information box. It can be a headache getting all the major browsers to do it right.

The approach used in BabyGenes is simple, but it depends on an external graphic. The information box is given no left border, and each of the tabs handles its own right border depending on its selection state, *and* the entire #tabs div is given a background image that fills in the border below the unordered list. The background image could be a 150px-wide transparent GIF with a vertical gray line running down its right side. Or, in the interest of keeping the graphics as general-purpose as possible, it could be a *single gray pixel* GIF that is positioned using the background-position property.

```
#tabs #buttons a { ... border-right:1px solid #999; ... }
#tabs #buttons a.selected { ... border-right-width:0px; ... }
#tabs { ... background:url(pixel.gif) repeat-y 149px 0px; ... }
```

These three rules take care of the vertical border. Tabs get a right border, except the selected tab, which gets no right border, and the area below the tabs is covered by the background image.

Now that the rules are in place, let's get to the dynamic aspect of the tabs. The great thing about CSS is that it can be dynamically manipulated—you can change attributes, change classes, or even change stylesheets all based on user input. To change tabs in this dynamic information box, all it takes is a simple JavaScript function:

```
function selectTab(num) {
  for (var i=1; i <= 4; i++) {
    document.getElementById("tab" + i).className = "";
    document.getElementById("box" + i).className = "infobox";
  }
  document.getElementById("tab" + num).className = "selected";
  document.getElementById("box" + num).className = "infobox enabled";
}
```

This function is called from the "onclick" event in the tab links, and it's referencing the following classes:

```
#tabs .infobox { display:none; }
```

```
#tabs .enabled { display:block; }
```

```
#tabs #buttons a.selected {
  color:black;
  background-color:#FDE9F0;
```

```
  border-right-width:0px;
  font-weight:bold;
}
#tabs #buttons a.selected:hover { background-color:#FDE9F0; }
```

By changing class from "infobox" to "infobox enabled," the JavaScript function is able to "turn on" one of the information boxes. Note the syntax of several class names separated by spaces. That's how you specify multiple class membership with CSS. Each class name overrides any rules preceding it, so in this case, `display:block` overrides `display:hidden`, and the `<div>` becomes visible.

Similarly, by setting a tab's class to "selected," the tab turns pink and loses its right border. When these two things happen simultaneously based on a user click, it creates the illusion of smoothly changing content that has a "snappy" feel because it occurs instantaneously on the click of a mouse.

The only problem now is IE5/Windows, which has a glitch in the way it displays unordered lists (see Figure 12-8). As you can see, it inserts 17px of padding below the anchors. There are workarounds, but they involve uglifying your clean CSS, and it's probably not worth it for purely cosmetic reasons. If you need pixel-perfect designs in IE 5, it would make more sense to use `<div>`s for the tabs instead of an unordered list.

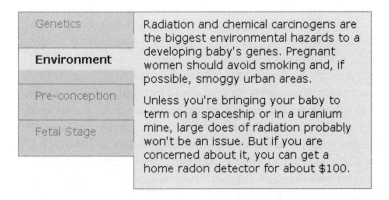

Figure 12-8. This is how the tabs would appear in IE5.x/Windows. Not right, but still functional.

Footer

The footer contains links that let you dynamically change the stylesheet:

```
<a href="#" onclick="document.getElementById('ss').href='';
  return false;">Stylesheet Off</a>
<a href="#" onclick="document.getElementById('ss').href='style.css';
  return false;">Stylesheet On</a>
```

```
<a href="#" onclick="document.getElementById('ss').href='structure.css';
  return false;">Demonstrate Structure</a>
```

Style.css is the default stylesheet. Structure.css is an alternate stylesheet, which includes all the rules from style.css, plus additional ones that illustrate the block structure of the document. To disable the stylesheet completely, the href is set to the empty string ''.

```
#footer {
  font-size:85%;
  margin-left:151px;
  padding-top:4px;
  color:#999;
  font-weight:bold;
  clear:left;
}
```

The style for #footer includes some basic formatting, plus clear:left. Because the dynamic pink tabs are floated to the left, the default behavior is for other elements to wrap around them. I want to insure that the footer appears below the tabs, not alongside them, so I clear it of all left-floating elements. It's the direct equivalent to <br clear=left> in HTML.

Summary

Although this is only a single-page project, I managed to touch on many of the issues involved in using CSS exclusively for layout and formatting. You saw how to use floated and absolutely positioned blocks instead of tables for layout and how to use padding and background-image in conjunction as an alternative to the <img> tag. You looked at a couple of browser compatibility issues and learned how to manipulate CSS dynamically using JavaScript. Even though current CSS support isn't perfect, it's well worth dealing with some minor hassles for the sake of having readable and maintainable code.

Buffalo Philharmonic Orchestra Site

by Michael Switzer
Annually, the Buffalo Philharmonic Orchestra (BPO) redesigns its website in line with its marketing materials. Prior to this year, the website was developed using noncompliant, browser-hacked HTML. As you can imagine, because of this, each redesign was extremely time-intensive.

In 2003, the BPO was offered an opportunity to have a fully standards-compliant redesign done. The benefits of faster load times, higher search engine rankings, and better access for users with disabilities made the decision an easy one.

Before getting into the actual redesign, though, let's take a look back at the old design to get an idea of where we're coming from.[1]

Laying the Groundwork

As you can see from Figure 12-9, the BPO home page's layout is similar to the front page of a newspaper. Horizontally across the top is the header, with some images and the BPO season slogan.

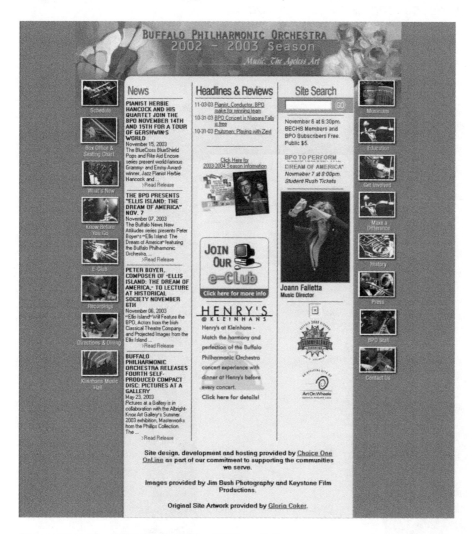

Figure 12-9. The 2002 design of the BPO's website

---

1. Credits: The layout for the BPO website was originally designed by Rob Schuster. Charlynda Winkley reworked the layout with the new design for 2003. Michael Switzer provided coding and development.

The navigation is on the right and left sides. Between these columns are three additional columns: News, Headlines & Reviews, and Site Search (along with miscellaneous information). The navigation is made up of photos of musicians in action, with the text below identifying the section each photo links to. When users place their mouse pointer over a button, the photo changes to a monochrome-hued version, with text highlighting content of that section.

Each year the design is based on this layout.

Bringing the Site Up to Date

Consideration of the previous layout and the 2003-2004 season's marketing materials led to the look shown in Figure 12-10.

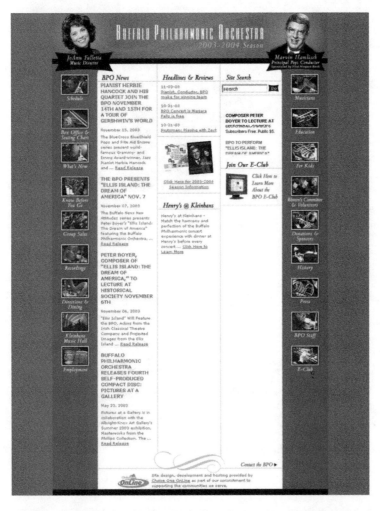

Figure 12-10. The new design based on the existing layout and new marketing material

You may think that with the five-column home page a typical HTML, table-based layout is ideal. Initially that is how the site was designed, but one look at the resultant file size should make you reconsider. Note that the file sizes in Table 12-1 include all images, scripts, style sheets, and markup.

Table 12-1. File Size Comparison

Markup	File Size
HTML 4.01 Transitional	201.2KB
XHTML1.0 Transitional and CSS	26.9KB

Using standards-compliant markup with CSS for presentation and layout reduced the file size by over 85%. The original design used CSS for some presentation already, so 85% is less than what many receive by replacing deprecated font tags and other markup with streamlined, standards-compliant CSS, especially in graphics-heavy layouts.

Let's walk through the project step by step to see where CSS comes into play. You may find it beneficial to download the complete code listings and refer to them while you read.

Finding a Middle Ground

The first item of business is centering the layout in the browser window. If you are using a table-based layout, your code might look something like this:

```
<body background="images/bg.gif" topmargin="0" leftmargin="0" marginwidth="0"
marginheight="0">
<center>
<div align="center">
<table width="772" border="0" cellpadding="0" cellspacing="0" align="center">
    <tr>
        <td colspan="5">
            ... header cell ...</td>
    </tr>
    <tr>
        <td rowspan="2">
            ... left nav cell ...</td>
        <td>
            ... news cell ...</td>
        <td>
            ... reviews cell ...</td>
```

```
            <td>
                ... search and misc cell ...</td>
            <td rowspan="2">
                    ... right nav cell ...</td>
    </tr>
    <tr>
        <td colspan="3">
            ... footer cell...</td>
    </tr>
</table>
</div>
</center>
</body>
</html>
```

For this layout, all you need is this in the CSS file:

```
body {
    padding: 0;
    margin: 0;
    border: 0;
    background: #B2D1E0 url(/images/bg.gif) top left;
    text-align: center;
}

#header, #container {
                position: relative;
                margin: 0 auto 0 auto;
                width: 772px;
                }
```

and this in the XHTML file:

```
<body>
<div id="header">
    ... header ...</div>
<div id="container">
    ... the rest ...</div>
</body>
</html>
```

Notice that you can conserve code by applying the same style to multiple selectors. In the case of the header and container <div>s, both have the same style rules. The zero in margin applies to the top and bottom, whereas auto applies to the left and right margins. Coupled with a width, this centers the two <div>s. For IE 5.*x*, the text-align: center; rule in the body is necessary, but other browsers don't need it. The relative positioning is necessary because you're centering multiple <div>s instead of using one container for the entire site. In IE 5+, the first <div> won't be centered if relative positioning isn't used.

Heading in the Right Direction

Now that the layout is centered, the first item to address is the header area. This contains three items: the site identifier, the conductor, and a special guest conductor who the BPO wanted to highlight as a drawing point for the coming season. Each conductor photo is linked to a page within the site that contains the conductor's biography.

The XHTML for this is pretty straightforward:

```
<div id="header">
    <h1><span>Buffalo Philharmonic Orchestra</span></h1>
    <p id="ja"><a href="/musicians/featured.php?musicianID=1" title="view more
    information about JoAnn Falletta"><span>JoAnn Falletta - Music
    Director</span></a></p>
    <p id="mh"><a href="/musicians/featured.php?musicianID=3" title="view more
    information about Marvin Hamlisch"><span>Marvin Hamlisch - Principal Pops
    Conductor [sponsored by First Niagara Bank]</span></a></p>
    <hr />
</div>
```

But where are all the images? For a multitude of reasons, I chose to use the FIR technique for all the images used in the layout. There are a number of benefits to this—most notably better search engine results and better access for wireless devices without requiring separate markup. There are drawbacks to FIR as well—most notably affecting those who surf the Web with images off. However, when weighing the number of users who would be negatively affected against the positive effects on the majority of users, I felt the pros outweighed the cons.

Let's take a look at the CSS to see how this works:

```
#header {
  height: 171px;
}

#header h1 {
  display: block;
  position: absolute;
  top: 0;
  left: 172px;
```

```
    width: 429px;
    height: 171px;
    padding: 0;
    margin: 0;
    background: url(/images/ihdbpo.gif) no-repeat;


#ja a:link,
#ja a:visited,
#ja a:hover,
#ja a:active {
    display: block;
    position: absolute;
    top: 0;
    left: 0;
    width: 172px;
    height: 171px;
    padding: 0;
    margin: 0;
    background: url(/images/hdjf.gif) no-repeat;
    text-decoration: none;
}

#mh a:link,
#mh a:visited,
#mh a:hover,
#mh a:active {
    display: block;
    position: absolute;
    top: 0;
    left: 601px;
    width: 171px;
    height: 171px;
    padding: 0;
    margin: 0;
    background: url(/images/hdmh.gif) no-repeat;
    text-decoration: none;
}
```

I used absolute positioning to place the elements in the proper order for display, although the code has them structured logically. Then I applied as a background the image that I wanted to appear. By wrapping the text in a <span> and adding display: none; as a rule to the span selector, I effectively hide the text from any standards-compliant browser, instead displaying the beautiful images in the layout.

Notice that I included all pseudo classes for anchors to eliminate some "flashing" that occurs in IE when the mouse passes over the links.

Speaking of Pseudo Classes

What an opportunity to segue into the navigation. It wraps the content and contains JavaScript-less mouseovers.

First I had to create the two wrappers for each side of the content. Here's the XHTML:

```
<div id="nav1">
    ... left side navigation... </div>
<div id="nav2">
    ... right side navigation ...</div>
```

Here's the CSS:

```
#nav1, #nav2 {
  display: block;
  width: 127px;
  text-align: left;
}
#nav1 {
  float: left;
}
#nav2 {
  float: right;
}
```

I added a horizontal rule after the second navigation div to provide a break between the navigation and the content in non-standards-compliant browsers. You may have noticed the <hr /> in the header code as well, which I used for the same effect. In my stylesheet, I used the <hr> as a selector and gave it the same treatment as the <span> tags, display: none;, effectively hiding this from the user agents that support this CSS-based layout.

The left navigation has float: left; in the rule, causing it to hug the left side of its parent element, container. The same effect is applied to the right navigation, except, of course, I want it to hang onto the right side, so I use float: right. Now what about the buttons?

There are many ways to create nice graphical navigation schemes using CSS that become text links in non-standards-compliant browsers. Many suggest using unordered lists, but I decided against that method. If you can imagine the length of an unordered list containing 18 items sitting at the top of the page, you can probably understand why I opted not to use that method.

What I did instead was place pipes before the anchors as separators, which allows non-standards-compliant browsers to show the navigation inline, whereas newer browsers will display it in all its glory. Here's the XHTML for one button:

```
<span> | </span><a id="btn_sched" href="/schedule" title="view the BPO
Schedule with Concerts, Dates and Times"><span
class="image"></span><span>Schedule</span></a>
```

and here's the CSS:

```
#nav1 a, #nav2 a {
  display: block;
  position: relative;
  width: 98px;
  height: 92px;
  padding: 0;
  margin: 0;
}

#nav1 a {
  padding-left: 15px;
}

#nav2 a {
  padding-left: 14px;
}

#nav1 span.image, #nav2 span.image {
    display: block;
    position: relative;
    width: 98px;
    height: 53px;
    padding: 0;
    margin: 0;
    border: 0;
    }

#btn_sched {
  background: transparent url(/images/btn_sched.gif) bottom right no-repeat;
}

#btn_sched:link span.image,
#btn_sched:visited span.image {
  background: transparent url(/images/btn_sched_p.gif) no-repeat;
}
```

```
#btn_sched:hover span.image,
#btn_sched:active span.image {
   background: url(/images/btn_sched_m.gif);
}
```

This is probably the least pleasing aspect of the code, and there are probably a million and one different ways to approach this, but here's a brief explanation of what's going on.

First, all anchor tags within nav1 or nav2 are made block-level elements and given the same width (98px) and height (92px). Next, I position the buttons so they appear centered in each navigation column.

The buttons are 29px narrower than the navigation columns, so I add 15px of left padding to all the buttons in the left column. That leaves 14px between the right side of the buttons and the content area. For the buttons on the right, I duplicate that 14px space between the content area and the buttons on the left side by adding 14px of left padding.

Then all <span> tags within nav1 or nav2 are hidden with the now familiar display: none; declaration. Confused yet? This is really the nitty-gritty of the CSS layout, so read it again if you need to. Once you understand it, you'll really have CSS down to a science.

Here comes the fun part. Each of the anchors is given an ID. The one in this example is the very first button, Schedule, to which I've given the id btn_sched. I assign to this a background image containing the text "Schedule." Pretty innovative, huh? This background is positioned bottom right and told not to tile with the no-repeat rule. I used shorthand CSS for this, but it could be written this way:

```
background-color: transparent;
background-image: url(/bpo2003/stdcomp/images/btn_sched.gif)
background-position: bottom right;
background-repeat: no-repeat;
```

You'll probably agree that shorthand is better. Regardless, it's time to move on to the wonderful CSS-based mouseovers. You may have noticed the empty <span> within the anchor. I've assigned a class image to this and use it to perform magic tricks.

First, I position it and make it a block-level element with a width (98px) and a height (53px). But wait, aren't the anchors 92px in height? Exactly! Hence the text "Schedule" won't be hidden by the image. Rather, I'm now going to use pseudo classes to make those nifty mouseovers appear above the button text.

I assign the plain image, again as a background, to the <span> using :link and :visited. Notice that the pseudo classes append to the parent element, because it's the anchor. (Translation: Apply this rule to the span with a class of image that is inside the anchor with an id of btn_sched, which is either in a state of link or visited.) Pretty long and wordy, but you get the point.

Next, I duplicate the rule, modifying the selector to use the :hover and :active pseudo classes, and changing the background image to the one I want to appear when the mouse is over the button.

Now is probably a good time to talk about love/hate relationships. Or merely the fact that when you're using pseudo classes, it really is a love/hate thing. You should always place your pseudo classes in this order: link, visited, hover, active. **Love/ha**te—get it?

Now that I have one button down, I can apply the same method to the 17 remaining buttons by merely changing the id of the anchor tag and the background images for the button text, basic image, and mouseover image. It's not that difficult after all.

Here's the Tricky Part

I'm all set with the header and navigation, and you might think I've reached the downhill portion of my journey. All I have to do is position the content element and I'm good to go. Here's my XHTML:

```
<div id="content">
    </div>
```

The CSS is straightforward:

```
#content {
  position: absolute;
  top: 0;
  left: 127px;
  width: 518px;
  padding: 0;
  margin: 0;
  border: 0;
  text-align: left;
  background: #fff;
}
```

That's simple enough. I know where I want my content to display and just base its position off the parent element container. The left navigation column is 127px wide, so I set the left coordinate to 127px and the top to 0, but there's a problem. It's invisible in IE 5.5.

Now what to do? The left navigation is floating left, the right navigation is floating right, and the content is supposed to be in the middle. I could change the markup and place nav2 after the content <div>, but then viewers would have to scroll past all the content to use any buttons in nav2 if they're using browsers that don't support standards.

My thought process says that I want the content <div> to float to the left of the right navigation. So I change the CSS to look like this:

```
#content {
    float: left;
    width: 518px;
    padding: 0;
    margin: 0;
    border: 0;
    text-align: left;
    background: #fff;
}
```

Now the beautiful white box floats to the left, but it starts *below* the navigation elements. That won't work. Therein lies the most confusing aspect of float. When you float an element, it's always with respect to the element preceding it in your markup. When I set float to left, I was telling the browser to position the *left* edge of this object against the *right* edge of the *preceding* object, but that's not what I want. In fact, I want just the opposite. So if I change float to right, what happens? You guessed it, now my content is positioned correctly. Here's the final working CSS:

```
#content {
    float: right;
    width: 518px;
    padding: 0;
    margin: 0;
    border: 0;
    text-align: left;
    background: #fff;
}
```

Float, Float, Float Your Boat, Gently Down the Screen . . .

Now that the outside three columns are set up with float, let's examine the inside three content columns. This actually works fairly easily. Here's the markup:

```
<div id="news">
    ... news items will go here...</div>
<div id="headlinesreviews">
    ... headlines and reviews ...</div>
<div id="misc">
    ... the third column ...</div>
```

Three columns and three divs. But there's something I want to do for non-standards-compliant user agents. I have a search box on the home page, but I don't want anyone to scroll to see it. Here's the new markup then:

```
<div id="search">
    ... the search will go here...</div>
<div id="news">
    ... news items will go here...</div>
<div id="headlinesreviews">
    ... headlines and reviews ...</div>
<div id="misc">
    ... the third column ...</div>
```

and here's the CSS:

```
#news {
  float: left;
  width: 170px;
}

#headlinesreviews {
  float: left;
  width: 177px;
  border-left: 1px solid #B8D4E3;
  border-right: 1px solid #B8D4E3;
  voice-family: "\"}\"";
  voice-family:inherit;
  width: 175px;
} html>body #headlinesreviews { width: 175px; }

#search {
  float: right;
  width: 171px;
  border-bottom: 1px solid #B8D4E3;
  text-align: center;
}

#misc {
  float: right;
  width: 171px;
  padding-top: 10px;
  text-align: center;
  background: #fff;
}
```

This time `float` behaves properly. BPO News is the leftmost column. Headlines & Reviews is the second column, which hugs the leftmost column quite nicely. As you look through the `headlinesreviews` rule, you may recognize a well-known box model hack. If you don't, look back through the book to get a good understanding of this method. It's vital because of the large number of IE 5.*x* users. Basically, the borders on the middle column modify the width of this column in IE 5.*x*, but the box model hack allows you to work around this flaw in IE 5.*x*'s behavior.

The `search` and `misc` objects are given a `float: right` rule. This is because the `search` appears before the news column in the markup, but I want it to be part of the right column. The `misc` <div>, if floated left, appears placed over the search box, which I don't want. Floating it right forces it below the search box.

One Last Item

The footer is the last item to appear within the content area. The footer actually contains three items: a fancy scroll graphic, a contact button, and some credit to the company that developed the website. Here's the markup to accomplish this:

```
<div id="scroll">
    <hr />
<a href="contact/" title="contact the BPO"><span>Contact the BPO</span></a></div>
<div id="footer">
    <hr />
    ... text...</div>
```

Here's the CSS:

```
#scroll {
  clear: both;
  display: block;
  width: 518px;
  height: 58px;
  padding: 0;
  margin: 0;
  border: 0;
  text-align: right;
  background: url(/images/hscroll.gif) no-repeat;
}
```

```
#scroll a {
  float: right;
  display: block;
  width: 117px;
  height: 58px;
  padding: 0;
  margin: 0;
  border: 0;
  background: url(/images/hcntct.gif) right bottom no-repeat;
}

#footer {
  clear: both;
  display: block;
  width: 518px;
  padding: 0;
  margin: 0;
  border: 0;
  text-align: center;
  background: #fff;
}
```

The only new item in this code is `clear: both;`, which I use to tell the browser to ignore any preceding float declarations. I want the scroll and the footer at the bottom, not next to the last column.

I use the now familiar FIR technique to replace the anchor text with an image and float the anchor to the right inside the scroll `<div>`. There's no need to use pseudo classes on this anchor because there is no mouseover image to swap in or out.

It's a Wrap

When you look through the code download, you'll likely notice some additional items not covered in this case study. Much of this focused specifically on the tableless layout because that's an area providing the most challenges to designers today. Figure 12-11 shows how the tableless layout displays in a legacy browser such as NN4.*x*.

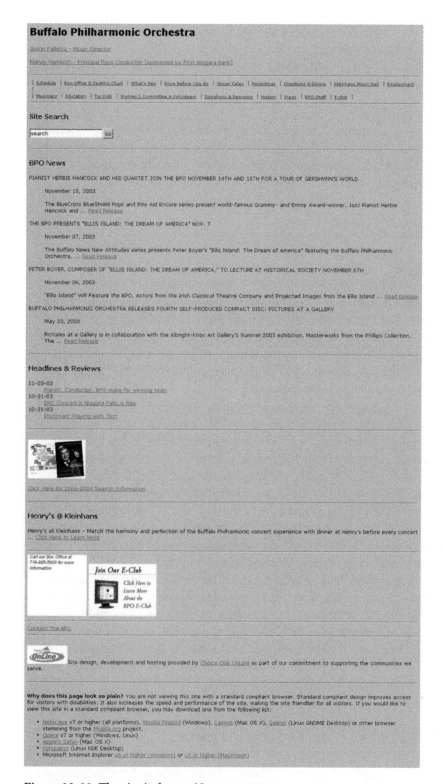

Figure 12-11. The site in legacy Netscape 4.8

If you see something and you just don't know what it does, try it out. The best way to learn is by doing.

Summary

This section of the chapter covered some of the more difficult aspects of a multi-column layout. Special attention was given to the float property because it often poses a great degree of challenge to developers. Additionally, one method of JavaScript-less mouseover navigation was considered in some detail.

Photo Gallery

by Dan Rubin

I want freedom. Is that too much to ask? As a graphic designer, I spend most of my time in Photoshop and Illustrator, *creating*. I don't want to be limited by technologies that I have to design for; I want those technologies to be flexible enough to work with my designs, so I'm free to create, to design. As a web developer, I don't want to jump through markup hoops just to make a great visual design work with the content of my page. CSS combined with XHTML gives me the freedom to do everything I want to do.

Since taking the plunge into the dark and mysterious world of XHTML and CSS (after many years of writing markup the "old way" using tables and spacer GIFs, and designing around the limitations), I haven't once looked back. Many technical reasons come to mind (semantic markup, separation of content and design, more accessible content, smaller page sizes, etc.), but the most exciting thing about this "new way" is that it has allowed me to change my approach to designing for the Web. I no longer have to think of how my design will break into sliced images, or how the tables will need to be nested to accomplish a certain aspect of the user interface (UI), or allow any markup-related restrictions to impact the aesthetic of a design—I now have the freedom to create.

This section of the chapter will show you the steps involved in designing a photo gallery, from paper sketch to Photoshop mockup to final working page. I'll explain how to create image rollovers using only CSS (no JavaScript!), describe an accessible image-replacement technique, and present tricks for getting a few problematic browsers to work properly. I'll also discuss some of the accessibility advantages gained from separating content from style, and I'll show an example of this design in a common text-only browser.

Project Description and Requirements

Every project, no matter how small, should always begin with an understanding of the goals and technical requirements involved, whether they come from you or someone else. This project will be based on a new photo gallery subsection of my personal site, SuperfluousBanter (http://superfluousbanter.org), dubbed "Superfluous Photos." I'll focus on just one page of what would normally be a larger, more involved site, so the description is simple:

The photo gallery features one main photograph per page, technical details about the camera and settings used, a short description of the main photo, thumbnails of other images within the same category, the site's name and logo, primary navigation links to other sections of the site, and a footer/copyright statement. The site must display properly in all modern browsers, and content must display properly in alternative browsers and devices. Navigation elements should be accessible to nonvisual browsers. Markup must validate XHTML 1.0 Strict and CSS, and highlight advanced CSS techniques, including CSS-only image rollovers.

This describes the purpose of the site and sets clear technical goals for the project.

Creating the Design

Now that I've set the basic technical requirements, I can forget about them for the moment. For a graphic designer, this is the best part about working with CSS.

Using Rough Sketches

I like to start every design with rough thumbnail sketches—these are small, quick drawings, no more than 2 inches square, that allow me to experiment with positioning without needing to fuss over details of the UI. In less than 2 minutes, I can fill a sheet of paper with eight to ten different layouts featuring the basic elements of the design (see Figure 12-12), and if I don't like any of them, it's easy and fast to draw some more.

Figure 12-12. Thumbnail sketches for this design

Polishing the Design

After creating a page or two of rough sketches, I fire up Photoshop and start compiling the visual elements of the design. During this stage, I create a color scheme, select the typographic style for each element (whether it will be rendered as an image or plain text), and hone the layout and positioning of each element, based on one or more of the thumbnail sketches. After incorporating the required visual and textual elements (the logotype in the header is set in Font Bureau's Interstate, and the logo itself is the \ [backslash] character from InterstatePi One), I add a few extras to the design (a background image of the site's logo for the body text, patterns for the page background and navigation bar, and a photo for the header of the page to accompany the site's logo), adjust the positioning of each element until I'm happy with it, and I'm done (see Figure 12-13).

Figure 12-13. The final mockup in Photoshop

Graphicus Minimus

Once you incorporate CSS into your design process, you start to learn how to use its capabilities to your advantage. Specifically, you discover that elements that used to require creating a bitmap image (GIF, JPG, or PNG) can now be created with a few simple rules in your stylesheet, thus decreasing your overall page weight, reducing the time it takes a user to download your site, and lowering your bandwidth bill substantially. Taking advantage of this capability depends on your particular design, and it just so happens that this photo gallery presents some good opportunities.

Compare the aspects of this design that require images (see Figure 12-14) with the CSS-styled elements (see Figure 12-15), and you can see that the majority of the visual presentation is controlled by CSS rules. Going one step further, if you remove the images that are specific to a photo gallery (the featured photo and the thumbnail images), you're left with only four bitmap images, two of which are the 4px-square background patterns for the page and navigation elements, each weighing in at less than 50 bytes!

Figure 12-14. Very few images are required for this design.

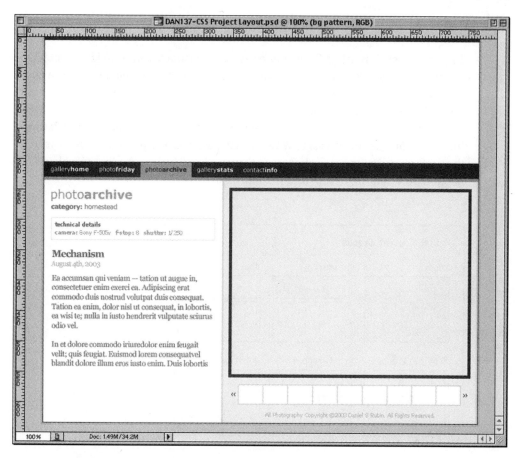

Figure 12-15. The rest is pure CSS, baby!

Defining the Structure

Now that I've finalized the visual design, it's time to translate my Photoshop layout into a logical structure for the XHTML. It's important to be mindful of the potential browsing devices and applications (user agents) that visitors might use to access your site while defining your document flow, because this is how the content will be presented to nongraphical browsers (text browsers such as Lynx or screen readers such as JAWS) and visual browsers that don't support CSS (in whole or in part, by design or by mistake).

Flow, Flow, Flow Your Doc

To write my site's markup, I need to convert the visual layout into logical blocks of content. This will help me determine where to place each element in the document flow, so the content will make sense when presented to user agents that don't display the visual design.

I like to tackle this step by grouping related visual elements and translating those groupings into <div>s, to which I then assign descriptive ids, which are then referenced in my stylesheet (see Figure 12-16). This is the first visual connection between the design and the markup.

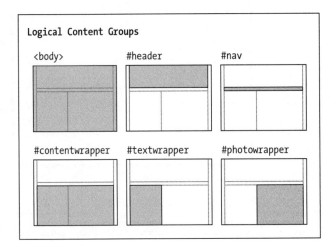

Figure 12-16. Creating logical content groups

From these groupings I can choose the best order to list the elements, and I've settled on the following basic flow and id naming:

1. #header

2. #nav

3. #contentwrapper

4. #textwrapper

5. #photowrapper

Now I can begin to write my XHTML, creating any additional <div>s along the way as needed.

Marking It Up As I Go Along

One of the requirements for this project is that its navigation elements are accessible to nonvisual browsers, so I've decided to mark up the #nav element as an unordered list, rather than a <div>. This is very friendly to nongraphical browsers, while still allowing me to style the <ul> and <li> elements to match my visual design (it's also semantically correct—the site navigation links are a list). With the same intent, I've also decided to make the #header element an <h1> heading.

> **TIP** *To get the unordered list to match my design, I must do two basic things. First, I need to display the list horizontally, and second, I need to remove the default list style. This is accomplished by the following CSS rule:* ul#nav li { display: inline; list-style-type: none; }. *To make sure the rollover effects line up properly within the list,* float: left; *must be applied to the navigation links using the* ul#nav li a *selector.*

After spending a little time in a text editor, but prior to adding the actual content (except for the navigation list items), my XHTML document now looks like this:

```
<!DOCTYPE html PUBLIC "-//W3C//DTD XHTML 1.0 Strict//EN"
"http://www.w3.org/TR/xhtml1/DTD/xhtml1-strict.dtd">
<html xmlns="http://www.w3.org/1999/xhtml" lang="en">
<head>
<meta http-equiv="content-type" content="text/html; charset=iso-8859-1" />
<title>superfluous photos</title>
</head>
<body>
<h1 id="header">superfluous photos</h1>
<ul id="nav">
<li><a href="/">gallery<strong>home</strong></a></li>
<li><a href="/photofriday/">photo<strong>friday</strong></a></li>
<li><a href="/archive/">photo<strong>archive</strong></a></li>
<li><a href="/stats/">gallery<strong>stats</strong></a></li>
<li><a href="/contact/">contact<strong>info</strong></a></li>
</ul>
<div id="contentwrapper">
<div id="textwrapper"></div>
<div id="photowrapper"></div>
</div>
</body>
</html>
```

After getting my basic markup in place, I needed to add a few more design-specific elements to the document flow (#frame and #wrapper; these will allow me to center the layout and set my double border), as well as the content (including another unordered list for the thumbnail images) and any required ids and classes. I've also elected to use an external stylesheet and import it into my XHTML document via @import (this hides the stylesheet from many older browsers that have poor CSS implementations, such as NN4). Now that everything is in place, it's time to start creating the stylesheet.

It's All About Style

I like to organize my stylesheets using comment-separated groups of like-styles: Global, Layout, Headings, Text, Lists, Links, Custom, and Miscellaneous. Within each group, ids and classes are listed in the order of appearance in the markup, and XHTML tags (<body>, <p>, <h1>, <h2>, etc.) are arranged to facilitate the cascading feature of CSS. When styling the elements in my design, I move from the top of the document to the bottom, so I can observe any inheritance of the rules I put in place.

Margins, Borders, and the Basic Layout

My design is intended to be a fixed-size layout—that is, the page won't resize to fit a user's browser window. I do, however, want the layout to be centered horizontally within the browser window, and I also need to style the two borders that adorn the left, bottom, and right edges of the design. Because I write my style rules in a particular order in the stylesheet, I need to take care of these issues first.

Under the Global style grouping, I first set the margin and padding of the page to 0 (and specify the background color and pattern), which will allow me to center the layout using the #frame element I created earlier:

```
/* global
------------------------------------------------ */
body {
  margin: 0;
  padding: 0;
  background: #d8d8d8 url(../i/bg_pattern.gif) top left;
}
```

Next, under the Layout group, I specify the width of my #frame and #wrapper elements (this requires use of the Tantek hack), and then set the left and right margins of the #frame element to auto, centering the layout evenly between the left and right sides of the browser window:

CSS Design Projects

```
/* layout
---------------------------------------------- */
#frame {
   width: 746px;
   margin: 0 auto 15px auto;
   background-color: #fff;
   border: 3px solid #c6c6c6;
   border-top: 0;
   /* box model hack a la Tantek: http://tantek.com/         */
   /* Include the rules below for any boxes with fixed widths or heights. */
   /* The width and/or height below is calculated by subtracting the    */
   /* border (x2) and padding (x2) from the width and/or height.        */
   voice-family: "\"}\"";
   voice-family: inherit;
   width: 740px; }


html>body #frame { width:740px; }
/* end box model hack */


#wrapper {
   width: 740px;
   margin: 0;
   background: url(../i/bg_content.gif) no-repeat bottom left;
   border: 1px solid #151f1c;
   border-top-width: 5px;
   /* box model hack */
   voice-family: "\"}\"";
   voice-family: inherit;
   width: 738px; }


body>#frame #wrapper { width:738px; }
/* end box model hack */
```

I also wanted a top border of 5px in the same color as my 1px border, so I added border-top-width: 5px; to the #wrapper style, which inherits the color (#151f1c) and style (solid) from the border rule the line before.

Image Replacement

I want the header graphic (photo and logo) to be visible to graphical user-agents, but I want screen readers and text-only browsers to have something to read too. I also prefer (in this instance) not to just plop an <img> into the document flow. This is the perfect opportunity to use a CSS image-replacement technique (structurally, an <h1> tag containing text is preferred to using an <img> tag in your markup, and image replacement allows you to produce a more structurally correct document while not relinquishing control over the visual presentation).

Image replacement specifies a background image for an element (in this case the <h1> heading at the top of the page) and hides the text within that element from graphical browsers. The text heading will be visible only to screen readers, text browsers, and users who prefer to use graphical browsers, but with images turned off. That last group is a special case, and a bit of nonsemantic, excess markup is required to make it work for them, but I believe it's a worthwhile compromise. A number of other image replacement techniques exist, but this version, thought up by Tom Gilder (http://blog.tom.me.uk/2003/08/07/), is the only one that supports users who surf without images.

The process is quite simple: Set the height of the element to that of the background image, then assign the background image to a <span> element (this is the aforementioned excess markup), and voila:

```
#header {
  height: 200px;
  position: relative;
}

#header span {
  background: url(../i/header.jpg) no-repeat top left;
  width: 100%;
  height: 100%;
  position: absolute;
}
```

The markup now looks like this:

```
<h1 id="header"><span></span>superfluous photos</h1>
```

CSS Image Rollovers

JavaScript has long been the tool of choice for manipulating image rollovers. Everyone knows CSS can control text links, and in this design I've used it to style the tab rollovers in the navigation bar (no images required), but you can also use CSS to eliminate the need for JavaScript image rollovers. The best thing about this method is that users who browse with JavaScript turned off will still get the visual feedback that makes links easier to use, but it also allows the removal of the images from the document flow (using image replacement) and is therefore more accessible.

Before I create the CSS, I first need to have alternate images for each state: passive/no action, active/hover, and current/"You Are Here" (see Figure 12-17).

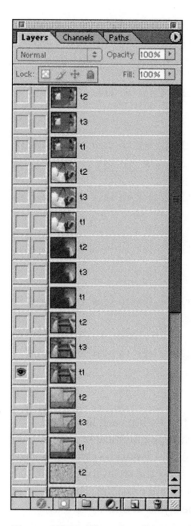

Figure 12-17. Thumbnail image layers in Photoshop

Now that the images are created, it's time to style the markup. Just as with the primary navigation for the site, I've decided to use an unordered list for the thumbnails, which will format nicely in nongraphical browsers:

```
<ul id="thumblist">
<li id="thumb01">
<a id="thumb01a" href="?c=homestead p=01" title="click to view this image">
<span class="hide">1</span></a></li>
<li id="thumb02">
<a id="thumb02a" href="?c=homestead p=02" title="click to view this image">
<span class="hide">2</span></a></li>
```

```
<li id="thumb03">
<a id="thumb03a" href="?c=homestead p=03" title="click to view this image">
<span class="hide">3</span></a></li>
<li id="thumb04">
<a id="thumb04a" href="?c=homestead p=04" title="click to view this image">
<span class="hide">4</span></a></li>
<li id="thumb05">
<a id="thumb05a" href="?c=homestead p=05" title="click to view this image">
<span class="hide">5</span></a></li>
<li id="thumb06">
<a id="thumb06a" href="?c=homestead p=06" title="click to view this image">
<span class="hide">6</span></a></li>
<li id="thumb07">
<a id="thumb07a" href="?c=homestead p=07" title="click to view this image">
<span class="hide">7</span></a></li>
<li id="thumb08">
<a id="thumb08a" href="?c=homestead p=08" title="click to view this image">
<span class="hide">8</span></a></li>
<li id="thumb09">
<a id="thumb09a" href="?c=homestead p=09" title="click to view this image">
<span class="hide">9</span></a></li>
</ul>
```

Each link is assigned its very own id, and the text within each link is surrounded by a span that will be used to hide the text from graphical browsers.

The CSS is the same for each thumbnail, but each id must be styled individually for the effect to work (to conserve space, I'll show the styles for the first thumbnail only, though some rules are combined where possible). The <li> elements are all the same, however, so they can be styled at once:

```
ul#thumblist li {
  margin: 0;
  padding: 0;
  width: 38px;
  height: 28px;
}
```

And here are the styles for the thumbnail background image:

```
/* backgrounds are applied here */
#thumb01a, #thumb02a, #thumb03a, #thumb04a, #thumb05a,
#thumb06a, #thumb07a, #thumb08a, #thumb09a {
  float: left;
  display: block;
  width: 40px;
```

```
    height: 30px;
    margin-right: 2px;
    padding: 0;
    border: 1px solid #FEFEFE;
    background: url(../p/h/homestead/homestead_01_t1.jpg) no-repeat 0px;
    /* IE/Mac positions the background images with a 1px offset compared with
    most other browsers, so after setting the value above for IE/Mac, we use a CSS
    parsing hack to hide the corrected values from IE/Mac (hack credited to James
    Craig; details can be    found at
    http://www.sam-i-am.com/work/sandbox/css/mac_ie5_hack.html) */
    /* start hiding from IE/Mac using the 'commented backslash' hack \*/
    background-position: -1px; /* stop hiding */
    /* box model hack */
    voice-family: "\"}\"";
    voice-family: inherit;
    width: 38px;
    height: 28px; }
/* end box model hack */


html>body #thumb01a, html>body #thumb02a,
html>body #thumb03a, html>body #thumb04a,
html>body #thumb05a, html>body #thumb06a,
html>body #thumb07a, html>body #thumb08a,
html>body #thumb09a { width:38px; height:28px; }


/* remove the right margin from the last thumbnail */
#thumb09a {
  margin-right: 0px;
}
```

Now I style the :hover state:

```
/* set the hover images */
a#thumb01a:hover {
  background-image: url(../p/h/homestead/homestead_01_t2.jpg);
}
```

Finally, I hide the text links:

```
/* hide alt text for rollovers */
.hide {
  display: none;
}
```

This takes care of the passive and active states, but I also mentioned a "You Are Here" marker to provide some additional visual feedback to the user. This is accomplished by specifying a class for the <body> element:

```
<body id="photoarchive" class="current01">
```

> **TIP** *Notice the* id="photoarchive" *in the* <body> *element? The same technique used for the thumbnails can be used (as it is in this project) to style the current tab in the primary site navigation. See the "You Are Here" rule in the stylesheet.*

Then I add the following rules for each thumbnail (these must be placed before the :hover rules in the stylesheet, so the rollovers will work on the "You Are Here" image):

```
/* set alternate images to show the current page based on the CLASS of <body> */
body.current01 #thumb01a {
   background-image: url(../p/h/homestead/homestead_01_t3.jpg);
}
```

That's all there is to it! I now have triple-state image rollovers without using a single drop of JavaScript, providing further separation between content and design.

The Completed XHTML and CSS

After testing the site in current versions of all major browsers, as well as older versions (see the "Squashing Bugs et al." section for solutions to some minor display bugs discovered during testing), and adding comments to explain the markup, the XHTML and CSS are ready to go.

Accessibility and the Separation of Style and Structure

I've mentioned nongraphical browsers quite a bit, and frankly, an image gallery doesn't feature highly accessible content. However, even though the images themselves aren't accessible, every other element of this design *is*, from the navigation to the page headings and description of the photo. This is possible because the visual style and layout of the page isn't embedded in the markup (a la nested tables of old), so alternate browsers are presented with only the content, not the design.

Text-Only Browsers

text-only web browsers;text only web browsersLynx is a very popular text-only web browser, and though it can't display the photos nor the visual design of the page, the page is still navigable and the textual content easily accessible (see Figure 12-18).

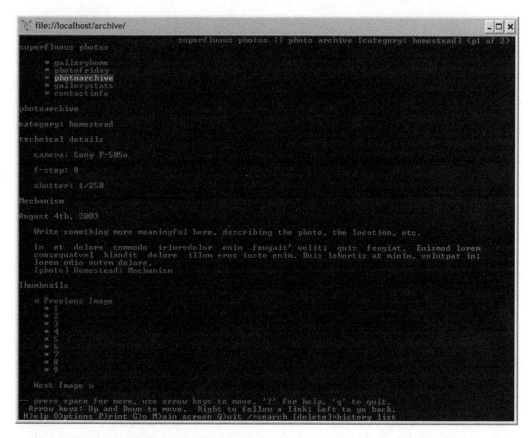

Figure 12-18. This design as displayed by Lynx

CSS-Challenged Browsers

There are some user agents that have a limited understanding of CSS (NN4.*x*, anyone?). Thankfully, it's possible to hide the stylesheet from most of those browsers by using @import instead of linking a stylesheet:

```
<style type="text/css" media="all">@import "c/basic.css";</style>
```

Users of such browsers will see something very similar to those who use Lynx: as an unstyled version of the page, except for the featured photo, which is visible because it isn't inserted by CSS (see Figure 12-19).

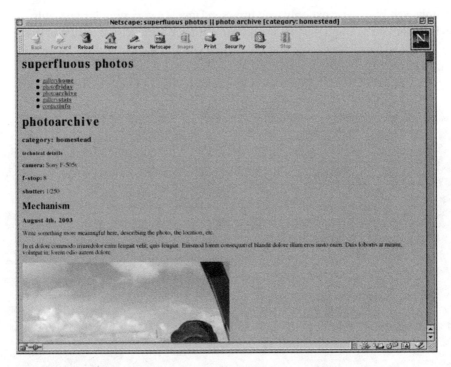

Figure 12-19. This design as displayed by Netscape Communicator 4.77

Squashing Bugs et al.

Comprehensive browser testing is an often-overlooked step in too many web projects. Although developing with XHTML and CSS will reduce the number of cross-browser and cross-platform display issues (especially when dealing with modern browsers), you may still discover a few small bugs by properly testing your site. It's always better to find and fix the problems *before* you present your site to the public.

Display/Rendering Issues

I ran into very few display issues while browser testing, but two of them are worth mentioning, if only for your future reference should you ever find a similar problem.

Background Image

Browsers in the Mozilla family (Mozilla, Netscape, Firebird, Camino) and Safari/
Konqueror wouldn't display the background image of the site's logo when applied
to the #textwrapper element. After some experimenting, I found that applying the
background-image to the #wrapper element and changing #textwrapper to background:
transparent; fixed the problem.

Mysterious *<div>* Clone in IE 6

IE 6 (tested on Windows XP Professional) had a strange problem with the
#details element when <h5> margin-bottom was set to a negative number:
A mysterious ghost image of the bottom border appeared further down the
page running through the date (see Figure 12-20). Removing margin-bottom
fixed the problem (see Figure 12-21).

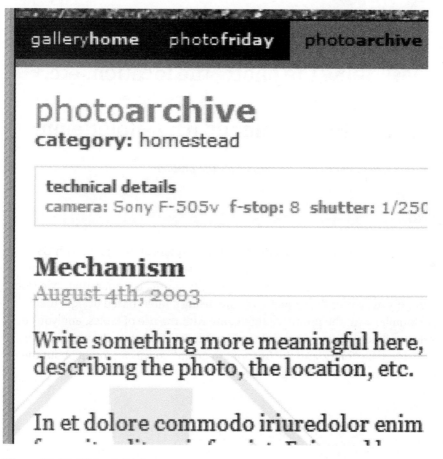

Figure 12-20. IE 6 exhibiting a strange reaction to a negative margin-bottom *value*

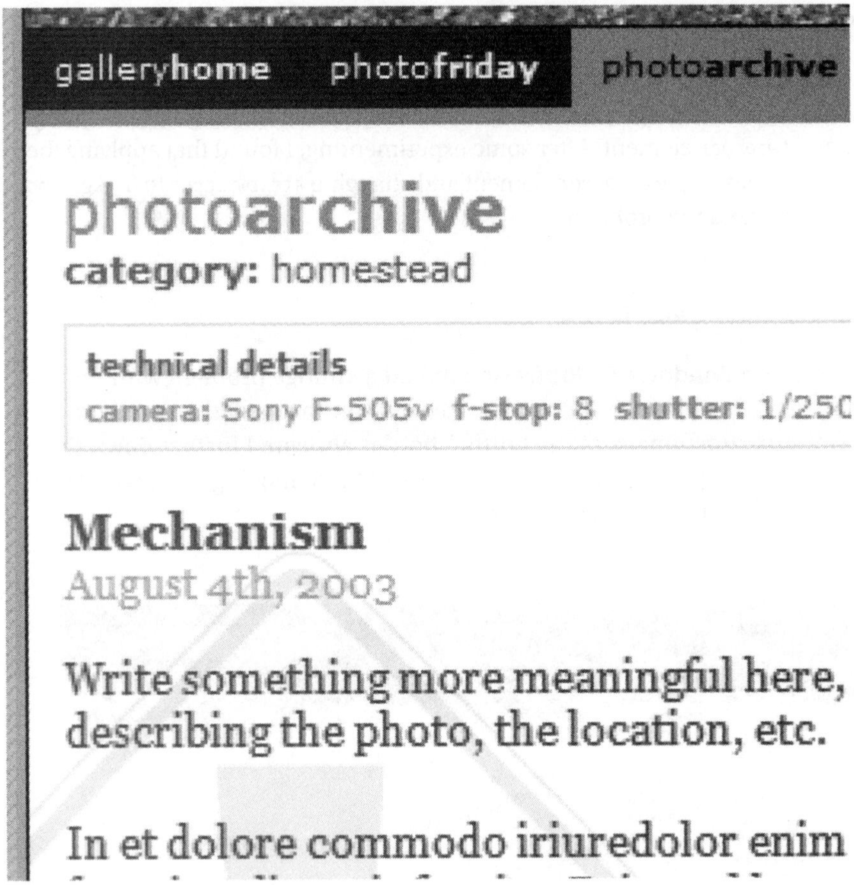

Figure 12-21. Removing margin-bottom *fixes the problem.*

Summary

I've shown you just a small percentage of the wonders of designing with CSS: more flexibility in your design, less reliance on JavaScript for interactivity and user feedback, and a higher level of accessibility simply by separating style from content. If you've ever developed a website using a table-based design, then you're familiar with the problems that come with the use of tables, and you've experienced sacrificing your artistic independence. CSS gives designers more control, more flexibility, and the freedom to create, so we can forget about the code and concentrate on being designers.

Image Viewer

by Michael Pick

The aim of this project is to provide a compact image viewer with a clean, attractive interface and some interesting features. You'll often see this kind of piece on news outlets such as the New York Times or BBC News websites. Inexplicably, they're often authored in Flash, even though they take no real advantage of Flash features. Using CSS, you can make up for the lack of animation and built-in rollovers with the addition of rendering speed. The resulting code also makes for easier updating and can be integrated quite seamlessly into a content management system such as Movable Type. The interactive capabilities of CSS are extended through the use of some simple JavaScript.

The goals are to provide the user with basic features: a clean image window, a simple system of navigating backward and forward through the image sets, a list of categories that the photographs are sorted into, and a set of thumbnails so that the user might navigate out of the regular sequence of the images. However, the additional features must not distract from the presentation of the images. Ideally, the navigational elements must also maintain consistent positioning so that the user doesn't have to search for them as the pages change. In keeping with the way this type of gallery is usually presented, the photographs will be displayed in a pop-up window launched from the main browser window, as shown in Figure 12-22.

Figure 12-22. Photograph displaying in a pop-up window

Design and Layout

Like most web designers I know, I like to assemble my layouts in Photoshop before the coding stage. By doing this, I can decide on placement, scale, color, type styles, and all the other layout decisions quickly and easily. By keeping all of the elements on layers, I can quickly change and move them around the layout. When a layout is finished, I can also use the mockup file to create any images I'll need for my pages.

When designing an image gallery, I like to make sure my images are a consistent size, which makes the gallery flow more smoothly. I also ensure that a layout can accommodate both landscape and portrait photographs, and that the navigation is in a consistent location from page to page, so that the user doesn't have to move the mouse quickly through the sequence, for instance.

In the layout phase, I decided to give the photos a background to simulate the kind of filed-out negative frame that a photographer might use in printing from film, giving a strong focus to each image. I also decided to keep the navigation and title information in simple black-and-white to avoid distraction from the photograph and to put it at the bottom of the pop-up window. The window leaves enough space to view landscape or portrait images. The most interesting decision lay in the positioning of the thumbnail images. In the end, I decided to lay them over the photograph like a television picture-in-picture, because it actually decreased the amount of distraction from the main image.

Coding

Once the layout is firmed up in the image editor, it becomes very easy to translate it into HTML and CSS code using a text editor. I can then make decisions about the structure of the CSS based on the layout and the intention of the pages.

I chose to use absolute positioning for this project for a number of reasons. For one, it tends to be well supported in general among browsers, and it's well suited to consistent size and placement of page elements. Because the gallery is to be presented in a fixed-size pop-up window, I don't have to worry about the window contents being *liquid* (i.e., shifting depending on window size).

There is one exception to this, however: the index.html file that the user initially sees when visiting the site and that is used to launch the pop-up window (see Figure 12-23).

```
<!DOCTYPE html PUBLIC "-//W3C//DTD XHTML 1.0 Transitional//EN"
    "http://www.w3.org/TR/2000/REC-xhtml1-20000126/DTD/xhtml1-transitional.dtd">
<html xmlns="http://www.w3.org/1999/xhtml" xml:lang="en" lang="en">
<head>
  <meta http-equiv="content-type" content="text/html; charset=iso-8859-1" />
  <title>Michael Pick &middot; Trans-Atlantica</title>
```

```
<style type="text/css" >
  body {
    background: url(images/front-bg.jpg) no-repeat top right #ffffff;
  }

  #titleBox {
    margin-right: 110px;
    margin-top: 210px;
    text-align: right;
  }
</style>

<script type="text/javascript" language="Javascript">
  function openViewer (w) {
    win = window.open(w, 'viewer', 'width=500, height=536,
scrollbars=no, status=no')
  }
</script>

</head>

<body>

<div id="titleBox">
  <a href="#" onclick="javascript:openViewer('london-1.html')">
<img src="images/front-title.png" width="280" height="60" border="0"
title="click to launch gallery" alt="Trans-Atlantica Click to Launch" />
</a></div>
</body>
</html>
```

Figure 12-23. The index page used to launch the pop-up window

I can't know this window size in advance, and because the layout calls for right-positioned elements, it needs to flow depending on the window size. Because it's a simple page with few rules, I simply embedded the style declaration in the <head> of the document.

These rules put the camera background at the right and top of the document and set a background color of white. The <div> #titleBox will contain the title of the project, which is also a link to launch the pop-up window using JavaScript. The title image ("Trans-Atlantica") used to launch the pop-up window is aligned right and given margins to keep its distance from the top and right side of the page. The pop-up window I'm launching has a size of 500×536px.

The next step is to divide up the gallery pages into blocks of content. Again, this is where the mockup comes in handy, because I can use it to get measurements for positioning.

Here's the main CSS file gallery.css:

```css
body {
  background: url(images/body-bg.png) repeat-x #ffffff;
  font-family: Helvetica, Arial, sans-serif;
  font-size: 11px;
}

a {
  text-decoration: none;
  color: #ffffff;
}

/* absolute position boxes for the photographs */

#horzPicBox {
  position: absolute;
  top: 20px;
  left: 20px;
  background: url(images/horz-bg.png) #000000;
  height: 350px;
  width: 460px;
  z-index: 0;
}

  #horzPicBox img {
    padding-top: 10px;
    padding-left: 10px;
  }

#vertPicBox {
  position: absolute;
  top: 20px;
  left: 20px;
  background: url(images/vert-bg.png) #000000;
  height: 460px;
  width: 350px;
  z-index: 0;
}

  #vertPicBox img {
    padding-top: 10px;
    padding-left: 10px;
  }
```

```
/* titlebox holds the tile and navigation widgets at the bottom of the page.
div widgets floats the widgets to the right in title */

#titleBox {
  position: absolute;
  background-color: #000000;
  color: #ffffff;
  top: 500px;
  left: 0;
  width: 500px;
  height: 36px;
  z-index: 0;
  font-weight: bold;
}

  #titleBox .photoInfo {
    display: block;
    padding-top: 11px;
    padding-left: 20px;
  }

  #widgets {
    float: right;
    padding-top: 11px;
    padding-right: 20px;
  }

  #widgets a {
    padding-top: 11px;
  }

  #widgets a:hover {
    background: url(images/tab.png) no-repeat top center;
  }

/* picInPic is the container for the thumbnails and the drop-down menu */

#picInPic {
  position: absolute;
  display: none;
  width: 110px;
  top: 40px;
  left: 40px;
  z-index: 1;
}
```

```
/* thumbnails is the thumbnails box. the divs that follow give rules for the
image thumbnails in the thumbnail div, including the rollover effect */

#thumbnails {
  display: block;
  width: inherit;
  height: 76px;
  overflow: auto;
  background: url(images/trans.png);
  border: 1px solid #aaaaaa;
}

  #thumbnails img {
    display: block;
    margin-top: 10px;
    margin-left: 10px;
    margin-bottom: 10px;
    border: 4px solid #ffffff;
  }

  #thumbnails a img {
    border: 4px solid #dddddd;
  }

  #thumbnails a:hover img {
    border: 4px solid #ffffff;
  }

/* div to hold the category dropdown */

#category {
  font-weight: bold;
  font-size: 9px;
  width: 112px;
  background: url(images/dark-trans.png);
}

  #category a {
    display: block;
    padding-left: 10px;
    background: url(images/drop-down.png) no-repeat center right;
    border: 1px solid #aaaaaa;
    padding-top: 6px;
    padding-bottom: 5px;
  }
```

```
  #category a:hover {
    background: url(images/drop-down-over.png) no-repeat center right;
  }


/* dropMenu is the drop-down menu for the category titles */

#dropMenu {
  visibility: hidden;
  font-weight: bold;
  font-size: 9px;
  width: 112px;
  color: #ffffff;
}

  #dropMenu a {
    display: block;
    padding-left: 10px;
    background: url(images/trans-blue.png);
    border: 1px solid #aaaaaa;
    border-top: 0;
    padding-top: 6px;
    padding-bottom: 5px;
  }

  #dropMenu a:hover {
    background: url(images/dark-trans.png);
  }
```

Here's a sample gallery page, london-1.html (all gallery pages are the same except for linked images and title information):

```
<!DOCTYPE html PUBLIC "-//W3C//DTD XHTML 1.0 Transitional//EN"
        "http://www.w3.org/TR/2000/REC-xhtml1-20000126/DTD/xhtml1-
transitional.dtd">
<html xmlns="http://www.w3.org/1999/xhtml" xml:lang="en" lang="en">
<head>
    <meta http-equiv="content-type" content="text/html; charset=iso-8859-1" />
    <title>Michael Pick &middot; Trans-Atlantica Gallery</title>

    <link rel="stylesheet" href="gallery.css" type="text/css" />

    <script src="scripts.js" type="text/javascript"
language="Javascript"></script>

</head>
```

```
<body onload="javascript:setState('picInPic','thumbsOff'); return false"
onunload="javascript:setPref('picInPic'); return false">

<div id="horzPicBox"><img src="photos/brompton_road.jpg" height="330"
width="440" title="Brompton Road" alt="Brompton Road" /></div>

<div id="picInPic">

    <div id="thumbnails">
        <a href="london-2.html"><img src="photos/watched_thumb.jpg" width="60"
height="50" title="Load This Image" alt="load" /></a>
<a href="london-3.html"></a><a href="london-3.html"><img
src="photos/stand_thumb.jpg" width="60" height="50" title="Load This Image"
alt="load" /></a><a href="london-4.html"><img src="photos/train_thumb.jpg"
width="60" height="50" title="Load This Image" alt="load" /></a>
<a href="london-5.html"><img src="photos/tate_thumb.jpg" width="60"
height="50" title="Load This Image" alt="load" /></a><img
src="photos/brompton_thumb.jpg" width="60" height="50" title="Load This
Image" alt="load" /></div>

    <div id="category">
    <a accesskey="m" title="toggle category (m)enu" href="#"
onclick="javascript:showvis('dropMenu'); return
false;">LONDON</a></div>

    <div id="dropMenu">
        <a href="new-york-1.html">NEW YORK</a><a href="rome-1.html">
ROME</a></div></div>

<div id="titleBox">

    <div id="widgets">
        <a accesskey="t" title="(t)oggle picture in picture" href="#"
onclick="javascript:showhide('picInPic'); return false;">thumbs</a> : <a
accesskey="p" title="(p)revious image" href="london-5.html">prev</a>
&middot; &sect; &middot; <a accesskey="n" title="(n)ext image"
href="london-2.html">next</a></div>

    <span class="photoInfo">BROMPTON ROAD &middot; London
07/2003</span></div></body>
</html>
```

I started by defining some basic page characteristics:

```
body {
  background: url(images/body-bg.png) repeat-x #ffffff;
  font-family: Helvetica, Arial, sans-serif;
  font-size: 11px;
}


a {
  text-decoration: none;
  color: #ffffff;
}
```

This simply sets a global `font-family` and `font-size` for the page, and defines its background and text color. There is also a background image defined, which is a 10×560px image of white with a black end where the title information and navigation widgets reside. This became necessary to add, because some browsers were leaving an extra pixel of white at the bottom or right edges of the title area, even though I had defined the proper dimensions to fill the space. There are also two global rules for the links: `color: white` and `text-decoration: none`, which displays them without the standard underline.

The next blocks to define are obviously the photograph areas:

```
#horzPicBox {
  position: absolute;
  top: 20px;
  left: 20px;
  background: url(images/horz-bg.png) #000000;
  height: 350px;
  width: 460px;
  z-index: 0;
}


  #horzPicBox img {
    padding-top: 10px;
    padding-left: 10px;
  }


#vertPicBox {
  position: absolute;
  top: 20px;
  left: 20px;
  background: url(images/vert-bg.png) #000000;
  height: 460px;
  width: 350px;
  z-index: 0;
}
```

```
#vertPicBox img {
  padding-top: 10px;
  padding-left: 10px;
}
```

The photo blocks are straightforward—they're specified as `position:absolute` and assigned their top and left coordinates on the page, plus their respective widths and heights (which is necessary to ensure that all of the background image—the rough black photo border—shows properly). The reasoning behind using two different blocks is to give different backgrounds and sizes for portrait and landscape photographs.

Notable here is the use of `z-index: 0`, which puts the photo block on the bottom layer of the page. Also notable is the use of a descendant selector such as `#horzPicBox img`, which assigns padding to the `<img>` tags that make up the content of the photo blocks. My usual practice is to assign padding to the contents of a block rather than to the block itself to avoid problems with IE and the box model.

Next up is the photo title and navigation block:

```
#titleBox {
  position: absolute;
  background-color: #000000;
  color: #ffffff;
  top: 500px;
  left: 0px;
  width: 500px;
  height: 36px;
  z-index: 0;
  font-weight: bold;
}

#titleBox .photoInfo {
  display: block;
  padding-top: 11px;
  padding-left: 20px;
}

#widgets {
  float: right;
  padding-top: 11px;
  padding-right: 20px;
}
```

```
#widgets a {
  padding-top: 11px;
}

#widgets a:hover {
  background: url(images/tab.png) no-repeat top center;
}
```

Again, it's fairly straightforward. The container #titleBox is specified position:absolute and given coordinates and a black background, and assigned to the bottom z-index layer like the photo block. The following <span> and blocks are inline content for #titleBox, and as before padding is assigned to the content rather than the container. The <span> #titleBox .title is set as display:block and the block #widgets is assigned float: right, meaning that it aligns itself to the right edge of the parent container #titleBox. Note that you should always put floated HTML code before the code to which it aligns—that is, the #widgets box appears in the HTML file before the .photoInfo information, like so:

```
<div id="titleBox">

    <div id="widgets">
        <a title="toggle picture in picture" href="#"
onclick="javascript:showhide('picInPic'); return
false;">thumbs</a> : <a title="previous image" href="london-5.html">
prev</a> &middot; &sect; &middot;
<a title="next image" href="london-2.html">next</a></div>

        <span class="photoInfo">BROMPTON ROAD &middot; London
07/2003</span></div>
```

The final two style blocks for #widgets define the rollover effect for the navigation. The rule #widgets a sets an 11px padding above any links in the #widgets block, and the #widgets a:hover assigns a new background when the mouse rolls over the link. In this case, it creates a little white triangle that is flush with the top of the black #titleBox area on rollover, as shown in Figure 12-24.

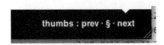

Figure 12-24. Navigation widgets close up

Now on to the more interesting bits: the picture-in-picture thumbnail and category blocks. Creating this block is actually easier than you might think—it's just a few inline blocks inside an absolute position container. The reasoning behind enclosing all of these into one block becomes clearer later, when the JavaScript is created to show and hide the picture-in-picture block.

```
#picInPic {
  position: absolute;
  display: none;
  width: 110px;
  top: 40px;
  left: 40px;
  z-index: 1;
}
```

The container is again very simple. Note that it is assigned a z-index of 1, which causes it to be rendered as a layer above the photo block. Now let's look at the style for the thumbnail images:

```
#thumbnails {
  display: block;
  width: inherit;
  height: 76px;
  overflow: auto;
  background: url(images/trans.png);
  border: 1px solid #aaaaaa;
}

  #thumbnails img {
    display: block;
    margin-top: 10px;
    margin-left: 10px;
    margin-bottom: 10px;
    border: 4px solid #ffffff;
  }

  #thumbnails a img {
    border: 4px solid #dddddd;
  }

  #thumbnails a:hover img {
    border: 4px solid #ffffff;
  }
```

First up is #thumbnails, the small box that holds the thumbnail images. The key here is overflow: auto, which gives the box a scroll bar if the content is larger than the assigned size of the #thumbnails container. Also notable is the background image, which is a 24-bit PNG with an alpha channel that gives it partial transparency. This

works only in browsers that properly support PNG alpha transparency—basically
every one of the modern browsers excluding IE/Windows, which renders a gray
background instead.

The following descendant selectors deal with the margins and rollovers for
the thumbnail images. As usual, margins are assigned to the content to avoid box-
model confusion, but here I use margin rather than padding. The reasoning is that
padding gets counted in the hover effect, whereas margin doesn't. The selector
#thumbnails img gives images a white 4px border by default—basically to highlight
the image that the user is currently viewing. The selectors #thumbnails a img and
#thumbnails a:hover img are used to give the images a border rollover effect.

For Mozilla-based browsers, it's possible to assign mouseover effects to the
thumbnail links simply by specifying styles for #thumbnails a:hover. In this way it's
possible to change the border color on mouseover, for example. The previous code
specifies rules for #thumbnails img, thumbnails a img, and #thumbnails a:hover img,
in order to make the mouseover effects work for IE. Essentially it needs to be
spelled out carefully for IE to render the mouseover as desired.

The next block is the category label (see Figure 12-25):

```
#category {
  font-weight: bold;
  font-size: 9px;
  width: 112px;
  background: url(images/dark-trans.png);
}

  #category a {
    display: block;
    padding-left: 10px;
    background: url(images/drop-down.png) no-repeat center right;
    border: 1px solid #aaaaaa;
    padding-top: 6px;
    padding-bottom: 5px;
  }

  #category a:hover {
    background: url(images/drop-down-over.png) no-repeat center right;
  }
```

Figure 12-25. The category label and drop-down menu link

The #category <div> is assigned font information and a background, and the
link part of the block, the text, is also assigned a background that is positioned

at the right center of the block—the drop-down indicator. The link is defined `display: block` so that it takes up a block of space rather than just appearing inline. When the mouse rolls over the link, the background (the drop-down indicator) changes to another image with a different color.

After #category comes #dropMenu—but where is it?

```
#dropMenu {
    visibility: hidden;
    font-weight: bold;
    font-size: 9px;
    width: 112px;
    color: #ffffff;
}
```

```
    #dropMenu a {
        display: block;
        padding-left: 10px;
        background: url(images/trans-blue.png);
        border: 1px solid #aaaaaa;
        border-top: 0px;
        padding-top: 6px;
        padding-bottom: 5px;
    }
```

```
    #dropMenu a:hover {
        background: url(images/dark-trans.png);
    }
```

The key to #dropMenu is the first rule: `visibility: hidden`. Because #dropMenu is a CSS menu made to simulate a drop-down menu, it must be hidden until the user activates it (see Figure 12-26). The rule `visibility: hidden` ensures that the item is rendered but not displayed when the document is loaded. (See the "A Tangent: Visibility vs. Display" section for more information.)

Figure 12-26. The drop-down menu toggled

The visibility rule is what is accessed and changed dynamically when the user clicks the link in #category. Using JavaScript, the rule is changed to visibility: visible and the menu appears.

A Tangent: Visibility vs. Display

While working through this project, I discovered a few critical differences in the behavior of the display and visibility rules, in terms of how they work to show and hide CSS elements in the pages.

The first difference lies in how they affect rendering when the document loads. Specifying display: none does indeed hide the element, but it does so by telling the browser not to render it at all. In a page of continuous content, this would cause the content to expand and collapse as the display state of the block is toggled; with an absolute positioned block, this isn't a problem.

The rule visibility: hidden, however, tells the browser to render the element but not show it, exactly as you would expect. This means that in a continuous page, an empty space will be left for the invisible block. One problem with visibility lies in that it doesn't seem to hide system widgets associated with the block in every browser, but only the content of the block. For example, using visibility: hidden dynamically on the thumbnails block hides the thumbnail images and the block background, but the scroll bar remains visible on top of the photograph! (Note that this behavior affected Mozilla 1.4/Mac but not Safari in my testing.)

Bugs and Workarounds

I work on a Mac using Mozilla primarily for testing when coding CSS/HTML, and therefore it should be no surprise when bugs crop up in IE (both Windows and Mac platforms) when testing compatibility.

Width Problems

Originally I was letting the #picInPic block size itself by specifying no width for one of the blocks and then 100% for the other, so that the wider block determined the width of #picInPic using the size of its content, and the other expanded to fit the same size.

However, setting width: 100% can cause problems in IE for Mac and Windows, as shown in Figure 12-27.

Figure 12-27. Width problems with the category label

In Figure 12-27 you can see #category interpreting its width as 100% of the viewport width (the browser display space) rather than inheriting it from its parent block as it should (using IE5/Mac). The solution is to specify fixed widths for all #picInPic blocks.

Paragraph Problems

I had originally used the paragraph tag to enclose the title information for each image like so:

```
<p>BROMPTON ROAD &middot; London 07/2003</p>
```

However, IE/Windows didn't render the margin above the paragraph like Mozilla, and the top of the title was therefore flush with the top of the #titleBox <div>. This seems to be IE deciding whether to render the top margin depending on whether or not the paragraph is the first in a block. The solution is to create the <span> photoInfo and use it like so:

```
<span class="photoInfo">BROMPTON ROAD &middot; London 07/2003</span>
```

Note that to have the <span> render assigned margins, it must be specified as display: block.

Float Problems

Originally, I used margin as a rule for the #widgets block that's floated to the right edge in the #titleBox block. It's important to note that a serious float bug in IE 6 causes it to render side margins at double their assigned sizes for floated blocks. The solution here is to use padding to create the desired margin at the side, rather than margin.

Usability Concerns

As I worked through the project I had to make decisions about the presentation based on what I thought might benefit the end user.

One concern is the use of a CSS-based drop-down menu instead of the standard system drop-down widget created by using `<select>` tags. In reality, it would be preferable to use the standard widget, because it's more recognizable as a menu. Using a CSS menu gives more control over its appearance at the expense of easy recognition. Drop-down menus can be written using pure CSS for the effect, such the pure CSS menus on Eric Meyer's site (`http://www.meyerweb.com/eric/css/edge/menus/demo.html`), although the menus described there don't work in IE/Windows—an advantage for these hybrid JavaScript menus.

Another usability discovery lay in the presentation of the thumbnails in the `#picInPic` block. Originally, I had them ordered by their numeric file order. Each page displayed the thumbnails in the same order, so that each page showed the same thumbnail first in the block. In some cases, it showed the same thumbnail as the image in the window. This meant that the user had to scroll every time to see a thumbnail different from the initial one. It seemed a much better method to order the thumbnails so that they always showed the next image in the sequence, which put the thumbnail for the current image *last* in the sequence.

Finally, an easy usability win comes through using access keys for important links in the presentation. Simply adding `accesskey="x"` to your links like so:

```
<a accesskey="n" title="(n)ext image" href="london-1.html">next</a>
```

can make for much faster navigation and is an accessibility plus for disabled users, although I have negated that effect somewhat by indicating the access key in the tool tip title rather than by underlining (mostly for aesthetic reasons).

JavaScript and Cookies

JavaScript is the final necessary component for this project to make it work properly. Actions taken in one block can't change styles in another block directly using only CSS, so I need another method of dynamically changing styles on demand, without reloading pages.

```
/* function to show and hide the thumbnails */

function showhide (id){
  if (document.getElementById) {
    obj = document.getElementById(id);
```

```
      if (obj.style.display == "block") {
        obj.style.display = "none";
      } else {
        obj.style.display = "block";
      }
    }
  }
}

function showvis (id){
  if (document.getElementById) {
    obj = document.getElementById(id);
    if (obj.style.visibility == "visible") {
      obj.style.visibility = "hidden";
    } else {
      obj.style.visibility = "visible";
    }
  }
}

/* function to set a cookie */

function setCookie (name, value, expires) {
  document.cookie = name + "=" + escape(value) + "; expires=" +
expires.toGMTString() + "; path=/";
}

/* function to set user prefs for thumbs using the cookie to store it on the
client machine */

function setPref (id) {
  if (document.getElementById) {
    obj = document.getElementById(id);
    var toSet = "";
    if (obj.style.display == "none") {
      toSet = "true";
    } else {
      toSet = "false";
    }
  }
  var expdate = new Date (); // create date object
  expdate.setTime(expdate.getTime() + 1000 * 60 * 60 * 24 * 365); // get
current and add one year to it
  setCookie("thumbsOff",toSet,expdate);
}
```

```
/* function to read cookie and set display of picInPic */

function setState (id, name) {
  var cookies = document.cookie;
  var startpos = cookies.indexOf(name)+name.length+1;
  var endpos = cookies.indexOf(";",startpos)-1;
  if (endpos == -2) endpos = cookies.length;
  var result = cookies.substring(startpos,endpos);
  if (document.getElementById) {
    obj = document.getElementById(id);
    if (result == "false") {
      obj.style.display = "block";
    }
  }
}
```

JavaScript allows for an easy solution by enabling you to target blocks by ID, and access and change the style rules for those blocks. For example, to show or hide the thumbnails block, a JavaScript function requests the display state of the #picInPic block. If the state is display: block, JavaScript changes it to display: none, or vice versa. Similarly, the link in the #category block toggles the visibility state of the #dropMenu block to show or hide the menu.

JavaScript is also used to preserve the state of the #picInPic block between pages by using a cookie. The JavaScript function is called using an onunload statement on the <body> tag in the HTML. When the user leaves the page, the function checks the state of #picInPic and writes a cookie on the user's machine to record it. When a page is loaded, an onload statement in <body> calls a function that checks for the cookie and then sets the display rule of #picInPic accordingly.

One more note regarding the JavaScript: Instead of you writing it inline, it's linked like the style sheet, giving you the advantage of working with one script file to alter the behavior of all pages in the project.

```
<script src="scripts.js" type="text/javascript" language="Javascript"></script>
```

Summary

In the end, this is a fairly easy project to implement, and what you get is a very fast image viewer that would be suitable to use with a content management system. The viewer could also be extended to include slide-show functionality fairly easily using JavaScript, and it's easy to update by hand if necessary. The clean, fast rollovers are much faster than more antiquated image-swapping methods. It's a simple application, but it does show how you can use some interesting and well-supported CSS methods to create a clean, interactive, cross-platform solution.

Real Estate Portal

by Cornelia Lange

I'd like to introduce an existing project: imapa.de, a portal for people to buy and sell real estate privately, without the services of a real estate agent. Imapa.de (http://www.imapa.de/) is a joint project of mine (http://www.clkm.de/) and Olaf Gleba's (http://www.creatics.de/). First, I'll summarize the initial considerations for the planning of the project, and then I'll move on to describe the essential parts of the project. The main topics are as follows:

- Project description and requirements

- Building the main template

- Building the template for a real estate listing

- Something special: creating a CSS image map without JavaScript

- Summary

Project Description and Requirements

The project's target group is property owners and potential property buyers who meet on imapa.de and who wish to interact with each other directly, without the involvement of a real estate agent. We assume that this target group has varying skills and experience in dealing with the Internet. For this reason, the website has to be as simple and accessible as possible, particularly with regard to navigation.

The project should fulfill the following requirements:

- It should have a CSS design (tableless).

- The layout should be centered.

- Usability and accessibility should be taken into account.

- It should be completely scalable in terms of not only the text sizes, but also the entire layout (i.e., it should be "elastic").

- It shouldn't include horizontal scroll bars at 800×600.

A couple of words about **browser compatibility**: We would, of course, like the site's layout to be presented without problem on as many browsers and operating systems as possible. However, in practice, we can't test all browsers, without limit, to fully satisfy everyone. We'll focus on the mainstream browsers because of time and money constraints involved (testing lesser-used browsers is time and cost intensive; let your client decide if they wish to do so after you explain this), and often the use of CSS features is rather limited.

We'll therefore confine this discussion to IE starting at version 5, Netscape version 7, and one current gecko browser (Mozilla). We'll also look at the latest versions of Opera (6 and 7). This website won't serve NN4.*x* with a graphical layout, but the site's content will be accessible without restriction. We hope that our graphical design supports good usability, though NN4.*x*-users will have to make do without it.

Building the Main Template

This section will take you step by step through the process of building the main template of imapa.de. You'll learn how we centered the outer box; built the site structure; added content, content navigation, and pictures; and created the main navigation.

Centering the Outer Box

As a first step, we built the outer boxes and centered the layout:

```
<!DOCTYPE html PUBLIC "-//W3C//DTD XHTML 1.0 Strict//EN"
"http://www.w3.org/TR/xhtml1/DTD/xhtml1-strict.dtd">
<html xmlns="http://www.w3.org/1999/xhtml" xml:lang="de">

<head>
<title lang="en">Main template - Step 1: Centered layout</title>
<meta http-equiv="content-Type" content="text/html; charset=iso-8859-1" />
<meta name="author" content="Cornelia Lange" />
<meta name="publisher" content="Cornelia Lange - clkm und Olaf Gleba -
 creatics Media&amp;Systems" />
<meta name="copyright" content="imapa.de" />
<link rel="stylesheet" type="text/css" href="fouc_nn4.css" />
<style type="text/css" media="screen">
<!--
@import url("main.css");
-->
</style>
</head>
```

```
<body>
<div id="container">
<div id="main">

<!--main--></div>
<!--container--></div>
</body>
</html>
```

Here's the basic CSS (see also http://cssproject.clkm.de/main.css):

```
/* to reset browser-specific settings */

* {
  margin: 0;
  padding: 0;
  border: 0 solid;
}

/* basic elements */
body {
  color: #000;
  background: #b3bfbc;
  font: 90% Arial, Helvetica, sans-serif;
  text-align: center; /* this is asking IE to center the container ;) */
}
a {
  text-decoration: none;
}

/* basic divs centering the layout */
#container {
  width: 51em;
  margin: 0 auto; /* to center the box */
  border-left: 1px solid #b3bfbc;
}
#main {
  position: relative;
  width: 100%;
  text-align: left; /* to revoke the body definition to please IE */
  border-right: 20px solid #fff;
}
```

To save time, we overruled the most important browser CSS to get a clean foundation for development. IE needs `text-align:center` in the body in addition to `margin:auto` for the left and right sides of `div#container`. Because of inheritance, we have to take back the text centering later; here we took care of it in the `div#main` box. The left border in `div#container` is set to avoid a special behavior of Mozilla. If the size of the screen is narrower than 800px or scaling is bigger than the screen size in Mozilla, the content begins to disappear off screen on the left side and becomes inaccessible. The border eliminates that behavior.

The layout is centered now, so we can look forward and take care of the inner structure. Because we have the restriction of no horizontal scrollbars at a resolution of 800×600, we develop from the outermost box to the inner ones. There are many situations in which it's better to build the structure from the outer to the inner boxes.

The Site Structure

Imapa.de was my first attempt to get familiar with using ems not only on text sizes, but also on box widths. I like that kind of scaling in Opera, so my aim was to rebuild this effect for all the other main browsers. To describe this special effect of scaling behavior, I use the term "Opera scaling." Patrick Griffith, who designed the CSS Zen Garden (http://www.csszengarden.com/) contribution "Elastic Lawn" (http://www.csszengarden.com/?cssfile=/063/063.css) uses the same effect and terms it "elastic design," which I like very much. (See also his article "Elastic Design" [http://www.alistapart.com/articles/elastic/] on A List Apart.)

Although we know that users with a screen size of 800×600 have to scroll horizontally, statistics show that in Germany more than 85% of users use a size bigger than that (http://www.webhits.de/deutsch/webstats.html). For this reason, we assume that the majority of users find this type of scaling very comfortable. At the beginning we started writing the layout in pixels to match a width of about 720px to ensure that there was no horizontal scrolling needed at a screen size of 800×600. As soon as we made all the declarations for the text sizes, as em responds to them, we changed the "width" declarations to em. The contents are structured as shown in Figure 12-28.

We serve NN4.*x* best by hiding `main.css` from it. To do that, we include the CSS as per the `@import` directive (as explained in Chapter 6). When using the `@import` directive, it's necessary to include an additional external stylesheet with a special purpose. We included `fouc_nn4.css` with no more inside than a CSS comment, `/* */`, to avoid the Flash of Unstyled Content (FOUC) effect that appears in IE 5+ whenever there's only an import style listed in the header. Doing it this way, we'll have a good look at the semantic structure by using NN4.*x* during testing as soon as we add the content because NN4.*x* can't process the `@import` directive. Another way of avoiding FOUC is to have an external JavaScript file, because the presence of a `<script>` tag in the `<head>` also gets rid of this nasty IE phenomenon.

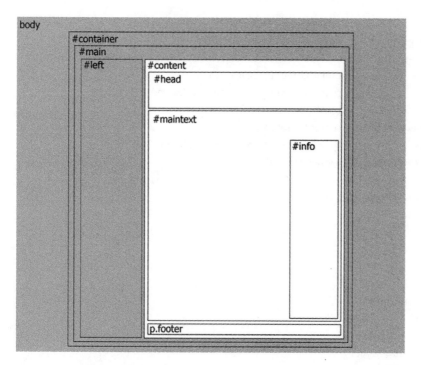

Figure 12-28. The basic structure of the HTML page

I've found for myself that a good practice is to return to this special stylesheet at the end of the project when all styles are written, proved, and validated for the website's current browsers. The advantage is that I don't need to worry about NN4.*x* for now, and can instead concentrate on the CSS contained in main.css, which is our ideal design that modern browsers will be able to render. I can then go back to fouc_nn4.css later and add some basic CSS that will make the page render acceptably for NN4.*x* users.

A few declarations styling the elements of the pages will be enough to improve the appearance of the website in NN4.*x* considerably. This way, the contents aren't only accessible, but also properly designed. But be careful: Don't forget that the styles chosen for the NN4.*x* are read by current browsers too. If you introduce a declaration for the NN4.*x* that isn't overruled by the following styles and isn't desired in the main design, you have to add the missing declarations to the imported styles accordingly.

Here's the markup for the structured page:

```
<!DOCTYPE html PUBLIC "-//W3C//DTD XHTML 1.0 Strict//EN"
"http://www.w3.org/TR/xhtml1/DTD/xhtml1-strict.dtd">
<html xmlns="http://www.w3.org/1999/xhtml" xml:lang="de">
```

```
<head>
<title lang="en">Main template - Step 2: Building the site structure</title>
<meta http-equiv="content-Type" content="text/html; charset=iso-8859-1" />
<meta name="author" content="Cornelia Lange" />
<meta name="publisher" content="Cornelia Lange - clkm und Olaf Gleba -
 creatics Media&amp;Systems" />
<meta name="copyright" content="imapa.de" />
<link rel="stylesheet" type="text/css" href="fouc_nn4.css" />
<style type="text/css" media="screen">
<!--
@import url("main.css");
-->
</style>
</head>

<body>
<div id="container">
<div id="main">
  <div id="content">
      <div id="header">
      <!--header--></div>
      <div id="text">
        <div id="info">
        <!--info--></div>
      <!--text--></div>
    <p class="footer"></p>
  <!--content--></div>
<div id="left">
<!--left--></div>
<!--main--></div>
<!--container--></div>
</body>
</html>
```

Here's the CSS (http://cssproject.clkm.de/main.css):

```
/* the site structure */
#content {
  width: 40em;
  margin: 0 0 0 11em;
  color: #000;
  background: #fff;
}
```

```css
#header {
  height: 142px;
  color: #000;
  background: transparent;
  text-align: left;
  margin-bottom: 60px;
}
#text {
  color: #000;
  background: transparent;
  padding: 0 10px;
  margin: 0 10px 0 20px;
}
.footer {
  font-size: 0.80em;
  padding: 10px 10px 10px 20px;
  margin-top: 5px;
  border-top: 1px dashed #6e7d8d;
  clear: both;
}
#info {
  float: right;
  width: 12em;
  margin: 0 0.2em 0 0.8em;
  color: #000;
  background: none;
  text-align: center;
}
#left {
  position: absolute;
  top: 0;
  left: 0;
  width: 11em;
  color: #000;
  background: #b3bfbc;
  padding-top: 200px;
}
```

For testing, it's helpful to define different background colors, as shown in Figure 12-29 (see also http://www.cssproject.clkm.de/structure_colored1.html).

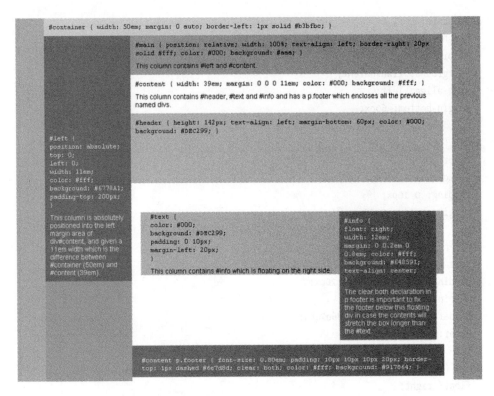

Figure 12-29. The basic structure of the site

Play around with the different settings. You'll see, for example, that the declaration clear:both; of p.footer, set as part of div#content, is important in case the floating of div#info is longer than div#text. clear:both is set (in p.footer) to encompass both div#text and div#info, as you can see. Figure 12-30 (see also http://www.cssproject.clkm.de/structure_colored2.html) shows what happens if clear:both is missing.

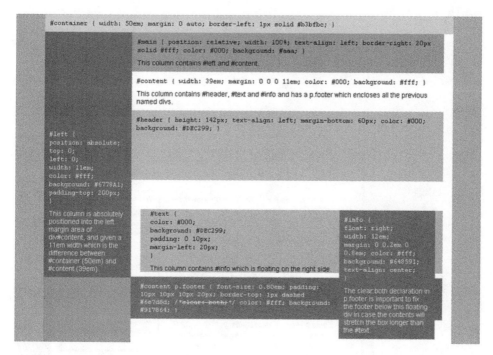

Figure 12-30. Missing `clear:both` *in* `p.footer`

div#left is positioned absolutely into the left margin area of div#content. Please be aware that this works only if you insert a declaration for positioning other than the default `position: static` of div#main into the surrounding <div> of div#left and div#content. Otherwise, the absolute positioning of div#left would refer to the body. Here we use `position:relative`. div#left becomes part of the surrounding div#main.

Remember to scale the text when building your own projects of this type. We defined all <div>s and text sizes in ems, so the whole layout will be scalable or, as Patrick would say, elastic.

Content, Content Navigation, and Picture Embedding

Adding the text for the home page in div#text, embedding the main pictures as background images per the stylesheet, and styling the infobox will complete the content section of our home page (see Figure 12-31).

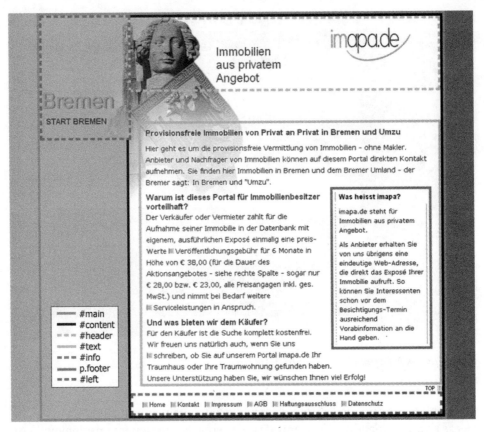

Figure 12-31. The home page with outlined boxes

Here's the relevant part of the markup (http://cssproject.clkm.de/homepage1.html):

```
<div id="content">

  <div id="header">
  <h2>Immobilien<br /> aus privatem<br /> Angebot</h2>
  <!--header--></div>

<div id="text">
<h1>... [headline main section] ...</h1>
<p>... [text main section] ...</p>

<div id="info">
<div class="infobox">
<h4>... [headline infobox] ...</h4>
<p>... [text infobox] ...</p>
<!--infobox--></div>
<!--info--></div>
```

```
<h2>... [headline main section] ...</h2>
<p>... [text main section] ...</p>
<!-- [...] -->
<!--text--></div>
<p class="footer">... [links] ...</p>
<!--content--></div>
```

Here's the CSS (http://cssproject.clkm.de/main.css):

```
/* adding the background image to body */
body {
    color: #000;
    background: #b3bfbc url(img/body.gif);
}
/* adding the background image to div#header (logo)*/
#header {
    color: #000;
    background: transparent url(img/imapa2.gif) 24.5em 0.5em no-repeat;
}
#header h2 {
    font: 1.4em Arial, Helvetica, sans-serif;
    color: #129;
    background: none;
    text-align: left;
    margin: 0;
    padding: 53px 0 0 180px;
}
/* adding the background image to div#content */
#content {
    color: #000;
    background: #fff url(img/roland_right.jpg) top left no-repeat;
}
#text {
    color: #000;
    background: transparent;
    padding: 0 10px;
    margin: 0 10px 0 20px;
}
#text h1 {
    font-size: 1em;
    color: #129;
    background: transparent;
    margin: 10px 0;
}
```

```
#text h2, #text h3 {
  font-size: 1em;
  color: #129;
  background: none;
  padding: 10px 0 0 0;
}
#text p {
  font: 0.82em/160% Verdana, Arial, Helvetica, sans-serif;
  color: #000;
  background: none;
}

/* Link icons in the main section */
#content a { /* Link icon for internal link */
  color: #000;
  background: transparent url(img/linkhover.gif) left no-repeat;
  padding-left: 14px;
}
#content a:link, #content a:visited {
  color: #000;
  background: transparent url(img/link.gif) left no-repeat;
}
#content a:hover, #content a:active {
  color: #000;
  background: transparent url(img/linkhover.gif) left no-repeat;
  text-decoration: underline;
}
#content a.top { /* link to the top of the page */
  font-size: 0.78em;
  color: #000;
  background: transparent url(img/tophover.gif) right no-repeat;
  padding-right: 16px;
}
#content a:link.top, #content a:visited.top {
color: #000;
background: transparent url(img/top.gif) right no-repeat;
}
#content a:hover.top, #content a:active.top {
  color: #000;
  background: transparent url(img/tophover.gif) right no-repeat;
  text-decoration: none;
}
/* content div#info */
#info .infobox {
```

```
    display: block;
    padding: 5px;
    color: #000;
    background: none;
}


#info h4 {
    font-size: 0.86em;
    border-left: 1px solid #ff8c00;
    padding: 2px 7px;
    margin: 0 0 5px 0;
    text-align: left;
}
#info p {
    color: #000;
    background: #fff;
    font-size: 0.80em;
    line-height: 140%;
    text-align: left;
    border-left: 1px dashed #9faba8;
    border-right: 1px solid #ff8c00;
    margin: 0;
    padding: 5px 7px;
}
/* adding the background image to div#left */
#left {
    position: absolute;
    width: 11em;
    left: 0;
    top: 0;
    color: #000;
    background: #b3bfbc url(img/roland_left.gif) top right no-repeat;
    padding-top: 200px;
}
/* taking bremen.gif out of the normal document flow */
#bremen {
    position: absolute;
    top: 150px;
    left: 0;
}
```

In an earlier version we made the picture bremen.gif part of the roland background-picture. In case of a decrease in scaling, the image was cut as shown in Figure 12-32.

Figure 12-32. Problems with scaling

Due to design issues, we didn't want to push "Bremen" further to the right. To solve the problem, we extracted this part as `bremen.gif` and took it out of the normal flow with `position:absolute`.

I've heard many people say that using CSS will result in a loss of design control. The opposite is true. With some inspiration, using CSS design correctly opens a variety of possibilities to convert almost every design suitably for web issues.

The Left Navigation

We now only have to add navigation to complete the first page. The completed home page is shown in Figure 12-33.

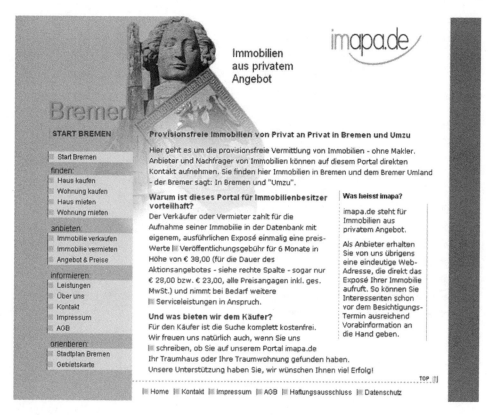

Figure 12-33. The completed home page

We use two nested lists to ensure good accessibility. Here's the markup
(http://cssproject.clkm.de/homepage2.html):

```
<div id="left">
<div id="bremen">
<img src="img/bremen.gif" height="37" width="154" alt="Immobilien in Bremen" />
<!--bremen--></div>
<h1>START BREMEN</h1>
<ul>
<li class="immonav"><a href="index.html">Start Bremen</a></li>
</ul>
<ul>
<li class="headernav">finden:
<ul>
<li class="immonav"><a href="hauskauf.html">Haus kaufen</a></li>
<li class="immonav"><a href="wohnungskauf.html">Wohnung kaufen</a></li>
<li class="immonav"><a href="hausmieten.html">Haus mieten</a></li>
<li class="immonav"><a href="wohnungmieten.html">Wohnung mieten</a></li>
</ul></li>
```

```
<!-- [...] -->
<li class="headernav">orientieren:
<ul>
<li class="immonav"><a href="stadtplan.html">Stadtplan Bremen</a></li>
<li class="immonav"><a href="gebietskarte.html">Gebietskarte</a></li>
</ul></li>
</ul>
<!--left--></div>
```

Here's the CSS (http://cssproject.clkm.de/main.css):

```
#left h1 {
  font-size: 1em;
  color: #129;
  background: none;
  margin: 15px 0 22px 2px;
  padding: 2px 2px 2px 4px;
  border-left: 2px solid #ff8c00;
}
#left ul {
  list-style: none outside;
}
#left .headernav {
  padding: .5em 0 .25em 0;
  width: 10em;
  color: #000;
  background: transparent;
  text-align: left;
  text-indent: 6px;
}
.immonav a {
  font-size: 0.82em;
  display: block;
  width: 11.7em;
  padding: 2px 2px 2px 1.4em;
  text-align: left;
  text-indent: 0;
  color: #000;
  background: #129;
}
.immonav a:link, .immonav a:visited {
  color: #000;
  background: #DBE7E4 url(img/navlink.gif) left no-repeat;
  border-left: 1px solid #129;
}
```

```
.immonav a:hover {
  text-decoration: none;
  color: #fff;
  background: #129;
  border-left: 1px solid #ff8c00;
}
.immonav a:active {
  text-decoration: none;
  color: #fff;
  background: #129 url(img/navlinkhover.gif) left no-repeat;
  border-left: 1px solid #129;
}
```

Building the Template for a Real Estate Listing

We will use the home page as a starting point from which we will develop the real estate listing overview page, but first, let's take a look at Figure 12-34 to see what the finished listing page will look like.

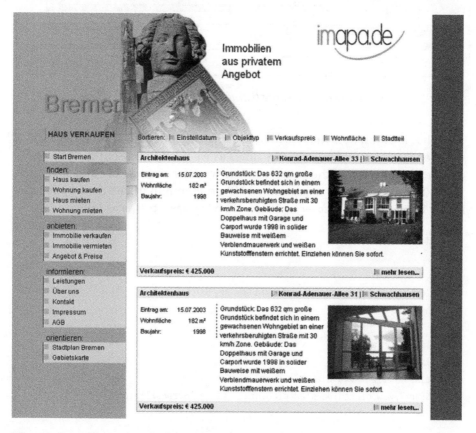

Figure 12-34. The web page for real estate listings

To build the page we just have to replace the div#text box from the home page. We replace it with a box that displays a quick preview of the property on offer. As you can see from Figure 12-35, building the template for the property overview isn't very different from creating the main page.

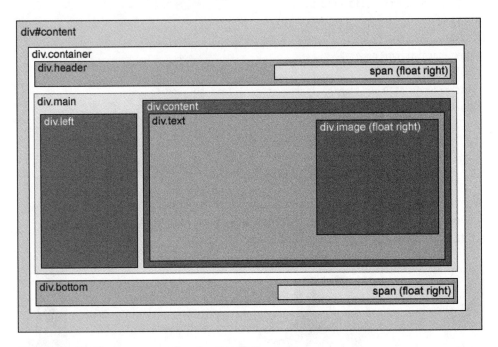

Figure 12-35. The structure of real estate listings

What is different is that we're now using classes instead of ids because we'll repeat this template as many times as we need to present the objects on our page. On top of the overview page we offer some select and sequence fields (to be added later using some PHP programming). The markup for the listing box (http://cssproject.clkm.de/listingpage.html) is as follows:

```
<div id="content">

  <div id="header">
  <h2>Immobilien<br /> aus privatem<br /> Angebot</h2>
  <!--header--></div>

<div class="container">
<div class="header">
<span class="fright"><a class="extern"
href="http://www.bremen.de/stadtplan.html" title="Stra&szlig;ensuche
```

```
bei www.bremen.de - ein neues Browserfenster wird ge&ouml;ffnet.">Konrad-
Adenauer-Allee 33</a> | <a
href="schwachhausen.html">Schwachhausen</a></span>Architektenhaus
<!--header--></div>
<div class="main">
<div class="content">
<div class="image">
<img class="rand" src="img/immoobject.jpg" height="135" width="180"
alt="Immobilienobjekt" />
<!--info--></div>
<div class="text">
<p>Grundst&uuml;ck: Das 632 qm große Grundst&uuml;ck befindet sich in einem
gewachsenen Wohngebiet an einer verkehrsberuhigten Stra&szlig;e mit 30 km/h
Zone. Geb&auml;ude: Das Doppelhaus mit Garage und Carport wurde 1998 in
solider Bauweise mit wei&szlig;em Verblendmauerwerk und wei&szlig;en
Kunststofffenstern errichtet. Einziehen k&ouml;nnen Sie sofort.</p>
<!--text--></div>
<!--content--></div>
<div class="left">
<table>
<tr><td>Eintrag am:</td><td class="fett right">15.07.2003</td></tr>
<tr><td>Wohnfl&auml;che</td><td class="fett right">
182 m&sup2;</td></tr>
<tr><td>Baujahr:</td><td class="fett right">1998</td></tr>
</table>
<!--left--></div>
<!--main--></div>
<div class="bottom">
<span class="fright"><a class="besucht" href="expose0010.html">mehr
lesen...</a></span>Verkaufspreis: &euro; 425.000
<!--preis--></div>
<!--container--></div>
<!-- next listing box [...] -->
<p class="footer">... [links] ...</p>
<!--content--></div>
```

Some of you will complain that we use too many <div>s to realize the layout
and will consider it as bad as using nested tables. But there's a difference: We're
aware of the structural semantics of our document and use <div>s only for logical structural grouping. This way, the markup structure isn't affected. Using tables
for layout is using HTML for an incorrect purpose, which loses the structural
semantics of a page.

The CSS (http://cssproject.clkm.de/listings.css) is included as a separate stylesheet because it's relevant to the pages with listings only:

```
/* css for the real estate preview box */
.fright {
  float: right;
}
.container {
  width: 37em;
  margin: 20px 0 5px 20px;
  color: #000;
  background: #fff;
  border-left: 1px solid #ff8c00;
}
.header {
  font-size: 0.82em;
  font-weight: bold;
  padding: 2px 5px;
  color: #000;
  background: #f2f4f4;
  text-align: left;
  border-top: 1px solid #ff8c00;
  border-right: 1px solid #ff8c00;
}
.main {
  position: relative;
  width: 100%;
  margin: 5px 0 0 0;
  color: #000;
  background: none;
  text-align: left;
}
.content {
  margin: 0 0 0 11em;
}
.image {
  float: right;
  padding: 7px 1px 5px 5px;
}
.text {
  margin: 0;
  padding: 0;
}
```

```
.text p {
  font-size: 0.82em;
  line-height: 140%;
  padding: 5px;
  margin: 0;
  color: #000;
  background: none;
}
.left {
  position: absolute;
  left: 0;
  top: 0;
  width: 10.5em;
  border-right: 1px dashed #000;
  padding: 0;
  margin: 5px 0 0 0;
}
.left td {
  font-size: 0.78em;
  padding: 2px 5px;
}
.bottom {
  clear: both;
  font-weight: bold;
  color: #000;
  background: #F2F4F4;
  font-size: 0.82em;
  border-right: 1px solid #ff8c00;
  border-bottom: 1px solid #ff8c00;
  text-align: left;
  padding: 2px 5px;
  margin-bottom: 0;
}
```

Something Special: Creating a CSS Image Map Without JavaScript

Now we look at something slightly more complicated—creating pop-up boxes with CSS instead of JavaScript. Eric Meyer presents some nice examples of this on his site at http://www.meyerweb.com/eric/css/edge/popups/demo2.html. We have implemented an example on imapa.de to show and name the different districts and areas of a city using pop-up information boxes. We'll explore how we accomplished this in this section.

First let's have a look at the completed page, which is shown in Figure 12-36 (see also `http://cssproject.clkm.de/citymap.html`).

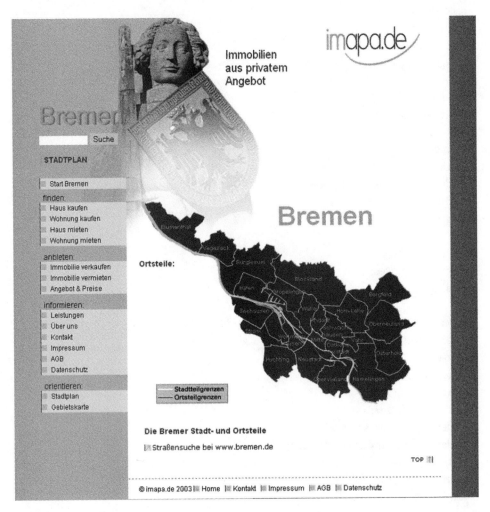

Figure 12-36. The city map of Bremen unhovered

Figure 12-37 shows what happens when the mouse is moved over the map.

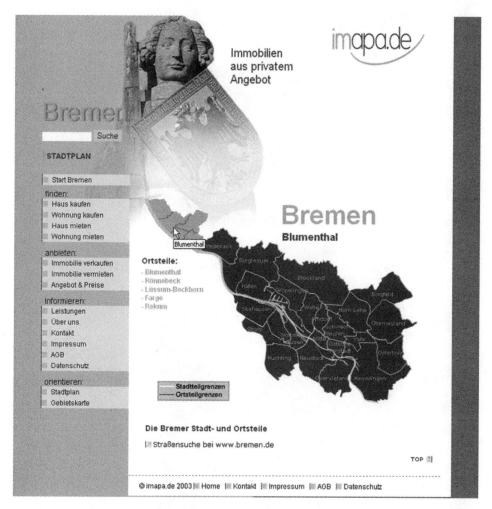

Figure 12-37. The city map of Bremen hovered

Impressive, huh? The color of the district hovered over changes, the name of the district appears below the name "Bremen," and a listing of the district areas displays below the word "Ortsteile" (which is "areas" in English).

So how did we achieve this? We'll go through the procedure from scratch here. First, we have to prepare our images with transparent backgrounds. The plain city map is shown in Figure 12-38.

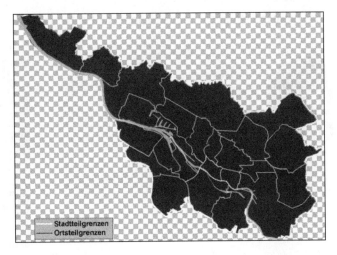

Figure 12-38. The plain GIF of the city map of Bremen

The different sized images for hovering status are shown in Figure 12-39.

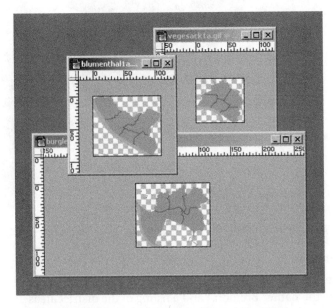

Figure 12-39. Some of the GIFs for hovering status

As you might have already guessed, we use our home page again and insert the headline in div#text and a paragraph with a hyperlink to the street search of Bremen to provide more detailed information—a service of bremen.de:

```
<div id="text">
<h1>Die Bremer Stadt- und Ortsteile</h1>
<p><a class="extern" href="http://www.bremen.de/stadtplan.html">
Stra&szlig;ensuche bei www.bremen.de</a></p>
<p class="ontop"><a class="top" href="#top">TOP</a></p>
```

Besides our imported `main.css`, we add another stylesheet, `citymap.css` (`http://cssproject.clkm.de/citymap.css`). To push the `<h1>` headline to the bottom of the page (this way, the paragraphs follow as they have the default declaration of `position:static`), we overrule the padding declaration:

```
#text h1 {
    padding-top: 500px;
}
```

The city map gets its own `<div>` and is positioned absolutely (`http://cssproject.clkm.de/citymap.css`):

```
#citymap {
    position: absolute;
    top: 320px;
    left: 12.5em;
    display: block;
    width: 500px;
    height: 355px;
    background: transparent url(img/citymap/citymap.gif);
}
```

The width and the height of `div#citymap` has the same dimensions as `citymap.gif`, which we included as a background image. Within `div#citymap`, we add further static elements:

```
<div id="citymap">
<div id="city">Bremen</div>
<div id="area">Ortsteile:</div>
```

The positioning of our `<div>`s is in pixels instead of ems. That isn't surprising because our reference is the pixel-sized `citymap.gif`. We add the following CSS (`http://cssproject.clkm.de/citymap.css`):

```
#city {
    position: absolute;
    top: 0;
    left: 250px;
```

```
  font: bold 3.2em Arial, Helvetica, sans-serif;
  color: #FF8c00;
  background: transparent;
}

#area {
  position: absolute;
  top: 100px;
  left: 0;
  font: bold 1em Arial, Helvetica, sans-serif;
  color: #129;
  background: transparent;
}
```

Let's look at what we've done so far (see Figure 12-40).

Figure 12-40. The static elements are ready now.

Now we're ready to get the image map into action. For each district we have to define a `<div>` id and embed an individual set of rules. To give you an example, we'll show how to manage the hovering for the Blumenthal district. Here's the HTML code:

```
<div id="blumenthal"><a href=""><span
class="districtname">Blumenthal</span><span class="showblum1"><img
src="img/citymap/blumenthal1a.gif" alt="Blumenthal" width="109" height="91"
/></span><span class="showblum2">- Blumenthal <br />
- R&ouml;nnebeck<br />
- L&uuml;ssum-Bockhorn<br />
- Farge<br />
- Rekum </span><span class="showblum3">Blumenthal</span></a></div>
```

As you can see, we're using four <span> elements inside the link that's enclosed by div#blumenthal. First, we define common link behavior to save a lot of declarations we would otherwise have to define to each of the individual district <div>s (and there are a lot):

```
#citymap a, #citymap a:link, #citymap a:visited, #citymap a:hover,
#citymap a:active {
  display: block;
  text-decoration: none;
  font: bold 10px Arial, Helvetica, sans-serif;
  color: #ff8c00;
  background: transparent;
  padding: 0;
  cursor: pointer;
  cursor: hand;
}
```

The next step is to position div#blumenthal absolutely onto the city map and to define the click area:

```
#blumenthal {
  position: absolute;
  top: 38px;
  left: 40px;
}
#blumenthal a {
  width: 60px;
  height: 20px;
}
#blumenthal a:hover {
  width:60px;
  height:18px;
}
```

If you take a close look at the preceding code, you'll notice there are different settings for height. You might wonder why we did this. The reason is that IE 5,

IE 5.5, and IE 6 don't show pop-ups if the settings are 100% the same on a and a:hover—it's a bug. Peter-Paul Koch has tested it seriously and found out that different settings in border, display, position, overflow, and background defeat this bug (see http://www.quirksmode.org/css/ie6_purecsspopups.html). You can add width to this list too, as certain width CSS declarations can be used to solve the problem as well (the height declaration works in IE 5.5 and IE 6, but not in IE 5).

To visualize the settings of div#blumenthal and its link declarations, please consider Figure 12-41.

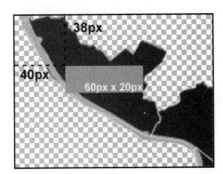

Figure 12-41. The measurements for positioning

In this case, defining the width of the click area isn't really important because the width stretches automatically with the length of the text ("Blumenthal"), but you can imagine other situations in which it might be helpful to cover a bigger area. We don't need the text as far as we make our mouseover work, so we have to hide the text. This is easy because we can address the text by means of the class name .districtname:

```
#blumenthal a:hover .districtname  {
   display: none;
}
```

Instead of the text, we now want to show the orange district GIF of Blumenthal, which is already part of the HTML code (blumenthal1a.gif, wrapped in the <span> element with the class .showblum1) but hidden with display:none at mouseout status:

```
#blumenthal a .showblum1 {
   display:none;
}
#blumenthal a:hover .showblum1 {
   position: absolute;
   top: -38px;
```

```
    left: -29px;
    display: block;
    width: 109px;
    height: 91px;
}
```

The width and the height settings will match the size of the GIF image. To understand the negative settings (top: -38px and left: -29px), have a look at Figure 12-42.

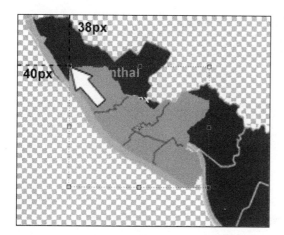

Figure 12-42. Placing the mouseover image

The starting point for the placement of the GIF is the position of div#blumenthal (top: 38px and left: 40px). We have to push the image 38px back to the top and 29px back to the left to exactly cover the area on the background image. You might think that this could be made a lot easier by putting div#blumenthal at a position of top:0 and left:0, and positioning the text with some padding. However, doing this will expand the click area and cause bad results.

To provide the user with more information, we show the names of the areas of the selected district Blumenthal below the heading "Ortsteile" (.showblum2) and the name of the district below the name of the town Bremen (.showblum3). As described earlier, the starting point for the measurements is div#blumenthal, but we don't refer to the image map any longer. To calculate the top and left measurements, we have to know where exactly we want to place the text. For the area names, it will be 20px below the div#area, so we perform the calculations shown in Table 12-2.

Table 12-2. Image Map Measurement Calculations I

Description	Top	Left
#blumenthal	38px	40px
#area	100px	0
20px below div#area	120px	0
.showblum2	120px – 38px = 82px	0 – 40px = –40px

Now we're able to make the necessary declarations:

```
#blumenthal a .showblum2 {
   display:none;
}
#blumenthal a:hover .showblum2 {
   position: absolute;
   display: block;
   width: 250px;
   top: 82px;
   left: -40px;
   font: bold 1.2em Arial, Helvetica, sans-serif;
   color: #ff8c00;
   background: transparent;
}
```

If we have this, it's easy to go on with placing the district name 55px below div#city, because on hovering status that name is hidden on the map itself. Table 12-3 shows the calculations for this.

Table 12-3. Image Map Measurement Calculations II

Description	Top	Left
#blumenthal	38px	40px
#city	0	250px
55px below #city	55px	250px
.showblum3	55px – 38px = 17px	250px – 40px = 210px*

We'll add 2px because of the difference in sizes (3.2em to 1.8em)—it looks much better.

```
#blumenthal a .showblum3 {
  display:none;
}
#blumenthal a:hover .showblum3 {
  position: absolute;
  top: 17px;
  left: 212px;
  display: block;
  font: bold 1.8em Arial, Helvetica, sans-serif;
  color: #129;
  background: transparent;
}
```

The district names aren't part of the background image; rather, they're written in HTML and placed via CSS. The result is a pure CSS image map with more accessibility than a JavaScript-based image map. To make it fully accessible, we only have to add a longdesc page to each district image. CSS can't provide multiple rectangular boxes, but there isn't just an image change happening. We can determine the size of the mouseover field independent of the size of the district image.

Play around for a while with the online version (http://cssproject.clkm.de/citymap.html) to get a feel for whether or not you like it.

Summary

This last project covered how to build a centered and elastic CSS design from the beginning stages. You learned how to create a basic CSS layout and change it to meet different purposes—for example, building listing blocks without using tables. You also learned that the thinking involved in CSS design is a bit different from the thinking involved in table-based layout design. The CSS image map shows that you can use CSS design to build some advanced dynamic effects, and use of the image map will help to make the page more accessible too.

After I finished the design part of the project, Olaf took over and added the bulk of the dynamic functionality using PHP. The fact that I had completely separated the presentation from the content by using CSS made it easy for him to plug in the server-side logic.

Index